Kings and Presidents

Kings

and

Presidents

Saudi Arabia and the United States
since FDR

BRUCE RIEDEL

BROOKINGS INSTITUTION PRESS
Washington, D.C.

The Brookings Institution is a private nonprofit organization devoted to research, education, and publication on important issues of domestic and foreign policy. Its principal purpose is to bring the highest quality independent research and analysis to bear on current and emerging policy problems. Interpretations or conclusions in Brookings publications should be understood to be solely those of the authors.

Library of Congress Cataloging-in-Publication data are available.
ISBN 978-0-8157-3137-5 (cloth : alk. paper)
ISBN 978-0-8157-3138-2 (ebook)

9 8 7 6 5 4 3 2 1

Typeset in Fournier MT

Composition by Westchester Publishing Services

To Gloria

Contents

Prologue

It was a bitterly cold day in December 2001. The terrible tragedy of September 11 was still fresh in our minds. The attack on America by al Qaeda had stunned the world. It had also created a crisis in America's relations with its oldest ally in the Middle East and the Islamic World. Fifteen of the nineteen terrorists were Saudi citizens and the leader of al Qaeda was another Saudi, Osama bin Laden. Indeed, bin Laden had wanted to create a crisis between Americans and Saudis and deliberately chose his countrymen to attack the World Trade Center, the Pentagon, and the Capitol to damage the relationship.

My wife, Elizabeth, and I were going to the Virginia residence of the Saudi ambassador to the United States, His Royal Highness Prince Bandar bin Sultan bin Abdul Aziz, for lunch. I was leaving the White House after almost five years on the National Security Council staff under Presidents Bill Clinton and George Bush for another assignment with the Central Intelligence Agency. For more than a decade I had worked closely with Prince Bandar, and he wanted to host us for a farewell lunch. His wife Haifa bint Faisal, the daughter of the former king of Saudi Arabia, was joining us.

The son of the late crown prince Sultan bin Abdul Aziz al Saud, Bandar is a graduate of the Royal Air Force College in Cranwell in the United Kingdom. Bandar later received additional military training in the United States and a master's degree from the Johns Hopkins University School for Advanced International Studies (as did Elizabeth). King Fahd appointed him defense attaché to the United States in 1982 and then ambassador in October 1983. He served in that post until 2005; his twenty-two years in office were longer than any other current ambassador, and this made him the dean of the diplomatic corps in Washington.

His skills as a diplomat, conspirator, and spymaster are legendary. A colleague of mine called Bandar the "greatest show in Washington" for his ability to insinuate himself into American decisionmaking and to influence American foreign policy toward policies that the Kingdom wanted. He worked with five American presidents, ten secretaries of state, and eleven national security advisers during his two decades as the king's man in Washington. The king provided him with his own four-engine wide-bodied Airbus 3000, fitted out with three bedrooms and a lounge so the ambassador could travel quickly and in comfort around the world.[1]

Of course Bandar also had his setbacks and detractors. A plane accident during his Royal Saudi Air Force flying days left him with chronic back pain, which often led to lengthy rehabilitation absences from his job. He sometimes exaggerated his ability to influence his boss's thinking and over-reached beyond his brief. Even his critics admitted, however, that he was a major player both in Washington and Riyadh.

Our lunch was served in a small room in the residence decorated to remember the Battle of Britain, the RAF's historic victory over the Luftwaffe in 1940 that saved England from Nazi invasion. Much of our lunch was a social occasion. Over more than a decade I had spent considerable time with Bandar at his homes in America, England, Switzerland, and in the Saudi kingdom. We had dined on fine meals at luxury restaurants as well as on McDonald's Big Macs, a shared passion, in his residence and at the Saudi embassy. I briefed him in August 1990 on the Iraqi threat after the invasion of Kuwait, shared meetings with three presidents and two Saudi monarchs together, and even stood by him to help explain to his father, then Defense Minister Prince Sultan, why a Saudi conspiracy to divide Yemen had failed. Bandar had sent flowers to celebrate our wedding and had attended a party after it, so we had had previous social encounters. He wanted to wish Elizabeth and me well in our next assignment in London.

Bandar is a great storyteller. He regaled us with one story about a trip he and Haifa took to a spa in England a few years earlier to detoxify their systems with healthy food and country air. After a few days of the regime, Haifa and Bandar slipped out one night to the local Chinese restaurant and indulged in a food binge. They both giggled like teenagers at the memory of their little adventure.

But inevitably work and 9/11 came into the conversation. Bandar was highly agitated that his years of trying to bring the Kingdom and America together as allies were jeopardized by al Qaeda's murderous attack. Bandar had spent his life seeking to persuade Americans, especially American presidents, that the Kingdom is America's most reliable and influential ally in the Islamic world—an ally that could deliver on issues ranging from fighting the Soviet Union in Afghanistan in the 1980s; stopping Saddam's aggression in Kuwait in the 1990s; and helping make peace between Arabs and Israelis over many decades to ensuring the reliable and affordable supply of oil to the world market.

Bin Laden's attack on America jeopardized all of Bandar's work. Instead of an ally, the Kingdom suddenly appeared to many Americans as an enemy. Saudi Arabia was increasingly portrayed in the American media as a hothouse of terrorism, an extremist Islamic state that provided the ideological base for al Qaeda, and a fertile recruiting ground for terrorists. The Kingdom's many enemies were quick to jump on the bandwagon of Saudi phobia. A prominent Israeli author, for example, quickly wrote a book titled *Hatred's Kingdom: How Saudi Arabia Supports the New Global Terrorism*. A former CIA officer wrote another, *Sleeping with the Devil: How Washington Sold Our Soul for Saudi Crude*. There were demands that Washington investigate the Saudi role in allegedly sponsoring al Qaeda in general and to determine what role it played in the 9/11 conspiracy itself. Haifa, Bandar's wife, was even accused of helping to finance the plot.

Bandar found himself accused of being the enemy. A man who had spent decades working with America in the Oval Office, a super fan of "America's team," the Dallas Cowboys, and a generous supporter of many humanitarian causes in the United States, now was suspected of being secretly in bed with America's worst enemy.

Ambassador Prince Bandar bin Sultan greeting the author and his wife,
September 8, 2001, just days before the events of 9/11. (Author's collection)

His problems were not only in Washington, D.C. In Riyadh the royal
family was in denial about al Qaeda. Most of the senior princes simply refused
to believe a band of Arab and Muslim terrorists in Afghanistan could be so
formidable as to attack the American heartland. Two key princes, the minister
of interior, Prince Nayef, and the governor of Riyadh, Prince Salman (who
became king in 2015), blamed the Israeli secret intelligence service, the
Mossad, for the attack. The American ambassador in Saudi Arabia had to get
a CIA briefer to Riyadh to show the princes compelling evidence of al Qaeda's
culpability.[2]

All this was especially painful for Bandar because just days before 9/11 he
had appeared to have helped resolve a falling out between his boss Crown

Prince Abdallah, who was ruling the Kingdom because his brother Fahd had suffered a major stroke, and President George W. Bush. The president had been eager to have the crown prince visit the White House since his inauguration in January, but the crown prince was angry at American support for Israel. Bandar had repeatedly told Bush and his aides the crown prince would not come to Washington as long as Bush did not take a stand supporting a Palestinian state. Secretary of State Colin Powell and I had met with Abdallah in Paris in the summer at the George V Hotel. The Saudi prince gave the secretary a photo book of dead Palestinian children killed in the intifada, or uprising, that was raging in the occupied West Bank and Gaza Strip. He accused Israel of war crimes and America of abetting them. Visibly angry, he categorically refused to see Bush until American policy changed. Our ambassador in Riyadh later characterized the crown prince as "livid" and "bitter" toward Bush due to the Palestinian issue.[3]

At Bandar's suggestion Bush wrote the crown prince in August 2001 and pledged American support for a two-state solution to the Israeli-Palestinian conflict. He promised to make his pledge public at the next session of the United Nations General Assembly, in September. The letter broke the impasse with Abdallah, and he agreed to a future visit to the United States. Then the al Qaeda attacks intervened, the General Assembly was postponed, and the immediate prospect for movement on the Palestinian issue was lost. Bush did promise American support for an independent Palestine at the UN General Assembly when it was rescheduled in November, but for Bandar his success in persuading the Bush administration to be the first to publicly call for a Palestinian state was entirely overshadowed by 9/11. Now Bandar was trying to put back together the Saudi-American alliance under enormous pressure from American public opinion, which saw Saudi Arabia as the root source of terrorism.

There is a basic conundrum at the core of the American relationship with Saudi Arabia. It has always been an uneasy alliance between two very different countries. America is a superpower democracy that aspires to be a tolerant home to a diverse multiethnic and multireligious population, all of whom are equal in the eyes of the law. Saudi Arabia is the world's last absolute monarchy and also is a theocracy with a fundamentalist religious faith, dominated by a Wahhabi clergy that is intolerant and suspicious of outsiders.

This book seeks to tell the story of this conflicted partnership from its origins in 1943 to today. It is not a diplomatic history of the relationship or a comprehensive study of all their interactions. Rather, it focuses on a select number of case studies of interaction between American presidents and Saudi kings to illustrate the nature of the uneasy alliance. For example, it begins with the famous meeting between President Franklin Delano Roosevelt and the founder of the modern Kingdom of Saudi Arabia, King Abdul Aziz al Saud, better known as Ibn Saud, on Valentine's Day in 1945 that forged the American-Saudi entente. That meeting focused heavily on American support for Zionism, the movement advocating the creation of a Jewish state, which FDR supported and the king adamantly opposed. The meeting was a success of sorts. The two men established a personal bond and agreed on an alliance that eventually was based on American security assistance and access to Saudi oil. The contradictions inherent in the partnership have been managed since that meeting by American presidents and Saudi kings for decades. This book focuses on the presidents and kings who have been the managers of the relationship—and how they managed the tensions in the alliance.

This book also looks at the fundamental areas of common interests and differences between Washington and Riyadh that create the dynamic of the alliance. It seeks to answer these questions: Is Saudi Arabia a force for order in the world or a force for chaos? Is the Kingdom an ally in promoting stability and order in the world? Does it promote peace between nations and the goals of the United Nations for a peaceful world order? Or is it a force for chaos, whose Wahhabi ideology is a root base of the global jihad? To try to answer these questions we must begin with an exploration of the Kingdom's origins and the unique alliance between the House of Saud and the al Shaykh family, the successors of Muhammad Ibn 'Abd al Wahhab, the founder of Wahhabism. That story begins two centuries earlier than the American-Saudi alliance, back to 1744 in the Nejd region of the Arabian Peninsula.

The book also looks to the future. Saudi Arabia today is in the midst of a complex generational transition. The sons of Ibn Saud have ruled the Kingdom since his death for over a half-century; now they are preparing to transfer power to his grandsons. It is a potentially destabilizing period. The Kingdom also is surrounded by a region in profound turmoil, with civil wars, failed states, and terrorism on the rise. In the United States a new president, Donald

Trump, is advocating what he calls an "America First" foreign policy, which is significantly different from the policies of any of his predecessors. The Kingdom has a new swashbuckling ambassador in Washington, Prince Khalid bin Salman, another former Royal Saudi Air Force pilot in his late twenties, who also is the son of the current king. Thus, it is a propitious moment to reexamine the American-Saudi relationship and assess its future.

Many of my colleagues at Brookings have been generous with their time and thoughts as I researched and drafted this book. Strobe Talbott, Martin Indyk, Bruce Jones, Michael O'Hanlon, Tamara Wittes, Suzanne Maloney, Kenneth Pollack, Bradley Porter, and Shaqaiq Birashk were all tremendously helpful. The staff of the Brookings library made my life much easier with their assistance. The Brookings Institution Press was, as always, a pleasure to work with and is a fine, professional institution. My wife, Elizabeth, was a constant companion and inspiration.

Any errors of fact or interpretation are solely my responsibility. The Central Intelligence Agency has reviewed the manuscript to ensure there is no inadvertent disclosure of classified information. The views in this book do not represent the views of the CIA or the United States government, nor does the CIA validate any facts or judgments in the book. This does not constitute an official release of CIA information. All statements of fact, opinion, or analysis are those of the author and do not reflect the official positions or views of the Central Intelligence Agency or any other U.S. government agency. Nothing in the contents should be construed as asserting or implying U.S. government authentication of information or CIA endorsement of the author's views. This information has been reviewed solely for classification.

There are many Saudis who contributed to my thinking about their country over many decades. They will know who they are, and I thank them for their insights and friendship.

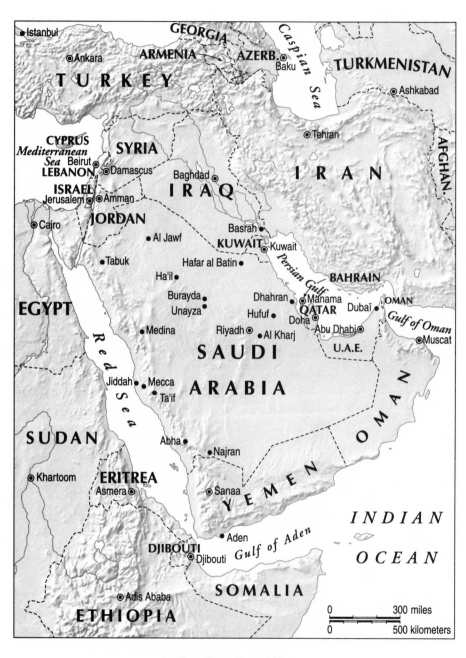

Saudi Arabia and its neighbors

Chapter One

FDR AND IBN SAUD,
1744 TO 1953

t was an extraordinary meeting during an extraordinary trip. On January 22, 1945, President Franklin Delano Roosevelt left the White House secretly by train for Newport News, Virginia, where he boarded an American naval cruiser, the USS *Quincy*. Ten days later, on February 2, the *Quincy* docked in Malta, where the president transferred to the first presidential aircraft, the *Sacred Cow*, to fly to Yalta in the Crimea for a top-secret conference with Soviet leader Joseph Stalin and British prime minister Winston Churchill. FDR hoped this meeting would build a new world order to prevent another global catastrophe like the Second World War. The Yalta summit finished on February 11 and FDR flew to Cairo for one more vital meeting.[1]

On February 14, 1945, as the Second World War was coming to an end, President Roosevelt met with King Abdul Aziz bin Abdul Rahman al Saud in Egypt, and the two forged a partnership that has endured, despite occasional severe strains, for the last seventy years. Even today, every Saudi official recalls the meeting vividly. Photos of the two leaders together are ubiquitous in

1

Franklin Roosevelt and Ibn Saud meeting aboard the USS Quincy,
February 14, 1945. (FDR Presidential Library)

Saudi embassies, and the American ambassador's residence in Riyadh is named after the cruiser on which the two held their summit.

The American-Saudi summit meeting was a closely held secret for security reasons; only a handful on each side knew it was coming. Germany was in the final agony of defeat, but it still had sharp claws, U-boats and jet fighters that could surprise an unwary opponent. FDR and Ibn Saud, as the king was known in the world by 1945, met on the USS *Quincy*, the cruiser that brought FDR across the Atlantic and then back again to America, in the Great Bitter Lake along the Suez Canal.

Roosevelt's health was very poor and he had only a few weeks to live. The trip was grueling and dangerous; FDR would travel 13,842 miles through a chaotic war zone. Churchill would later write that FDR "had a slender contact with life." His blood pressure was 260 over 150.[2] The USS *Quincy* was surrounded by other cruisers and destroyers with an air cap overhead of fighter planes. German U-boat submarines were a constant menace. The president stayed in constant contact with the White House map room by cable, and through the map room's cables he was kept up-to-date on the progress of the war.

Ibn Saud had come from Jidda on an American destroyer, the USS *Murphy*, with an entourage of bodyguards, cooks, and slaves, plus an astrologer, a fortuneteller, and other retainers—and some sheep. The *Murphy* was the first-ever American Navy vessel to visit Jidda. The Navy's only available charts dated from 1834. The king only reluctantly agreed to leave his wives behind in Jidda when he was told their privacy could not be assured in the crowded space of a destroyer. His brother Saud accompanied him as well as his son, Crown Prince Saud, and his interpreter. A senior member of the *ulema*, or clergy, was also in the king's party. Another son, Prince Faisal, stayed behind in Jidda to run affairs and communicated with the king's party every hour by radio to assure Ibn Saud that all was well in the Kingdom. It was the king's first trip outside the Arabian Peninsula aside from a brief visit to Basra in Iraq and his first time to travel at sea.

The two leaders were remarkably different. FDR was the scion of one of America's most famous families. He had grown up in the most modern country in the world and the oldest democracy. After a failed run at vice president in 1920 and a paralyzing polio attack in 1921 he had gone on to win four elections for the presidency. He had led America out of the Great Depression and then through the fire of World War II. He had traveled the world and was, in 1945, undoubtedly the most powerful man in the world.

Ibn Saud had been born in the deserts of the Arabian Peninsula, one of the most backward and impoverished lands in the world. He, too, was a scion of a famous family, but it had fallen on hard times and was living in exile in Kuwait. Ibn Saud had restored his family's rule in the Arabian Peninsula, fought numerous battles, and had gone on to expand the borders of the Kingdom of Saudi Arabia to dominate the peninsula. He had a prodigious sex life, producing forty-three acknowledged sons and at least fifty-five daughters. He told a confidant, the Englishman Harry St. John Philby, that he had "married no fewer than 135 virgins."[3] His kingdom was an absolute monarchy, desperately poor but sitting on incredible riches in oil. FDR was the first foreign head of state Ibn Saud had ever met. In 1945 there were only 400 foreigners in all of Saudi Arabia, about one hundred of whom were Americans in the oil fields near Dhahran.[4]

FDR came to the Great Bitter Lake to see Ibn Saud as part of the mission that had taken him to Yalta, fashioning the postwar world. At Yalta he had focused on creating the United Nations to provide the framework for the new political order that would come after the worst war in human history. In the

Suez Canal he was seeking to ensure Saudi support for that order through a bargain that would trade American security guarantees for access to Saudi oil, and Saudi political support for stability in the Middle East.

Oil was very much on Roosevelt's mind. The huge armies, air forces, and navies of the Second World War were fueled by oil—no longer by coal and horsepower, as their predecessors had been. At the peak of military operations in 1944 in Europe, for example, the daily requirement of oil for the U.S. Army and Air Force in just that theater of the global conflict was fourteen times the total amount of gasoline shipped to Europe in the First World War. By 1945, some 7 billion barrels of petroleum had been required to support the allied war effort. American domestic production provided two-thirds of the global output and American refineries almost the entire refined product. Already American experts believed Saudi Arabia would prove to be the home of vast quantities of as yet unproven oil reserves. The Kingdom mattered enormously for postwar energy.[5]

Oil was also on the king's mind. He and his country were broke. The depression and the war had hurt Saudi Arabia badly. The British had been subsidizing the Saudis for years, but they, too, were broke. Only the United States had the resources to help the Saudi economy cope until oil production grew sufficiently to make the Kingdom solvent. Americans had found oil in Saudi Arabia and were exploring for more.

The king was also worried about the Kingdom's security as well as its economy. The Middle East was a rough neighborhood then and remains so now, and the king was well aware of his many enemies. The Hashemites, who ruled Jordan and Iraq and claimed their lineage had a direct family connection to the Prophet Muhammad, longed to recover the two holy cities of Mecca and Medina that Ibn Saud had seized from them two decades earlier. Yemen was a constant source of tension; Ibn Saud had taken territory from its rulers, as well. Even his putative ally Great Britain was an avaricious empire that might yet want Saudi oil. The Kingdom was vulnerable and needed an ally.

Roosevelt and Ibn Saud agreed to work together to ensure stability in the postwar Middle East. The United States would ensure security for the Kingdom, and the Saudis would ensure access to their oil fields. The United States acquired use of Dhahran air base for operations in the Middle East; U.S. oil companies were already operating in the Kingdom. Saudi Arabia declared war on Nazi Germany and Imperial Japan two weeks later, thus securing a seat in the United Nations.

The *Quincy* summit was carefully planned in advance. Ibn Saud's son Prince Faisal, the future king, had visited the United States in November 1943 to begin the courtship. Faisal flew from the Kingdom through Africa to arrive in Miami before heading to Washington. Prince Faisal and his brother Prince Khalid, another future king, stayed at Blair House while meeting with President Roosevelt and senior executive and legislative officials. Faisal was only thirty-seven, but he had been serving as his father's top diplomat since 1919, when he was twelve and had traveled to London to discuss the future of the region after the First World War. After visiting Washington, Faisal and Khalid traveled to Texas, New Mexico, Arizona, California, Colorado, Michigan, New York, New Jersey, and Maryland before flying to London. It was during Faisal's visit that the plans for the Dhahran air base were agreed upon and the United States began providing military assistance to the Kingdom.[6] By the end of the war American lend-lease assistance to the Kingdom amounted to almost $100 million.[7] An American chargé d'affaires arrived in the Kingdom in 1943, the first American diplomat accredited to Saudi Arabia.[8]

Aboard the USS *Murphy* the king and his entourage slept and ate on the deck. They slaughtered a lamb they had brought with them and prayed five times a day, relying on the destroyer captain to tell them the direction to Mecca. Ibn Saud was introduced to apple pie à la mode and loved it. The king saw his first movie, *The First Lady*, a documentary about the aircraft carrier USS *Yorktown* fighting in the Pacific against the Japanese Imperial Navy. The one-hour Technicolor film had exciting scenes of aerial dogfights and crashes on the flight deck. Another American movie was shown to the king's entourage later, *Best Foot Forward*, a Lucille Ball musical comedy that featured a scene where her dress was ripped off. Ibn Saud's sons decided it was not fitting for their father.

Also on board the USS *Murphy* was America's consul to Saudi Arabia, Colonel William Eddy, a Marine hero of World War I. Eddy was born in Lebanon and spoke fluent Arabic. After his service in the First World War he taught at Dartmouth College and the American University of Cairo, then went on to be a college president. At the start of World War II he returned to active duty in the Marines and was assigned as naval attaché, first in Cairo and then in Tangier. After the creation of the Office of Strategic Services (OSS), the forerunner of the Central Intelligence Agency, Eddy was assigned to the OSS. He played a central role in collecting intelligence in French North Africa before the Allied invasion in 1942, but his proposals to arm the Arab population against the French Vichy colonial government were regarded as too dangerous by the Allied military command, which did not want to encourage Arab nationalism.[9] He acquired a reputation for espionage daring and expertise in Arabia. In 1943 Eddy was assigned to Saudi Arabia and in November 1944 he was promoted to the position of American chargé to the kingdom. After the war Eddy would play a part in the early development of the Central Intelligence Agency.

Eddy's account of the summit on the *Quincy* is the principle firsthand source of what happened there. On board the *Murphy* and the *Quincy* Eddy had the difficult duty of reconciling two strong traditions, those of the U.S. Navy and the House of Saud. He did so brilliantly.

On February 14 the two ships came together and Ibn Saud transferred to the USS *Quincy*. FDR sent his daughter Anna Roosevelt Boettiger, who was traveling with him, to Cairo for the day to shop, telling her that "this king is a Muslim, a true believer with lots of wives. As a Muslim he will not permit women in his presence when he is talking to other men."[10] No guns were fired to salute the king, to maintain the secrecy about the meeting, and the two men began an informal discussion on the deck.

The king raised one issue at the start. He had received a message that British prime minister Winston Churchill wanted to see him in Egypt. Churchill had learned from FDR on the final day of the Yalta summit of FDR's upcoming visit to see Ibn Saud. Churchill was determined that the Middle East remain the sole preserve of the British Empire when the war ended, and he was not going to let FDR get a jump on London. The Saudis had had a difficult relationship with the British for decades, largely because the British backed their Arab rivals, the Hashemites, and sought domination of the Arabian Peninsula. Ibn Saud wanted FDR's advice: Should he meet with Churchill? The president, who increasingly regarded Churchill as a Victorian imperialist antique wedded to keeping the empire intact, told the king to see Churchill. He was, undoubtedly, confident that Churchill would misplay his meeting with the Saudis and only reinforce Ibn Saud's inclination to tilt to Washington.

Ibn Saud told the president that the two of them shared much in common, including infirmity. The king could walk only with difficulty, due to his age and many war wounds. FDR was paralyzed from the waist down. FDR gave Ibn Saud one of his extra wheelchairs on the spot to assist the king. It was to become a prized possession even though the king was too large to fit comfortably in the chair.

Lunch was served in the captain's mess below decks. On the way down in the elevator, FDR stopped the lift and smoked two cigarettes, having refrained from smoking in the king's presence. Lunch was prepared by the president's Filipino chefs from the White House. On the menu were curried lamb, rice, grapefruit, eggs, raisins, tomatoes, olives, pickles, chutney, and coconut. The king was so pleased that he asked if he could be given the chef as a gift. In the Kingdom, royal chefs were slaves. FDR cleverly told the king the chef had a contract with the U.S. Navy and could not break it.

After lunch the two went back on deck for a four-hour meeting with only Eddy present as the translator. Now that the two had established a personal connection and agreed that America and Saudi Arabia should be allies in the postwar world, Roosevelt wanted to raise another issue: the fate of Europe's Jewish survivors of the Holocaust and of a Jewish homeland in Palestine.

In Yalta the president had told Stalin he was going to see Ibn Saud and raise the question of a Jewish homeland for the survivors of the German concentration camps. Stalin said the Soviets had tried to create a Jewish homeland in Birobidzhan in Siberia. Stalin had created the Jewish Autonomous Oblast of Birobidzhan in 1934 as a bid to increase support for the Soviet Union among Russia's Jews, but the idea had never gotten much support, in part because Stalin was a notorious anti-Semite. FDR told Stalin he was a Zionist and that he hoped to convince Ibn Saud to support a Jewish homeland in Palestine.[11]

In 1945 Saudi Arabia and Yemen were the only independent countries in the Arab world. The rest were colonies or protectorates of Britain, France, or Italy, their governments pawns of the European imperial powers. Egypt, for example, had a king put in power by the British army. FDR did meet with King Farouk on his trip to the Suez Canal, but Farouk had no credibility as an Arab leader and was rightly regarded as a British puppet.

Ibn Saud, on the other hand, was a credible defender of Arab and Islamic interests. He was not under British protection, although London liked to regard itself as the preeminent power in the peninsula, and as a Wahhabi Muslim Ibn Saud was rightly seen as a "true believer," as FDR had told his daughter Anna. If Ibn Saud could be persuaded to support a Jewish homeland in Palestine, it would be a major diplomatic coup for Zionism and for Roosevelt.

The president opened by saying he wanted to get the king's advice on the question of Palestine and the Jews' desire for a state there. The Auschwitz concentration camp in Poland had been liberated by the Red Army three weeks earlier, and the full extent of the Nazis' mass murder was now becoming clear to the world. FDR argued the survivors should go to Palestine, where the Zionist movement had been building the basis for a Jewish homeland for decades.

The king was firm in his reply. "The Jews should return to live in the lands from which they were driven. The Jews whose homes were completely destroyed and who have no chance of livelihood in their homelands should be given living space in the Axis countries which oppressed them." Roosevelt argued the Jews of Europe did not want to live in Germany. The king was unpersuaded, saying, "make the enemy and the oppressor pay; that is how we Arabs wage war. Amends should be made by the criminal, not by the innocent bystander. What injury have the Arabs done to the Jews of Europe? It is the Christian Germans who stole their homes and lives. Let the Germans pay."[12]

Roosevelt tried another tack. The Arabs were numerous and their lands extensive; the Jews were few in number and sought only Palestine. The king looked FDR in the eye and quietly uttered one word: "No."[13] Then the president tried an idea that Churchill had suggested, that the Jews could build their state in Libya. Libya had been an Italian colony before the war and had a small population. Once again Ibn Saud rejected the notion of any part of the Arab world being ceded to the Jews. It would not be fair to the Libyan Arabs. "Give them [the Jewish survivors] and their descendants the choicest lands and homes of the Germans who oppressed them."[14]

FDR decided to end this part of the conversation with a commitment to the king. He told Ibn Saud that as president "he wished to assure His Majesty that he would do nothing to assist the Jews against the Arabs and would make no move hostile to the Arab people." His government "would make no change in its basic policy in Palestine without full and prior consultation with both Jews and Arabs."[15] The king was pleased with the president's commitment.

The conversation finished with a discussion of the future of Syria and Lebanon, French trusteeships since 1919. Roosevelt assured the king that the United States would press the French to give them independence just as the United States was giving the Philippines its independence after the war. Ibn Saud said: "The USA never colonizes nor enslaves."[16]

The meeting then almost collapsed into failure. Roosevelt said he must start his voyage home (it would take sixteen days to sail back to Virginia). The king was appalled. Under Arab custom it was imperative that the king now host the president for a meal on the USS *Murphy*. The president had hosted him for lunch, now honor demanded the king host the president.

Always astute to the needs of his interlocutors, FDR said for security reasons the USS *Quincy* must leave. Ibn Saud turned to Eddy and blamed him for this insult, not the last time an ambassador was to take the blame for a decision he had no role in making. Then the king suggested a compromise: he would serve the president Arabian coffee. Two coffee servants appeared in minutes and poured the king and president cardamom-scented Arabian coffee.

Gifts were exchanged. The king gave FDR four complete sets of Arab robes, a solid gold knife, and a vial of perfume. His retainers also gave Anna and Eleanor Roosevelt Arab gowns, perfumes, bracelets, anklets, rings, pearl earrings, and belts. Roosevelt gave the king a gold medal and told him that he was also arranging for a twin engine DC3 to be provided to the Kingdom with an American crew for the king's use. When it arrived later it had a swivel throne chair so the king could always face Mecca while airborne. Finally, the president's navy physician gave the king's doctor a small box containing the new medicine penicillin. The king's doctor asked if it would cure venereal disease, and the physician said it would. The king was very impressed.[17]

Despite his poor health, FDR had been a masterful host. He used his famous charm with the king, he engaged intensively on the issues, and was keen to make a connection with the king. Eddy said later the president was in fine form although the strains of his years in office were also clear.[18]

When the two-day voyage ended, the king gave the *Murphy*'s captain a gold dagger, the other officers' Arab robes and watches engraved with Ibn Saud's name, and every member of the crew money in sterling. In return the destroyer's captain gave the king two submachine guns and a pair of Navy binoculars. It was a small start to America's arms relationship with the Saudis.

There was one final moment of drama. After the president's party had departed and the king was transferred to Cairo, his personal physician approached Eddy to report that the king's medicines had been inadvertently left on the *Murphy*. They had to be retrieved. Eddy immediately sent word to get them and also asked the chief medical officer of the U.S. Army in Cairo to review the list of medicines and see if they could be reproduced from U.S. military stocks. The army doctor reviewed the list and reported 210 of the 240 items on the list were aphrodisiacs, most of which were entirely phony and unavailable. Fortunately, the crew of the USS *Murphy* found the original medicines on the ship and they were returned without the king ever knowing of their loss. His doctor went on to be Saudi Arabia's ambassador to France.[19]

FDR found Ibn Saud to be a fascinating figure but a tough negotiator. After the five-hour meeting the president told his special adviser Bernard Baruch that "among all the men that I had to deal with during my lifetime, I have met no one than this Arab monarch from whom I could extricate so little: the man has an iron will."[20] In April, just a week before he died in Georgia, FDR wrote Ibn Saud a letter reaffirming his promise that he "would take no action, in my capacity as Chief of the Executive Branch of this Government, which might prove hostile to the Arab people." He promised full consultation on Palestine. The king believed Roosevelt's promise was binding on the American government.[21]

After the king and his entourage went back to the USS *Murphy*, they traveled to see Churchill in Egypt. The two met at the Hotel Auberge du Lac on the shore of Lake Karoun fifty miles south of Cairo. The meeting took place over lunch. During their luncheon Churchill smoked and drank champagne, and the Saudis felt insulted. Churchill's aides had told him smoking and drinking alcohol were offensive, but the prime minister responded, "No, I won't pull down the flag. I feel as strongly about smoking as His Majesty feels about not smoking." He told the king, "My religion prescribes as an absolute sacred rite smoking cigars and drinking alcohol before, after and if need be during all meals and intervals between them." The king offered Churchill a glass of water from a well in Mecca.[22]

The Anglo-Saudi summit's substance was as troubled as its ambiance. Churchill also pressed for Saudi support for a Jewish state in Palestine. The prime minister told the king that the British Empire had been his ally for twenty years, subsidizing the Kingdom for many of those years, and now wanted Saudi help as it dealt with the difficult situation in Palestine, which had been a British trusteeship since 1919. Churchill had helped implement Britain's commitment to a Jewish state in Palestine when he was minister for colonial affairs in the 1920s—indeed he had designed the British Empire's domination of the Middle East at a conference in Cairo in 1921.

As he had been with FDR, the king was blunt. He told Churchill that "promotion of Zionism from any quarter must indubitably bring bloodshed, widespread disorder in the Arab lands with certainly no benefit to Britain or anyone else." Instead of agreeing to help smooth the way to a Jewish state, Ibn Saud asked for assurances from London that Jewish immigration to Palestine be stopped completely.[23]

The king told Consul Eddy later that he was impressed at "the contrast between the President and Mr. Churchill. Mr. Churchill speaks deviously, evades understanding and changes the subject to avoid commitment, forcing me repeatedly to bring him back to the point. The President seeks understanding in conversations, his effort is to make the two minds meet, to dispel darkness and shed light upon this issue." He concluded, "I have never met the equal of the President in character, wisdom and gentility."[24]

Even the British-Saudi parting was unpleasant. The king gave Churchill a sword and dagger set with jewels and a large diamond for Mrs. Churchill. Churchill gave the king a Rolls Royce automobile, but it was a right-hand drive. The king liked to sit in the front when he rode in a car, but if he sat to the left of the driver, in Arab culture he would be dishonored. The king never used the car. He also complained that the food on the British Royal Navy cruiser that took him home to Jidda was unpalatable.[25]

Overall, Roosevelt's trip to Egypt to meet Ibn Saud was a success despite the differences over Palestine. The king's meetings with FDR and Churchill, in retrospect, can be seen as the initial passing of the torch of power in the Middle East from the United Kingdom to the United States. It would mark the beginning of the U.S. alliance with the Kingdom, America's oldest ally in the Middle East. Every king and every president since 1945 has reaffirmed the partnership begun on the *Quincy*.

The most concrete result of the summit on the *Quincy* was the construction of an American airfield in Dhahran. The formal agreement to build the base was signed on August 5, 1945, by Eddy. The United States Air Force built more than fifty buildings, all air-conditioned, including a restaurant, hospital, movie theater, and housing for 500 personnel. The original agreement leased the Dhahran base to the USAF for three years. It also provided for the American civilian airline TWA to use the airfield for commercial air traffic on the New York-Cairo-Bombay route. It was the first American military facility in the Arabian Peninsula, previously the exclusive preserve of the British Empire.[26]

FDR's genius was to see the future. In the midst of a global war, the president looked to the future and recognized Saudi Arabia's huge potential importance not only for oil but for what we now call soft power in the Islamic world. Roosevelt sought to harness that importance to America, detaching it from Britain, as America prepared to be the guardian of the postwar peace. It is unlikely any other American in 1945 was as far-sighted as FDR.

The meeting on the *Quincy* also illustrated what has become the fundamental paradox in the relationship. Aside from commerce Saudi Arabia and the United States have few values in common. The Kingdom is an absolute monarchy named after the ruling family; the United States is a vibrant democracy. Saudi Arabia is one of the most intolerant countries in the world regarding religious freedom; the United States prizes freedom of religion. Saudis cannot criticize the king or the ruling family; Americans exercise their freedom of speech. Absent a bedrock of shared values, the alliance has always been defined primarily by shared threats and enemies. Even the first summit was dominated by argument over Palestine's future. It has always been an uneasy partnership.

The Kingdom's Origin

The beginnings of what was to become today's Kingdom of Saudi Arabia can be traced to 1744. The heart of the kingdom's leadership is an alliance of two families. One is the al Saud family, which has provided political leadership in an absolute monarchy since 1744. The second is the al Shaykh family, which has provided religious leadership and spiritual guidance for the kingdom since 1744, when the two families sealed an agreement to work together as partners in building a state in the Arabian Peninsula. This partnership between a governing royal family and a family with its own special claim to a set of theological beliefs is the crucial glue in the political and religious chemistry that makes Saudi Arabia.

Two men created Saudi Arabia. Muhammad ibn Saud, the founder of the dynasty of the House of Saud, was, in the mid-eighteenth century, the amir of Diriyya, a town in the Nejd, the center of the Arabian Peninsula. The Nejd was a barren backwater of the Islamic world, so poor that no outsider wanted to waste the resources to govern it. It was divided among a number of local leaders. Muhammad ibn Saud was one of many local potentates.[27]

But Muhammad ibn Saud would prove to be more than just another Arabian potentate. Between 1744 and his death in 1765 he gradually expanded Saudi control beyond the agricultural town of Diriyya to most of the Nejd, including the town of Riyadh, today the Kingdom's capital. He is now remembered as the founder of the first Saudi kingdom, and the Imam Muhammad ibn Saud Islamic University in Riyadh is named in his honor.

Central to Muhammad ibn Saud's success in conquering the Nejd was his alliance with the second key figure, Muhammad ibn 'Abd al Wahhab. Wahhab is one of the most controversial figures in the history of Islam. To devout Saudis he is the man who restored Islam to its origins, a preacher who taught the right path for believers. The current king, Salman, has created a center for the study of Wahhab's life and preachings on the site of the original Saudi capital, Diriyya; Salman's personal palace is nearby. The center has museums depicting life in the first Saudi state, a library of books by Wahhab and his descendants, and a Memorial Hall illustrating his contribution to Islam. At the center of the complex is a reconstruction of the first house of worship Wahhab built.[28] King Salman's son Sultan, Saudi Arabia's only astronaut, has been the driving force behind the reconstruction of Diriyya at his father's behest.[29] Qatar, also a Wahhabi state, named its state mosque after him, the Muhammad ibn 'Abd al Wahhab mosque in Doha.

To his many enemies, Wahhab is the archvillain of intolerance and the spiritual father of al Qaeda and the Islamic State. Efforts have been made to paint him as a tool of British imperialism, with one conspiracy theory alleging that he was recruited by a British spy in Basra to encourage conflict between Muslims.[30] Even the name of his movement is controversial. Wahhabis generally do not like to be called Wahhabis because it elevates Muhammad ibn 'Abd al Wahhab to the rank of a prophet or a holy figure, an elevation that borders on the idolatry that Wahhab preached against his entire life. They prefer to be called Unitarians or *muwahiddun*, or just Muslims.

Because of his central role in the creation of Saudi Arabia and its ideology, it is crucial to study Muhammad ibn 'Abd al Wahhab in some depth. More than any other figure, Wahhab set the ideological base for what Saudi Arabia stands for. He lived in a backwater of Arabia on the edge the Ottoman Empire, and his life story has many gaps and uncertainties. His enemies vilified him effectively. Only recently has Muhammad ibn 'Abd al Wahhab been the subject of a detailed biography by a British scholar, who drew on original sources to paint a portrait of one of the most revolutionary and radical figures in the history of Islam.

Muhammad Ibn 'Abd al Wahhab was born in the Nejd in 1703, the son of a local preacher and judge. He traveled to Mecca and Medina to perform the holy pilgrimage and to study. His first mentor was an Indian scholar, Muhammad Hayat al Sindhi, who emphasized a return to the original sources of Islam, the Quran, and the early accounts of the prophet's life. In the middle 1730s Ibn 'Abd al Wahhab traveled to Basra, a major city in southern Iraq. Basra was much more cosmopolitan then than any city in Arabia and was home to a large Shia population, as well as many Persians. Christians and Jews lived in Basra as well as traders and merchants from India. Representatives of the English and Dutch East India Companies were engaged in global trading deals there. The city was under the nominal control of the Ottoman Empire but was often threatened by the Safavid Empire in neighboring Iran.

Basra had an important impact on Wahhab's thinking and development. He may have begun writing his first book during his time in Basra. He certainly began preaching against the diversity of Islamic practice while in the city. Ibn 'Abd al Wahhab denounced the worship of Ali, the nephew of Muhammad, who is the central figure in Shia Islam. He also denounced the practice of worshipping local Muslim saints and clerics; he spoke against mystical Sufism and the veneration of the tombs of respected Muslim clerics. He was expelled from the city at some point in the 1730s and moved to what is now the Eastern Province of Saudi Arabia, also known as al Ahsa or al Hasa. This region along the Persian Gulf has a significant Shia presence and, like Basra, apparently played an important part in Wahhab's hostility to Shi'ism. He was expelled from al Hasa for his views and returned to the Nejd.

He did not travel outside that region for the rest of his life.[31] Some biographies claim Wahhab traveled much further, perhaps to Damascus, Baghdad, and even into Persia. The best recent scholarship, by Michael Crawford, a British scholar whose biography is the most credible to date, dismisses these reports as inaccurate and invented by Wahhab's detractors.[32]

In the Nejd, Wahhab aligned himself at first with the ruler of his own native town. Again he spoke out against what he called polytheists who venerated local tombs and even trees. He destroyed these false idols with help from his followers. He said that Arabia had fallen out of grace since the death of the prophet and had returned to the state of ignorance that had preceded Muhammad's prophecy in the seventh century. He ordered stoned to death a woman who publicly announced her adultery. He was expelled from the community and left for Diriyya, where he came under the protection of Abdul Aziz.

The eldest son of Muhammad al Saud, Abdul Aziz had already become a follower of Ibn 'Abd al Wahhab, as were several of his brothers and probably his favorite wife. Taking in the radical preacher was a dangerous move because it put the small Saudi community at war with its neighbors and the Ottoman Empire itself. For the rest of Muhammad al Saud's life he was engaged in battles to defend Diriyya and, ultimately, expand his realm to seize Riyadh and the rest of the Nejd. After his father's death, Abdul Aziz continued the process of expanding the borders of what is now called the first Saudi kingdom.

Muhammad ibn 'Abd al Wahhab's most important book is *Kitab al Tawhid*, and it deals with the central message of his preaching. Wahhab taught that the oneness of God, *tawhid*, is the most important essence of Islam. By this he meant two things. First, God is the sole creator, provider, giver of life and death, and orderer of affairs in the universe. Second, God alone should be the addressee of prayers, supplications, sacrifices, and all other forms of worship. There should be no intermediary between a believer and God, no intercessor to appeal to for help with prayer or devotion. The Prophet Muhammad, as important as he is to Islam, should not be worshipped. Those who pray to Ali (Shia) or Jesus (Christians) or some local, venerated Muslim cleric or saint are infidels even if they claim to be Muslims.

From his perspective almost all Muslims in the world were, thus, infidels or at least polytheists and idol worshippers. The illiterate nomads of Arabia, the Bedouin, were especially ignorant in Wahhab's view because they knew nothing about their beliefs other than what their local cleric told them and often venerated trees or sacred tombs. The Shia were especially ignorant, with their elaborate ceremonies celebrating the struggles of Ali and his son Husayn, their veneration of senior clerics called ayatollahs, and their failure to understand the importance of *tawhid*. Wahhab's own experiences in Basra and al Hasa had bred a deep antagonism toward all Shia. When the first Saudi state conquered al Hasa after his death, the Saudis tried to convert the Shia population to the new Wahhabi viewpoint or at least destroy any vestige of Shi'ism in the mosques and public space.

Given the centrality of *tawhid* in the narrative of Ibn 'Abd al Wahhab it was inevitable that a second major element of his thinking concerned the nature of the Wahhabi community. It must be a community apart, separated from the ignorant. It was essential that infidels not be allowed to travel in the community because they would corrupt it. Equally important, the believers should not travel among the ignorant, again because they might be corrupted. Thus the early version of Wahhabi Islam was very xenophobic and aloof from the outside world. It guarded its righteousness by staying apart from the unbelievers. The believers must be isolated from the infidels.[33]

A final key principle was the importance of jihad or holy warfare to expand the community of the faithful. It was incumbent on every believer, and especially those in positions of leadership, to expand the boundaries of the believers and defeat the ignorant. As a result, "the obligation to wage jihad was absolute" for the community and the Saudi leadership especially.[34] War between the Saudis and the Ottomans was virtually inevitable.

After the conquest of Riyadh, Muhammad Ibn 'Abd al Wahhab largely retired from everyday public life and devoted himself to writing and preaching. He wrote an extended biography of the Prophet Muhammad and several other books about the teachings of other key Islamic figures. He died in June 1792 at the age of eighty-five. He left six sons who would continue his work and founded the al Shaykh family dynasty that is the al Saud family's most crucial partner.

Muhammad Ibn 'Abd al Wahhab did not try to develop a concept of an Islamic political order or of a state. Such concepts were simply unknown in the Nejd in the eighteenth century. He was content to leave governance to the Saudi family. He did not call for the creation of an Islamic caliphate or an empire uniting all Muslims. Wahhab's vision was rather simple: the power of *tawhid* was the basis for understanding everything else. The contradictions between a simple and radical worldview and the realities of governance and diplomacy were challenges for Wahhab's successors, not for the first Saudi state. The first Saudi state made no compromises with the ignorant and waged war relentlessly against them.

In the last decade of the eighteenth century the first Saudi state grew to become much larger than the current Kingdom of Saudi Arabia. At its peak in 1808 it included all the territory that is today Saudi Arabia except for the port of Jidda, which remained an outpost of the Ottoman Empire. It also included what is today Qatar, Bahrain, the United Arab Emirates, and parts of northern Oman. The Hadramawt region in south Yemen was a Saudi vassal. Only two parts of the peninsula with unique Islamic sects of their own, Zaydi Shia Yemen and Ibadi Oman, held out against the Saudi state. Mecca and Medina were under Saudi control, an enormous humiliation to the Ottomans who regarded themselves as the true defenders of Islam and the holy cities. In the north, Saudi armies raided Iraq, capturing the wealthy Shia holy city of Kerbala and destroying the tomb of Husayn. They also laid siege to Najaf and Basra in Iraq and Sana'a in Yemen. For a brief moment it appeared the Saudis would dominate the entire Arabian Peninsula. At its peak, the first Saudi state ruled some 2.4 million people.[35]

The Ottoman Empire, meanwhile, had been under attack from Napoleon and France. The French had invaded Egypt in 1798 and marched into Palestine. The French threat was not fully defeated until late in 1801, and even then the Ottomans were preoccupied with the Napoleonic wars in Europe for several more years. The Ottomans, in 1811, dispatched an army from Egypt, which regained control of Mecca and the Hijaz. In 1818 they marched into the Nejd and captured Diriyya. The senior members of the Saud family that survived the siege and capture of their capital were imprisoned and sent to Cairo. King 'Abd Allah al Saud was sent on to Istanbul where he was executed. After storming out of the Nejd and creating a state, the House of Saud's fortunes had collapsed and the family was all but destroyed.[36]

The Second Saudi Kingdom

The Turkish-Egyptian army that destroyed the first Saudi state did not stay long in Arabia. Political challenges at home required the use elsewhere of the resources that had conquered Arabia. In the 1820s the Ottomans withdrew the bulk of their forces from the Nejd. One of the surviving members of the House of Saud, Turki ibn Abdallah, began to rebuild the Saudi empire. Turki recovered Riyadh from the Turks in 1824. He was assassinated by a cousin in 1834, and his son Faisal bin Turki al Saud succeeded him. The current Saudi leadership are direct descendants of Faisal.

Faisal was forced into exile in 1838 by another Ottoman army, only to return in 1843 to resume Saudi rule of Riyadh and the Nejd. He was successful in bringing the bulk of central Arabia back under Saudi and Wahhabi rule. His forces retook control of the Eastern Province, or al Hasa, from the Turks. Most of what is today the United Arab Emirates and all of Qatar also fell under the control of the second Saudi state. In 1861 Faisal threatened to seize Bahrain, as well, but the British Royal Navy intervened to protect the island from Saudi conquest. The British raj in India felt keeping Bahrain out of the orbit of the Saudis was in the interest of the empire.

Otherwise Faisal was careful not to provoke the British. Unlike the first Saudi state, the second did not try to reach beyond the Arabian Peninsula into Iraq or to fight the Ottomans for the Hejaz and the British in the Gulf states. The Saudis had learned there were some limits to their power and that accommodation with the dominant powers of the day was a necessary constraint enabling their survival. The British gradually consolidated their influence all along the southern shore of the Persian Gulf from Kuwait to Oman, leaving only al Hasa out of their orbit.

Faisal died in December 1865. Infighting among his four sons was the hallmark of the next thirty years of the second Saudi state. Each claimed the right to the throne, and some were prepared to make tactical alliances with the Turks to defeat their brothers. Power and control of Riyadh passed from one to another. In 1871 the Turks recovered control of al Hasa, and in 1887 the Saudis were driven out of Riyadh. By 1893 the House of Saud was in exile in Kuwait where the amir gave them sanctuary.

Between 1744 and 1893 there were fourteen successions in the House of Saud, as power passed from one king to another. The first two, from Muhammad bin Saud to his son Abdul Aziz and then to his son Saud, were smooth and uncontested. The three kings ruled from 1744 to 1814, and they oversaw the great growth of the first Saudi Kingdom. The next twelve successions witnessed eleven power struggles within the family as power was transferred from one monarch to another. Of fourteen successions in the first two Saudi states, eleven were contested. The founders avoided succession struggles; the generations that followed were consumed with them.[37]

The long history of the first and second Saudi states is largely unknown in America. The intricacies of their rise and fall has not been taught by many American scholars, even to students of the region. For Saudis, of course, the history of their kingdom is very much a part of their national identity, and the narrative of the rise, fall, rise, fall, and rise again of their state is central to their worldview. Saudis look back on their past, as all nations do, and see lessons learned—or in some cases, lessons learned but later forgotten or set aside.

If Saudis today study the first Saudi state for inspiration about their faith and their roots in the eighteenth century, the second state is a lesson in the dangers of family disharmony. Surrounded by powerful enemies like the Ottomans and the British, the family prospered when its enemies were distracted and the family was united. When the regional powers were able to deploy forces into Arabia and the family was split, the House of Saud was on the defensive if not defeated. The nineteenth century was a time of peril for the family and their Wahhabi ally because the royal family was divided and let the door open to foreign conspiracy against them. In the twentieth century the Saudis would not repeat this mistake.

Ibn Saud and the Third Saudi State

Abd al Aziz ibn Saud was born in Riyadh in 1880. The city was anarchic during much of his childhood as the various factions of the al Saud family competed for power. As one biography notes, "The young Abd al Aziz was aware of an all pervading atmosphere of insecurity and sense of impermanence during his early years."[38] It was a searing experience that guided him through the rest of his life.

In 1891 under pressure from the Turks and their Arab allies, his father Abd al Rahman al Saud took the family out of Riyadh and into exile. At first they tried to survive in the harsh desert of the Rub al Khali, a huge expanse in what is now southern Saudi Arabia. In 1894 they moved to Kuwait. The local amir in Kuwait was constantly trying to balance the strength of his more powerful neighbors, and giving the Saudis protection in the mid-1890s was temporarily in the interest of the Ottomans who claimed Kuwait as their territory and did not want the rivals of the al Sauds to get too powerful in Arabia.

Kuwait was a much more cosmopolitan place than Riyadh, with merchants from around the world trading and dealing in the port. Ibn Saud was tutored by the members of the al Shaykh family who accompanied the Saudi exiles. The young Ibn Saud was exposed to a world much more complex than that of the Nejd, and he befriended up-and-coming members of the Kuwaiti royal family. The port of Kuwait was also a sought-after prize in the competition between the rival European empires of the late nineteenth century, including Germany and Britain. The British won the battle, and Ibn Saud maneuvered deftly between factions in the Kuwaiti ruling family and backed the group aligned with the British.

With the support of Kuwait, Ibn Saud decided to return to Riyadh and re-establish Saudi control of the Nejd. With a handful of supporters he captured the central fort in the town on January 15, 1902. Ibn Saud's elderly father Abd al Rahman came back from Kuwait and presented his son with a sword that had belonged to Muhammad ibn 'Abd al Wahhab and had been handed down from one Saudi leader to the next for generations. Abd al Rahman would nominally serve as the ceremonial leader of the new Saudi state until his death in 1928, but in practice Ibn Saud ran the kingdom. He fought in over fifty battles between 1902 and 1932.

In the dozen years after taking Riyadh, Ibn Saud gradually restored Saudi authority over the Nejd. He also began a dialogue with the British consul in Kuwait, Captain William Henry Irvine Shakespear, a fluent Arabist and ad-venturer who reported to the British viceroy in India who had responsibility for Persian Gulf affairs in the empire. Shakespear took the first photographs of Ibn Saud, and the two forged a strong friendship. Ibn Saud was interested in a dialogue with the British to deter the Turks and his other enemies. In this he was breaking with the Saudi and Wahhabi tradition of seeing all foreigners as infidels who could not be dealt with. It was dramatic evidence that the third Saudi state was going to be a more pragmatic and realistic state than its two predecessors.

In 1913 the Saudis invaded and occupied al Hasa, which had been an Ottoman province. Preoccupied with wars in the Balkans and Libya, the Turks had no resources to defend a faraway desert province. The local Shia community was suppressed, although Ibn Saud granted some local notables in the main Shia towns of Qatif and al Hasa a measure of local rule. Saudi discrimination against the Shia minority (perhaps as many as 10 to 15 percent of Saudis today) is deeply entrenched in the Wahhabi faith. No Shia has ever been a minister in the Kingdom, and only once has a Shia been a Saudi ambassador (to Iran in 1999–2003). The region was renamed the Eastern Province.[39]

With the outbreak of the First World War in August 1914, Ibn Saud's fledgling state found itself in the middle of a global power struggle. When the Ottomans joined the war on the side of the Germans, the allies began planning to carve up the Turkish Empire between them. The British were eager to get the Saudis on their side. Shakespear offered Ibn Saud a treaty guaranteeing Saudi independence under the protection of the viceroy of India and the British Empire. In return Ibn Saud would not support Ottoman calls for a Muslim jihad against the allies. Saud agreed to the proposed treaty, which was dispatched to India and London for review.

Before an answer was returned, Shakespear was killed in a battle between the Saudis and a rival pro-Turkish tribe, the Rashids, in January 1915. His death removed the urgency behind British dealings with Ibn Saud. The Saudi file receded into the background for the British, and they, instead, found a different Arab ally in the sharif of Mecca and his Hashemite family that ruled the Hejaz, the area of current-day Saudi Arabia bordering the Red Sea. The British did, ultimately, sign a treaty with Ibn Saud in 1916 and provided him with some rifles and a small monthly stipend to pay his supporters, but the main focus of British policy in Arabia shifted from the Saudis to the Hashemites.

Ibn Saud stayed on the British side in the war and greatly expanded his territory at the expense of the pro-Turkish Rashid tribe. When the war ended, the Saudis and Hashemites fought their own war to determine control of Arabia. Ibn Saud relied on his tribal army's shock troops, called the *Ikhwan*, or brothers. These were extreme supporters of Wahhabism who were dedicated to expanding the borders of the Saudi-Wahhabi state, much like the early Muslims had in the golden age of Islam or the Wahhabi armies of the first Saudi state in the eighteenth century. They were settled in oases and practiced a stern and extreme puritanism.

In 1925 Ibn Saud's Ikhwan army took Mecca and Medina. The Hashemites were expelled from the Hejaz, although thanks to their British connection they remained in Jordan and Iraq. In Mecca and Medina the Saudis purged the holy cities of what they considered idols. Mosques or other structures built to remember members of Muhammad's family or those of his key supporters were destroyed. In particular, the Jannat al Baqi cemetery in Medina—the burial site adjacent to the prophet's mosque for many of his family members, close companions, and other central figures of early Islam—was leveled, destroying many sites revered especially by Shia. The site also had been destroyed by the first Saudi state and then restored by the Ottomans. The destruction of the Baqi cemetery remains an outstanding source of friction between the Saudis and Shia today.

In January 1926 Ibn Saud was proclaimed king of the Nejd and Hejaz. The British negotiated a new treaty with Ibn Saud a year later, recognizing him as an independent king and accepting his conquest of the Hejaz. In return Ibn Saud accepted British control of the Gulf emirates and their position in Jordan and Iraq. He also accepted the transfer of part of the northern Hejaz to Jordan, especially the cities of Aqaba and Ma'an, which had historically been ruled as part of the Hejaz. In addition, Ibn Saud ceded claims to the narrow eastern wing of Jordan that connects it to Iraq.[40] Relations with the Hashemite monarchs in Amman and Baghdad remained strained well into the 1950s.

The Ikhwan were dissatisfied with Ibn Saud's decision to accept British primacy in the region and to halt the expansion of the Saudi state further to the north and east. After a bloody two-year-long rebellion, they were crushed as a military force. The British Royal Air Force helped Ibn Saud defeat the Ikhwan by bombing its raiding parties whenever they moved close to Jordan or Kuwait. The Wahhabi clerical establishment stayed loyal to the Saudi monarchy, and in return its hegemony over domestic and social issues was confirmed.[41]

While the Ikhwan was crushed, another institution of the Wahhabi establishment flourished. These were the religious police, or *mutawween*. These were official enforcers of the religious rules and rituals of Wahhabi Islam. No one was beyond their authority. Most mutawween were Nejdis even in the Hejaz and al Hasa, where they were brought in to enforce discipline. Later they were given the official title of the Committee for the Propagation of Virtue and the Prohibition of Vice.[42]

The Saudis fought another war in 1934 with the only other independent state in the Arab world, Yemen. After the nominal Ottoman control of Yemen ended in 1918, the Zaydi Shia monarchy proclaimed the country's independence. The Wahhabi and Zaydi monarchies were uncomfortable neighbors. In the war Ibn Saud's forces defeated the Yemenis and then took several border regions in the resulting peace agreement, expanding the Saudi state to the southwest. Many Yemenis have never accepted the outcome of the 1934 war as legitimate.

The Kingdom of Saudi Arabia was formally proclaimed in 1932. The conquest of the Hejaz had made Ibn Saud the defender of the holy cities and provided a modest income from fees paid by pilgrims coming to the holy cities, especially during the annual Hajj. But the Great Depression of the 1930s sharply reduced the number of pilgrims each year with a resulting significant decline in the Kingdom's income. In the boom years of the 1920s, about 100,000 pilgrims came each year for the Hajj; by 1940 the number had dropped to only 37,000.[43]

Ibn Saud was increasingly desperate for another source of income. Oil had been discovered decades earlier in Iran, Bahrain, and Iraq, and the global oil companies were eager to explore the Kingdom, especially al Hasa, now known as the Eastern Province. The king in 1933 turned to an American oil company, Standard Oil Company of California, and signed a deal for exploration. This signing took place in his new palace in Riyadh, which had just been built for him by a young emigrant from the Hadramawt in Yemen, Muhammad bin Laden.[44]

The Americans found oil in 1938. Ibn Saud had chosen Standard Oil in large part because it was American and he did not want a British or other European oil company exploring the Kingdom for fear it would lead to the British or French trying to gain political control of the Kingdom. The Saudi fear of British imperialism was deeply rooted. Ibn Saud and others knew they needed to accommodate London, but they had no faith that Britain had abandoned plans for the further expansion of the empire, especially if there was oil to be gained.

In the Second World War Ibn Saud was officially neutral but, in fact, tilted toward the Allied cause. Surrounded by the British Empire, he had little choice. Italy inadvertently bombed Dhahran in October 1940; the intended target had been British bases in nearby Bahrain.[45] The Germans tried to tempt Faisal to join their side. In early 1941 a pro-German coup took place in Iraq; the Germans suggested Ibn Saud support the coup but he refrained. In April 1941 Adolf Hitler sent Ibn Saud a personal, private message suggesting that if Saudi Arabia joined the Axis powers against Britain, Berlin would recognize Ibn Saud as "King of all the Arabs." The message was sent via the Saudi ambassador in Switzerland. Ibn Saud not only rejected Hitler's offer, he recalled the ambassador in Bern for dealing with the Nazis.[46] As we have seen, near the end of the war Saudi Arabia officially declared war on both Germany and Japan.

In the postwar era Saudi oil income and wealth gradually expanded, but for the majority of the residents the Kingdom remained a desperately impoverished backwater through the remainder of Ibn Saud's life. He did consolidate power in his own hands. He had demonstrated a pragmatic foreign policy much more sophisticated than his predecessors in the first two Saudi states, making treaties with the British and welcoming American oil prospectors. Ibn Saud had total power over life and death in his kingdom. His alliance with the United States sealed on the USS *Quincy* on Valentine's Day 1945 further strengthened his posture as the undisputed master of Arabia. On his death on November 9, 1953, Ibn Saud's legacy was firm: the third Saudi state was an absolute monarchy rooted in its commitment to practicing Wahhabi Islam.

The American "Betrayal" of Ibn Saud

The last years of Ibn Saud's life were as tumultuous as the earlier years. After 1945 the British, French, and Italian empires in the Middle East were in retreat. Arab states like Egypt, Syria, and Iraq gradually got their independence. The Zionist movement triumphed in Palestine and created the state of Israel, with important support from Roosevelt's successor, Harry S. Truman. For Ibn Saud and his family the latter was a betrayal of the promise the king thought he had secured aboard the USS *Quincy*. This Saudi sense of betrayal would have a longstanding and bitter residue in U.S.-Saudi relations.

As noted earlier in this chapter, President Roosevelt sent the king a letter after the summit in Egypt in response to a message from the king dated March 10, 1945. FDR's April 5, 1945, letter was addressed to GREAT AND GOODFRIEND. It stated: "Your majesty will recall that on previous occasions I communicated to you the attitude of the American government towards Palestine and made clear our determination that no decision be taken with respect to the basic situation in that country without full consultation with both Arabs and Jews . . . and that I would take no action, in my capacity as Chief of the Executive Branch of this Government, which might prove hostile to the Arab people." The letter concluded with FDR reassuring Ibn Saud that those commitments were "unchanged."[47]

Great Britain, exhausted by the cost of the world war, turned Palestine's future over to the United Nations to decide. A UN special commission recommended in 1947 that the country be partitioned between the Jews and the Arabs. The Arabs rejected the recommendation and requested, instead, full independence for a unified Palestine, which would elect its own government. Since Arabs were still a majority in the area, that would have been an Arab government.

President Truman, for a variety of reasons, including domestic politics but also a keen sense of responsibility to assist the survivors of Hitler's Holocaust, chose to support the UN recommendation. In 1947 the United States lobbied the UN Security Council to endorse the partition plan. Both the State Department and the military pressed Truman not to support partition, because they feared it would provoke an Arab, especially Saudi, backlash. But Truman's White House advisers told him, accurately, that the Saudis needed the American oil companies and their oil income too much to afford to take any action against Washington. Clark Clifford, Truman's legal counsel, argued, "The fact of the matter is the Arab states must have oil royalties or go broke. Military necessity, political and economic self preservation will compel the Arabs to sell their oil to the United States. Their need of the United States is greater than our need of them."[48]

The Saudis were deeply angered by Truman's decision, which they saw, right or wrong, as a repudiation of the FDR commitment to take no action harmful to the Arabs. The Roosevelt letter was not a personal communication, as the language in it makes clear it was an official commitment of the presidency and the government. Prince Faisal, who had been the architect of the American-Saudi alliance in 1943, now urged his father to cut diplomatic relations with the United States. Ibn Saud did not, largely because he needed the income from the American oil company in the Eastern Province. Instead, Ibn Saud instructed all provincial governors to raise volunteers to fight in Palestine alongside the other Arab armies. At least a thousand joined the war in 1947–48, the first instance of Saudi volunteers going abroad to fight for a Muslim cause.[49]

The American role in the creation of Israel left a bitter residue in the minds of many influential Saudis, especially Faisal. For Faisal and others in the royal family, Truman had betrayed Roosevelt's commitments and the Kingdom was too dependent on America to do anything about it. This would prove to have lasting implications.

Chapter Two

FAISAL, KENNEDY, JOHNSON, AND NIXON, 1953 TO 1975

The Great Mosque of Brussels is set in one of Belgium's most beautiful and monumental parks, Le Parc Cinquantenaire or Jubelpark, which opened on the fiftieth anniversary of Belgium's independence in 1880. Originally the mosque was the Oriental Pavilion in the complex of museums built throughout the park to mark the anniversary. It was not a house of worship but a museum to teach Belgians about Islam and the Middle East. For many years after the celebrations in 1880 the building was neglected and deteriorated.

In 1967 King Baudouin of Belgium gave the building as a gift to King Faisal bin Abdul Aziz of Saudi Arabia who was on a goodwill visit to Europe. Faisal had become king three years earlier as the result of a protracted succession struggle with his brother Saud. The Saudi Wahhabi clergy, the *ulema*, had been critical to Faisal's victory in the power struggle, and Faisal was eager to demonstrate his piety and religious devotion to Wahhabi Islam to keep the favor of the clerics.

Over the next decade Faisal and then his successor, King Khalid, provided generous funding to restore the original building and turn it into a major religious center in Brussels, the Centre Islamique et Culturel de Belgique. It officially opened its doors to the faithful in 1978 at a ceremony presided over by Khalid and Baudouin. Today it is the largest and most influential mosque in the capital of the European Union. It propagates Saudi Islamic values, notably the religion of Wahhab, including its intolerance. The director of the Centre Islamique and most of the staff are Saudis. Indeed, the Belgian authorities in April 2012 quietly asked Riyadh to replace the director with another Saudi because his views were so extreme.[1] The mosque is only a few hundred meters away from the EU's headquarters in the city. My own home for more than three years was directly across the street from the mosque, on Avenue de la Renaissance, giving me a close-up view.

The mosque in Brussels is symbolic of King Faisal's decisive influence on both the Kingdom of Saudi Arabia and the Islamic world more broadly. It was during his reign that the Kingdom began aggressively exporting its own brand of Islam around the world. Faisal commissioned great mosques in many countries, from Belgium to Pakistan, to help spread the faith as practiced in the Kingdom. The Kingdom's rapidly expanding oil revenues paid for this export of the faith. Faisal rightly is regarded as the architect of modern Saudi diplomacy based on the "legacy of strong puritan Islamic values maintained by descendants of Wahhabi reformers with the al Shaykh" family, as his biographer wrote. Indeed Faisal's mother was an al Shaykh, a direct descendant of Muhammad Ibn 'Abd al Wahhab, the founder of Wahhabism. Faisal literally embodied the unity of the two great families that created the Kingdom, the Sauds and the al Shaykhs.[2]

Faisal's oil-funded export of Saudi Islamic values helped strengthen Muslim communities around the world. Much of his work benefited the global community of Islam, the *umma*, providing schools, hospitals, and mosques for many faithful. But it also fueled the least tolerant and most extreme elements within the *umma*. Within the puritanical version of Islam that Saudi Arabia values so much, some have exploited their faith for political purposes to justify global jihad and terrorism. Osama bin Laden is only the most famous Saudi to make the journey from faithful citizen of Saudi Arabia to mass murderer. Faisal would undoubtedly denounce bin Laden and al Qaeda if he were alive, but his propagation of an intolerant version of faith cannot escape some culpability for the problems besetting Islam today.

Belgium has become a hotbed of Islamic militancy and extremism. The small Muslim community at the time of Faisal's visit in 1967 has grown enormously with the arrival of migrants, mostly from Morocco—from 100,000 to more than 600,000 in 2017. Perhaps a quarter of the city's population is now Muslim. More Belgians have joined groups like al Qaeda and the Islamic State per capita than in any other country in Europe. The district of Molenbeek, across the city from le Parc Cinquantenaire, has achieved dubious fame as "jihad central" in Europe.[3] The mosque Faisal created is still the center of Islamic teaching in the city. Ninety-five percent of the courses offered on Islam for Muslims in Brussels are operated by young preachers trained in Saudi Arabia under the mosque's supervision, according to a European think tank based in Brussels.[4]

Faisal was the architect of modern Saudi Arabia. He inherited a still-impoverished kingdom with an almost medieval government and turned it into a modern state with a global reach. He ensured that out of the ashes of a dangerous succession struggle, the passage of power from one of his brothers to another would provide stability in the Kingdom for fifty years. That stability provides the basis for the Kingdom's remarkable achievements.

Three American presidents dealt with Faisal as king: John F. Kennedy, Lyndon Johnson, and Richard Nixon. The interaction of each with the king illustrates the contradictions and complexity of the uneasy alliance.

For all his importance in the history of the Kingdom, Faisal has been the subject of little rigorous scholarly research in English to date. One scholar stands out, Joseph A. Kechichian, whose biography, *Faysal: Saudi Arabia's King for All Seasons*, is considered by the king's heirs as the most authoritative, and it benefits from unique access to his papers. Prince Turki al Faisal, the son who became head of Saudi intelligence and ambassador to both the United States and the United Kingdom, recommended it to me. Indeed when he graciously came to speak to my class studying Middle East history at Georgetown University, he gave every student a copy.

*President John F. Kennedy meets with Crown Prince Faisal bin Abdul Aziz
in Washington, D.C., September 1962. (Diomedia)*

Training for the Job

Faisal bin Abdul Aziz al Saud was born April 9, 1906, in Riyadh, the third son
of Ibn Saud. His mother was Tarfah bint al Shaykh, a direct descendant of
Muhammad Ibn 'Abd al Wahhab. Faisal was the only son born of this marriage; Tarfah died in 1912. The young Faisal was raised by the al Shaykhs, so

he epitomized the union of the House of Saud and the al Shaykh Wahhabi *ulema* more than any other modern Saudi monarch. His upbringing under the tutelage of his maternal grandfather, Abdallah bin Abdukl Latif al Shaykh, anchored him firmly in the Kingdom's faith.[5]

Ibn Saud recognized his son's talents early and put him to work as the Kingdom's diplomat. At the age of twelve Faisal was sent by his father in 1919 to London to represent Saudi interests as the allies prepared to divide the Ottoman Empire among them. The king believed Faisal was a good choice for the mission in part because his impeccable Wahhabi credentials ensured he would not be accused of selling out to Western influence. Ibn Saud called Faisal the *walad* of the al Shaykh, the boy from the al Shaykh family.[6] The young prince toured the United Kingdom, France, and Belgium, meeting with British and French diplomats, visiting the battlefields of Flanders, and experiencing the modern world of Europe as no Saudi had ever before. He visited armaments factories, watched plays, climbed the Eiffel Tower, and became a symbol for the Kingdom.[7] It was an extraordinary change from the early Wahhabis, who shunned the outside world as evil.

Upon his return Faisal was appointed commander of Saudi forces fighting in Asir, a southern province bordering Yemen. Then he commanded the year-long siege of Jidda, where the Hashemites were finally defeated and ousted from the peninsula for good. His father made him the viceroy of the Hejaz in August 1926. He traveled again to Europe to secure diplomatic recognition of the Saudi conquest of the Hejaz from Britain, France, and the Netherlands, the three countries with diplomatic legations in Jidda.

A third trip to Europe in 1932 included stops in Italy, Switzerland, France, Britain, Holland, Germany, Poland, and Russia. In Moscow Faisal met with senior officials of the Union of Soviet Socialist Republics after the USSR recognized Saudi Arabia and opened a consulate in Jidda. On the way home Faisal visited Turkey, Iran, Iraq, and Kuwait. Just twenty-six years old, Faisal was, without question, the most experienced and widely traveled Saudi prince.[8]

So it was no surprise that Ibn Saud sent Faisal to Washington in 1943 to lay the foundation for the Saudi alliance with America two years before the famous meeting on the USS *Quincy*. The prince met with President Roosevelt twice, stayed in Blair House, met with many members of Congress, and then toured the country to California and back. He visited Princeton and met with American Arabists.

Two years later he was back in the United States to attend the San Francisco conference establishing the United Nations. Saudi Arabia became one of the original signers to the UN Charter, and Faisal gave a speech hailing Roosevelt's leadership in securing the Allied victory in World War II. In 1947 Faisal represented the Kingdom in the deliberations of the UN Palestine committee in New York; as noted earlier he was profoundly disappointed in Truman's support for the establishment of Israel.

Troubled Transition

On November 9, 1953, Ibn Saud passed away in Taif. His eldest son Saud succeeded him as king with Faisal as crown prince. This began what would become a decade-long transition as the two brothers engaged in a prolonged power struggle for the crown. This succession struggle took place against the backdrop of a deeply troubled Middle East and the American-Soviet Cold War. Within the Arab world, the independent states recently freed from European colonial rule fought with each other over their individual regional ambitions, and they fought with Israel. The Arab Cold War, as it was called, pitted the revolutionary Arab nationalist republics against the conservative monarchies. The Arab states also became pawns in the Cold War, and at the same time exploited the war to secure favors from the Americans and Russians.

King Saud had difficulty maneuvering in these tricky waters. It did not help that he lacked good financial judgment and spent the Kingdom's oil wealth on too much luxury for himself and his cronies. The national debt more than doubled between 1953 and 1958, from $200 million to $480 million despite increased oil exports and earnings. Like his father he was a prodigious father, with fifty-three sons and fifty-four daughters.[9] He was torn between his commitment to the conservative values of his father and the new wealth of the oil boom. He was also torn between the appeal of Arab nationalism and the reality of heading an absolute monarchy. Saud also placed his sons in important cabinet positions, like defense minister, before they had experience, suggesting that he might try to have a son succeed him as king. This alienated many of his important brothers, who were also sons of Ibn Saud and who had their own aspirations for higher office and more experience and qualifications for office than did Saud's sons.

In the end Faisal would win the power struggle because he had strong support from the *ulema*, the Wahhabi establishment, as well as the backing of most of the royal family. The struggle between Saud and Faisal inevitably involved Washington, as well, not just as an important observer but as an occasional participant. Saudi Arabia was firmly in the anti-communist camp during the Cold War, not just because it is a deeply Islamic country, which regards atheist communism as anathema, but also because the House of Saud recognized that only the United States could provide security against the Soviet Union, British imperialism, revolutionary Arab nationalists, and other perceived threats.

Saud turned to the United States in November 1955 to secure a five-year military training program for the Saudi military. The training mission was linked to the Dhahran air base agreement and helped begin the modernization of the Saudi armed forces. President Dwight Eisenhower was determined to build a network of alliances around the Soviet Union and Communist China to contain the communist menace. "In American eyes the Dhahran facility was vital for regional defense."[10]

The rivalry between Saud and Faisal first came to a boil in July 1956 when seven of Saud's brothers signed a letter criticizing his stewardship of the Kingdom. They charged Saud with financial incompetence because of his spending, which risked bankrupting the Kingdom. The chief of the Royal Guard and Faisal were among the signers. A month later, Saud sacked the head of the Royal Guards and asked for American training for the guards.[11]

In November 1956 the British, French, and Israelis—operating in secret collusion—attacked Egypt. All felt threatened by the growing influence and power of Egypt's charismatic revolutionary leader Gamal Abd al Nasser. He had been a key player in the coup that overthrew the British-backed Egyptian monarchy and had thrown the British out of Egypt and the Suez Canal. Saudi Arabia broke diplomatic relations with both London and Paris as a consequence of the Suez crisis. Eisenhower also opposed the conspiracy against Cairo, fearing that it threatened to turn all the newly independent states of Africa and Asia against the West. If the old imperial powers behaved as colonial predators,

Eisenhower reasoned, only the Soviets would benefit. As a consequence of Ike's firm stand against the British, French, and Israeli conspiracy, his popularity in the Kingdom grew substantially.

Both King Saud and Crown Prince Faisal traveled to Washington the next year, 1957, to see Eisenhower, and both had extensive conversations with him.[12] During this official state visit to the United States, King Saud signed a five-year renewal of the Dhahran air base agreement. This would prove to be the final extension, and the base would revert to the Saudis in early 1962. While in the United States Faisal had two operations to remove his gallbladder and a small tumor.

At the start of 1958 the Arab Cold War between Nasser and the monarchies escalated. On March 5, 1958, Nasser accused Saudi Arabia of plotting to assassinate him and called, in turn, for the overthrow of the House of Saud.[13] This precipitated a wave of propaganda across the Arab world as the revolutionaries sought to bring down the monarchs and unite the Arab states into a single state. The Soviets enthusiastically backed the revolutionaries.

Against this background, the internal struggle in Riyadh came to a head. On March 24, 1958, Prince Fahd bin Abdul Aziz al Saud, a future king, along with eleven other senior princes, confronted Saud directly in the palace and demanded that Saud turn power over to Faisal. Within an hour a royal decree was published stripping Saud of political power and making Faisal regent. But Faisal did not demand Saud's abdication. With executive power now in his hands, Faisal quickly moved to cut government spending, end the purchase of luxury cars and other items for the princes, restore financial health to the Kingdom, and reduce corruption.

Later that year a revolutionary coup in Baghdad that overthrew the Hashemite monarchy in Iraq seemed to herald a decisive turn in the Arab world toward the nationalist forces. Nasser created the United Arab Republic, unifying Egypt and Syria. To forestall further coups, the United States sent U.S. Marines to Lebanon to shore up its pro-Western Christian government, and the United Kingdom sent paratroopers to Jordan to save the last Hashemite monarchy led by King Hussein bin Talal. But the nationalist forces were deeply divided; for example, Nasser did not control the revolutionary government in Baghdad. The wave of revolutions seemed to ebb for the moment.

Another major threat to the Kingdom came in 1961 when the revolutionary regime in Baghdad threatened to attack and occupy Kuwait. Kuwait had offered the Saud family asylum seventy years earlier and had hosted Ibn Saud for a decade. The House of Saud felt a bond of loyalty to the Kuwaiti al Sabah family. When two Iraqi divisions threatened to invade Kuwait in July 1961 the British send a battalion of Royal Marines to deter them, with full support from the United States.[14] Saudi Arabia also sent a small paratroop battalion to assist the Royal Marines. Only Jordan's King Hussein backed the Iraqi claims to Kuwait, because they dated back to the old Hashemite monarchy in Iraq. By the end of July the British were withdrawing and the Saudis took command of a joint Arab League force, including 1,500 Saudi troops, to defend the emirate. It was a harbinger of a future crisis that would test the Saudi-American alliance in 1990.[15]

At home Saud mounted a countermove against Faisal in December 1960, working with the so called Free Princes—a small number of more liberal Saudi royals who were attracted to Nasser's Arabist posture. Saud regained control of the executive powers from Faisal in this struggle. The leader of the Free Princes, Prince Talal, called for the closing of the United States Air Force base in Dhahran, leading to the nonrenewal of the U.S. lease. Saud's return to power was short-lived, however, as his health deteriorated and he had to travel to America for medical attention. Faisal was again made de facto regent and acting prime minister in November 1961.

Yemen, Kennedy, and Faisal

In 1961 America had a new president, John F. Kennedy, who would have a complex and uneasy relationship with Faisal and the Kingdom. Kennedy came into office determined to do better than Eisenhower at managing the Cold War. He wanted to avoid Eisenhower's black-and-white approach to third world nationalism. Kennedy appreciated that many of the newly independent states in Africa and Asia did not want to join either camp in the Cold War and, instead, wanted to be independent and aligned with neither great power. Leaders of these states also were determined to end colonialism and free any remaining colonies.

Kennedy had recognized the importance of appealing to the nationalist current in the so called Third World. In a major speech delivered in July 1957 titled "Imperialism—the Enemy of Freedom," Kennedy called on the Eisenhower administration to cease supporting France in its war to keep Algeria as a colony. Despite France's historic support for the United States, Kennedy argued that Paris's determination to hold on to Algeria only served Soviet interests by alienating Arabs and Africans from the free world. He cited Algeria's war for independence as a cause consistent with American principles. Kennedy also argued that the Algerian case was symptomatic of a broader imperative: the need to align America with nationalist forces and movements across what was then known as the Third World.[16]

In the Middle East this approach dictated an effort to reach out to Nasser's Egypt to see if Cairo could be a partner in stabilizing the region, not an opponent. A dialogue with Nasser would also keep Egypt from drifting further into the Soviet's orbit, Kennedy and his advisers believed. They had doubts that the traditional American allies in the region—the monarchies of Saudi Arabia, Iran, Libya, Yemen, and Jordan—could survive. There seemed a significant risk those monarchs would be toppled as had the kings of Egypt and Iraq. The ongoing power struggle in Riyadh between Saud and Faisal seemed to suggest the Kingdom was dangerously unstable and in urgent need of reform. If that were the case, Kennedy felt it would be wise to have a dialogue with the progressive nationalist forces in the Arab world. Not surprisingly, this approach "badly startled America's traditional Arab friends, especially Saudi Arabia."[17]

For the first two years of his administration Kennedy engaged in a delicate courtship of Nasser, with the two exchanging letters and emissaries to see if they could reach an accommodation. Riyadh followed the dialogue with great unease. The process came to a moment of truth in the fall of 1962, when a nationalist coup toppled the monarchy that ruled Yemen, the most backward country in Arabia. Egypt swiftly came to the aid of the nationalist forces with a massive troop deployment facilitated by the Soviet Union. Saudi Arabia, the United Kingdom, and Israel backed the royalists. Kennedy tried to find a middle ground but, ultimately, backed the Saudis. In the course of the Yemen crisis the power struggle between Faisal and Saud was also resolved, finally, in Faisal's favor.

The autumn of 1962 was an extraordinarily tense moment in the Cold War. The Soviets were introducing intermediate-range ballistic missiles and nuclear weapons into Cuba, deploying some 50,000 Russian troops to the Caribbean island. The Cuban missile crisis dominated world attention for most of October. At the same time China invaded India and defeated the Indian army in a border war in the Himalayas. Kennedy began an urgent airlift to resupply the Indians and stiffen their defenses.

Concurrently, Egypt and Russia intervened in Yemen. On September 19, 1962, the king of Yemen, Imam Ahmad bin Yahya, died. British prime minister Harold Macmillan later described his rule as "notorious for cruelty and despotism on a truly oriental scale . . . a combination of medieval squalor and obedience."[18] His thirty-six-year-old son, Muhammad al Badr, took the throne, but within a week the army mounted a coup. The Royal Palace was surrounded by tanks and demolished, but the young monarch escaped and fled to the northern mountains along the border with Saudi Arabia and joined his uncle, Prince Hassan, who was already mounting a tribal rebellion against the new republican government that set itself up in Sana'a and the other major cities.

The Egyptians were widely believed to be behind the coup and quickly moved to support the new government led by Abdallah al Sallal. The revolutionaries made clear from the beginning that their ambitions extended beyond Yemen. They openly called for revolution both in Saudi Arabia and in southern Yemen, which was then still a British colony centered around the port of Aden. In the view of both Riyadh and London, the coup was an existential threat. Prime Minister Macmillan, while noting the notoriety of the Yemeni royalists, told Kennedy from the beginning of the crisis that Nasser's goal was Saudi Arabia, "a great prize," and Aden the linchpin of British security in the Arab world.[19]

The royalists quickly rallied many of the Zaydi Shia tribes of northern Yemen to their side. The republicans controlled the cities and coastal lowlands. As early as October 2, 1962, the Central Intelligence Agency told Kennedy in his daily briefing that a "civil war is shaping up with direct backing from the United Arab Republic (Egypt) for one faction and from Saudi Arabia for the other." The agency reported the Saudis were arming and financing the royalists while Egypt and Russia backed the republic.[20] On October 4, 1962, the CIA told Kennedy two Saudi army battalions were actively assisting the royalists along with "a small Jordanian detachment."[21]

Nasser sent a battalion of Egyptian paratroopers to Sana'a in northern Yemen to strengthen the coup almost immediately. Within weeks the Egyptian deployment grew to 25,000 troops. The Egyptians did not have sufficient transport aircraft to lift them to Yemen and resupply them, so Cairo asked Moscow for help. The Soviets gave Egypt fifteen AN-12 transports (similar to the American C-130) with Russian crews to create an air bridge carrying the Egyptian army into Arabia. The CIA told Kennedy on October 16, 1962, that the Egyptians were receiving the AN-12s, the pilots were mostly Russians but also some Czechs, and the operation was tricky given the primitive nature of Yemen's airfields.[22] The planes had Egyptian markings on them, and by 1965 Egyptian pilots were trained to fly them, but for all intents and purposes they were Russian transport aircraft with Russian pilots under Egyptian command for most of two years.[23] The AN-12s were doing five to seven sorties a day to supplement ship deliveries from Egypt to the Yemeni port at Hudaydah. By March 1963, 30,000 Egyptian troops were in Yemen, later reaching 70,000, one-third of the Egyptian army.

Moscow also provided Nasser with long-range heavy bombers to strike the royalists. Two squadrons of TU-16 bombers were deployed in Egypt with Russian crews to fly combat missions in Yemen in support of the Egyptian and republican Yemeni ground forces. The Soviets built a military airfield outside Sana'a for smaller fighter aircraft and transports; some 500 Soviet combat engineers supervised its construction. The Russian bombers attacked targets across the border in Saudi Arabia, where the Saudis were assisting the royalists.[24] The Royal Saudi Air Force was unprepared and unequipped to respond; even worse, several of its pilots defected with their aircraft to Egypt. The Jordanians sent six Hawker Hunter jet fighters to Taif in Saudi Arabia to help deter air attacks by the Egyptians and Russians.[25] To the enormous embarrassment of King Hussein, the Jordanian squadron commander and two of the pilots defected to Egypt. The Jordanian deployment did help Faisal and Hussein tone down significantly the historic Saudi-Hashemite rivalry.[26]

The Kennedy administration monitored the rapidly deteriorating situation in Yemen even as it was coping with the Cuban missile crisis and the Chinese invasion of India. The Kennedy team still wanted to see if dialogue with Nasser could resolve the crisis. They also had grave doubts about the stability of the remaining Arab monarchies. Kennedy's top aide on the Middle East in the National Security Council was Robert W. Komer, a CIA officer with a "sharp pen, keen wit, abrasive spirit and ceaseless energy." Komer argued for trying to engage Nasser, as did the State Department. In time Kennedy would refer to the struggle in Yemen as "Komer's war."[27] The immediate question was whether to recognize the new republican government as the legitimate Yemeni government. London, Riyadh, and Amman all urged Washington to stall and not give this symbol of approval to Nasser and Sallal.

Faisal's Response

Faisal responded to the crisis in Yemen with determination and clarity. His response can be broken into three components. Most immediately, he backed building a coalition of states to support the royalists in Yemen. He wanted Kennedy to join this coalition but was also prepared to accept American security support for Saudi Arabia if he could not get active American help for the royalists. Second, he embarked upon building an Islamic alternative to Nasser's Arab nationalist movement. This would be manifested in Saudi support for Islamic institutions around the world, like the mosque in Brussels, and in the creation of an Islamic conference of states led by Saudi Arabia to act as a global representative of the Islamic world and to convene periodic Islamic summits. Finally, at home, he consolidated his power and, ultimately, ousted Saud and replaced him as king.

When the Yemen crisis began Faisal was in New York to attend the annual meeting of the United Nations General Assembly. He met with Secretary of State Dean Rusk at the Waldorf Astoria hotel. Faisal portrayed the coup and the Egyptian and Russian intervention as a threat to the Kingdom. He asked for a meeting with the president and urged the United States not to recognize the republican government.

Kennedy and Faisal met at the White House on October 5, 1962. Kennedy had met Saud a year before and was unimpressed. Faisal was a much more impressive figure. The two leaders began with a working lunch with their aides. Faisal said the Abdallah al Sallal regime was getting military aid "not only from the United Arab Republic but also from the Soviet Union." This was a major challenge to the stability of the entire Arabian Peninsula. Faisal noted that Sallal in his first communiqué had called for the overthrow of all the monarchies in the Arabian Peninsula and the creation of a single republic. If the royalists were not supported firmly, the Kingdom, Aden, and the Gulf states would be at risk.[28]

After lunch Faisal and the president went upstairs in the White House to the family quarters to continue their discussion in a more private and intimate setting. In the family living room Kennedy pressed Faisal to make reforms in the Kingdom. He suggested that the Kingdom's most serious threat came from the same internal problems that had destroyed the monarchies in Yemen, Iraq, and Egypt. He pressed the crown prince to consider allowing Jews to visit the Kingdom in a gesture of tolerance.[29] Kennedy also assured the prince that "the United States would consider its pledge of general support for the Kingdom to apply to threats activated from without and from within." This was a crucial expansion of America's commitment to Saudi security.[30]

Kennedy's pressure also represented a highly unusual direct American intrusion into Saudi internal affairs, reflecting the president's deep concern about the sustainability of the monarchy. None of Kennedy's predecessors and few of his successors would be so direct in suggesting the Kingdom needed to change for its own good.

Faisal responded positively. "Then and there he promised Kennedy that he would abolish slavery, institute basic civil rights and strive to eliminate corruption."[31] The Kingdom was one of the last countries in the world where slavery was legal. Faisal said: "I concur with your ideas and I intend to implement precisely this kind of reform."[32]

Faisal kept his promise to Kennedy and in November 1962 made public a reform program of ten points. The judiciary and the *mutawween* (religious police) were reformed and the government promised to provide free medical care and education. Slavery was made illegal, despite some objections from the clerics. The Saudi government paid slave owners to encourage them to free their slaves: $700 for a male slave and $1,000 for a female, until July 7, 1963, after which all slaves were considered free and there was no further compensation for owners.[33]

This was a unique example of an American president convincing a Saudi leader to make major internal reforms in the Kingdom, with no president before or since having done so. Kennedy's timing was excellent. Faisal knew the revolutionary tide was strong and that he needed to reform the Kingdom. The president also used discretion and tact; by making his case privately in the intimacy of the White House family quarters he spared Faisal any public embarrassment. Kennedy feared the royal family was heading toward collapse from internal and external pressures. In fact, the CIA told Kennedy after the White House sessions that Faisal was returning to a Saudi Arabia "heavily overshadowed by foreboding for its future."[34]

In addition to his reforms, on returning to Riyadh Faisal consolidated his position as chief executive. Saud's sons were removed from the council of ministers and replaced by Faisal loyalists. Prince Fahd became Interior Ministry, Prince Sultan took on the Defense Ministry, Prince Abdallah became commander of the Saudi National Guard, and Prince Salman became governor of Riyadh. All would hold those positions for the next half-century except Fahd, who would become king in 1982. Again, King Saud was not asked to abdicate but he was stripped of most of his power.

Faisal also appointed a commoner to be oil minister. Ahmed Zaki Yamani was only thirty-two in 1962, an Hejazi from Mecca whose father had been grand mufti in what is today Indonesia. Educated in Cairo, New York, and at Harvard Law School, Yamani was the king's protégé and would be his expert adviser on oil issues and international law and would serve as an effective diplomat for his monarch.[35]

The power struggle took place against a backdrop of unrest in the military. Between October 2 and 8, 1962, the crews of four Royal Saudi Air Force aircraft defected to Egypt with their planes. The entire RSAF was grounded in response. A month later, when the air force was allowed to fly again, seven more pilots defected with their planes to Egypt. The pilots had been part of a conspiracy to overthrow the king and establish a pro-Nasser republic. Again the RSAF was grounded, and Faisal strengthened the standing and power of the National Guard, which was more loyal than the regular military. Another coup plot by factions of the RSAF in 1969 prompted Faisal to ground the air force a third time.[36]

Faisal also moved to back royalists elsewhere. In January 1963 he broke relations with Cairo and restored relations with London. Saudi intelligence proposed to the British that they embark on a joint secret project to assist the royalists in Yemen. The British would provide a small number of former military specialists in guerilla warfare to advise and assist the royalists, which Saudi Arabia would fund. There would be no official British government role, but behind the scenes the United Kingdom would provide the expertise to help the royalists bog down Egypt and Russia in a quagmire. The entire operation would involve fewer than fifty experts and be run out of an office on Sloane Street in London.[37]

A third party joined the coalition. Israel also felt threatened by Nasser and was also eager to bog him down in Yemen. The royalists directly approached Israel for help. The Israeli intelligence service, Mossad, proposed that the Israeli Air Force would fly clandestine missions from southern Israel across the Red Sea to drop military supplies to the royalists. The British coordinated the supply missions with the royalists and the Saudis. Code-named Operation Rotev, *gravy* in Hebrew, the Israelis flew fourteen supply missions to Yemen in the next couple of years. Most of the weapons dropped to the royalists were Russian-made equipment captured by Israel from Egypt in the 1956 war, intended to ensure there was no obvious connection to Israel.[38] The arms appeared to be captured from Egypt in Yemen; this allowed Israel to maintain plausible deniability of any involvement in the war. A future head of the Mossad, Nahum Admoni, ran the operation, which was authorized by Prime Minister David Ben-Gurion.[39]

The Saudis avoided direct meetings with the Israelis, using the British as intermediaries. The Saudi operation in Yemen was run by Kamal Adham, head of Saudi intelligence, a graduate of Cambridge University and a brother of Faisal's wife. The one time the British tried to arrange a direct meeting at the Dorchester Hotel in London, Adham was very nervous.[40] Nonetheless, it was a remarkable example of Saudi realpolitik in action and Faisal's willingness to go to any partner to stymie Egypt in the early 1960s.

The United States did not join the coalition backing the royalists. In part this reflected Kennedy's continued strong preference for dialogue with Nasser. He and his key aides, including Komer, still wanted to find common ground with Egypt. As a result, after some delay, the United States gave official recognition to the new republican government in Sana'a, against the advice of Riyadh and London. Kennedy's reluctance to embrace the royalists probably also stemmed from their reactionary history. In a piece published after the death of Imam Ahmed in September 1962, the CIA characterized him as a ruthless monarch who ruled Yemen's 5 million people by keeping tribal leaders' sons as hostages, conducting mass beheadings of dissidents, and even publicly executing his own brother. The heir, Mohammad Badr, was described as eager "to drag Yemen out of the eleventh century but certainly not into the twentieth."[41]

Instead of backing the royalists, Kennedy proposed a compromise. Egypt would withdraw its army from Yemen while Saudi Arabia would cease providing arms to the royalists. Yemenis would then decide their own future without foreign interference. The devil, of course, was in the details. Who would go first, who would monitor the arrangements—and could either side be trusted?

In March 1963 Kennedy dispatched Ellsworth Bunker, a senior State Department diplomat, to the region to try to sell a deal. Bunker met with Faisal and offered to send a squadron of American fighter aircraft to the Kingdom to symbolize American security support as part of a mediated solution to the crisis.[42] Faisal was frustrated by the American mediation and had hoped for a more assertive line against Nasser. But he needed American support and agreed to Bunker's plan. He doubtless expected Nasser to fail to withdraw his troops and, thus, scuttle the initiative.

The Kennedy initiative never produced success. Although both Faisal and Nasser paid lip service to it, neither was prepared to retreat from Yemen. For the Saudis it was a matter of survival, and they had no qualms about the royalists. For Egypt the Yemen intervention was a chance to defeat the Saudis and British and consolidate Egyptian hegemony in the Arab world.

The United States did send jet fighters to Saudi Arabia after repeated Egyptian air attacks on Saudi border towns. Over the objections of United States Air Force Commander Curtis Lemay, who thought it a diversion from more important missions, eight F100D jet fighters, six KB-50 air-to-air refueling tankers, and more than 500 U.S. military personnel were deployed in mid-1963 to Dhahran and Jidda to fly combat patrols over the border. Operation Hard Surface was the only deployment of American troops into the Middle East on Kennedy's watch.[43] The mission lasted only six months, and the planes left Saudi Arabia in January 1964.[44]

After Kennedy's assassination in November 1963, President Lyndon Johnson continued the dialogue with Nasser but with much less conviction. In April 1964 Nasser made his only visit to Yemen during the war and gave a bellicose speech calling for revolution in Aden. That was the last straw for Johnson; the dialogue with Nasser petered out.

Before Nasser's visit to Sana'a, the power struggle in Saudi Arabia had reached its finale. In March 1964 Faisal persuaded the Wahhabi *ulema* to issue a formal call for Saud's abdication. Saud resisted and surrounded the royal palace with his Royal Guards. Faisal mobilized the regular army under Prince Sultan and the National Guard led by Prince Abdallah to surround the Royal Guards. A tense standoff ensued, but Saud was completely outnumbered on the ground and outmaneuvered by the clerics' alliance with Faisal. No blood was shed, but "the threat of force was necessary to depose the King."[45] He reluctantly abdicated and went into exile in Switzerland, Egypt, and Greece until his death in 1969.[46] During his exile in Egypt, Saud made pro-Egyptian radio broadcasts on Radio Cairo against his brother, but these ceased when Egypt was defeated by Israel in the 1967 war and Nasser needed desperately to make peace with Faisal.[47]

To solidify the Saudi family grip on power, Faisal developed a clear line of succession for the future. His brother Khalid was made crown prince in 1965, removing any suspicion that Faisal's sons might inherit the throne. In 1967 Prince Fahd, the interior minister, was made deputy prime minister, in effect, third in line to the throne. This ensured the line of succession for the next two kings and created a precedent for Faisal's successors.

Faisal created the modern Saudi political system. His choice of his brothers Khalid, Fahd, Abdallah, Sultan, and Salman for key positions in the council of ministers created bureaucracies run by powerful princes that could provide patronage and jobs to loyal retainers. The system gave the Kingdom its first modern government and worked effectively for over half a century. In time other senior princes would gain positions, for example, Prince Nayef as Fahd's successor as interior minister. With the infusion of oil money as Saudi production increased, the Kingdom became much more stable. Faisal had inherited a kingdom in disarray, still desperately poor, under siege from Nasser and beset with royal family intrigue. He would leave to Khalid a much more stable and secure kingdom. Another key to that transformation was the propagation of Saudi Islam.

Faisal's Islamic Mobilization

King Faisal was a true believer in the Islam practiced since Muhammad Ibn 'Abd al Wahhab. He was brought up in the family of Wahhab, the al Shaykhs. Despite his extensive exposure to the outside world, unique for a Saudi of his age and time, he remained a believer. As king he intended to use Islam as a practical force to strengthen Saudi Arabia's foreign policy and create an alternative to the secular world of Arab nationalists like Nasser. In the process he would begin the large-scale export of Saudi Islamic values and teaching to the *umma* across the world.

In May 1962 Faisal created the Muslim World League as a nongovernmental organization dedicated to propagation of Islam and Islamic values. The league became a mechanism for the creation of mosques and religious schools propagating Saudi Islam; that is, Wahhabism.

Faisal wanted to do more; he sought the creation of an organization of Islamic states to be a global player akin to the United Nations.[48] The cold war with Egypt and the hot war in Yemen made this difficult. Nasser could rally a substantial number of nationalist regimes against Faisal. Consequently it required time and extensive travels for the king to build support for his pan-Islamist dream. In December 1965 he went to Tehran and secured the backing of the shah of Iran. Additional trips followed to Morocco, Jordan, Pakistan, Turkey, Sudan, Guinea, Mali, and Tunisia in 1966.

The Saudi and Jordanian partnership in Yemen helped to reduce the rivalry between the two great families of the Arab world, the Saudis and Hashemites, and Faisal and Hussein became friends and confidants. This helped the nascent Islamic movement to grow. In 1965 the two kings signed a new border treaty that expanded Jordan's access to the Gulf of Aqaba, Jordan's only seaport and only access to the outside world.

The key turning point was the Arab-Israeli war in June 1967. Egypt was defeated in six days by the Israelis and lost the Sinai Peninsula. Jordan lost the West Bank and East Jerusalem, while Syria lost the Golan Heights. The Suez Canal was closed. It was a catastrophe for Nasser. At an Arab League summit in Khartoum, Faisal and Nasser reconciled. Egypt committed to withdrawing its army from Yemen; in return Saudi Arabia provided significant economic assistance to Egypt and Jordan. The Arab Cold War that had dominated the region from the 1950s ended.

In December 1967 Faisal created the Popular Committee for Aiding Martyrs, Families, and Mujahedin in Palestine. It was an organization dedicated to raising funds to support the Palestinians fighting Israel. Faisal turned to his half-brother Prince Salman, already the governor of Riyadh, to head the committee. He still heads it today. It began soliciting funds from Saudi citizens for the Palestinian cause and also received contributions from the state. It had a modest $5 million budget in 1968, which doubled to $10 million by 1978 and grew to $45 million in 1982 during the Lebanon war.[49] It was the first time the Kingdom, backed by the *ulema*, enthusiastically initiated fundraising for a political cause abroad and explicitly for fighting a jihad with mujahedin. Prince Salman, now king, was a central figure in the funding of the Afghan mujahidin in the 1980s, as we will see later. He plays a key role in funding the Palestinians today. In the second intifada in 2000 his Popular Committee raised funds for the families of martyrs killed by the Israelis. He personally wrote a check for $100,000 to the family of Muhammad al Durrah, a Palestinian teenager whose death in 2000 was caught on camera and became a symbol of Palestinian resistance.[50]

In September 1969 the first Islamic summit was convened in Rabat, Morocco. The summit created the Organization of Islamic Cooperation, which has its headquarters in Saudi Arabia. This became another instrument for promoting Islam. At its second summit in February 1974 in Lahore, Pakistan, it created the Islamic Solidarity Fund, another mechanism for promoting mosques and religious institutions of education.

At home Faisal also promoted religious education and created the modern Saudi educational system. In 1952 there were only 316 schools in the Kingdom, with fewer than 40,000 students, all boys. By 1973 there were 6,595 primary and secondary schools with over 700,000 students, many of them girls. Several universities were established. All these schools had a significant amount of the curriculum devoted to Islamic studies. Nonetheless, securing clerical support for girls' education was a challenge for Faisal. His wife, Queen Iffat, was a strong supporter of education for girls and the king and queen made an example by sending their daughters to school.[51]

Faisal needed teachers and professors to fill the new academic community he created. Far too few capable Saudis were available for the jobs needed. So the king turned to Egypt, especially the opposition Muslim Brotherhood. Nasser had outlawed the Brotherhood as a danger to his secular regime, depriving hundreds of Muslim Brotherhood professionals of their jobs. Now Saudi Arabia hired them to teach its children. Naturally they brought their own strict form of Islam with them, but that was acceptable to the Wahhabi clergy. As one Saudi intellectual later said, "The Muslim Brotherhood literally built the Saudi state and most Saudi institutions," especially in education, thanks to Faisal.[52]

Johnson and Faisal

Lyndon Johnson met with Faisal only once, on June 21, 1966, when Faisal came to Washington on an official visit. Johnson was told before the meeting by his staff that behind "this bearded robed desert king" is a man "a lot more modern than he looks. Under those robes you will find a sharp mind and deep devotion to educational and social progress." The king was looking for assurance that "we will not let Nasser swallow up Saudi Arabia." LBJ was reminded: "Our largest single overseas private enterprise is the Arabian-American Oil Company's $1.2 billion investment in Saudi Arabia."[53]

Johnson met privately with Faisal in the Oval Office for one hour and twenty minutes after the formal welcome to the White House. The two leaders spent a good deal of time discussing education in the Kingdom. Faisal described the progress the Kingdom had made on his watch, noting it was a "smooth evolutionary development" that accepted Saudi Arabia's "built-in peculiarities and checks." President Johnson was effusive in his praise for the king's efforts, likening them to his own efforts to build a great society in America. On Nasser and the Soviet threat, the two were in agreement; Johnson made clear he had given up trying to work with Cairo. The two leaders came away from the meeting in complete harmony.[54]

Washington was increasingly confident that Faisal had transformed the Kingdom from an unstable regime ripe for revolution into a stable and reliable ally. "Faysal's domestic position is strong. Mounting oil revenues will bring continued prosperity and economic advance" was the conclusion of a National Intelligence Estimate on the prospects for the Kingdom prepared by the CIA in December 1966.[55]

The short war between Israel and its Arab neighbors a year later, in June 1967, transformed the Middle East and profoundly changed the American-Saudi relationship. Faisal no longer saw Egypt as his top security challenge; the defeated and humiliated Nasser was now a threat to no one. Instead, Israel became Faisal's top concern, and he spent the rest of his life trying to undo the results of the June war.

It was deeply ironic that Egypt's swift defeat by Israel owed so much to Faisal's successful campaign to bog down the Egyptians in Yemen. The best of Egypt's military was still in Yemen when the 1967 crisis erupted in May. The CIA told LBJ that Israel had overwhelming military superiority over its Arab neighbors, and the Egyptian quagmire in Yemen only added to Israel's advantage.[56] Saudi Arabia sent an infantry brigade to help Jordan in the war but it arrived too late to see any fighting.[57]

Nasser blamed his defeat on the United States and the United Kingdom, claiming their air forces had assisted Israel. This false claim put enormous pressure on the other Arab states to take action against Washington and London. Iraq immediately cut off oil exports to the two countries on June 6, 1967. Arab oil ministers met in Beirut, Lebanon, later in June and passed resolutions calling for an embargo on oil sales. The Saudis were reluctant participants in the embargo because they recognized it would hurt their economy; Faisal was told by his economic advisers the embargo was damaging Saudi finances. At the Khartoum Arab summit where Faisal and Nasser had their public reconciliation, the Arabs agreed to end the embargo at Saudi initiative.[58]

The brief oil embargo in 1967 had little impact on the American economy because the United States did not import much oil at the time. The impact on the United Kingdom was much more significant because it imported almost all of its oil from the Persian Gulf. The closure of the Suez Canal due to the Israeli occupation on the east bank of the canal further damaged the UK's economy. The CIA, on June 7, 1967, predicted that a prolonged oil embargo would create a "severe economic depression" in Britain.[59] The embargo's economic impact played a key role in the subsequent decision of the British government to announce in January 1968 the withdrawal of British military forces from "east of Suez" by 1971, a decision that ended Britain's role as the preeminent outside power in the Gulf.[60] It would fall to Johnson's successor, Richard Nixon, to deal with the ramifications of the 1967 war and the British decision to quit the gulf.

Nixon, Kissinger, and Faisal

President Nixon and his national security adviser, Henry Kissinger, were not focused on the Arab world when they came into office in 1969. Vietnam was their first concern, and reordering America's relationship with Russia and China was their big objective. The Arab-Israeli conflict seemed frozen, with Israel the dominant power in the area. The White House followed Arab-Israeli events through the prism of the Cold War; the Soviets favored the Arabs and America backed Israel. Since Israel was the preeminent military power, the United States held the winning hand. The oil weapon was regarded in Washington (but not in London) as proven ineffectual by the 1967 case.

However, the withdrawal of the British forced some rethinking of American security policy for the Persian Gulf. Instead of reliance on the United Kingdom Nixon chose to rely on what was called a "twin pillars" strategy. Saudi Arabia and Iran would be the two regional powers armed and backed by the United States and responsible for maintaining order and stability.

In practice, Nixon and Kissinger regarded the shah of Iran as the main pillar of their strategy in the Gulf. When Nixon visited the region in May 1972, he stopped in Tehran and met with the shah, Mohammad Reza Pahlavi, but he did not visit Saudi Arabia.[61] Nixon was a long-time admirer of the shah. As vice president, he had first visited Iran in 1953 after the coup that ousted the leftist prime minister, Mohammad Mossadegh. The shah visited the White House three times during the Nixon administration. In contrast, Nixon never visited Saudi Arabia until the last days of his administration.

The shah was eager to modernize his country and project power in the region. He sent an expeditionary force to Oman to help the sultan of Oman defeat a communist insurgency based in South Yemen. He built a large army, air force, and navy to deter any regional or Soviet aggression. The shah backed Kurdish rebels in Iraq to keep the leftist government in Baghdad off balance. He also occupied several small islands in the Persian Gulf claimed by the United Arab Emirates when the British pulled out to enhance Iran's dominance of the region.

Faisal was more focused on the Arab-Israel conflict. He now was in the midst of his Islamic mobilization. The first Islamic summit took place on Rabat in 1969 and was called to action by Israel's annexation of East Jerusalem.

Faisal was deeply committed to the goal of returning Jerusalem to Arab and Muslim control. For him the loss of Jerusalem in 1967 was a great injustice. He had hoped the Johnson administration would behave like Eisenhower in 1956 and press for an early Israel withdrawal from captured territory. By 1969 the king realized that was not in the cards, and he began mobilizing an Islamic and Arab coalition to fight.

The king signaled his unease early to President Nixon. Just days after Nixon took office in 1969 Faisal met with the American ambassador and urged the new administration to take a "more balanced" approach to the Arab-Israeli conflict. Faisal bemoaned the spread of pro-Soviet governments in the Arab world, arguing Saudi Arabia was the only bulwark against the entire region becoming clients of Moscow. The Israeli victory in 1967 had enraged the Arab world, pushed many Arab leaders toward the Soviets, and weakened America's position in the region. He argued that Zionism was a partner with communism, pointing to the famous book, *The Protocols of the Elders of Zion*, as evidence. When the ambassador noted that *Protocols* was a forgery created by the Russian czar's secret police in 1905, Faisal not only rejected the allegation of forgery, he admitted the Kingdom was printing copies of the book in numerous languages to broaden its circulation.

The Saudi leader indicated his top priority was to end the Israeli occupation of Jerusalem. He signaled he was prepared to agree to give Israel "secure and recognized boundaries" that might differ from the 1948 cease-fire lines. Saudi Arabia would encourage other Arab states to accept such a settlement, Faisal said, but "the Israelis must leave old Jerusalem," meaning East Jerusalem, which they had occupied in June 1967. The Kingdom would never accept any agreement that failed to return East Jerusalem to Arab and Islamic control.[62] Faisal also summoned the American executives in the oil company Aramco and urged them to tell Nixon the status quo of Israeli occupation was unacceptable and unsustainable.

By the time the Middle East erupted again in the October 1973 war, which caught both Israeli and American intelligence napping, Nixon was immersed in the Watergate scandal and fighting to save his presidency. He was focused on his own political survival and left most of the foreign policy management to Kissinger. Nixon's vice president, Spiro Agnew, resigned from office during the first week of the war after corruption charges led to his indictment. "Nixon's drinking to excess became routine," one biographer has written, and Kissinger no longer "trusted Nixon to deal with the Middle East" crisis.[63]

In the months leading up to the war, Faisal began warning Nixon and Kissinger that he would use the oil weapon, cutting off oil exports, if the United States did not take action to resolve the Arab-Israeli conflict and compel Israel to withdraw from the territories occupied in 1967. In April 1973 he sent his son Saud al Faisal and his oil minister, Ahmed Zaki Yamani, to Washington; for the first time they linked the future of oil production and exports to American policy on Israel. Without a change in the U.S. policy of supporting Israel, Saudi oil policies would be used to punish the United States. The Nixon administration dismissed their message as bluster.[64]

King Faisal went public with the message himself in the summer of 1973, telling *Newsweek* that "Saudi Arabia would use its oil as a political weapon if the United States continued to support Israel's policy of aggression against the Arab world."[65] Egypt's president, Anwar Sadat—who had succeeded Nasser after his death in 1970—and Syria's president, Hafez Assad, visited Riyadh in August 1973. The two leaders were well advanced in planning a joint attack on Israel, and they wanted to ensure that Faisal would support their war and use the oil weapon if the United States backed Israel.[66] Faisal agreed to use the oil weapon, asking Sadat to ensure the war lasted long enough for this weapon to be credible.[67] Sadat later praised Faisal in his memoirs as "always a rational and stable character and, above all, a real friend."[68]

Within days of the outbreak of conflict the United States initiated a massive airlift of supplies to Israel in response to a massive Soviet airlift and sealift of supplies to Egypt and Syria. On October 17, 1973, the oil ministers of the Organization of Arab Petroleum Exporting Countries (OAPEC) met in Kuwait and announced a 5 percent cut in oil production and exports to punish the United States for the airlift, promising that every thirty days that went by without a change in American policy would produce another 5 percent cut. The Saudis cut production 10 percent immediately. Ironically, Iraq, which had led the oil embargo in 1967, refused to participate in the 1973 cutback, arguing that it was too weak a gesture. Saddam Hussein, Iraq's dictator, actually increased oil production to take advantage of the Arab embargo.

On October 19 Nixon announced a $2.2 billion emergency military aid package for Israel. The next day Saudi Arabia cut all oil exports to the United

States, the Netherlands, Portugal, South Africa, and Rhodesia for helping Israel.[69] In December 1973 another OAPEC meeting in Kuwait cut oil production by 25 percent. Oil prices quadrupled, causing severe disruption in the United States and long lines at gas stations.[70] Yamani was the public face of Saudi oil policy but Faisal was the decisionmaker. The impact on the American economy was devastating. American gross domestic product fell 6 percent due to the Arab embargo between 1973 and 1975 and unemployment doubled to 9 percent; later in the 1970s, inflation soared well into the double digits, prolonging the economic impact of the embargo long after it had ended.

Faisal understood that a fundamental shift had occurred in the global oil markets. Ever since the end of the Second World War the world market had an excess of supply, largely due to the fast expansion in oil exports from the Middle East. The United States, moreover, had large oil resources of its own, and for many years had been only a marginal importer. That situation changed dramatically in the early 1970s. According to Daniel Yergin, the author of the best book on the oil market, U.S. oil imports grew from 3.2 million barrels per day (mbd) in 1970 to 6.2mbd in 1973. Saudi Arabia filled the demand. Its oil exports grew from 5.4mbd in 1972 to 8.4mbd in 1973, a staggering rise.

As Yergin puts it, Saudi Arabia replaced Texas as the global swing producer of oil, meaning it was the oil producer with sufficient excess oil production capability to meet global demand.[71] The Arab reduction in oil exports cut Arab oil exports from 20.8mbd on October 1, 1973, to 15.8mbd by December 15, 1973. Although Iran and Iraq increased production by 600,000 barrels per day, they could not fill the gap, and the global market lost 5mbd, or 10 percent, of global production. Unlike in 1967 America was no longer invulnerable. Oil prices soared from $2.90 a gallon in July 1973 to $11.65 in December.[72] The shah of Iran was the biggest price hawk despite not participating in the embargo and quietly shipping Iranian oil to Israel.

Kissinger visited Riyadh in November 1973, his first trip to the Kingdom and his first meeting with Faisal. It was also the first visit to the Kingdom by an American secretary of state since John Foster Dulles visited during the Eisenhower administration.[73] The king repeated his familiar remarks on the communist and Zionist collusion, the importance of Jerusalem, and the need for a comprehensive settlement to the Arab-Israeli conflict. On Nixon's instructions, Kissinger invited the king to Washington for a summit with the president. Nixon, although preoccupied with Watergate, realized the American public was focused on the oil crisis and desperately hoped that if he could engineer an end to the oil embargo it would benefit his flagging domestic position. Faisal turned down Kissinger and lectured him on the twin evils of Zionism and communism.[74] Nixon made another bid to end the oil embargo in January, asking Faisal to let him announce in the annual State of the Union address to Congress that the oil embargo would end; again Faisal rebuffed his request and demanded an end to the occupation of Syrian territory captured by Israel in the 1973 war. Nixon told Kissinger the oil embargo is "the only thing the country is interested in."[75]

The conclusion of a Kissinger-brokered Syrian-Israeli disengagement agreement—returning a token piece of Syrian territory occupied in 1967 and all the territory seized in 1973—finally led to an end of the embargo in the spring of 1974. Faisal had imposed a serious price on the American economy for American support for Israel. The global oil market had been radically transformed, oil was now in short supply, and prices were four times higher than before the war. An enormous transfer of wealth began from the oil-importing countries to the oil exporters, especially Saudi Arabia. The Saudis were the key to global oil economics.

Nixon traveled to the Middle East in June 1974 trying to build on Kissinger's success in disengaging the Syrians and Israelis on the Golan and the Egyptian and Israelis in the Sinai to boost his standing with the American public. Nixon became the first American president to visit the Saudi Kingdom; indeed, his three immediate successors had not visited the Kingdom in their presidencies. The reception in Jidda was subdued at best. At the state dinner on June 14, 1974, Nixon paid tribute to Faisal's extraordinary career in diplomacy from 1919 onward. He praised the king's wisdom and vision. He acknowledged the United States needed Saudi oil but stressed he wanted Saudi support on a wide variety of issues.[76]

In his remarks Faisal was direct. "Mr. President, the injustice and aggression which were wrought upon the Arabs of Palestine are unprecedented in history, for not even in the darkest ages had a whole population of a country been driven out of their homes to be replaced by aliens," the king argued. While thanking the president for the disengagement agreements, he went on to say, "We believe that there will never be a real and lasting peace in the area

unless Jerusalem is liberated and returned to Arab sovereignty, unless liberation of all the occupied Arab territories is achieved, and unless Arab people of
Palestine regain their rights to return to their homes and be given the right to
self-determination."[77] Faisal was confident the oil weapon gave him leverage
for the first time to achieve these goals.

Faisal's Assassination

Nixon resigned in disgrace two months later. His successor, Gerald Ford, kept
Kissinger on as secretary of state. On February 14, 1975, propitiously the
thirtieth anniversary of FDR's meeting with Ibn Saud, Faisal and Kissinger
had their last meeting together. By this time Faisal had come to distrust Kissinger who, the king believed, was interested in arranging a separate peace
between Egypt and Israel rather than a comprehensive settlement of the
Arab-Israeli conflict. Kissinger, in the king's mind, did not want to resolve
the Palestinian issue or restore Arab rule in East Jerusalem but, instead, wanted
to defuse the conflict by a separate Egyptian-Israeli agreement that would
significantly reduce the Arab states' strength and their capacity to make war.
The Riyadh meeting went poorly.[78]

The king also suspected Kissinger was behind press articles proposing an
American invasion of Saudi Arabia to grab its oil. In January 1975 *Commen-
tary*, a right-wing journal, had published an article suggesting the United
States should invade and occupy Kuwait, the Eastern Province, Bahrain, and
Qatar. Two months later, in March 1975, *Harper's* published "Seizing Arab
Oil," which advocated an American seizure of the Eastern Province in collu-
sion with Iran taking Kuwait. The royal family saw these articles as inspired
by Kissinger. Prince Fahd was especially worried.[79]

The Saudis were also unhappy with Kissinger's continued preference for
Iran as the chief pillar of stability in the Gulf. Their deep-seated aversion to
Persia was reinforced by America's tilt to the shah. Saudi oil minister Yamani
told the American ambassador in Riyadh in 1975 that all the rhetoric about
close American-Iranian ties "was nauseating to him and other Saudis." Yamani said the shah was a "megalomaniac" and predicted, "if the Shah departs
from the stage, we could have a violent anti-American regime in Tehran."[80]

On March 25, 1975, on the anniversary of the Prophet Muhammad's birthday, King Faisal was assassinated. In many Islamic countries the prophet's birthday is a holiday but in the Kingdom, keeping with its strict Wahhabi faith, it is celebrated only with special prayers. After his prayers the king went to a meeting with Yamani and a visiting Kuwaiti oil delegation. Among those in the audience chamber was one of his nephews, twenty-seven-year-old Prince Faisal bin Musa'id Abdul Aziz al Saud. When the two met, the prince pulled a revolver from his robes and shot the king three times, fatally.

The assassin had been educated in the United States, first at San Francisco State College, then at the University of Colorado, and finally at the University of California, Berkeley. This led to speculation that he was hired by the CIA on Kissinger's orders to kill Faisal in retaliation for the oil embargo. But the truth was more local. His brother had been killed in 1965 when Saudi police opened fire on a demonstration protesting the introduction of television into the Kingdom, which the protesters believed was an un-Islamic invention that would corrupt the values of the country. After a trial by religious authorities, the assassin who had sought revenge for his brother was beheaded in front of the Great Mosque in Riyadh.

With the assassination of Faisal, his brother Khalid bin Abdul Aziz al Saud became king. Vice President Nelson Rockefeller represented the United States at the funeral, becoming the first vice president to visit the Kingdom.[81]

Faisal's Legacy

King Faisal transformed Saudi Arabia. He inherited from his father a kingdom that had reached its historic borders dominating the Arabian Peninsula. But it was a backwater, desperately poor and almost entirely illiterate. His brother Saud had taken the kingdom to the edge of disaster by spending recklessly. The military was rife with coup plots, the Royal Saudi Air Force useless due to nationalist cabals and plots. Meanwhile, Egypt's Nasser seemed poised to bring down another monarchy.

By the time Faisal died, the Kingdom was truly transformed. The monarchy was solidly in place, the economy booming, and the country had become a world player. Faisal appointed his half-brothers to positions of authority, which they would hold for the next half-century, including four who would go on to be kings: Khalid, Fahd, Abdallah, and Salman. He created the modern ministerial system that runs the kingdom to this day. The military became a loyal institution of the state. Schools opened for millions of young Saudis, including women, and others enjoyed the opportunity to study abroad.

The oil boom of the 1970s accelerated all of Faisal's programs. The Saudi economy became an engine of growth, transforming the country with airports, shipping ports, and superhighways. At home and abroad huge sums were poured into building mosques and other religious institutions. Faisal made the country the leader of the Islamic world, giving the Kingdom enormous influence, what is now called "soft power."

Faisal was also the architect of the special relationship with America. His trip to Washington in 1943 set the stage for his father's famous meeting with FDR. Faisal negotiated the Dhahran air base deal. At President Kennedy's urging, he began reforms inside the Kingdom that would help stabilize the monarchy and solidify its hold on power. He oversaw the clandestine operations that bogged Egypt down in a Yemeni quagmire that left Egypt vulnerable to catastrophic defeat by Israel in 1967.

After 1967 Faisal tried to urge Washington to accommodate Arab interests, but neither Johnson nor Nixon listened to him. In 1973 he used the oil weapon against the United States, imposing a major penalty on the American economy and forcing Washington to alter its policies toward Israel and the Arabs.[82] The man who had created the uneasy alliance in many ways was also prepared to use the economics of energy to make America pay greater attention to Saudi interests.

Chapter Three

KHALID AND CARTER, 1975 TO 1982

King Khalid bin Abdul Aziz ruled the Kingdom of Saudi Arabia for seven of its most critical and eventful years. He was confronted by two major events in the first half of his reign: the fall of the shah's monarchy in Iran and the separate Egyptian peace with Israel, both of which reached their climax in early 1979. These two events dramatically shook Saudi relations with the United States. Then in November 1979 the Grand Mosque in Mecca was seized by a group of religious fanatics, and the king had to authorize the use of deadly force to regain control of the holiest site in Islam. Almost immediately after the crisis in Mecca, the Soviet Union invaded Afghanistan in December 1979, and nine months later Iraq invaded Iran. The latter two crises pushed the Kingdom closer to America.

Khalid was born on February 13, 1913, in Riyadh. He was Ibn Saud's fifth son. In 1932 he was appointed viceroy of the Hejaz and served with the Saudi army in the war with Yemen, and later helped negotiate the treaty that ended the war. Ibn Saud then made him minister of the interior. He accompanied his older brother Faisal to London in 1939 for talks on the future of Palestine, and he accompanied Faisal again when they visited Washington in 1943 to lay the groundwork for the American-Saudi alliance.

The king had a history of heart trouble, and he had a serious heart incident in 1970, which led to heart surgery in Cleveland in 1972. As king he would return to Cleveland for more surgery in October 1978. Illness impacted his ability to rule, and Khalid delegated most of the day-to-day administration of the Kingdom to his younger brother, Crown Prince Fahd, giving him a major role in governing the Kingdom. Khalid remained the ultimate decisionmaker, however, and confronted alone the most serious challenge of his reign, the Mecca uprising, as Fahd was attending an Arab summit in Tunisia.

A CIA assessment prepared for the incoming administration of Jimmy Carter provides an American intelligence estimate of Khalid and his kingdom at the start of his turbulent reign. The assessment noted Fahd's day-to-day governance but said the king retained "the final authority." The CIA believed the "regime faces no threats of any consequence" at home. The Kingdom was stable although it would face daunting challenges as oil money led to rapid modernization of infrastructure and education. The CIA judged Khalid's top priority was a comprehensive settlement of the Arab-Israeli conflict, especially the Jerusalem issue. That would stabilize the region and reduce the dangers of war and terrorism. The king and crown prince believed "the U.S. is the key to a solution of the Arab Israeli problem because of its influence over Israel." The Saudis hoped President Carter would be their partner in peacemaking.[1]

John West, the new American ambassador to the Kingdom and friend of Carter, sent in his impressions of the royal family a few months later. He characterized Saudi Arabia as "presently undergoing an almost fantasy like experience similar to 'A Thousand and One Nights'—the whole country is changing overnight as though someone had rubbed Aladdin's lamp and said, 'Take this place into the Twentieth Century.'" He forecast this rapid change would "create tensions and frictions at all levels." The family was broadly divided between "liberals" led by Fahd and "conservatives" led by Prince Abdallah, third in line to the throne and a half-brother of Khalid and Fahd. He was more pious than most of his generation. Both factions were pro-American but the conservatives were more suspicious of Washington and worried that the pace of change was too fast. West warned Carter that "a failure of the Arab

Israeli peace negotiations coupled with continued U.S. support for Israel" was the most likely event to "cause real problems in U.S.-SAG [Saudi Arabia government] relations."[2] Carter read the report and wrote on it "superb report."

Twin Shocks Shake the Alliance

The Saudis were eager to get off to a good start with Carter after the bitterness of dealing with Henry Kissinger. In December 1976, at an Organization of Petroleum Exporting Countries (OPEC) summit in Doha, Qatar, the Kingdom refused to go along with Iran's push to raise oil prices again. Except for the United Arab Emirates, the rest of OPEC backed the shah. Saudi Arabia not only refused to increase its prices, it flooded the market by pumping more oil than ever before. The price remained constant, Iran was humiliated, and King Khalid and Oil Minister Ahmed Zaki Yamani had demonstrated who was really in charge of the global energy picture. Yamani publicly linked the oil decision to Saudi Arabia's hopes that Carter would take serious and decisive action to promote a comprehensive Arab-Israeli peace agreement. They were privately also pleased to see Iran lose clout.[3]

For his part, Jimmy Carter came into office in 1977 committed to achieving a comprehensive peace agreement to resolve the Palestinian issue. Carter was critical of Kissinger's diplomacy in general and his step-by-step approach in the Middle East in particular. He sought to convene jointly with the Soviet Union a peace conference in Geneva with all the Arab states and Israel to conclude a comprehensive peace. In May 1977 Crown Prince Fahd came to Washington to see Carter and engage in discussions on how to secure peace. The Saudis were prepared to live with Israel if the territories that Israel had occupied in 1967 were returned to the Arabs with minor border rectifications. Riyadh wanted the Palestinians to have their own independent state. Carter wrote in his diary that Fahd was very friendly and eager to find a settlement. He noted that the Saudis are "more interested in the Palestinian question than all the other problems" in the Middle East.[4]

On November 19, 1977, Egyptian president Anwar Sadat traveled to Jerusalem to meet directly with Israel's leaders and to address the Knesset. Sadat was frustrated by the slow movement of the Geneva process, which he felt gave too much leverage to the Soviets and Syrians. No Arab leader had ever met publicly with Israeli leaders before, especially not in Jerusalem. His unprecedented trip split the Arab world. Syria, Iraq, Algeria, Libya, and South Yemen accused him of seeking a separate peace with Israel that would return the Sinai Peninsula to Egypt, end the credible threat of an Arab military option against Israel, and leave the other Arab states abandoned to deal with a strengthened Israel. The Saudis, by contrast, were extremely reluctant to break with Sadat; they believed Egypt was central to the peace process. Sadat assured Khalid he did not want a separate peace. The Saudis cautiously waited to see what Sadat and Carter would do. Fahd told Secretary of State Cyrus Vance after Sadat's trip that it "was an impulsive act" but also an "important step."[5]

Carter traveled to the Middle East at the end of 1977. His Middle East trip began in Iran where he was received by the shah. On New Year's Eve Carter famously gave a toast declaring, "Iran, because of the great leadership of the Shah, is an island of stability in one of the most troubled parts of the world." His words, as he later wrote, "understandably, were derided when the Shah was overthrown thirteen months later."[6] In Iran, Carter met also with King Hussein of Jordan. Both the shah and the king urged Carter to pursue a comprehensive peace agreement.

After visiting India, Carter arrived in Riyadh on January 3, 1978, the second American president to visit the Kingdom. Carter was "pleasantly surprised at the vigor and involvement of King Khalid. Each day he has open court, so any citizen of his country can come and visit with him." Carter was especially impressed that Khalid ate with "common people" and "each evening when he goes back to his home palace he permits women to come in to meet with him."[7]

The detailed discussion of the region's problems was left to Crown Prince Fahd. Carter and Fahd reviewed Soviet activities in the region, oil policy, and bilateral relations. The Saudis were eager to get new American fighter aircraft, sixty F15s, for the Royal Saudi Air Force. They had raised this request at the beginning of the administration when Secretary of State Cyrus Vance met with Fahd in February 1977.[8]

The F15 sale was a political problem for Carter because it was opposed by the pro-Israel lobby in Congress. Israel was offered fifteen F15s (it already had sixty) and seventy-five F16s for itself and, after a bruising fight on the Hill, Carter was able to get the sale through the Congress by May 1978. The battle for the F15s was also Prince Bandar bin Sultan's maiden voyage into American politics. He had been training in Texas as an RSAF pilot when his father, Defense Minister Sultan bin Abdul Aziz al Saud, sent him to Washington to assist the lobbying campaign for the sale of the F15s. Bandar was good at working the Congress. Carter later recalled, "He was urbane, he was westernized adequately, he was eloquent, and he obviously had direct ties to the highest level of the royal family."[9] To reassure the Israelis, the prince conveyed an assurance via Washington that the RSAF would not deploy its F15s to Tabuk, its major air base near the Israeli state.[10]

But the major issue for Carter in Riyadh was the Arab-Israeli conflict. The Saudis pressed for Carter to commit to seeking a comprehensive agreement, not just an Egyptian peace treaty. Carter promised he would do so. Carter noted that the Saudis were "the only leaders I've met who want to see an independent Palestinian nation formed. Others [Arab states] only pay lip service to this, because of their reluctance to antagonize the Saudis." Carter said he was "very frank about this point. We [the United States] saw a real danger in an independent Palestinian state." Fahd told Carter the Kingdom wanted Sadat to succeed and was "eager to accommodate us on almost anything I request."[11]

Meanwhile, internal unrest began to snowball inside Iran. The Pahlavi dynasty faced many of the same socioeconomic frictions as the Saudis in modernizing rapidly. But Iran was also a more complex society with a much older history as a united nation. In Carter's diary the descent of the shah's regime can be traced over the course of 1978. Looking back later, Carter dates the beginning of the shah's downfall to the demonstrations that accompanied the monarch's visit to Washington in November 1977, which was marred by dramatic demonstrations across the street from the White House. In the summer of 1978 unrest became more frequent and violent. In October 1978 Carter noted the shah had broken all relations with Israel to appease the opposition, but this had no impact on the situation. On November 4, 1978, Carter notes in his diary that the shah was a weak and indecisive leader. On November 20 the president wrote, "We are concerned about the Shah's courage and forcefulness, and he seems to be excessively isolated." Carter found the Iranian situation to be a "quandary," but he was determined to give the shah as "much support as possible."[12]

The Saudis were shocked at what was developing across the Gulf in Iran. They were no fans of the shah, whom they regarded as arrogant and abrasive. His Pahlavi dynasty was founded by his father after World War I and had little legitimacy despite its pretensions to be the heirs of 4,000 years of Persian empires. The shah had seized several islands in the Gulf claimed by the United Arab Emirates when the British withdrew in 1972, an action that all the Arab states found threatening. His government had longstanding claims to Bahrain. Iran was also a close ally of Israel. Oil Minister Yamani once speculated that if there were another Arab-Israeli war, "Israel would occupy Tabuk in northern Saudi Arabia and Iran would occupy the Eastern Province and the small Gulf States." He told James Atkins, a previous American ambassador to Saudi Arabia, that the shah was "highly unstable mentally."[13]

Nonetheless, the unrest threatened a key U.S. ally against the Soviet Union and its radical Arab allies, like Iraq. Worse, the protests were a genuine national uprising against a monarch, orchestrated by the clerical establishment led by long-exiled Ayatollah Ruhollah Khomeini. The parallels to the Saudis' own position were all too obvious, although the Saudis argued they were fundamentally different situations. The Saudis were also convinced the Soviets were the real source of the opposition to the shah, somehow manipulating the situation behind the scenes to weaken an American ally and gain control of Iran. They were especially appalled that America seemed unable to smash the opposition and keep the shah, or at least a military government, in power. The Saudis had no formula for how to accomplish these goals, however.

The fall of 1978 proved to be a turning point for the Middle East. First, Carter hosted Sadat and Israeli prime minister Menachem Begin for a summit at the president's retreat at Camp David in Maryland. The result was a "framework" for an Egyptian-Israeli peace treaty and a much more vague agreement calling for autonomy for the Palestinians living in the West Bank and Gaza Strip. King Hussein of Jordan was to be the major interlocutor for negotiating autonomy, although he had not been invited to Camp David or informed about the negotiations as they were under way. Not surprising, he refused to take part in the Egyptian-Israeli autonomy talks. While the Camp David agreement was widely acclaimed in the United States and much of the world, it was almost universally seen in the Arab world as a betrayal by Sadat of the Palestinian cause and of Arab solidarity against Israel.

An Arab summit was convened in Baghdad on November 2, 1978, to discuss the Camp David agreement. Fahd attended for the Kingdom. The Baghdad summit agreed the Camp David agreements harmed the Palestinian cause, and the Arab leaders urged Sadat not to sign the peace treaty with Israel, freezing Egypt's position in the Arab League. For the Saudis it was an agonizing choice between Arab unity and the Palestinian cause on the one side and breaking with Egypt and the United States on the other. The king chose the Palestinian cause.

As the fall continued, the unrest in Iran escalated rapidly. By November massive demonstrations were sweeping Iranian cities, the oil industry was closed due to labor strikes, and the shah was isolated and confused. On the Shia holy day of Ashura that month, the day that commemorates the martyrdom of Ali's son Husayn in 680, millions of Iranians marched in massive demonstrations calling for the shah to abdicate or be overthrown. He went into exile in Egypt on January 16, 1979. The Saudis were stunned to see a monarchy collapse so quickly across the Gulf. By the end of February the monarchy was abolished and replaced by an Islamic Republic led by Ayatollah Khomeini, who promised publicly to overthrow the other monarchs in the region. The CIA told the White House that "Saudi reaction to Iranian developments is heavily colored by the conviction that the USSR is successfully engaged in a strategic effort to encircle Saudi Arabia," and the Saudis believed that Washington "does not appreciate the urgency of the situation."[14] The analysis argued a "conservative tide" was moving the ruling family away from close ties to the United States because of Camp David and the fall of the shah.

The Carter team tried to reassure the Saudis that America was still a reliable ally. Secretary of Defense Harold Brown traveled to Riyadh in February 1979 to propose closer military ties. A squadron of American F15 jets carried out a training mission in the kingdom, but to avoid raising tensions it was not armed with its usual complement of missiles. By the middle of 1979, the embarrassment of sending unarmed jets to defend the Kingdom, the U.S. support for Sadat's go-it-alone strategy, and the deteriorating situation in the Gulf had created "the most serious juncture in U.S.-Saudi relations since the 1973 Middle East War and oil embargo. Ties between the two appear to be marked by deepening frustration, conflicting goals and misunderstandings," reported the *Washington Post*.[15]

Sadat signed the formal peace treaty with Israel in Washington in March 1979. On March 31, 1979, the Arab summit in Baghdad was reconvened. Just before the Arab summit the two most hardline Arab states, Syria and Iraq, negotiated an end to their long-simmering feud over leadership of the Baath Party (a pan-Arab party with different factions ruling in Damascus and Baghdad). The temporary unity between Syria and Iraq greatly strengthened the anti-Sadat camp. As one expert notes, the Syria-Iraq rapprochement "forced the Saudis, privately reluctant to censure Egypt or antagonize Washington, to fall into line behind them."[16] Egypt's membership in the Arab League was suspended, and almost all the Arab states, including Saudi Arabia, withdrew diplomatic recognition from Egypt and closed their embassies in Cairo.

Crown Prince Fahd's standing in the Kingdom suffered seriously as a consequence of the twin setbacks. Fahd was rightly seen as the foremost advocate of close ties with both Carter and Sadat. He took an extended vacation in Europe from the end of March until the end of May 1979. This is a typical Saudi approach to the problem of being associated with an unpopular or unsuccessful policy gambit: escape the fallout by taking time out in your palace in Spain or elsewhere. Fahd's protégé, the head of royal intelligence, Kamal Adham, was relieved of his job, and Prince Turki bin Faisal became head of the General Intelligence Directorate.[17]

Khalid's decision to break with Cairo and Washington was consistent with Saudi policy toward the Arab-Israeli conflict. Since Ibn Saud's meeting with FDR in 1945, Saudi policy had been to support the Palestinians. In 1978 and 1979 Khalid was undoubtedly influenced by the legacy of his older brother Faisal. Given Faisal's actions during his own life, there is every reason to believe that if Faisal had been alive in the late 1970s he would have broken with Sadat and Carter over Camp David. Khalid, Abdallah, and a more reluctant Fahd were only doing what they expected Faisal would have done.

Officials in the Carter White House were highly critical of the Saudi decision to break with Sadat and not support Camp David. Gary Sick, Carter's National Security Council staff director for the Middle East, wrote a memo to the president characterizing Fahd's performance at the first Baghdad summit as "indecisive" and indicative of "a deeper malaise currently afflicting the

Saudi Royal Family." Khalid's well-known health issues kept him from day-to-day business, and now those problems reportedly were getting worse. "He has become very difficult to wake up in the morning and his concentration is said to be poor," Sick wrote. Faced with dramatic developments in the region, the Saudi leadership "is ill, indecisive and distracted by the succession struggle." The NSC experts recognized that Saudi Arabia was not Iran, but they raised concerns about the stability of the Kingdom and doubts about the CIA's ability to track unrest there.[18]

The perception that Saudi Arabia was ripe to follow Iran as the next monarchy to collapse into revolution was widespread in the United States in the wake of the shah's demise. A public opinion poll taken in early 1980 asked Americans about the chances of the Kingdom of Saudi Arabia being taken over by enemies of the United States in the new few years. Forty-three percent of those surveyed thought it was almost certain or somewhat likely, 29 percent thought it possible but not likely, and only 12 percent thought it not likely at all (17 percent answered "don't know").[19] Scholars at think tanks and universities wrote papers about the Kingdom's future, and many were bleak.

The White House convened a meeting of the national security team on April 27, 1979, to review ties with the Kingdom. The summary of the meeting's conclusions noted "a general consensus that the U.S. relationship with Saudi Arabia is undergoing a period of severe strain."[20] So with the U.S.-Saudi relationship in turmoil due to differences on the peace process and the collapse of the shah, an unprecedented domestic incident was about to shake the Kingdom. Washington would be almost entirely a bystander—a very worried bystander— in the next chapter in Khalid's reign.

The Assault on Mecca

The Grand Mosque in Mecca is Islam's holiest site, because at its center is the *Kaaba*, believed to be the first house of worship, built by Abraham. Muslims pray toward Mecca and the mosque five times a day and are buried with their heads pointing toward it. Only Muslims are allowed inside the city; it is a crime for non-Muslims to enter the city or its environs. For the House of Saud no role is more important than their responsibilities as custodians of the holy mosques. The Saudi conquest of Mecca from the Hashemites consolidated the modern Kingdom's hold on the Arabian Peninsula and made it a major power in the Arab and Islamic worlds. Between 1955 and 1973 the Saudis engaged in a major expansion of the mosque to increase its size and remove most of the vestiges of Ottoman or older architecture. Since 1979 the Saudis have engaged in three additional large-scale projects to expand the mosque's capacity.

On November 20, 1979, several hundred extreme fanatics entered the holy mosque. They secretly brought in weapons, ammunition, and food in coffins and other hiding places. Some of the local police and security guards were bribed into allowing in more weapons and supplies by back gates. There are no reliable numbers on how many extremists were involved in the assault (300 is a good guess), but they definitely took the security forces by complete surprise and had much more advanced small arms than the poorly trained and poorly armed police.[21] At dawn they brought their weapons out of hiding, quickly subdued the police, and took control of the mosque and several thousand hostages who had been worshiping that morning.

Our knowledge of the mosque's seizure and subsequent recapture by the Saudi authorities owes a great deal to Yaroslav Trofimov, an enterprising investigative journalist who published *The Siege of Mecca* in 2007 based on years of interviews inside the Kingdom, France, and the United States. He obtained access to the American ambassador's diary, a critical source for understanding the U.S. perception of the crisis from John West's pivotal position. Trofimov also secured considerable assistance from the then head of Saudi intelligence, Prince Turki bin Faisal, who was present at the battle and was a key interlocutor in securing help from the French for the final assault on the rebels.[22]

I was the Saudi analyst in 1979 in the CIA's office responsible for political analysis so I had a direct view of what the American intelligence community knew—and didn't know—about what was going on in the Kingdom. Some of that information recently has been declassified by the State Department. It was an extraordinary period. On November 4, just two weeks before the takeover of the mosque in Mecca, the American embassy in Tehran was seized by Iranian radicals, who would hold most of our diplomats hostage for the next 444 days. Shortly after the seizure of the mosque in Mecca, Iranian leader Ayatollah Khomeini accused the United States and Israel of responsibility for the attack. U.S. diplomatic posts across the Islamic world were the target of demonstrations and, often, violence. The embassy in Islamabad was sacked by a mob on November 21, and the embassy in Tripoli attacked by another mob on December 2.

When the mosque was seized, the first question asked by everyone was: who are these guys? An employee of the Haj Research Center in Mecca, Ziauddin Sardar, who was in Mecca that morning, later wrote:

> Saudi Arabia is a police state and bad news is buried quickly and permanently. There was a total blackout and no one had any idea what was happening. Mecca was under attack by Zionist and American imperialist plotters, said some. The Sacred Mosque had been taken over by renegade Shia from Ayatollah Khomeini's Iran, others speculated. A third theory postulated a split in the royal family, with Crown Prince Fahd's men trying to overthrow King Khalid.[23]

The Saudi authorities cut all communications to the Kingdom from the outside world. The mosque and the city were surrounded by concentric rings of security forces from the Saudi Ministry of the Interior run by Prince Nayef, the Saudi Arabian National Guard run by Prince Abdallah, and troops from the regular army run by Prince Sultan.

The rebels soon identified themselves to the authorities. They were Islamic radicals who believed the Mahdi had arrived. In Islamic eschatology, the Mahdi is a prophesied redeemer who will rid the world of evil and set the stage for the Final Day of Judgment. The Mahdi is not specifically referred to in the Quran, but there are many references to a Mahdi in the hadiths, the accounts of the Prophet Mohammad's life that are studied by Islamic theologians and scholars for insights into the religion. Not surprisingly, Sunni and Shia Muslims have very different visions of the Mahdi.

The insurgents in the Grand Mosque were led by two men. One was Juhayman al Utaybi, a former soldier in the Saudi National Guard who was the mastermind of the attack. The other was the self-proclaimed Mahdi, Muhammad Abdallah Qahtani, Juhayman's twenty-seven-year-old brother-in-law. Most of the rebels were Saudis, primarily from the Utaybi tribe, but others were followers of Juhayman from across the Islamic world. He had a particularly strong following in Kuwait. They freed most of the worshippers in the mosque after a few hours of trying to convince them of the legitimacy of their religious claims.

Juhayman had written a series of letters after he left the National Guard in which he attacked the House of Saud for its close ties to America and for widespread corruption, citing Wahhabi scholars to justify his arguments. His focus was on the concept of the Mahdi. Juhayman said it was revealed to him in a dream in late 1978 that his brother-in-law was the Mahdi because he had the right family heritage to be the redeemer and his physical appearance was as foretold in the hadiths. Juhayman's letters were published and circulated widely in the Kingdom and in Kuwait.[24]

It quickly emerged in the royal court that members of the Saudi religious clergy were well aware of Juhayman and his group. In fact, the top cleric in the Kingdom was their patron and protector: the blind shaykh Abdul Aziz bin Baz, who was a very conservative leader of the Wahhabi clergy. Baz was notorious for believing the world was flat and that high heels were evil. He intervened with Prince Nayef to keep Juhayman's followers out of prison at least once before 1979—not because he believed the Mahdi was coming imminently but because he believed Juhayman's followers were pious Muslims. Born in 1910, bin Baz had been chancellor of the Islamic University of Medina and the chairman of the Scientific Research and Religious Edicts group that issues edicts for the Kingdom. In 1992 he became grand mufti of Saudi Arabia. Bin Baz had been a patron of dozens of what one observer in Mecca then called "irrational zealots."[25] Bin Baz was not aware of Juhayman's plans to attack the mosque or to use force, but he knew exactly who Juhayman was.[26]

The mosque was a natural fortress that had been built and rebuilt over the centuries. Six large minarets, 292 feet high, provided excellent observation points and positions for snipers and machine gunners to control the inside and outside of the mosque. Under the surface is a series of tunnels and rooms called the *Qaboo* that made for an excellent hiding area and an almost impenetrable bunker to fight from, especially for fanatics ready to die for their Mahdi. In the early hours after the takeover, with no architectural plans for the site, the Saudi authorities were able to get the assistance of the bin Laden construction company, which was in charge of the mosque's expansion and had detailed plans for the mosque and the Qaboo. The Hajj Research Centre in

Mecca also provided detailed plans that could be used for the recapture of the mosque.[27]

King Khalid was in Riyadh when the attack occurred. It was the first day of Muharram in the Islamic year 1400—the Islamic New Year and the start of the fifteenth century for Muslims. Khalid was home alone, to a certain extent. Crown Prince Fahd was in Tunisia at another Arab summit to condemn Sadat; with him were Foreign Minister Prince Saud al Faisal and the intelligence chief, Prince Turki al Faisal. Deputy Crown Prince and National Guard Commander Abdallah was in Morocco on vacation. Khalid quickly convened the available senior princes: Prince Sultan and Prince Nayef, as well as Mecca governor Prince Fawwaz.

The royal family was relieved to learn there were no other uprisings in the Kingdom. The Sunni majority was quiet. The other holy city, Medina, was calm. Later, unrelated violence would break out in the Shia towns in the Eastern Province, but they were not believers in the Mahdi. On November 25 large demonstrations in those towns protested Saudi discrimination against Shia. Three days later, the National Guard used massive force to break up Ashura commemorations in Qatif, the stronghold of Shia in the province, which had turned into anti-monarchy protests. The National Guard's suppression was brutal and effective. The historic center of the old city of Qatif was totally demolished and replaced with a parking lot and a large Sunni mosque. However, the Shia unrest did not affect the siege in Mecca.[28]

The royal family asked the clerical establishment, the *ulema* headed by bin Baz, for a religious edict authorizing the use of force to retake the mosque. It took several days to gather the clerics together and for them to debate. On November 23, 1979, they issued a document authorizing the Kingdom to use "all measures" necessary.[29] Even then the family refrained from use of the Royal Saudi Air Force or bombing.

The ground assault was hampered by multiple chains of command. The Interior Ministry forces were directed by Prince Nayef, the National Guard by Abdallah or his subordinates, and the regular army by Prince Sultan. It was a bloody and messy affair as none of the three services was trained in urban warfare or well equipped for the battle. The Saudis attempted to use tear gas against the rebels, some of it provided by the United States, but the troops were untrained in how to use the gas and were poorly equipped with gas masks to defend themselves from it. By the end of the first week of the siege, however, the surface level of the mosque was back in Saudi hands, the remaining rebels having been driven into the Qaboo.

It took another week, with help from the French, to reclaim the underground chambers and capture Juhayman and the rest of his followers. Prince Turki secured the help of the French intelligence community to defeat the holdouts. Both Prince Turki and Prince Nayef had close relations with their French counterparts. Khalid took their advice and appealed to Paris, discreetly, for help. French president Giscard d'Estaing sent three French commandoes along with the chemical agent dichlorobenzylidene-malononitrile, or CB. The French commandoes never went into the Grand Mosque but they trained Saudis in how to use the agent, and it worked. The Qaboo was secured and all the remaining rebels killed or captured by the end of the second week of the siege.[30]

The Saudis had specifically turned down an offer of assistance from Jordan. King Hussein visited Riyadh on November 28, 1979, while the Qaboo was still in Juhayman's hands and offered the use of his elite special forces. Khalid and Abdallah met with Hussein and politely refused his offer. The last thing the Saudis wanted was to have the Hashemites recover Mecca for them from religious zealots.[31]

On December 6, 1979, King Khalid visited the mosque and was shown on Saudi television walking safely inside the holy site. Prince Nayef announced that seventy-five rebels and sixty Saudi soldiers had died in the battle. Ambassador West later reported to Washington that the real fatality toll was closer to 1,000. The self-proclaimed Mahdi had died in the battle, but Juhayman was captured. On January 9, 1980, sixty-three rebels were executed publicly in eight Saudi cities. Forty-one were Saudis, ten were Egyptians, six were South Yemenis, three Kuwaitis, and one each came from North Yemen, Iraq, and Sudan. Juhayman's organization was destroyed in Saudi Arabia by a ruthless crackdown by the Interior Ministry. A remnant survived in Kuwait for a few years.[32]

The governor of Mecca, Prince Fawwaz bin Abdul Aziz, resigned his post in late December, serving as the scapegoat in the royal family for the failure to see what Juhayman was planning and for the botched initial attempts to stop the takeover. He was an easy scapegoat since he was a fairly liberal prince and had flirted with Egypt's Nasser in the 1960s. Juhayman had criticized him for drinking alcohol and gambling. Several military commanders were also fired, including, for no obvious reason, the commander of the Air Force.[33]

President Carter and his team in Washington were worried observers to the Mecca mosque siege. The Saudis provided critical information about events in the first few days of the attack, despite their embarrassment about losing control of the mosque. The U.S. Embassy in Jidda was able to get some firsthand accounts of the situation from an American helicopter pilot who worked for the Saudi civil defense system and was flying reconnaissance missions over the mosque. He privately briefed the embassy on what he had seen and learned. The petroleum minister, Shaykh Zaki Yamani, was the first Saudi government official to brief Ambassador West on the attack and revealed that the attackers were Sunni zealots led by a self-proclaimed Mahdi.[34]

The day after the attack began, November 21, 1979, the embassy in Jidda reported (in a recently declassified cable to Washington) that the twenty-six-year-old self-proclaimed Mahdi, Muhammad Abdallah, had seized the mosque with between 200 and 500 followers. The mission reported that "there is no repeat no direct relationship with Iran and Muhammad and his followers deny any Khomeini influence in their actions." According to a senior Saudi cabinet official (Yamani), the Saudi authorities did not see the mosque attack as a fundamental danger to the monarchy because the attackers "lacked sophisticated leadership sufficient to translate their religious principles into overthrow of a civil government." Aside from a few minor incidents in Medina, the rebels had no broader support, the embassy reported.[35] The embassy reporting provided the basis of the intelligence community's assessment for the White House.

Reacting to the events in Tehran, Mecca, and Islamabad, the Carter administration in late November sent a United States Navy carrier battle group, led by the nuclear carrier the USS *Kitty Hawk*, to the Persian Gulf as a show of force. In announcing the deployment, the administration press spokesman reported that "some kind of disturbance, apparently a seizure of a mosque by a group" had occurred in Mecca at the Grand Mosque. This was the first public statement by any government about the takeover, breaking the Saudi efforts to keep it a secret.[36] The Saudis were livid. Prince Nayef, the head of the Interior Ministry, said later that the American announcement helped trigger the wave of violence against American diplomats that followed. He even speculated "about the reason why the Americans announced the report the way they did." Nayef would not be a friend of the United States for many reasons as he rose in prominence in the royal family, and this was one of those reasons.[37]

There was much speculation in Washington that Iran must be behind the attack in Mecca given the heated atmosphere over the U.S. hostages in Tehran and the unrest among Shias in the Eastern Province. The CIA fairly quickly concluded the mosque takeover was not an Iranian provocation, however: "The attack appears to have been the isolated act of a small group of religious fanatics. The Saudis have had to quell uprisings by similar groups in the past, most notably in the 1920s and 1930s when dissident elements of the Ikhwan— the military arm of the Wahhabi religious movement—rose against the Saudi monarchy. In 1975 King Faysal was assassinated by a religious fanatic."[38] The embassy reports and the Saudis' own reporting all confirmed that no Iranian hands were involved.

Despite the huge shock of the Mecca attack, the rebels never posed an existential threat to the survival of the House of Saud. Juhayman and his band of about 300 (the CIA estimated "several hundred")[39] could not have overthrown the monarchy. They got no assistance from others in the Kingdom. Their connections with clerics like bin Baz were covered up quickly, and the Wahhabi clergy not only condemned them but sentenced them to execution. As the CIA noted in its retrospective shortly after the mosque was recaptured, the rebels enjoyed no mass support in the Kingdom: "On the contrary, most Saudis appear to be outraged by the desecration of the mosque and there have been numerous calls, especially from the Saudi religious establishment, for quick punishment of the attackers."[40]

Nonetheless, the attack on the holy mosque had a profound impact on the royal family. It symbolized the reality that the danger to the family's hold on power no longer came from Egyptian-inspired leftist nationalists like in the 1960s but, rather, extremist Islamic zealots outraged by corruption and change. The rapid modernization of the country inevitably produced resistance from those who were attached to core Wahhabi principles. As one Saudi historian has written, "The mosque siege unveiled the tension between the state and its own religion."[41] Even if the clerical establishment reluctantly agreed to modernization, some dissidents were ready to use arms to fight change and resist the royal family. Senior family leaders concluded, therefore, that the best assurance against such dangers was to embrace the faith even more vigorously, slow down social changes, bring the clerics closer to the family, and find causes for Faisal's global Islamic movement to support and encourage.

Only weeks after King Khalid's triumphal walk through the Grand Mosque such an opportunity would present itself. The Soviet Union would invade its Muslim neighbor Afghanistan and set the stage for the final and decisive battle of the Cold War. The invasion would present the occasion for America and Saudi Arabia to work together to defeat Moscow and international communism. It would, of course, have other consequences as well.

The Saudis spent billions restoring the mosque after the battle in November 1979 and then vastly expanding its size and transforming the neighborhoods around it. After Khalid's death, King Fahd expanded the mosque with fourteen more gates and two more minarets. A million worshippers could be accommodated during the hajj season. New roads and tunnels were built to speed traffic into Mecca and make the hajj more orderly. A third massive expansion began in 1988 with Fahd building a royal palace overlooking the mosque.[42] The contract for the expansion was given to the Saudi Bin Laden Group, the huge construction company founded by Osama bin Laden's father, the largest construction company in the Middle East. One of the most recent projects built more than 300 retractable canopies to shelter worshipers from the sun. From 1979 to 2016 the Saudis spent $26.6 billion on the mosque.[43]

Some Muslims have been critical of the Saudi expansion projects, arguing they have destroyed many old Islamic architectural treasures that could have been preserved. Some argue that the many accidents that have plagued the hajj in the last quarter century are due in part to the hasty expansion and the creation of tunnels and overpasses that become death traps for tired, thirsty pilgrims, especially the elderly. One critic called the reconstruction a Saudi "nightmare vision of modernity, turning Mecca into Disneyland."[44]

Today the largest bell tower clock in the world looks down on the Grand Mosque. Built at a cost of $15 billion, the Makkah Royal Clock Tower, part of Abraj al-Bait, a development in the heart of Mecca, is the third-tallest building in the world. The bin Laden group was the contractor; an Ottoman fortress was demolished to build it. The clock is visible for miles and is illuminated at night. The structure includes a shopping mall and the Hotel Fairmont Mecca, a five-star, luxury 800-room hotel for Muslims only. It has 1.5 million square meters of floor space and two helicopter landing pads on the roof. A one-room studio apartment sells for $650,000.[45] The minarets of the Grand Mosque are now overlooked by a much taller skyscraper.

Afghanistan and Iraq

Events in late 1979 outside the Kingdom quickly and dramatically altered the picture for King Khalid. On December 24, the Soviet Union invaded Afghanistan. The Soviet air force launched a massive airlift of troops into Afghanistan's capital, Kabul, to overthrow a failing Marxist government and replace it with another entirely beholden to Moscow. The 105 Guards Airborne Division, one of Russia's most elite military units, led the assault. Some 300 transport flights delivered the division to Bagram air base outside the capital. The previous regime was deposed, its leader killed, and a new Soviet-backed government imposed. Soviet armored forces also crossed the border from Soviet Central Asia and occupied all of Afghanistan's main cities in a couple of days. Over the Christmas holiday, the Soviet Union's Fortieth Red Army invaded and occupied Afghanistan.

President Carter was caught by surprise. His private diary shows he was at Camp David to celebrate Christmas and was shocked by the Russian attack. The American intelligence community had carefully monitored the buildup of Soviet forces in the months preceding the invasion but assessed that a Soviet invasion was unlikely because it would lead to a prolonged insurgency like Vietnam. The CIA thought the Soviet leadership was too smart to fall into such a quagmire.[46]

Immediately after the Soviet invasion, the president of neighboring Pakistan, General Mohammad Zia ul Haq, called King Khalid to discuss the Soviet threat, then urgently sent his intelligence chief to Riyadh to meet with King Khalid and Prince Turki. Zia was convinced the Soviet invasion of Afghanistan was the first step in a larger plan of Russian aggression. Zia believed Pakistan or Iran would be next, giving Moscow a warm-water port on the Arabian Sea and the Straits of Hormuz, along with control over the Persian Gulf and its oil resources. His fears matched those of the Saudis. The king agreed immediately to support Pakistan and assist its efforts to arm and train an Afghan resistance, the mujahedin, to fight the Soviet occupation.[47]

Carter scheduled a National Security Council meeting at the White House for December 28. His national security adviser, Zbigniew Brzezinski, set the stage with a memo to the president the day before the meeting. In it he argued that whatever Moscow's immediate motives for the invasion, once they were in Afghanistan the Soviets' motives and ambitions might grow, given the instability in Iran and Pakistan. Moscow's advances "could produce a Soviet presence right down on the edge of the Arabian and Oman Gulfs." To stop the Russians it was essential to provide "money as well as arms shipments to the rebels" in Afghanistan in "concert with Islamic countries in a covert action campaign to help the rebels." The Saudis would be a crucial partner in the struggle, and China should be enlisted, as well as European allies like the United Kingdom and France. Aid to Pakistan, which had been suspended because of the country's work to acquire nuclear weapons, must be restored as well.[48]

As he wrote in his diary, the president and his team decided to regard the Soviet invasion as "a radical departure from the reticence which the Soviets had shown for the last ten years since they overthrew the government of Czechoslovakia" and "to make this action by the Soviets as politically costly as possible." Carter said he "sent on the Hot Line the sharpest message that I have ever sent to [Soviet leader Leonid] Brezhnev, telling him the invasion of Afghanistan would seriously and adversely affect the relationship between our two countries." The president decided to impose economic sanctions on Russia: interrupting grain sales and high technology sharing; canceling fishing rights; restricting negotiations on culture, trade, commerce, and other bilateral exchanges; canceling visits to the Soviet Union; and establishing differences in technology and trade transfers that would benefit Communist China at the Soviets' expense. These moves were announced in January.[49]

The president also decided to sign a secret "Presidential Finding" authorizing a new covert action by the CIA to supply lethal weapons to the mujahedin through the Pakistani government. Signed on December 29,[50] this document notified the Congress of the covert action so it would be able to conduct oversight of the program.[51]

The chief of the Near East Division in the CIA's Directorate of Operations at the time was Charles Cogan, a longtime veteran of the CIA with years of experience in clandestine activity. Cogan quickly turned the Presidential Finding into action. Cogan had just become head of the division the previous summer, and he would stay in that key post until 1984. His officers were ready to act. As he relates in his memoir, "The first arms—mainly .303 Enfield rifles—arrived in Pakistan on January 10, 1980, fourteen days after the Soviet invasion." The initial goal was "for the purpose of harassing the Soviet occupation forces in Afghanistan."[52]

The arms were carefully chosen so their origin could not be traced to the United States, thereby allowing the operation to remain secret and giving the president plausible deniability that a secret war was under way. Carter wanted to emphasize Soviet-origin weapons so they would appear to be simply weapons captured on the battlefield. The CIA's professional operators saw the same need to keep hidden the CIA role.

Pakistani cooperation was essential to Carter's plan to resist the Soviet takeover. Carter called General Zia after the December 28, 1979, NSC meeting to ask him to receive Deputy Secretary of State Warren Christopher with an urgent message. According to Carter's diary, Zia was "reluctant" to have Christopher come immediately as the situation was "delicate, tragic and sensitive" in Pakistan, but he made clear that he wanted American aid for Pakistan and the Afghan resistance. Zia told Carter that Pakistan now faced an "onslaught" by the Soviets, but that Pakistan was determined to resist. Zia also wanted plausible deniability of the role to be played by Pakistan's intelligence service—just as Carter did for the CIA. The basis of American-Pakistani covert cooperation was established in the call.[53]

The president wanted to build a large global alliance against the Soviets and supporting Pakistan. Moscow blocked any significant action in the United Nations Security Council with its veto, but the UN General Assembly was urgently convened. Pakistani foreign minister Agha Shahi led the campaign to condemn the Soviets in the General Assembly, with strong support from Saudi Arabia's Prince Saud al Faisal. The General Assembly voted 104 to eighteen, with fourteen abstentions, to condemn the Russian action. It was a stunning diplomatic defeat for Moscow, which got support only from fellow members of the Soviet bloc.

The president convened another high-level meeting at a White House breakfast on January 4, 1980, to review aid to Pakistan and the Afghan rebels. His preference, as he outlined in his diary, "was to send them the kind of weapons they could use in the mountains in a portable condition, primarily against tanks and armored personnel carriers. We need to get as many other nations as possible to join us in a consortium so that the Paks won't be directly seen as dependent on or subservient to us."[54] The Saudi Kingdom was the key to the consortium.

Pakistani foreign minister Shahi was invited to visit Washington after the UN vote. Carter and Zia spoke on the phone again on January 8, 1980, and Carter met with Shahi four days later in the Oval Office. Carter proposed a $400 million aid package in combined economic and military assistance over a two-year period. Washington would also urge aid for Islamabad "from the Saudis, European allies, and Japan," Carter recounts in his diary.

In February 1980 Deputy Secretary of State Christopher and Brzezinski went to Islamabad and Riyadh. The two American envoys presented General Zia and then King Khalid with a broad overview of Washington's post-invasion thinking. Brzezinski later said that he found Zia very self-confident and assured despite the dangerous waters around Pakistan. The Saudis were deeply alarmed by the Soviet threat and, despite the disappointments over Camp David and Iran, eager to work with Washington.[55] In a meeting of the national security principals on February 6, 1980, Brzezinski and Christopher reported a "change of mood in Saudi Arabia from a year ago" due to the Soviet invasion of Afghanistan and renewed Soviet subversive actions elsewhere in Yemen and East Africa.[56]

The centerpiece of the strategy was covert aid to the mujahedin. The CIA and the Saudi intelligence service, led by Prince Turki, would give money to the Pakistani intelligence service, the Inter-Services Intelligence Directorate (known as the ISI), to arm and train the Afghan insurgents in camps inside Pakistan. The ISI would also assist the mujahedin in carrying out attacks inside Afghanistan against the Soviets. The CIA and Saudi intelligence would have no direct presence in Afghanistan. Instead, Washington and Riyadh would be the financiers and arms suppliers for the war.[57]

The Christopher and Brzezinski mission was a success in both Islamabad and Riyadh. The Saudis agreed to match American funding for the mujahedin, and the partnership among the three intelligence services was set in place. "Zbig reported privately to me that his trip to Pakistan and Saudi Arabia was successful," Carter wrote in his diary on February 6, 1980. Both Zia and the Saudis also wanted American "protection," but they wanted it kept private. In public they would be defended by "unanimity among the Muslim world," Carter wrote. The secret war would stay behind the scenes.[58]

The Saudis also asked Zia for help protecting the Kingdom at home. Beginning in 1982 Pakistan deployed a reinforced armored brigade to Saudi Arabia stationed in Tabuk. Its primary mission was to guard against an Israeli attack from the northwest, but it also served as a loyal Praetorian Guard force if the royal family needed assistance. The 12th Khalid bin Walid Independent Armored Brigade grew to 20,000 troops at its height. Saudi Arabia paid for all the costs of the Pakistani deployment, which lasted throughout the 1980s. It was a hedge just in case the Americans were not reliable.[59]

In his State of the Union address on January 23, 1980, Carter explained his strategy to the American people without discussing the covert operation. He said the Middle East was now threatened by "the Soviet troops in Afghanistan." They posed a direct threat to "more than two-thirds of the world's exportable oil. The Soviet effort to dominate Afghanistan has brought the Soviet military to within 300 miles of the Indian Ocean and close to the Straits of Hormuz, a waterway through which most of the world's oil must flow. The Soviet Union is now attempting to consolidate a strategic position, therefore, that poses a grave threat to the free movement of Middle East oil."

Carter announced that after careful thought and consultation with key allies in the region it was vital to "preserve the security of this crucial region." He said, "Let our position be absolutely clear: an attempt by any outside force to gain control of the Persian Gulf region will be regarded as an assault on the vital interests of the United States of America, and such an assault will be repelled by all means necessary, including military force." Carter did not specifically refer to the Kingdom of Saudi Arabia, but his speech was the clearest statement by any president to date that America would defend the Kingdom by force if it were threatened.[60]

The "Carter doctrine," as it was labeled immediately, was implemented by creating a new military command to rush American forces to the region in an emergency. This would become, in time, the Central Command with its headquarters in Tampa, Florida. Carter also announced the United States would boycott the 1980 Olympic Summer Games in Moscow; eventually sixty-five countries joined the boycott.

The Saudi response to the Soviet invasion was not limited to the official financing of the covert war. Saudis, both royals and commoners, were enthusiastic supporters of the mujahedin and the fight against communism. Khalid appointed his brother Salman to lead a private fundraising campaign to raise more money for the Afghan resistance. Prince Salman bin Abdul Aziz was born on December 31, 1935, and had been governor of Riyadh province since 1962. Since most royals lived in Riyadh, Salman was closely connected to the family, literally knowing all its secrets. When the Kingdom had begun in the early twentieth century, Riyadh had only 10,000 inhabitants. By 2017 it had 7 million, with most of the growth occurring on Salman's watch.

Salman's impressive skills as a top administrator led Khalid and Fahd to select him to establish a "private" committee to raise funds for the mujahedin from Saudi princes and the public. The head of the Saudi Wahhabi clerical establishment, Shaykh Abdul Aziz bin Baz, issued a religious order, or fatwa, charging Salman's committee to raise funds from across the Kingdom to fund the jihad in Afghanistan. As a result, the Kingdom would contribute both official money and private money to the war.[61]

The private Saudi funds were especially critical in the first years, when American support was small. As the head of the Pakistan intelligence service's Afghan cell has written, "It was largely Arab money that saved the system. By this I mean cash from rich individuals or private organizations in the Arab world, not Saudi government funds. Without these extra millions the flow of arms actually getting to the mujahedin would have been cut to a trickle" before 1983.[62] One American estimate is that private Saudi donations through Salman's committee averaged around $20 million to $25 million a month.[63]

The cleric bin Baz was also active in the propaganda side of the war in Afghanistan. He wrote the foreword to an influential book published in 1984 titled *The Defense of Muslim Lands*. The author was a Palestinian, Abdallah Azzam, who had lived and studied in the Kingdom before moving to Pakistan after the Soviet invasion. Azzam's book argued that the war in Afghanistan was a jihad, a holy war that should be supported by every Muslim as a holy obligation to defeat Russian aggression against a Muslim country. It was an enormously successful book read by Muslims around the world and remains a major ideological statement of the global jihad today. Bin Baz's endorsement of it was a major statement of the Wahhabi and Saudi commitment to the jihad in Afghanistan.[64]

Other Saudis also volunteered to help the Afghan cause. The most famous today is Osama bin Laden, a son of Mohammad bin Awad bin Laden, the wealthiest construction mogul in the Kingdom. Born in 1908 in Hadramut Province of Yemen, Muhammad had immigrated to the Kingdom and built a construction empire. He was the builder of Ibn Saud's palace in Riyadh, the airports and seaports of the Kingdom, its modern highways, and, most important, the expansion of the holy mosques in Mecca and Medina. He also was in charge of the restoration of the third-holiest mosque in Islam in Jerusalem in the early 1960s at the request of Jordan's King Hussein.

Muhammad bin Laden was a pious man who funded the improvements to the Dome of the Rock and the Noble Sanctuary—the Haram al Sharif in Jerusalem—from his own pocket and hosted many pilgrims visiting Mecca at his own home. Among those were prominent Afghans and Pakistanis like Burhanuddin Rabbani, the future president of Afghanistan, and Qazi Hussain Ahmed, the leader of Jamaat e Islami, Pakistan's leading Islamist party. These men were "common faces" to Osama bin Laden, well before the Soviet invasion, because he had met them with his father and during their visits to Mecca after his father's death.[65]

In December 1979 the young Osama bin Laden flew to Pakistan to help the fight against the Russians. He arrived in Peshawar, Pakistan, on the Afghan border even before the first arms from the CIA arrived in Karachi. Just twenty-two-years-old in 1979, Osama bin Laden met with the leadership of Jamaat e Islami immediately after arriving in Pakistan. He established a close working relationship with the Islamists, who were also close to Zia ul Haq.[66] At first bin Laden's principle work was in facilitating the flow of the private Saudi money from the Kingdom's donors to the Afghans in Pakistan. He was perfect for the job since he was so well connected, through his father's company, with the powerful and wealthy leadership in the Kingdom and, on the other end, with the Pakistani Islamists and Afghan party leaders. His contacts in the Kingdom included not just Prince Turki bin Faisal, the intelligence chief, but the very powerful minister of the interior, Prince Nayef bin Abdul Aziz, brother of both Fahd and Salman.[67]

Osama bin Laden was ambitious and eager to be more than a financier. By 1985 he had recruited other Saudis to help him in creating an Arab fighting force that would join with the mujahedin in fighting inside Afghanistan. With the help of the bin Laden construction empire, bin Laden assisted in the building of the Zhawar base camp, the largest base inside Afghanistan for the Pakistani intelligence service and mujahedin, as well as underground fortresses for the mujahedin. In late 1985 he built a fortress for his own band, which he called the Lions' Den. Like the Zahwar camp, it was in eastern Paktia province, adjacent to the border with Pakistan. On August 17, 1987, bin Laden's small band fought an intense firefight with Soviet troops at the camp, known as the battle of Jaji. It was his first combat experience.[68]

Bin Laden was joined by hundreds of other Saudis eager to wage jihad. Thousands of Muslims from other countries came, as well, many inspired by *The Defense of Muslim Lands*. The Afghan Arabs, as they became known, were a trivial part of the military campaign against the 40th Red Army. Perhaps 500 Arabs and other Muslims died in the war against the Russians in the 1980s, according to the estimate of a senior CIA analyst who worked on the war at the time.[69] Tens of thousands of Afghan mujahedin died in combat with the Russians and over a million Afghan civilians died as a result of the war. Ultimately, it was Saudi money, not Arab jihadists, who contributed most to the victory. We return to Osama bin Laden's remarkable story in the next chapter as the war in Afghanistan comes to its climax under President Ronald Reagan and King Fahd later in the 1980s.

As 1980 developed, the Carter administration was increasingly consumed with the Iran problem. A rescue mission to free the American hostages in Tehran failed disastrously on April 24, 1980, with eight American soldiers killed. The hostages were immediately removed from the embassy compound where they had been incarcerated since November 1979, and dispersed in small groups around Iran, making another rescue attempt impossible. The Iranians secretly brought them back to Tehran during the summer and put most of them in Komiteh prison, where they were held until their eventual release.[70]

That same summer the Soviets conducted a secret military exercise in preparation for a possible invasion of Iran. It was entirely a Moscow headquarters exercise; no troops were actually deployed to simulate an invasion, but it caused serious worry in Washington. It was unclear then whether this exercise indicated a new Soviet interest in a possible invasion or was simply a routine Russian military drill.[71]

A Special National Intelligence Estimate prepared in August 1980 concluded that "the Soviets are indeed developing plans for military contingencies in Iran." The exercise involved an invasion force of sixteen divisions and would include elements of the 40th Red Army in Afghanistan. Brzezinski pressed for an explicit warning to Moscow that "any Soviet military action in Iran would lead to a direct military confrontation with the United States."[72] Again, most analysts at the CIA thought an invasion unlikely, but the exercise and modest increases in the readiness status of Soviet forces in Turkmenistan and the Caucasus region were worrisome.[73]

Then in September 1980 a series of clashes began along the Iraq-Iran border. The CIA warned the White House on September 17, 1980, that major hostilities were imminent. This would further complicate the hostage situation, disrupt Iraqi and Iranian oil exports, and "would involve Iraq in costly and protracted struggle with Iran." Early Iraqi successes would not mean Iran's defeat. The agency warned, as well, that Iran "would probably step up its appeals to Shia in Iraq to revolt and might also urge the Shias in Saudi Arabia, Kuwait, Bahrain and other Gulf countries to attack Iraqi and U.S. interests."[74] Within days the Iraqi army invaded Iran, beginning what was to become the largest and longest conventional war anywhere in the world since Korea; it would last eight years and kill hundreds of thousands. The Carter administration was preoccupied for weeks with containing the war and keeping it from spreading throughout the Persian Gulf. The sultan of Oman seriously considered allowing Iraq to stage bombing raids from its territory into Iran, for example, and the Carter team had to persuade the sultan that such a move would only expand the war.[75]

Riyadh was friendly with neither Iran nor Iraq. Iran was a Shia theocracy dedicated to overthrowing all the monarchs in the Gulf, while Iraq was a radical Baathist republic also dedicated to overthrowing the monarchs. King Khalid told a family conclave in September 1980 to recall lines from an Arab poem: "maybe the snakes will die from the poisonous stings of the scorpion."[76] But from the perspective of the 1980s, Iran was the greater long-term threat, so the Carter administration almost immediately was asked by the Gulf states to tilt toward Iraq.[77]

Despite their ambivalence, the Saudis supported the Iraqi attack on Iran from the start. It is unclear if they had any prior notification from Saddam that the invasion was coming, but they clearly welcomed Saddam Hussein's attempt to destroy the Islamic Republic. By the fall of 1980 the Iranian regime was openly calling for the overthrow of the Saudi monarchy and training Saudi Shia dissidents at camps in Iran. Iranian radio stations and other propaganda mediums broadcast constant attacks on the king and the House of Saud. The Iranians directed much of their effort at encouraging unrest in the Eastern Province and nearby Bahrain.[78]

The CIA warned President Carter that Iran might escalate the war and strike oil targets in Saudi Arabia to force the United States and the Soviets to pressure Baghdad to end its offensive. CIA director Admiral Stansfield Turner told the National Security Council on September 27 that this was a "very real possibility." Carter agreed to send U.S. Air Force AWACs (airborne warning and control aircraft) to Riyadh to improve Saudi air defenses. The Saudis agreed not to share the data collected with the Iraqis. Saudi defense minister Prince Sultan and the Pentagon began contingency planning in case the war expanded.

At first Saudi support for Iraq was primarily diplomatic, including support at the United Nations. The Saudis also urged other Arab and Islamic states to break with Iran and sought to bring the Gulf monarchies closer together to combat Iranian subversion. In May 1981 Khalid convened a summit of the six Gulf states and announced the formation of the Gulf Cooperation Council, which then served as a forum for closer intelligence cooperation among the participants.

The Iraqi invasion soon bogged down. By early 1982 Iran had successfully evicted the Iraqis from its territory and threatened to invade Iraq. The Iranians appeared poised to defeat Iraq and dominate the region, an outcome that had seemed improbable only a couple years earlier.

On June 13, 1982, King Khalid finally succumbed to a heart attack in his palace in Taif. His body was immediately brought to Riyadh, and he was buried the same day. Crown Prince Fahd ascended to the throne and Prince Abdallah became the new crown prince. Khalid's relatively short but eventful reign was characterized by strong continuities with his predecessor Faisal. Both were eager to have good ties with America. Both had been present at the creation of the relationship in Washington in 1943, and both saw it as crucial to defending the Kingdom from foreign aggression, especially by the Soviet Union. Yet both found it difficult to reconcile their desire for security from the United States with their strong dedication to the Palestinian cause. Prince Abdallah told Ambassador West in June 1980, "Arabs all over the Mideast are now convinced your policies are set in Tel Aviv and Jerusalem." West commented to Carter that this Saudi perception of U.S. policy "strikes at the very heart of the bilateral relationship" and produced deep disillusionment within the royal family.[79] In 1973 and 1979 the American-Saudi relationship was battered by differences over Palestine in general and Jerusalem in particular. Of course, Ibn Saud and FDR had the same difficulty decades earlier.

Faisal and Khalid were also deeply committed to the defense of Islam and especially to the Saudi-Wahhabi vision of Islam. Khalid was shaken by the attack on Mecca but he recognized it was not an existential threat to his reign per se. The Mahdi was an imposter but also a symbol of the latent deep commitment of many Saudis to the faith of Ibn 'Abd al Wahhab. The Afghanistan war gave Khalid the perfect opportunity to channel his own deep commitment to the defense of Islam with that of his people. The Islamic revolution in Iran would pose a new challenge to the longstanding Saudi conflict with Shiism, a conflict that dates to Wahhab's time in Basra. The Saudi-Iranian, Arab-Persian, and Sunni-Shia conflict was rapidly becoming the Kingdom's most immediate challenge as Khalid passed away. Fahd would face a summer of clear, present, and immediate danger for the Kingdom.

Chapter Four

FAHD, REAGAN, AND BUSH, 1982 TO 1992

King Fahd bin Abdul Aziz al Saud ascended to the throne in a summer of extreme danger for the Middle East in general and Saudi Arabia in particular. The Israeli army was at the gates of Beirut seeking to destroy the Palestine Liberation Organization (PLO) and remake much of the Middle East. The Iranian army was at the gates of Basra seeking to destroy Saddam Hussein's Iraq and open the road to Jerusalem. Saudi Arabia's regional foes seemed on the cusp of establishing their primacy in the region to the detriment of Saudi interests. From Riyadh's perspective Washington was abetting Israel's actions and seemed powerless to stop Iran.

Fahd had been the Kingdom's day-to-day ruler for the last seven years under Khalid and was completely prepared to be king. Born March 16, 1921, in Riyadh, Fahd attended the signing of the United Nations Charter in San Francisco in 1945 with his brother Faisal. In 1953 Fahd led the Saudi delegation to attend the coronation of Queen Elizabeth II in London, and later that year he became minister of education. When Faisal became king in 1962 he appointed Fahd to the crucial position of minister of interior.

*President George H. W. Bush and King Fahd bin Abdul Aẓiẓ al Saud share a laugh
during bilateral meetings at the Royal Palace, Jeddah, Saudi Arabia, November 1990.
(George Bush Presidential Library and Museum)*

As a young prince, Fahd had a reputation for being a playboy. Tales of huge losses in his gambling in London and Monte Carlo were widely believed in the Kingdom. One story had him losing $8 million in one night in 1962.[1] His expensive palace in Marbella on the Costa del Sol in Spain was opulent and considered decadent by many. After becoming crown prince in 1975, and especially after the Mecca siege, Fahd sought to change his image to be more pious and conservative. Fahd began using the title "Custodian of the Two Holy Mosques" to convey his more religious image. A debilitating stroke in 1995 made him a recluse, but in 2002 Forbes estimated his personal wealth to be $25 billion.[2]

Perhaps as a legacy of his youthful days of indiscretion, Fahd was a night owl who preferred to work in the late evening and early morning. Even when traveling abroad he was notoriously late for even the most formal occasions. In May 1975 he showed up forty-five minutes late for a state dinner with President Ford at the White House.[3] He especially preferred to meet foreign visitors after midnight, and Americans often found this difficult. One senior American official I accompanied to see Fahd spent his two hours in the waiting room in the palace endlessly adjusting the chairs, tables, and pictures on the walls to pass the time. No doubt the Saudi protocol officials noticed this and told Fahd, who probably decided to let his guest wait a little longer.

Fahd and Reagan

The Saudis were convinced that Anwar Sadat's separate peace with Israel would encourage Israeli leaders to use their overwhelming military superiority to impose their will on Israel's Arab neighbors. Without Israel facing the danger of a war with Egypt, the Saudis expected Prime Minister Menachem Begin and his defense minister, Ariel Sharon, to try to destroy the PLO and impose peace agreements on Israel's weaker neighbors. The Saudis looked to Washington to restrain Begin.

The Israeli Air Force raid on June 7, 1981, on Iraq's nuclear reactor outside Baghdad reinforced Saudi concerns. The attack was carried out only days after a summit meeting between Sadat and Begin, underscoring how the Egyptians had been neutralized by the Camp David agreement. The eight F16s and six F15s overflew Saudi territory en route to attack the Iraqi reactor, underscoring Saudi vulnerability. Ronald Reagan's new administration issued a pro forma denunciation of the attack but made no serious move to restrain Begin and Sharon.

Reagan did agree to sell the Kingdom AWACs aircraft for the Royal Saudi Air Force to enhance and, ultimately, replace the U.S.-manned aircraft Carter had sent at the beginning of the Iran-Iraq war. Another difficult congressional battle ensued with the pro-Israel lobby. The arms deal won favor in the Senate by only a two-vote margin in October 1981; the key vote came from Maine Republican William Cohen, who switched his vote at the last moment. The deal also included air-to-air missiles for the F15s sold by Carter, along with Boeing 707 aerial refueling tankers. The total package came to $8.5 billion. Again, Prince Bandar bin Sultan, still a pilot in the Royal Saudi Air Force, played a role in the lobbying effort for the arms sale.[4]

By the spring of 1982 the Arabs expected Israel to launch a major military attack into Lebanon to destroy the PLO, defeat the Syrian army in Lebanon, and impose a peace treaty on Lebanon with the cooperation of the Maronite

Christian minority. The American intelligence community had reached the same conclusion and warned the Reagan team an attack was imminent.[5]

On June 3, 1982, the Israeli ambassador to the United Kingdom, Shlomo Argov, was badly wounded in an assassination attempt outside the Dorchester Hotel in London. The assailants were members of the Abu Nidal organization, an Iraqi-based Palestinian group that opposed the PLO. One assailant was an Iraqi intelligence officer.[6] The Iraqis wanted to retaliate for the nuclear reactor raid by killing Argov. They also sought to preempt an Iranian invasion of Iraq by creating an Arab-Israeli crisis that Saddam hoped would rally the Islamic world against Israel and persuade Tehran against invasion. It was a foolish and desperate gamble. The Begin government ignored its own intelligence community reporting about Iraq's role and blamed the PLO alone for the London attack. PLO Chairman Yasser Arafat flew from his base in Beirut to Riyadh on June 4, and Israel invaded Lebanon two days later.[7]

Fahd ascended to the throne one week after the invasion, and throughout the summer of 1982 he pressed the Reagan administration to restrain the Israelis. He had little initial success. Reagan's first secretary of state, Alexander Haig, supported the Israeli game plan and deflected Arab opposition to the war. Only after the Israeli army began to besiege the PLO in West Beirut in late June did Reagan fire Haig and start pressing Begin to accept a cease-fire and allow the PLO and Arafat (who had returned to Beirut) to evacuate the city and move to Tunis. The PLO evacuation was not completed until early September.

Prince Bandar played a role in the diplomacy between Fahd and Reagan. He was appointed defense attaché in Washington in early 1982. During the crisis in Beirut, Bandar delivered messages from Fahd to Reagan and Haig. His credibility as a protégé of Fahd who had the king's ear was established with the Reagan team.[8]

Under growing international pressure, President Reagan put forward his own plan for resolving the Palestinian issue on September 1, 1982, calling for Israeli withdrawal from the West Bank and Gaza Strip and the creation of a Palestinian confederation with Jordan. Israel, which had not expected Reagan's plan, immediately rejected it. Eight days later, King Fahd put forward a Saudi peace plan at the Arab summit in Fez, Morocco. The Fahd plan called for complete Israeli withdrawal from the West Bank and Gaza as well as East

Jerusalem and the creation of an independent Palestinian state with its capital in Jerusalem.[9] The Arab summit endorsed the Fahd plan.

The war in Lebanon consumed much of Fahd's attention during his first weeks in office, but it was overshadowed for Saudis by a greater danger closer to home in the Persian Gulf. The Iranians successfully evicted the Iraqi army from all the territory it had seized in 1980, capturing 30,000 to 40,000 Iraqi prisoners in the process. Saddam's army was collapsing as the Iranians advanced.[10]

In Washington and Riyadh there were dark predictions that Saddam's regime was about to fall. The CIA's National Intelligence Council warned the Reagan National Security Council on July 20, 1982, that Iran was seeking to replace Saddam with "a fundamentalist Islamic" government beholden to Tehran. The CIA warned that if the Iranians broke through at Basra in their next offensive, all of southern, Shia-dominated Iraq, including the holy cities of Kerbala and Najaf, would be occupied by Iran, threatening to arouse the Shia populations of Kuwait, Bahrain, and the Eastern Province of Saudi Arabia. The memo concluded Iran would, thus, achieve "dominance over the Persian Gulf Region and 35 percent of known world oil reserves."[11]

Reagan's national security adviser, William Clark, told the president that "an Iranian invasion will create shock waves throughout the Gulf and pose further dangers for U.S. interests in the Middle East which are already threatened because of Lebanon." Based on the intelligence estimates from the CIA, Clark told the president "the Iranians are massing 100,000 troops opposite Basra." If Basra fell the "Iranians will sit astride Kuwait, leaving the Kuwaitis very vulnerable to direct or indirect Iranian threats. The Saudis, Jordanians and Gulf States can be expected to turn to us for protection." Clark judged it was "likely that Iran will succeed in accomplishing its military objectives."[12]

Under strong pressure from the Saudis and Jordanians, Reagan authorized CIA director Bill Casey to share intelligence with the Iraqis on the Iranian buildup. A senior CIA officer, Thomas Twetten, traveled to Baghdad on July 27, 1982, with "satellite imagery, maps, battle line imagery and analysis" to help the Iraqis stop the Iranian attack. As Twetten later described the Iraqi reaction, "It was clear that they hadn't seen anything like it before, the intelligence made a big difference."[13] To follow up, Reagan sent Donald Rumsfeld to Baghdad to assure Saddam of American support.

For their part the Saudis began bankrolling Saddam's war effort. With much of his equipment destroyed or abandoned inside Iran, Saddam needed to rebuild and vastly expand his army and air force. Over the war's eight years Saudi Arabia would provide Iraq with $60 billion in loans and grants. Kuwait provided another $18 billion. It was a staggering amount of money for two monarchies to provide a left-wing republic, but it was essential to keeping Iraq in the war and keeping Iran out of Basra.[14]

The Iraqi army held, just barely, in 1982. Iran had launched a series of offensives in late 1981—code-named Path to Jerusalem, Undeniable Victory, and Jerusalem—that drove the Iraqi army out of Iran, captured thousands of prisoners, and created the image of an unstoppable juggernaut. In late July 1982 Iran began Operation Blessed Ramadan to take Basra and open southern Iraq to Iranian occupation. The Iraqis rallied, buoyed by American intelligence, and finally stopped the Iranian advance. The war then fell into a stalemate that would last six more years.[15]

The two crises in 1982 pushed Fahd and Reagan closer together. Washington encouraged Israel to gradually withdraw from most of Lebanon in 1983 and provided diplomatic support and intelligence to Iraq to maintain the stalemate along the Iran-Iraq border. Fahd agreed to provide financial assistance to Reagan's global campaign to combat the Soviet Union. Reagan's director of the Central Intelligence Agency, Bill Casey, provided money and arms to various anti-communist groups fighting Soviet-backed regimes around the world. The largest such covert action program was the one in Afghanistan and Pakistan begun in the Carter administration. In the first four years of the Reagan administration, Washington and Riyadh gradually increased their financial commitment to the Afghan mujahedin. In the second term Reagan and Casey, with the enthusiastic support of King Fahd and his intelligence chief Prince Turki, significantly increased the campaign against the Soviet army in Afghanistan.

King Fahd visited Washington after Reagan's November 1984 reelection victory to coordinate strategy even more closely. The February 1985 summit included meetings with the president and his advisers and a breakfast between the two leaders. The principle public message from the king was that "the Palestinian question is the cause of instability and turmoil in the region and the United States has a responsibility to make use of its powerful influence and to make a strong effort for achieving peace through a just solution to the Palestinian question."[16] The two leaders did not reconcile the Fahd and Reagan plans for resolving the Palestinian question, however, and there was no movement toward a peace agreement.

In private, however, there was much agreement on ratcheting up the pressure on the Soviets. The main battlefield was Afghanistan. The king and the president "agreed to keep the pressure on the Soviet Union to remove its occupation troops from Afghanistan," according to a Saudi account.[17] Casey pressed for an increase in the CIA budget for supporting the mujahedin to $250 million annually, with a matching Saudi contribution. Fahd agreed. Casey's deputy, Robert Gates, later wrote that "the character of U.S. policy toward Afghanistan changed dramatically" as a result of these consultations. The goal went from harassing the Soviets and tying them down in a quagmire to winning the war and driving the Soviet 40th Red Army out of Afghanistan.[18]

Within a year the United States began providing the mujahedin with Stinger shoulder-fired antiaircraft missiles, thus tilting the war toward the resistance. Other sophisticated equipment followed. At the same time the flow of volunteers from Muslim countries, including Saudi Arabia, expanded significantly. The Saudi religious establishment was encouraged by Fahd and Prince Salman to promote the jihad in Afghanistan as a religious obligation. Gates wrote later that the CIA "began to learn of a significant increase in the number of Arab nationals from other countries who had traveled to Afghanistan to fight in the Holy War against the Soviets in 1985." The CIA had little contact with the Arab fighters; that business was done by the Pakistanis.[19]

The war against the Russians in Afghanistan came to a conclusion in 1988 when Moscow withdrew its troops. While the war between the mujahedin and the communist regime in Kabul would continue for another three years, with the American-Saudi-Pakistani alliance backing the mujahedin and the Russians backing the communists, the defeat and retreat of the Soviet 40th Red Army was a dramatic and decisive victory for the allies. Within months of the defeat of the Russian army, the Berlin wall fell, the Warsaw Pact crumbled, and the Cold War ended.

The collapse of the Soviet occupation of Afghanistan amounted to a major propaganda victory for the Kingdom. King Fahd could rightly say that his government had played a crucial role in the defeat of communism and Soviet imperialism. The credibility of Saudi Arabia as a leader in the Islamic world was hugely advantaged by winning in Afghanistan. Without question the agreement between Fahd and Reagan at their 1985 summit to escalate the war in Afghanistan was the summit's most important and consequential decision.

Fahd wanted another arms deal with Reagan, but the administration was reluctant to engage in yet another bruising battle with Israel over arms to Saudi Arabia. Fahd turned, instead, to the United Kingdom. Prince Bandar later described the subsequent *al Yamamah* (dove of peace) deal as the easiest arms deal he ever arranged. Fahd dispatched Bandar to see British prime minister Margaret Thatcher while she was vacationing in Salzburg, Austria. The prince told her the king wanted to purchase advanced Tornado strike aircraft plus jet trainers and even the infrastructure to build air bases. The prime minister replied immediately, "You have a deal." It was done in twenty-five minutes. In time it became the largest military sale in British history, worth $86 billion, and included seventy-two jets, two air bases, and a host of service contracts.[20]

The Tornado deal also proved to be controversial. Allegations of kickbacks to Saudi defense minister Prince Sultan and to Bandar surfaced soon after the ink was dry. Ultimately, another British prime minister, Tony Blair, halted any investigation in the United Kingdom of the 1985 deal and various follow-up deals on the grounds that British relations with Saudi Arabia were too important strategically to be undermined by investigations of impropriety in arms deals.[21]

By turning to London for advanced aircraft, the king acquired jets with no limits on where they might be deployed. Unlike the F15s, which the United States sold with the proviso they would not be based at Tabuk air base in northwest Saudi Arabia near Israel, the Tornados could be deployed wherever the Saudi leadership wanted.

The Saudi quest for advanced weapons was rooted in the country's sense of vulnerability in the dangerous Middle East region. Events continued to underscore those dangers. On June 5, 1984, two Iranian F4 fighter jets penetrated Saudi air space on the Persian Gulf coast. Two Royal Saudi Air Force F15s shot the intruders down. Eleven more Iranian aircraft took off immediately from their base to respond, the Saudi Air Force scrambled more jets, and the Iranians then returned to base. Prince Bandar told the *New York Times* that "our sovereignty was violated and we are determined to defend our country."[22] Meanwhile, with the land war between Iran and Iraq still stalemated, the two countries began firing short-range missiles, known as Scuds, at each other's cities and attacking tankers in the Gulf carrying oil from each country.

The situation in the Levant also troubled Saudi security planners. On October 1, 1985, eight Israeli Air Force F15s attacked the headquarters in Tunis of the PLO leaders who had been evacuated three years earlier from Beirut. The attack demonstrated that Israel could project power 2,000 kilometers, or 1,280 miles, from its air bases. The Saudis saw the Tunis raid, like the earlier raid on Baghdad's nuclear reactor, as a vivid demonstration of their vulnerability to Israeli military operations.

King Fahd and Defense Minister Prince Sultan decided to seek a deterrent capability to discourage Iran and Israel from any military operations against the Kingdom. They were well aware the United States and Britain would not sell them an intermediate-range missile system that might be used against targets like Tehran or Tel Aviv. Prince Sultan turned to his sons, Prince Bandar, now the ambassador to the United States, and the head of Saudi air defenses General Prince Khalid bin Sultan, to find a solution. Their answer was China.

Bandar opened the initiative by approaching his Chinese counterpart in Washington, Ambassador Han Xu, and asking him privately if Beijing would sell missiles to the Kingdom. Riyadh did not have diplomatic relations with Beijing so this was an extraordinary request. The Chinese were eager to develop relations with Saudi Arabia and agreed in principle to consider the request. Bandar was invited to talk to more Chinese officials to pursue the idea. He stole a page from Henry Kissinger's playbook. When Kissinger secretly opened ties with China in 1970, he used Pakistan as an intermediary. Bandar flew to Pakistan for more conversations with Chinese officials who had the authority to discuss military sales. They agreed to sell missiles and invited the prince to visit Beijing secretly to work out details.[23]

In July 1985 Bandar made his first of three secret visits to Beijing to work the deal. The Chinese then sent a military delegation secretly to Riyadh to engage with the Saudi military on the details. Prince Khalid was their host. In December 1986 an agreement was reached on how to bring intermediate-range ballistic missiles, Chinese-made CSS2 missiles, code-named East Wind, to the Kingdom, install them, train Saudi crews to operate them, and do all of this without the American intelligence community discovering the plot. Khalid then made four trips to China to work out the details and coordinate everything. The missiles were delivered and installed in 1987.[24]

Prince Khalid later wrote that the purpose of the missiles "was to give us the capability to counterattack in the event of an attack on us by either Israel or Iran, both in their different ways hostile neighbors." Khalid cited the Israeli incursion in Lebanon in June 1982, the raid on Baghdad in 1981, and the raid on Tunis in 1985 as the reasons why the king "decided to seek Chinese weapons." The Iranian threat to Iraq and its neighbors, highlighted by the June 5, 1984, aerial combat, was the other reason.[25]

The CIA detected the CSS2 missile base in Saudi Arabia in early 1988. President Reagan was furious with Fahd and Bandar for the duplicity and the deal. Initially the United States pressed for the return of the missiles to China or for American monitors to be placed at their bases. Riyadh refused but did promise not to equip the missiles with nuclear warheads. The story quickly leaked to the press with a front-page article in the *Washington Post* on March 18, 1988.[26]

The Saudis were now worried that Israel would attack the missile sites. Bandar approached Reagan's national security adviser, General Colin Powell, asking him to tell Israel not to attack Saudi Arabia and explaining that the missiles were for defensive purposes only. According to Powell's recollection, the situation was very tense for a few days, with both the Israeli and Saudi air forces on high alert. Reagan made a public statement making it clear he was "totally opposed" to an Israeli attack. The Israelis did not attack and the Chinese missiles remain in Saudi Arabia to this day. To demonstrate his pique at the American reaction to the missile deal, Fahd asked that American ambassador Hume Horan be removed from his post. Since he would be unable to do his job against the king's wishes, Horan was brought home.[27]

The East Wind missile deal remains something of an enigma to this day. The missiles were designed by the Chinese to carry a nuclear warhead. When Khalid inspected them in China, they were equipped with nuclear warheads.[28] When armed with only conventional warheads the missiles' value as a deterrent was diminished significantly. Many observers have questioned whether the underlying Saudi plan was to get Pakistani nuclear warheads for the missiles in a crisis situation. No hard evidence of a Saudi-Pakistani agreement to provide such warheads has surfaced, even from the 1980s when King Fahd and General Zia were collaborating so closely in Afghanistan—or in the years since. Even so, the rumors of such a deal have not evaporated.

By 1988 the relationship between Reagan and Fahd had been deeply shaken by another secret deal, this time an American plot to sell arms to Iran in return for help in freeing American hostages in Lebanon held by the Iranian-sponsored terrorist group Hezbollah. The operation also funded aid to right-wing guerrillas fighting the leftist government of Nicaragua, aid that the Congress had banned. The secret dealings broke into the public domain in November 1986 when the Iranians leaked news about some aspects of them to a Lebanese magazine.

At first the president tried to deny any knowledge of the scheme, but he finally admitted some responsibility in a speech on March 4, 1987. In fact, Reagan was at the center of what came to be known as the Iran-Contra scandal. He drove the policy process toward a secret opening with Iran because he was obsessed with freeing American hostages taken by Iran's allies in Lebanon. It was Reagan's decisions, not some rogue operation run by the CIA's Bill Casey, that led to America selling arms to Iran in return for promises, never fulfilled, to free the hostages. Despite his later denials, Vice President George Bush was also deeply involved in the policy process and kept fully informed on the efforts to free the hostages. Casey and Reagan believed they had a valuable Iranian partner (arms dealer Manucher Ghorbanifar) in a man who failed catastrophically every lie detector test he took. Casey's senior advisers all told him the Iranian was a liar; he ignored their judgment and went ahead recklessly. Casey's deputy at one point cabled his boss, who was traveling, that "everyone at headquarters advises against this operation not only because the principal involved is a liar and has a record of deceit. But secondly we would be aiding and abetting the wrong people." Nonetheless, despite "our counsel to the contrary," the operation proceeded as the White House and Casey ordered.[29]

Behind the scenes Reagan had a crucial and enthusiastic partner in Israel. Israeli leaders, including Prime Minister Shimon Peres, desperately wanted to restore the cozy relationship Israel had with Iran under the shah, when the two states were aligned in a secret entente. The Israelis urged Reagan to try an opening with Iran. Peres and his colleagues refused to believe the ayatollahs would not sooner or later come back to partnering with Israel, even though their professional intelligence officers told them this was a fantasy. Instead, Israel became Iran's critical arms supplier during the Iran-Iraq war and enticed America into joining it in the madness. American diplomats were told to turn a blind eye to Israeli arms shipments to Iran even before Reagan got into his own arms deals. Israel helped the Ayatollah Khomeini survive the Iraqi war and persuaded Reagan to arm the Iranian regime.[30]

The Saudis and leaders of the other Gulf states were shocked by the Iran-Contra scandal. They had believed the United States was on their side in the confrontation with Iran, but now they discovered Washington was secretly dealing with Tehran. To add insult to injury, for the Arabs, Israel was the moving force behind the subterfuge. The longtime Saudi conviction that Israel manipulated American foreign policy was reinforced. The scandal produced a crisis in Saudi confidence in the Reagan administration.

Gulf War Escalates

The war in the Gulf also escalated. With the battle on the ground stalemated, the Iraqis and Iranians each began attacking oil tankers exporting its rival's oil in the Persian Gulf. With the Iran-Contra scandal damaging American credibility, the Reagan administration determined again to assist the Iraqi war effort. Kuwait asked Washington to protect tankers delivering oil from its facilities, and Reagan agreed to do so. The U.S. Navy became an active belligerent in the war during the spring of 1987 by defending oil traffic going to and from Kuwait and attacking Iranian naval vessels threatening the export of Gulf oil to the outside world. As Secretary of Defense Casper Weinberger told National Security Adviser Colin Powell, "We should be seen as supportive of Iraq. This is an opportunity to recoup some of our standing in the region and regain credibility with the Arab states."[31]

Over the course of the next eighteen months the U.S. military engaged in a series of operations to defend oil traffic to and from Kuwait, which had become Iraq's major access to the sea for its oil exports. Operations with code names Earnest Will, Prime Chance, Nimble Archer, and Praying Mantis gradually wore down the Iranian naval and air threat in the Gulf. Iranian oilrigs, frigates, and small ships were destroyed. At the same time Iraq began to gain the upper hand on the ground. Iraq launched a series of ground offensives, assisted by American intelligence support, which drove Iranian forces out of Iraq and began to destroy the Iranian ground forces.

As the war turned against it, Iran increased its support for subversion in Saudi Arabia. In late July 1987 Iranian pilgrims to the Hajj in Mecca staged political demonstrations that turned violent, and at least 275 Iranian pilgrims and eighty-five Saudi policemen died. The Saudi embassy in Tehran was attacked and Ayatollah Khomeini called for the overthrow of the Saudi monarchy. In August 1987 a new Iranian-supported terrorist group called Hezbollah al Hijaz attacked an oil facility in the Eastern Province. Hezbollah al Hijaz was composed of Saudi Shia trained by the Iranian Revolutionary Guards at camps in Lebanon, where they acquired battlefield experience by supporting the Lebanese Hezbollah fight against the Israeli army. The groups' military leader, Ahmad Ibrahim al Mughassil, was one of those trained in Lebanon fighting the Israelis. Mughassil traveled between Beirut, Tehran, and Damascus to organize operations. In Damascus Hezbollah al Hijaz operated from the Sayyida Zaynab mosque, which houses the tomb of Imam Ali's daughter Zaynab. The group called for an Islamic Republic in the Arabian Peninsula modeled on the Iranian example or the secession of the Eastern Province to form a Shia state aligned with Iran.[32]

More attacks on Saudi oil installations followed in 1988. An attempt was also made to attack the air base at Dhahran to destroy the AWACs aircraft stationed there. Hezbollah al Hijaz was also responsible for attacks on Saudi diplomats abroad in Ankara, Karachi, and Bangkok in 1988 and 1989. Several Saudi diplomats were killed and wounded in the attacks. In April 1988, in response to the attacks inside the Kingdom, the assassination attempts on Saudi diplomats, and the ratcheting up of the tanker war, Saudi Arabia broke diplomatic relations with Iran.[33]

The Saudis played a key role in the end game of the Iraq-Iran war. They were Saddam's bankers by this point. Saddam had built a million-man army and a military industrial complex that employed another million Iraqis. His army was flush with equipment purchased from Russia and China, his air force full of Russian and French aircraft. All this was expensive, and the Saudis and Kuwaitis had bankrolled all of it.

Saddam was now reluctant to end the war he was, at last, winning. The United States and other members of the United Nations Security Council were reluctant to stop him and had little leverage over Iraq even if they wanted to stop the war. Iran had no allies. On July 3, 1988, an American cruiser, the USS *Vincennes*, inadvertently shot down a civilian Iranian passenger jet, which the ship had misidentified as hostile Iranian military aircraft, killing 290 passengers and crew. By this point, Ayatollah Khomeini was finally ready for a cease-fire, and Iran used the shooting down of the airliner as justification for ending the war, citing aggression against it by "other countries," meaning the United States. Even so, Saddam was not yet ready.

UN Secretary General Javier Pérez de Cuéllar asked the Saudis to intervene. As his deputy, Giandomenico Picco, later recalled, the UN took its "cue from the Renaissance. Back then, in Florence, the great House of Medici resolved such disputes by applying a little financial pressure." Pérez de Cuéllar asked Prince Bandar and Foreign Minister Prince Saud al Faisal to use Riyadh's financial leverage to persuade Saddam. The Saudis were Iraq's banker and ally, but above all the Saudis wanted an end to a war that was escalating out of control. King Fahd called Saddam and then informed the secretary general that Iraq was ready to halt the war. Pérez de Cuéllar told Fahd he needed a call from Saddam himself. Within five minutes Saddam called the secretary general and said, "I would like you to know I concur with His Majesty."[34] Iran formally accepted an end to the war on July 18.

The Iran-Iraq war had cost a half-million lives, with another million wounded seriously. The economic cost was over a trillion dollars. The war also began the march of folly that would shortly lead to another war in the Gulf in 2003—the current American military engagement in Iraq. The Saudi decision to end the war with an ultimatum to Saddam was the right thing to do, but it would have grave consequences later as Saddam began to consider his next target.

Reagan's relations with Fahd had fluctuated wildly in the 1980s. After a difficult beginning due to the Lebanon war, the two became close partners in bringing the Cold War to a successful end by backing the mujahedin in Afghanistan, but the Iran-Contra affair badly damaged their relationship. Fahd felt betrayed by Reagan's foolish initiative with Iran, especially given its

Israeli inspiration. Fahd turned to London and Beijing for arms. Robust American military support for Iraq at the end of the war helped recoup some American credibility in Riyadh, but the Saudi distrust of Reagan never really diminished. It would be up to his successor, George H. W. Bush, to rebuild ties with King Fahd when the next great crisis came to the doorstep of the Kingdom, this one in Kuwait.

Desert Shield

The war for Kuwait in 1990–91 was a watershed moment for the American-Saudi alliance. Before the war the relationship was largely handled behind the scenes and was little known to most Americans and most Saudis. Diplomats, oilmen, and spies quietly ran the relationship for the most part. Only the oil embargo in 1973 had resonated with most Americans. The great collusion in Afghanistan was a covert project until some aspects of it became public knowledge in the late 1980s. The war for Kuwait finally brought the U.S.-Saudi partnership out of the closet and onto the front pages for everyone, Americans and Saudis. A half-million Americans, mostly soldiers, were deployed to the Kingdom by President Bush to first defend it from Iraqi aggression and then to liberate Kuwait. This marked the beginning of a decades-long American conflict in Iraq, and it marked the beginning of an increasingly violent blowback inside the Kingdom against the American alliance.

I had a ringside seat for the Kuwait war. At one in the morning on August 2, 1990, I was promoted from deputy division chief of the Persian Gulf Affairs Division at the CIA to deputy chief of the Persian Gulf Task Force. The task force was responsible for all intelligence analysis and production concerning the crisis and its implications for the agency. My good friend, colleague, and mentor, Winston Wiley, was the chief. Among my responsibilities was liaison with other intelligence services, including those in Saudi Arabia, whose de facto intelligence representative in Washington was Prince Bandar. When the fighting ended, I was promoted again to be the director of Persian Gulf and South Asian Affairs at the National Security Council for the remainder of the Bush term and the first year of Bill Clinton's administration. My bosses there included Brent Scowcroft, Bob Gates, Richard Haass, and

Martin Indyk, four good friends and fine colleagues. My daily interlocutor was Prince Bandar.

We are fortunate today to have a detailed account of the Persian Gulf crisis written by the Saudi commander Prince Khalid bin Sultan, along with a noted British expert on the region, Patrick Seale. Prince Khalid headed the Saudi Joint Force and had command over the regular Saudi military and the National Guard. Along with his American counterpart, General Norman Schwarzkopf, Prince Khalid commanded an international army with 750,000 troops from thirty-six countries.

Iraq ended its war with Iran deeply in debt. It owed billions of dollars to its creditors, especially Saudi Arabia, Kuwait, and the United Arab Emirates. But Saddam's enormous ambitions had not been reduced by the war. If anything, the Iraqi dictator emerged from eight years of conflict even more determined than he was in 1980, when he invaded Iran, planning to become the dominant player in the Middle East. He was still frustrated that the Saudis had reined in his army when it seemed to have Iran on the ropes in August 1988.

With Iraqi and Iranian oil back on the world market, the price of oil declined. Oil prices had been low throughout the 1980s, putting pressure on all the producers. With further decline in the wake of the war's end, Iraq was financially pressed even more. The creditor states, including the Saudis, did not press for immediate payment of Iraq's debts but did not want them forgotten or forgiven.

Saddam wanted to restore Iraq to the leadership position in the Arab world it had briefly enjoyed when it led the Arab opposition to Sadat's peace treaty with Israel. Ironically, Egypt's return to Arab politics from its isolation was facilitated by Iraq. Iraq had purchased large quantities of weapons from Egypt during the war with Iran. On February 16, 1990, Iraq, Egypt, Jordan, and Yemen formed an alliance called the Arab Cooperation Council, with Jordan's King Hussein as the principal mover. He backed Iraq enthusiastically in the war with Iran and had become close to Saddam. At the first summit of the council on February 24, 1990, Saddam gave a bellicose speech threatening Israel, and a few days later the CIA detected fixed launch sites were being developed in western Iraq within the range for Iraq to fire Scud missiles at Tel Aviv.[35]

None of the four partners told the Saudis their plan for the council. King Fahd had inklings that something was in the works but learned of the alliance only when it became public. From Riyadh's perspective the council looked like an alliance encircling the Kingdom, especially given Yemen's inclusion. Saudi-Yemeni relations were historically troubled. Fahd complained to Egypt's president Mubarak that the alliance looked to be anti-Saudi.[36]

Saddam paid a rare visit to Riyadh on March 17, 1990, to explain the council and to complain about low oil prices. Oil prices dropped from $22 per barrel in January to $16 in June. Saddam was especially angry with Kuwait for its high oil production, which contributed to the price decline. Inflation in Iraq rose to 45 percent as its economy came undone. In April Saddam called Fahd and asked him to send Prince Bandar to see him. Bandar met with Saddam in Mosul on April 5, 1990. Again, Saddam complained about Kuwait and oil prices, and Saddam asked Bandar to take a message to Washington and London that Iraq did not intend to attack Israel but was worried about an Israeli attack on Iraq.[37]

Against this backdrop of increasing tensions in the region, Saddam attacked Kuwait verbally at an Arab summit in late May 1990. He accused Kuwait of waging economic warfare against Iraq and colluding with the United States against Baghdad. In a private meeting with Fahd, Saddam called the Kuwaitis "rich, fat people" who came to Iraq to gamble, drink, and use prostitutes.[38] Saddam was right about Kuwait's wealth; the Kuwaitis had over $200 billion in reserves.

On the July 17 anniversary of the coup that had put him in power in 1968, Saddam publicly threatened Kuwait again. The American intelligence community quickly detected a massive buildup of Iraqi forces north of Kuwait. The elite of Iraq's army, the Republican Guard, dispatched an eight-division-strong force to the border with Kuwait.[39] The CIA warned the Bush administration an attack on Kuwait could come at any moment. Bush phoned key Arab leaders. All of them—King Fahd, King Hussein, and President Mubarak—assured the president that Saddam was just bluffing. They argued that at worse he might grab a couple of uninhabited mud islands in the Shatt al Arab waterway that belonged to Kuwait but blocked Iraq's access to the Persian Gulf. At Fahd and Mubarak's request, Iraq agreed to a meeting with the Kuwaitis in Jidda on August 1 to resolve the dispute. Instead, once they got to Jidda the Iraqis demanded that Kuwait forgive Iraq's war debts and provide Baghdad with $27 billion in reparations to help pay for the war's damage.[40] When Kuwait refused, the Iraqis left Jidda and returned to Baghdad.

The next week would be perhaps the most critical in the history of Saudi kings and American presidents. Shortly after midnight in the Persian Gulf on August 2, 1990, 120,000 Iraqi troops invaded Kuwait. The White House was surprised. Bush had relied too much on what the Arab leaders told him and too little on the intelligence that showed Saddam's buildup. Saddam was always a difficult person to read. He was impulsive, prone to bad decisions, and exercised poor judgment. The two wars he started were terrible mistakes. Some accounts, notably that of usually well-informed Egyptian journalist Mohamed Heikal, argue the final decision to seize all of Kuwait was made only two days in advance of the invasion.[41] Prince Khalid notes the invasion was poorly planned, as it did not provide for capturing the amir or rapidly controlling Kuwait's two air bases. It seemed hastily organized and not thought through carefully.[42] The CIA officer who debriefed Saddam after his capture in 2003, John Nixon, asked the Iraqi leader about this decision. Based on Saddam's statement, Nixon believes it was an impulsive decision. Saddam was broke, he needed money, and a very rich bank was next door. Certainly Saddam did not accurately assess the implications and reactions to his invasion.[43] It is difficult, if not impossible, to predict the moves of a leader who repeatedly makes such monumental mistakes.

President Bush convened a National Security Council principals meeting for August 3, 1990, but their discussion was inconclusive. The reality of what Saddam had done was not yet fully apparent. As Richard Haass later noted, it was too soon to be digested by the principals. The White House looked off-balance.

The next day, August 4, Bush convened his top aides again. At the start of the meeting, the director of central intelligence, William Webster, summarized a paper I had drafted for him. According to the recollection of General Colin Powell, by then the chair of the Joint Chiefs of Staff, "The CIA director gave us a bleak status report. The Iraqis," he said, "are within eight-tenths of a mile of the Saudi border. If Saddam stays where he is, he'll own twenty percent of the world's oil reserves. And a few miles away he can seize another twenty percent. He'll have easy access to the sea from Kuwait's ports. Jordan and Yemen will probably tilt toward him. Israel will be threatened. Saddam will be the preeminent figure in the Persian Gulf."[44] Brent Scowcroft, the president's closest confidant and national security adviser, remembered Webster saying that "this will fundamentally alter the Persian Gulf region. Saddam would command the second and third largest proven oil reserves with the fourth largest army in the world. His ego cannot be satisfied: his ambition is to have ever more influence."[45] Webster's opening brief put the issue clearly to the president and his team; they would be focused for the next few days on getting the Saudis to accept a massive American military expedition to save the Kingdom from a repeat of the Kuwaitis' mistakes of not taking Saddam seriously.

The Saudis had also been caught totally by surprise. At first, King Fahd did not believe the early reports from Kuwait. But then the Kuwaiti amir fled to the Kingdom in a rush, and Fahd was told by the Eastern Province governor, his son Prince Muhammad ibn Fahd, the complete truth about the invasion. Within weeks some 360,000 Kuwaitis flooded into the Kingdom seeking refuge. Prince Khalid was appointed to command Saudi forces on the border, where he found complete confusion. Only one brigade of the Saudi Arabian National Guard was deployed on the Saudi border facing Kuwait and Iraq. Some other Arab nations sent troops quickly, notably Morocco. Two more brigades from the Saudi army were rushed to the front from the borders with Jordan and Yemen, but even when they arrived the Saudis still would be outnumbered by more than twenty to one. "Our intelligence and our general military staff had paid little attention to Iraq, and no one had anticipated that a threat to the Kingdom would come from that direction," wrote Khalid.[46]

Prince Bandar was caught off guard by the invasion. On July 31, 1990, he left Washington for London to meet his wife Haifa and their children en route to what was planned to be a month-long vacation in China, Hong Kong, Singapore, and Thailand. He was confident the Jidda meeting would end the crisis. In London he learned of the Iraqi attack and turned back, rushed to the White House immediately, and began working to stop Saddam from invading his country.[47] Bandar's role would be critical in the crisis. Brent Scowcroft later said Bandar "became a de facto member of the National Security Council" during the crisis because of his unparalleled access to both Bush and Fahd.[48]

On August 5, 1990, the CIA detected that the Iraqis were moving the Republican Guard in force to the border. Logistics for an offensive were moving
to south Kuwait, just north of the border with the Kingdom. Four more armored and mechanized divisions from the regular Iraqi army were moving
into Kuwait. Bush convened the National Security Council again. I accompanied Webster to the meeting, briefing him on the latest information in the car
as we drove down the George Washington Parkway from CIA headquarters
in Langley, Virginia, to the White House. When he began the meeting, he
again said the threat to Saudi Arabia was immediate and dangerous. The president dispatched Secretary of Defense Richard Cheney to Saudi Arabia that
evening to press King Fahd to accept American military protection for the
Kingdom.[49]

The royal family was initially divided on how to respond to Saddam's
threat. Several senior princes, including Crown Prince Abdallah and governor of Riyadh Prince Salman, preferred an Arab solution that would be a
diplomatic option to gain a mediated compromise. Other princes were more
troubled. Prince Bandar, who had been briefed on the alarming intelligence
by Powell in the Pentagon, believed Fahd needed to agree to invite American
forces immediately.[50]

All week the Americans sensed Fahd was hesitating. Years later Bush told
his preeminent biographer, Jon Meacham, that in his conversations by phone
with Fahd and other Arab leaders after the invasion he detected an "openness
to an accommodation with Saddam that would expand Iraq's power and re-
ward Iraq's military strike." Cheney's trip, thus, in the American narrative,
became crucial to influencing Fahd to take American military help and stand
firm against Iraq.[51]

The Saudi version is different. According to Khalid bin Sultan's account,
the king recognized immediately after the invasion the magnitude of Saddam's
move. Once his son Prince Muhammad explained how the Iraqis had overrun
Kuwait, Fahd was determined not to repeat the Kuwaiti errors. When Fahd
asked the Iraqis on August 3, 1990, about Kuwait, they told him "the status of
Kuwait has now been rectified. The clock cannot be turned back." It was clear
that Iraq meant to annex Kuwait, which it now claimed as the nineteenth province of Iraq. Fahd had a "special feeling of consideration for Kuwait," because
the Kuwaitis had provided a safe exile for his father, Ibn Saud, in the nine-

teenth century. But most important, he understood "the occupation of Kuwait was little different from the occupation of Riyadh itself and the disappearance of Kuwait would, sooner or later, pose a great threat to the security and identity of Saudi Arabia." Fahd also knew from his brother, Prince Sultan, minister of defense and aviation, and from Prince Khalid that even if all the Arabs sent troops to help Saudi Arabia, it would be too few to stop Iraq. In his memoirs Khalid lays out the numbers in detail. Even if Egypt sent its entire army to reinforce the Gulf states, Iraq would still have more troops, tanks, and aircraft.[52]

Bandar played a key role in convincing the king to get Bush's help. He pressed the Bush team to tell him what exactly they would send to defend the Kingdom. Bandar did not want a token American force. Bush told General Powell to brief Bandar, who was an old friend by now. Powell recalls that he told Bandar on August 3: "We'll start by bringing in the 1st Tactical Fighter Wing and the 82nd Airborne Division and a carrier. All told about one hundred thousand troops for starters." After the prince left, convinced he could tell the king that the Americans were serious about defending Saudi Arabia, Secretary of Defense Cheney told Powell he had exceeded his brief with such specific pledges, but by then it was too late.[53]

Operation Desert Shield commenced immediately after Fahd told Cheney on August 6 to send the troops Powell had promised Bandar. In his memoirs, President Bush noted, "In retrospect if Saddam had wanted to make a go for Saudi Arabia he probably made a mistake in that he did not do it in this brief window (early August); if he had he would have had a free run."[54] By the end of August, at the latest, Saddam had completely missed his window of opportunity. Enough American forces were on the ground in the Kingdom or offshore to destroy the Iraqis if they came south from Kuwait. President Bush and King Fahd had brought America and Saudi Arabia closer than ever. American popular attitudes toward Saudi Arabia shifted, as well. A Harris poll in January 1991 reported 33 percent of Americans thought the Kingdom was a "close ally" and another 44 percent saw it as "friendly." This 77 percent approval rating for Saudi Arabia as an American partner was unprecedented.[55]

There are no polls about Saudi popular opinion. The deployment of tens of thousands of foreign, presumably Christian, soldiers to the Kingdom and the resulting war with a neighboring Muslim country sent shock waves through Saudi Arabia. Saudis were stunned to discover that their country, which spent billions on arms every year, needed massive outside—American and European—military assistance to cope with the Iraqi threat. A few hoped the Western presence would bring reform and change. On November 6, 1990, forty-five women drove cars in a demonstration in downtown Riyadh. They were arrested and lost their jobs.[56]

The more significant reaction came from the dissidents in the religious community. In September 1990 the dean of the Islamic College at Umm al Qura University in Mecca, Safar al Hawali, publicly charged that the real enemy was not Iraq but, rather, America. Hawali then wrote an open letter to Shaykh Abdul Aziz bin Baz, the blind shaykh and the most senior cleric in the country, attacking the United States as "an evil greater than Saddam." Another cleric, Salman al Awadah at Imam Muhammad al Saud University in Riyadh, also called for the withdrawal of Western troops and warned their presence would be dangerous to Saudi moral values; he cited the women's driving protest as a sign of the country's disintegrating values.[57] Bin Baz and the top *ulema* had already endorsed Fahd's decision to invite the Americans into the Kingdom, so the criticism did not alter Fahd's position.

The protests did not end with the liberation of Kuwait. In the spring of 1991 open letters were sent to the king to undertake reforms. Some called for greater public participation in governance, but the most popular came from clerics Hawali and Awadah and called for a more Islamic society and the creation of an Islamic army to defend the Kingdom. It was openly critical of Fahd's pro-American foreign policies. The most senior clerical establishment did not endorse the letter but was reluctant to openly oppose it.[58]

Another voice of opposition was Osama bin Laden, who was back from Afghanistan by the summer of 1990. In Afghanistan and Pakistan, bin Laden had been the Saudis' most famous mujahedin supporter. He was famous at home, as well. He worked closely with the Saudi intelligence services, including with Interior Minister Prince Nayef and with Saudi general intelligence and Prince Turki. Turki's deputy later said, "He was our man." Nayef, the deputy noted, "liked" bin Laden.[59]

In July 1990 bin Laden proposed to Prince Turki, the head of Saudi intelligence, that he would organize a mujahedin-like insurgency to overthrow the pro-Moscow communist regime in South Yemen. Turki, who knew the Peoples Democratic Republic of Yemen, as it was called, was collapsing on its own, demurred and rejected bin Laden's advice. When Saddam invaded Kuwait, bin Laden again urged a mujahedin response to the royal court. The idea was rejected as too little to stop Saddam. Bin Laden was disappointed but he did not break with the House of Saud while the war with Iraq was under way.[60]

Operation Desert Storm

Saudi Arabia was safe by September 1990, but Kuwait was still occupied. Bush and Fahd had another momentous decision to make: how to liberate Kuwait. The Saudis were reluctant, at the beginning, to use force. As Prince Khalid noted, although the Saudis wanted Saddam overthrown at home, "we had no wish to see Iraq itself devastated. Despite our quarrel with its leader, Iraq was a brotherly country whom we had helped in its war with Iran, and whose regional role we valued as a counterweight to both Iran and Israel."[61] The Saudis worried about Iraq's efforts to acquire nuclear and chemical weapons, Khalid writes, but were troubled that Washington regarded "Israel's own nuclear bombs, chemical weapons and long range missiles in whose grim shadow the Arabs have had to live for decades as legitimate weapons of self defense whereas any Arab attempt, however feeble, to achieve a modicum of deterrence must be considered a threat to the 'civilized world.' "[62]

Saddam's refusal to leave Kuwait, the intense lobbying of the Kuwait royal family in exile in Taif, and pressure from Washington combined to persuade the king that force was the only option. When President Bush announced on November 8, 1990, a massive increase in the American force presence in the Kingdom, more than doubling the size of the American expeditionary army to a half-million, the king was in agreement that Kuwait could only be liberated by force of arms. Bush benefited from the counsel and insights of his fine ambassador in Riyadh, Chas Freeman, one of the best representatives Washington has ever sent to the Kingdom.

The Saudis in general and Bandar in particular were very worried that their traditional foes in the region, especially Yemen and the Hashemite Kingdom of Jordan, would take advantage of the Iraq-Kuwait crisis at the

Kingdom's expense. Jordan's King Hussein was close to Saddam and tried to persuade the Iraqi dictator to avoid war by leaving Kuwait. Saddam was very popular in Jordan, and King Hussein was reluctant to break with the Iraqi dictator. For the Saudis and President Bush this seemed a weak, vacillating approach. The Saudis feared King Hussein wanted to regain the Hejaz for the Hashemites. This was Saudi paranoia at work, but they believed their fears were real. Bandar wrote a scathing column for the *Washington Post* in which he took Hussein to task for arguing the Iraq-Kuwait border was a product of British colonialism. Bandar said: "Your majesty, you should be the last one to say that. Not only your border, but your whole country was created by the colonial British."[63]

Yemen worried the Saudis even more. King Fahd and his advisers feared that President Ali Abdullah Saleh nurtured ambitions to regain the territory lost in the 1930s to Saudi Arabia. Prince Khalid, Bandar's brother, worried that "there was a strong chance that other fronts might open up. The Yemenis might seize the opportunity to cross our frontier and attempt to seize our border province of Asir."[64] In September 1990 Riyadh broke relations with both Amman and Sana'a.[65] To counter the potential Yemeni threat, the Saudis deployed the Pakistani armored brigade away from Tabuk to the Yemeni border to back up the weak Saudi National Guard forces in the south. Later, when Saudi fears of Yemeni adventurism eased, the brigade was redeployed facing Iraq.[66]

The Pakistani task force, which had been in the Kingdom since after the Mecca siege in the early 1980s, was quickly joined by other Muslim units. Thousands of troops from Egypt, Morocco, and other Muslim states gave the emerging coalition an Islamic dimension. For the Saudis it was important that the coalition army in the Kingdom have as many Arabs and Muslims as possible, even if the core of the fighting force was American. Fahd, especially, sought support from Syria, a frontline state against Israel with a history of being at the forefront of Arab nationalism. Fahd urged President Hafez Assad to join the coalition, and eventually the Syrians sent a division to fight in Kuwait.

President Bush and First Lady Barbara Bush visited the Kingdom to see Fahd and meet the troops for Thanksgiving in late November. Fahd greeted them at the airport and they stayed in the King's marble guest palace. "The

King hosted a late state dinner for us—ten o'clock, which I was told was an early hour for him. It was an unbelievable meal. The only way to describe the amount of food was to say that if ever there was an occasion when tables groaned under a feast, this was it," Bush recalled later. But the dinner was kept short, only an hour, so that Bush and Fahd could talk past midnight about their plans for taking the offensive against Saddam.[67] Prince Khalid relates that after the Bush-Fahd summit the Saudis were brought into the intense American planning already under way for what would be called Operation Desert Storm.[68]

Khalid and General Norman Schwarzkopf, the top American commander, had occasional disagreements on strategy and protocol but generally worked smoothly together. A key disagreement centered on the Iraqi missile threat to the Kingdom and Israel. The Saudis felt more attention should be paid to preventing Saddam from using his Scud missiles to attack Riyadh than did the Americans. The Saudis also worried that Saddam would attack Tel Aviv with his Scuds to try to draw the Israelis into the war, which would turn a conflict among Arabs into an Arab-Israeli conflict and place Saudi Arabia on the side of Israel. Khalid pressed to make eliminating the Scuds the top priority of the air campaign at the start of Desert Storm. Schwarzkopf disagreed, arguing the Scuds were not a significant military weapon because they were so inaccurate and carried small warheads.[69]

When the war began on January 17, 1991, Prince Khalid was proven right. Iraq almost immediately began attacking Tel Aviv and Haifa in Israel, as well as Riyadh, with Scuds. By the time the war ended, Iraq had fired more than eighty missiles at Israel and Saudi Arabia. One hit a U.S. Army barracks in Dhahran and killed twenty-eight American soldiers. Fortunately, casualties from the other missiles were relatively light, with two Israelis killed and 230 injured in thirty-nine missile attacks, and one Saudi killed and seventy injured.[70] Belatedly, the United States deployed Patriot air defense missiles to Israel and Saudi Arabia to shoot down the Scuds; it turned out they were good for morale but had little success in defending against the Iraqi attacks.

Despite the low casualty rate, the Israelis were deeply alarmed by the Scud attacks, which brought their economy to a halt and created considerable anxiety. Prime Minister Yitzhak Shamir proposed sending one hundred Israeli aircraft through Saudi airspace to attack the Scud launching sites in western Iraq, or sending aircraft and paratroopers through Jordanian airspace to attack them. Bush firmly rejected both ideas and refused to give Israel the codes that would identify the Israeli aircraft as friendly; they would be regarded as enemy aircraft if they entered the battlespace. Bush did send more Patriot missiles to help defend Israel's cities.[71]

To underscore their concern, the Israelis moved their Jericho intermediate-range ballistic missiles from their bunkers into the open, knowing American intelligence satellites would see them. This was a way to rattle Israel's never-acknowledged nuclear option without going public. The Saudis were informed of the Israeli move.

For their part the Saudis considered using their Chinese-supplied CSS2 missiles to retaliate against Baghdad. Prince Khalid, who had been instrumental in acquiring the missiles from China, ordered them placed on alert when the Scuds fell on Riyadh. They were to be prepared for launch upon order from the king. "But after some anxious hours, King Fahd decided not to escalate the conflict. He made a rational decision to reserve the missiles as a weapon of last resort," Khalid later wrote.[72]

The ground campaign, which began on February 24, proved to be anti-climatic. The previous thirty-four days of air war had decimated the Iraqi army and smashed its morale. Prince Khalid commanded the forces that liberated Kuwait City; he made sure that contingents from every Arab army fighting in the war participated in the return to the capital. Kuwaiti forces restored law and order. After just a hundred hours of ground war, Bush announced a cease-fire.

The allies had planned carefully for all kinds of contingencies in the war but had given surprisingly little thought to the peace that would follow. No one discussed marching to Baghdad and overthrowing Saddam. As Prince Khalid later wrote, "Any suggestion of marching on Baghdad was out of the question for the Arab members of the coalition, and indeed would have been vigorously opposed by Saudi Arabia."[73] General Powell writes that "in none of the meetings on the war I attended was dismembering Iraq, conquering Baghdad or changing the Iraqi form of governance ever seriously considered. We hoped Saddam would not survive but his elimination was not a stated objective. Our practical intention was to leave Baghdad enough power to survive as a threat to Iran."[74]

The assumption in the White House was that Saddam would fall from power without any more pressure from the allies. Instead, he held on to power and ruthlessly suppressed uprisings by the Shia majority in the south and the Kurdish minority in the north. Meanwhile, the large foreign army in Saudi Arabia went home. Only an air wing remained in Dhahran. From the air base there, American, British, and French aircraft patrolled a no-fly zone, to protect Shias in southern Iraq, for the next twelve years.

In the war's aftermath, Bush did engage in a major diplomatic effort to resolve the Arab-Israeli conflict. He believed the war had opened new opportunities for conflict resolution. Such an effort would also make it easier for the Saudis and other Arabs to work closely with the United States to foster regional stability. After a marathon diplomatic campaign led by Secretary of State James Baker, a peace conference was convened in Madrid, Spain, on October 30, 1991. The parties agreed to establish bilateral talks between Israel and its neighbors along with multilateral talks on regional issues like the environment and arms control.

Prince Bandar attended the Madrid conference to represent the Kingdom, along with the secretary general of the Gulf Cooperation Council.[75] The Saudis and the other Gulf states participated in the multilateral talks, marking the first time the Kingdom got directly involved in the peace process with Israel. But the Madrid process soon bogged down and no progress emerged from the bilateral talks. It would take a secret Israeli-Palestinian dialogue in Oslo, Norway, to create a breakthrough on the watch of Bush's successor in 1993.

The Kuwait war illustrated more clearly than ever before the strong ties between Saudi Arabia and America, but it also vividly exposed the Kingdom's weakness and its dependence on American security to survive. If Saddam had attacked in early August 1990 after invading Kuwait, the Saudi Eastern Province and Bahrain would have fallen quickly. To liberate Kuwait the Kingdom needed a half-million American soldiers as well as British, French, and Arab troops. The Iran-Iraq war had already exposed Saudi military weakness; now the Kuwait war highlighted its vulnerability in a dangerous neighborhood. Iran had threatened the Kingdom in the 1980s, and Iraq stood on the precipice of invading it in 1990.

One consequence of this vulnerability was a renewed Saudi effort to build legitimacy by exporting its own brand of Islam to the world. Fahd expanded

Faisal's support for mosques and educational establishments across Europe, Africa, and Asia after the Kuwait war. This was one way to answer the domestic critics of his decision to turn to Bush for help in 1990.

After Bush lost his bid for reelection in November 1992 to Bill Clinton, he sent American military forces to Somalia to try to restore order and deliver humanitarian relief. On December 31, 1992, the president paid a visit to Riyadh en route to Somalia to see King Fahd. It was a poignant symbol of how close the king and president had become over the years and the importance the Kuwait war had in the Bush presidency. Fahd gave Bush an enormous replica of the fort in Riyadh that Ibn Saud had seized back at the start of the modern Saudi Kingdom to symbolize his affection for the president.

Chapter Five

ABDALLAH, CLINTON, AND BUSH, 1993 TO 2008

The palace of Abdallah Abd al Aziz al Saud in Jidda is intended to impress. In May 1998 Abdallah, then the crown prince, was entertaining Vice President Al Gore for lunch. The luncheon was served in a room the size of six basketball courts, next to the palace's Olympic-size indoor swimming pool. The ceiling was painted blue with white stars to symbolize the desert sky in the evening. Behind the dining table was an enormous aquarium that extended from the floor to the ceiling and the length of the room. One guest at the luncheon estimated it was seventy-five feet long and thirty feet high. The glass wall was surrounded with pillars to appear as an ancient palace. The aquarium was filled with exotic fish swimming around what appeared to be ancient ruins. Several large sharks were among them.[1] I was accompanying the vice president as the National Security Council (NSC) representative. To me it was a scene right out of the first James Bond novel, *Doctor No*.

The lunch was an opportunity for Gore and Abdallah to get to know each other better. Much later Prince Turki, the Saudi intelligence chief, told the media that two of the 9/11 hijackers, Khalid al Mihdhar and Nawaf al Hazmi, were involved in a plot to attack Gore's party that day.[2] The Saudis captured anti-tank missiles the terrorists had smuggled in from Yemen to carry out the attack. This was months before al Qaida's first attacks on American targets: the U.S. embassies in Kenya and Tanzania in August 1998.

The Saudis did not tell the Americans about the plot until well after Gore had left the Kingdom. This was typical of the Saudi policy toward terrorism in the 1990s. The royal family was in denial about the fact that a significant infrastructure of terror had developed under the surface calm in the nation. Terrorist groups, especially al Qaeda but also Shia terrorists, had extensive underground networks inside the Kingdom. Saudi officials were convinced they knew how best to deal with any such problem, either through tough internal security measures, diplomacy abroad, or, if necessary, assassination. Above all, the Saudis did not want outsiders, especially Americans, dealing with the terror nexus in Saudi Arabia.

Abdallah Abd al Aziz al Saud was the tenth son of Ibn Saud. He was born in Riyadh; his date of birth is often cited as August 1, 1924, but it is not certain. His mother, Fahda bint Asi Al Shuraim, was from the rival al Rashid dynasty and the powerful Shammar tribe that dominates the northern Arabian Peninsula. She died when he was only six. He also suffered from a speech impediment. His half-brothers—Khalid, Fahd, Sultan, Nayef, Ahmed, and Salman—all had a different mother, Hussa bint Ahmed Al Sudairi, giving them the title of the Sudairis. The status of Abdallah's mother as an al Rashid made him somewhat of an outsider within the royal family.

But he overcame these issues early in life. In 1961 he was appointed mayor of Mecca, helping establish a lifelong reputation of piety. Unlike brothers Saud or Fahd, Abdallah was never considered a playboy. His image was of a pious Muslim with close connections to the tribal leadership. In 1962 Abdallah became commander of the Saudi Arabian National Guard, with the responsibility of regime protection. The National Guard is deployed in the holy cities, the capital, and the Eastern Province. The regular army is deployed on the frontiers. The National Guard was Abdallah's powerbase, and he kept command of it until 2010 when he passed control to his son Mutaib. The post gave Abdallah a special position in the family as the commander of what, in effect, was its Praetorian Guard and as the man most connected to the tribal elites. He, in turn, made sure the National Guard got the best training and best equipment needed to do its job. Most of that training and equipment has come from the United States or Canada.

King Khalid appointed Abdallah to be deputy crown prince in 1975 after Faisal was assassinated, and King Fahd made him crown prince in 1982 when Khalid died. For the next thirteen years Abdallah worked closely with Fahd. In 1995 Fahd suffered a massive, debilitating stroke, and for the next decade Abdallah ruled as de facto regent. On August 1, 2005, Abdallah ascended to the throne when Fahd passed away. He lived until January 23, 2015.

So for some twenty years Abdallah effectively ruled the Kingdom. While his half-brother Fahd was still alive he was careful to maintain the fiction that Fahd was in charge. When a senior American official like Gore visited the country, he went first to see Fahd in the royal palace. After picture taking and a few bland remarks, the official was dismissed and went on to see the crown prince. Abdallah always opened the substantive discussion that followed by asking how the visitor found Fahd's health. The correct protocol answer was that the king was in fine health.

Abdallah dealt with three American presidents: Bill Clinton, George W. Bush, and Barack Obama. Saudi-American relations during the Abdallah era began on the high note of the aftermath of Desert Storm in 1990–91. The 1990s represented almost a golden period of close cooperation on many issues, but underlying tensions would begin to emerge by 2000. Clinton's second ambassador to the Kingdom, Wyche Fowler, probably had the closest relationship to King Abdallah in the history of America's partnership with the Kingdom, in large part because the king liked Fowler, a former congressman from Georgia. In 2001 the storm broke when the towers collapsed with the 9/11 terrorist attack. For the remainder of the Abdallah era the relationship continued to be important and valuable to both sides but increasingly tense and contentious.

Clinton

It was inevitable that the successor to President George H. W. Bush would begin with a less intimate relationship with the Saudis. While Bush had saved the Kingdom via a war against Iraq, many of the Democrats elected with

Clinton in 1992 had voted against that war in the Senate. I was still the National Security Council's director for Gulf affairs, and my new bosses wanted a way to open a dialogue with the Kingdom and to begin to build relationships.

Prince Bandar bin Sultan bin Abdul Aziz, the Saudi ambassador, and I had an idea. Bill Clinton had graduated from Georgetown University in the same year that Prince Turki al Faisal, the Kingdom's intelligence chief, had attended the school. So Bandar and I worked to have a reunion of the two classmates to establish a bond. Turki visited the White House to meet with National Security Adviser Anthony Lake, and the president "dropped in" on the meeting to see his old classmate. It was a start to what became a strong working relationship between the Clinton White House and the House of Saud.

Bill Clinton pursued two major policy lines in the Middle East. First was enthusiastic and high profile support for negotiations to achieve a comprehensive and final peace settlement between Israel and all its Arab neighbors, including the Palestinians. Second was the dual containment of Iraq and Iran, which were judged threats to American vital interests and needed to be restrained from dangerous adventurism in the Middle East. The two policies were designed to reinforce each other. It would be easier to gather support among the Arabs to contain Iraq and Iran if the peace process involving Israel was vibrant and producing results. It would also be easier to get results in the peace process if two spoilers, Iraq and Iran, were successfully contained and marginalized in the region.

The Saudis were equally enthusiastic about the peace process although much less inclined to be as high profile in their efforts as Washington sometimes sought. They also agreed that Iraq and Iran were twin dangers but, worried that containment was unsustainable and costly, they preferred a coup that would remove Saddam and replace him with another Sunni strongman who would help rein in Iran. They had no capacity to affect such a coup, however, and neither did Washington.

The Clinton team inherited from Bush the Madrid peace process, which had become stalemated. Behind the scenes, however, Israel and the Palestine Liberation Organization (PLO) were engaged in secret diplomacy facilitated by Norway. The so called Oslo process achieved a breakthrough in mid-1993 when Israeli Prime Minister Yitzhak Rabin and PLO Chairman Yasser Arafat agreed to mutual recognition and the withdrawal of Israeli forces from most but not all of the Gaza Strip and the city of Jericho on the West Bank. The withdrawal from Gaza and Jericho was intended to initiate a process to end Israel's occupation of Gaza and the West Bank and produce a final peace treaty. The United States was not a party to the talks, but once briefed on the results, Clinton was eager to support the process and to host a signing ceremony at the White House.

As dean of the diplomatic corps in Washington (the longest-serving ambassador), Prince Bandar welcomed Arafat to Washington at Andrews Air Force Base in September 1993. Bandar attended the signing ceremony at the White House for the Oslo deal, representing the Kingdom. He also had the important, albeit somewhat unusual, job of persuading Arafat, behind the scenes, that he should not kiss the president or prime minister at the ceremony. Arafat had a fondness for embracing and kissing his interlocutors (I know from experience).[3]

The Saudis had long supported Arafat and funded the PLO. They were irritated at Arafat's tilt toward Iraq during the 1990–91 Kuwait crisis, but the Palestinian cause was deeply popular within the royal family, across the *ulema,* and among the Saudi public, so he was rehabilitated quickly after the war. Bandar hosted Arafat for every visit he made to Washington during Clinton's two terms in office, and the Palestinian leader called more often at the Clinton White House than any other foreign leader. Nonetheless, the Saudis were always distrustful of Arafat after 1990.

The Saudi preference was to be out of sight most of the time and keep a low profile, letting Arafat and his Syrian counterparts be in the public space. As one senior Clinton aide, Martin Indyk, later wrote, "The Saudis helped us quietly on the peace process, where they were willing to provide funding for Arafat's Palestinian Authority but were wary of engaging with Israel."[4]

Ironically the Israeli-Palestinian Oslo deal opened the door to an Israeli-Jordanian peace treaty. King Hussein was initially shocked at the Oslo agreements, from which he had also been excluded, but he saw in Oslo an opportunity to end Jordan's state of war with Israel and achieve a peace treaty. If the Palestinians had made a deal, so could Jordan. The critical negotiations were done secretly by the king and Efraim Halevy, the head of Mossad, the Israeli Secret Intelligence Service. Again, the Americans were largely excluded from the talks, but Clinton was invited to the signing ceremony. He insisted that he be the only witness, signatory, and guarantor of the treaty to underscore American centrality in the process.[5]

Clinton traveled to the region in October 1994 for the signing ceremony in Jordan. His itinerary included Egypt, Jordan, Syria, Israel, Kuwait, and Saudi Arabia. The Saudis still had not forgiven King Hussein for his tilt toward Iraq in 1990, but King Fahd welcomed Clinton to the Kingdom for a few hours in what would be the president's only visit to Saudi Arabia.[6] A year later Fahd suffered the debilitating stroke that removed him from managing the affairs of the Kingdom and placed Crown Prince Abdallah effectively in charge.

Abdallah continued Fahd's policy of quiet but effective support for the peace process. He was especially keen to secure a peace treaty between Syria and Israel. The Saudis believed such an agreement would take the Syrians out of their alliance with Iran and also permit Lebanon to sign a treaty with Israel, thus making the region more stable and weakening Tehran's influence. The election of former armed forces chief of staff General Ehud Barak to be Israeli prime minister in 1999 seemed to open the path to a deal with President Hafez Assad.

Clinton hosted Syrian and Israeli negotiators at the White House in late 1999. Bandar separately hosted the Syrian delegation at his Virginia home after the first day's talks. Syrian foreign minister Farouk Sharaa told the assembled representatives of the Arab states at Bandar's home that "they should inform their governments that Syria was about to make peace with Israel."[7] A deal seemed imminent, with the final negotiations to be hosted by Clinton at Shepherdstown, West Virginia.

Instead of a deal, Shepherdstown produced a "debacle."[8] The key problem was a disagreement on where to place the border between Syria and Israel on the northeast shore of the Sea of Galilee. Assad insisted it be on the lakeshore, where the Syrian army had been stationed on June 4, 1967, just before the Six-Day War. Barak insisted Israel control a narrow strip of territory along the shore, as had been the case when France and Britain had settled the border between their colonies in Syria and Palestine in 1919. Assad wanted to get access to the lake, but Barak was determined not to let his enemies' toes in the water at all. Clinton did not press Barak to give Assad the sliver of territory at stake. The talks ended in failure and damaged Clinton's credibility. In his memoirs Clinton wrote that "the Syrians came to Shepherdstown in a positive and flexible frame of mind, eager to make a deal." Barak was the obstacle, Clinton concluded.[9]

The Saudis played a central role in getting another chance at an Israel-Syria deal in March 2000 when Assad agreed to see Clinton in Geneva, Switzerland, at the end of Clinton's trip to India, Bangladesh, Pakistan, and Oman. Bandar traveled to Damascus to persuade Assad to go to Geneva. However, the small but crucial border problem scuttled the Geneva meeting, as well. When Assad saw the terms Barak was proposing, he said he was not going to agree. Clinton did not press Assad either, and it was all over in an hour. To add insult to injury, the president was suffering from the ill effects of food he had eaten in Islamabad the day before and was eager to get home to Washington.[10]

Assad died shortly after the Geneva summit. Prince Bandar hurried to Damascus to help Assad's son Bashar take power. Bandar used Saudi influence to persuade Syria's senior generals that Bashar was the best man for the job of replacing his father.

The Saudis were skeptical of Clinton's next major effort at peacemaking when, in July 2000, he convened another summit between Arafat and Barak, this time at Camp David, the presidential retreat in Maryland. As the president's special assistant for the Near East and South Asia, I was also skeptical that a deal was possible and advised both Clinton and National Security Adviser Samuel "Sandy" Berger about my skepticism. I was especially doubtful an agreement could be reached after the Assad failures—and particularly on the future of Jerusalem. Unfortunately, I was proven right and the Camp David summit failed. The two parties were far apart on all the issues going into the summit, and the gaps did not close significantly despite Clinton's sustained efforts. Almost immediately afterward the West Bank erupted into violence, marking the beginning of a Palestinian uprising, or intifada, in the occupied territories.

Clinton was not deterred from one last effort. In the closing days of his administration, he proposed his own "parameters" for a comprehensive Israeli-Palestinian peace agreement. Barak, facing a difficult election and under pressure because of the intifada, accepted them with considerable caveats. Bandar pushed Arafat to do the same when he came to the White

House in January 2001. Crown Prince Abdallah weighed in with Arafat, as well, according to Clinton's later account, but a deal simply was not possible at that point.[11] The Saudis were disappointed but hopeful that the newly elected president, George W. Bush, would continue the negotiating process his father had begun at Madrid. On this, Bandar and Abdallah were to be very disappointed.

Iraq

In the Persian Gulf, Iraq repeatedly challenged the cease-fire regime imposed at the end of the Kuwait war. The Iraqis were obligated by the United Nations Security Council resolutions following the armistice to destroy their weapons of mass destruction programs, under UN inspections and monitoring, and to agree to an official border demarcation with Kuwait. The sanctions imposed after the invasion in August 1990 were lifted only partially to allow Iraq to sell oil to purchase food and medicine for the Iraqi people.

Saddam Hussein interfered with the UN inspectors almost from the beginning, creating a series of mini-crises between Washington and Baghdad that began in the first Bush administration and continued through Clinton and into the next Bush administration. The Saudis were vital to American efforts to force Iraqi compliance with the UN resolutions since they hosted the largest American military air base in the region, at Dhahran. This meant U.S. forces remained in the Kingdom long after the liberation of Kuwait despite Bush's promises that American forces would leave once the war was over. It was an uncomfortable position for Fahd and Abdallah, but they backed both the United States and the UN.

Saudi support was particularly crucial for enforcing a no-fly zone in southern Iraq that Bush had established in 1992 to prevent Iraqi air strikes on Shia dissidents. American, British, and French aircraft patrolled southern Iraq to stymie such strikes. The no-fly zone also meant that the coalition partners controlled Iraqi air space bordering Saudi Arabia and Kuwait, thus making another Iraqi attempt at invasion of either country far more difficult and providing critical strategic depth for both. After losing his bid for reelection, Bush traveled to Kuwait in early 1993 to attend the second anniversary of the emirate's liberation. The Kuwaiti authorities discovered Iraq had smuggled a large car bomb into the country with the intent to kill the former president. They briefed the White House and, on June 26, 1993, Clinton ordered the launching of twenty-three Tomahawk cruise missiles to destroy the Baghdad headquarters of the Iraqi intelligence service that had plotted the assassination attempt.

Another major crisis came suddenly in October 1994 when Saddam sent two rebuilt and refurbished Republican Guard armored divisions to the Kuwaiti border, apparently threatening another invasion. By October 8, 1994, Iraq had 80,000 troops and hundreds of tanks just north of Kuwait. Clinton sent 350 aircraft to Saudi Arabia and Kuwait to deter Saddam and prepare to destroy the Iraqi tanks. He told the Saudis that if Saddam attacked, this time the United States would not stop the war until Saddam was finished. American ground forces, totaling over 50,000 people, were alerted to deploy to Kuwait and the Kingdom.[12] Iraq backed down and Saddam, in humiliation, formally accepted the UN-demarcated border with Kuwait.[13]

The most serious crisis between Clinton and Saddam came in the president's second term when I was his top Middle East adviser on the National Security Council staff and he was mired in the political scandal surrounding his relationship with Monica Lewinsky. Again, Saddam was interfering with UN weapons inspections. Sandy Berger and I urged the president to conduct a larger punitive air campaign to convince Saddam that the cost of these crises was serious. The main targets of the airstrikes would be those elements of the Iraqi regime that were Saddam's principal protectors: the Special Republican Guard and the intelligence services, both of which were also directly involved in thwarting the UN.[14]

Clinton agreed, and on December 16, 1998, after Clinton made a short trip to Jerusalem and Gaza, the United States and the United Kingdom began a four-day bombing attack from bases in Saudi Arabia and Kuwait, targeting eighteen command centers, eight Special Republican Guard barracks, six airfields, and nineteen intelligence sites in Iraq. Called Operation Desert Fox, this was the last major crisis between Iraq and the UN coalition in the Clinton era.[15]

The continuing danger posed by Iraq in the 1990s meant that Washington and Riyadh remained engaged in containing Saddam's regime. Crown Prince

Abdallah and Bandar were frustrated that Saddam survived in power, but they had no enthusiasm for another major war on Baghdad. Nor did Clinton and his team. That, too, would change under President George W. Bush.

Iran

Iran was the other half of Clinton's dual containment policy. The containment of Iran appealed to the Saudis' long-standing and deep concerns—dating to the shah's rule—about Iran's pursuit of regional hegemony in the Persian Gulf. But unlike Iraq, no United Nations resolutions limited Iranian ambitions and no sanctions kept Tehran under international controls. Indeed much of the world was eager to expand economic and trade relations with Iran and to sell products to Iran in exchange for oil.

Iran in the early 1990s was especially interested in buying a large number of civilian aircraft to replace aging civilian planes from the shah's time. The European consortium Airbus and the American company Boeing were the two suppliers most likely to make such a deal. Clinton did not want to block the Boeing company from a lucrative deal, and, thus, benefit its competitors, but he also did not want Iran's purchase of American jets to weaken his containment effort.

I proposed that Washington persuade Saudi Arabia to buy a large number of American civilian aircraft, to keep the airline business happy, while reaching a private understanding with the Saudis that we would then not compete for Iran's business. I raised the idea with Bandar, who was enthusiastic. So was the president, and several weeks later, in 1993, Clinton sent Secretary of Commerce Ron Brown and me to the Kingdom, where Fahd agreed, and the Saudis bought $6 billion worth of jets. The massive deal was formally announced (without mention of the Iran connection) in February 1994.[16]

On June 25, 1996, the most important U.S. military facility in the Middle East was attacked by terrorists. A large truck bomb (equivalent to 20,000 pounds of TNT) was detonated outside a barracks at the Dhahran air base, in a suburb called Khobar. The attack on the residence known as Khobar Towers killed nineteen United States Air Force personnel and wounded another 372. Several hundred Saudis and guest workers in the nearby town were also injured. Dhahran was a vital facility, home to the Operation Southern Watch aircraft that patrolled the no-fly zone in southern Iraq.

At the time I was deputy assistant secretary of defense for Near East and South Asia affairs and traveling in the region with Secretary of State Warren Christopher. We learned of the Khobar attack while we were in Jerusalem, and Christopher immediately decided to go to the scene of the attack. En route my boss, Secretary of Defense William Perry, instructed me to stay in Dhahran after Christopher left and wait for him to come to the region in a few days. I spent a week in Dhahran living in the consulate residence and working with the embassy and U.S. Air Force on the aftermath of the bombing.

Prince Bandar arrived on the scene shortly, as well. I met with him at the palace of the governor of the Eastern Province. Bandar said the Saudis were still developing information on the attack, but he clearly pointed a finger at Iran as responsible for the operation. When Perry arrived a few days later and met with the king, crown prince, and interior minister, they also suggested Iranian involvement but were quick to say the investigation was still in its early days.

It was not the first serious terrorist attack in the Kingdom against American targets. On November 13, 1995, a bomb detonated in the parking lot outside the headquarters of the Saudi Arabian National Guard training facility in Riyadh. Five Americans were killed and thirty wounded. The Americans were employed by the Vinnell Corporation, which had a $5.6 billion contract to train the National Guard. That attack apparently was the work of Sunni extremists who had fought in Afghanistan and were influenced by the speeches of Osama bin Laden. The Saudis captured four of the perpetrators and executed them after their confessions were aired on Saudi television. Minister of the Interior Prince Nayef bin Abdul Aziz refused to give the FBI access to the terrorists before their execution.[17]

Nayef resisted cooperation with the United States on the Khobar attack, as well. In part this was personal; Nayef was not a friend of the United States and he jealously guarded his prerogatives as interior minister. He did not want Americans involved in his investigation or in the Saudi judiciary process. But Nayef's reluctance was shared by the crown prince and other senior princes. Their concern was with what Washington would do with the results of the investigation. If an Iranian hand were involved, would Clinton attack Iran, as he had attacked Iraq for the Bush assassination plot? Would the situation escalate into another Gulf war with Saudi Arabia in the crosshairs of Iran's terrorist apparatus and missiles?[18]

The immediate shared requirement after the Khobar attack was to find a more secure base for U.S. Air Force operations in Saudi Arabia. Perry pressed Crown Prince Abdallah and Defense Minister Prince Sultan for a new location with better security than Dhahran. The Saudis provided the air force with Prince Sultan Air Base in the desert fifty miles southeast of Riyadh. That base was surrounded by miles of open desert, and it was enormous, eighty square miles. It also was isolated from Saudi civilians, and from a security perspective it had much better "stand off" distance than Khobar, which was right in the center of a busy metropolitan area.[19] The U.S., British, and French air forces all moved their aircraft and crews to the base before the end of 1996.

The Saudis gradually revealed that they had caught a Shia Saudi smuggling explosives into the Kingdom from Jordan a month before the Khobar attack; he said the terror group he was working for had surveilled the Khobar barracks. The group responsible was Saudi Hezbollah.

The Saudis, especially Nayef, were well acquainted with Saudi Hezbollah, or Hezbollah al Hijaz, from its terror attacks in the mid-1980s (see chapter 4). They knew the leader of the military wing of the group was Ahmed Ibrahim al Mughassil and that it was closely connected to the Iranian Revolutionary Guard Corps and its base in Syria. They determined that Mughassil was responsible for the Khobar attack and was in the truck bomb when it was parked outside the barracks.

The driver of the get-away car was another Saudi Shia, named Hani Abd Rahim al Sayegh, who had fled to Canada. The Canadian Security and Intelligence Service in March 1997 concluded that Sayegh was a "direct participant" in the attack and that Mughassil was the "mastermind." Sayegh admitted to having been provided with a false passport by the Iranian intelligence service and to having plotted in Syria and Iran with other members of Saudi Hezbollah.[20] Eventually Sayegh was extradited to the United States, but he refused to cooperate with the FBI and was, ultimately, sent back to the Kingdom.[21]

In February 1997 Defense Minister Sultan visited Washington. He was received by Perry's successor, former Maine senator William Cohen, and by other senior officials. He was given the rare privilege of a visit to the National Security Agency headquarters in Fort Meade, Maryland. Sultan was pressed to encourage more cooperation in the investigation.[22]

By the spring of 1997 the White House felt the evidence was sufficient to take some action against Iran. I had by then moved over to the National Security Council to become special assistant to the president and senior director for Near East and South Asia affairs. Richard Clarke, the senior director for counterterrorism, and I proposed that the United States take action against the Iranian intelligence service and the Iranian Revolutionary Guard Corps by disrupting their operations around the world. This would be a simple matter of "outing" their operatives around the world—letting them know that we knew who they were.[23]

Operation Sapphire, as it was called, was a big success. The Iranian intelligence chief in Saudi Arabia was among those "outed."[24] George Tenet, director of the Central Intelligence Agency, later wrote in his memoir that John Brennan (who would later become a CIA director) "handled the local Iranian intelligence chief in Riyadh himself. John walked up to his car, knocked on the window, and said, 'Hello, I'm from the U.S. Embassy and I've something to tell you.' The guy got out of the car, claimed Iran was a peace loving country, then jumped back in the car and sped away."[25]

Later that summer Ayatollah Mohammad Khatami was elected president of Iran. Khatami was a reformer who wanted to open Iran to outside influences and publicly called for better relations with the United States. Khatami attended the summit of the Organization of the Islamic Conference, which King Faisal had created, and argued for a revitalization of Islamic civil society and a reduction in tensions. Crown Prince Abdallah was present at the summit and was impressed. A Saudi-Iranian rapprochement followed, including signing of a security cooperation agreement. Former Iranian president Ayatollah Rafsanjani visited the Kingdom in 1998 and Khatami visited in 1999. In a very unusual gesture, the crown prince sent a Shia as ambassador to Iran.[26]

Khatami's election also changed the dynamics of U.S.-Iran relations. President Clinton wanted to engage Khatami, who clearly had no involvement in the Khobar attack himself and was the enemy of the hardliners in the Iranian Revolutionary Guard Corps. When Vice President Al Gore traveled to Saudi Arabia in May 1998, he carried an appeal from Clinton asking Crown Prince Abdallah to send a message to Khatami welcoming a change in American-Iranian relations and urging Iran to open a direct diplomatic channel to Washington.

Clinton continued to try to engage Khatami directly for the remainder of his presidency, but Khatami's domestic situation was too fragile to allow him to have a direct diplomatic opening to Washington. In June 1999 Assistant Secretary of State Martin Indyk and I traveled to France to see the sultan of Oman at his chateau outside Paris to give him a message to take to Khatami. Oman has long enjoyed good relations with both Riyadh and Tehran, so the sultan was an important intermediary.

The sultan has ruled his country since 1970, when the British engineered a coup against his father, who ruled almost as a medieval monarch, and put him on the throne. He is something of a recluse, only visiting Washington once in his reign. I've met him several times and always found him smart, insightful, and direct. On this occasion he immediately agreed to help Clinton.

At the meeting in Fontaine le Port I read a written message to the sultan and his foreign minister, Yusuf bin Alawi, that was focused on the Khobar attack. Subsequently declassified, the message said the United States government had acquired evidence that directly linked the Iranian guards to the attack. The United States sought a clear message from Khatami and the Iranian government that it would stop any further terrorist plots against American targets and bring to justice those involved in Khobar. Bin Alawi delivered the message to Khatami in Tehran on July 20, 1999, and explained that Clinton wanted good relations with Iran but needed assurance that Khobar would not be repeated. Khatami listened carefully to the foreign minister and said he was unaware of any Iranian involvement in the operation but would investigate.

The Iranians formally responded to the Omanis in September 1999. They categorically rejected the "allegations" of involvement as "inaccurate and unacceptable." But the message also assured that "there exists no threat from the Islamic Republic of Iran" to Americans, an implicit commitment that "there would be no additional Iranian terrorist attacks on American citizens," as

Indyk later wrote.[27] Until the American invasion of Iraq in 2003, that would be the case.

The president raised the Iran issue directly with Crown Prince Abdallah when he visited Washington on September 25, 1998. Unfortunately, that visit occurred in the midst of the Monica Lewinsky scandal. The crown prince spent the bulk of his meeting with the president assuring him of his personal support despite the scandal and suggesting that the Mossad was probably responsible for the affair.[28]

The Bush administration formally brought charges against Mughassil, his accomplices in Saudi Hezbollah, and Iran in June 2001. The Department of Justice issued an indictment that laid out the case against them. The Saudis were kept fully informed of the case, and Bandar quietly welcomed the formal indictment.[29]

Abdallah's close ties with Clinton had a price, helping exacerbate the tensions between extremists and the Kingdom. Osama bin Laden turned on the House of Saud as he embarked on his global jihad against America. In 1991 bin Laden left Saudi Arabia and went into exile in Khartoum, Sudan. He kept a low profile until 1994, although he was active privately in support of dissident critics inside the Kingdom.

In December 1994 bin Laden sent an open letter to Chief Mufti Shaykh al bin Baz of Saudi Arabia who had endorsed his work in Afghanistan a decade before. In this open letter, bin Laden's first public statement evoking his new jihad, he attacked bin Baz and the clerical establishment for endorsing the Oslo accords. The cleric had issued a statement endorsing the Oslo agreement and the Saudi support for the peace process. Bin Laden attacked this as "conferring legitimacy on the contracts of surrender to the Jews that were signed by traitorous and cowardly Arab tyrants," a reference to the House of Saud.[30] He repeated his earlier criticism of the Saudis for allowing American troops into the Kingdom in 1990, but he made clear that the breaking point with the royal family and their clerical allies was the peace process with Israel. As one expert wrote later, "The letter makes it plain that Palestine, far from being a late addition to bin Laden's agenda, was at the center of it from the start."[31]

Under pressure from Washington and Riyadh, the Sudanese government encouraged bin Laden to leave in 1996, and he moved to Afghanistan where he reconnected with his mujahedin friends from the past. On August 23, 1996, he issued a statement calling for the expulsion of "the polytheists from the Arabian Peninsula," meaning the American base in Saudi Arabia. This public document justified attacks, such as the Riyadh and Dhahran bombings, because of Israel's occupation of Palestine and Jerusalem and America's presence in the Kingdom and the two holy cities. While mentioning the two attacks in Riyadh and Dhahran, bin Laden did not take credit for them. This was his declaration of his coming jihad.[32]

It was another two years, however, before words became action. On August 7, 1998, bin Laden's al Qaeda attacked simultaneously the U.S. embassies in Kenya and Tanzania. Two hundred and fifty-seven people were killed, most of them locals but twelve of them Americans, and hundreds more were injured, mostly Africans. A plot to blow up the American embassy in Tirana, Albania, was foiled at the same time.[33] The CIA quickly told Clinton that al Qaeda was responsible. According to Clinton's recollection, "The CIA also had intelligence that bin Laden and his top staff were planning a meeting at one of his camps in Afghanistan on August 20 to assess the impact of their attacks and plan their next operations." Berger was instructed to plan a missile strike to "wipe out the al Qaida leadership."[34]

On August 15 the president told his wife Hillary and his daughter Chelsea that he had lied about his relationship with Monica Lewinsky, and two days later he told the nation he had misled it. Then the first family went on vacation in Martha's Vineyard in Massachusetts. From there he issued the executive orders for the missile strike designed to kill bin Laden. Several al Qaeda operatives were killed as well as "some Pakistani officers," but as Clinton recalls bin Laden had either left the camp early or was never there.[35]

From August 1998 Clinton put fighting al Qaeda at the top of his agenda. Berger organized an interagency effort to hunt down and fight al Qaeda around the world. The Saudis were skeptical that bin Laden was as dangerous as the Americans argued, but they did provide some support in the campaign. Prince Turki went to Pakistan to try to use Pakistan's leverage with the Afghan Taliban, bin Laden's host in Afghanistan, to have him extradited to Saudi Arabia. Instead, the Pakistanis let Turki deal directly with Taliban leader Mullah Omar, who rejected any move against bin Laden. Turki and Omar ended their meeting in a shouting match, Turki later told me.

The Saudis may have also tried to assassinate bin Laden. After the Clinton cruise missile attack failed, bin Laden claimed that his security detail had foiled a plot ordered by the Saudi governor of Riyadh, Prince Salman (the future king), to kill him. As governor of Riyadh, Salman was responsible for "policing" aberrant behavior in the royal family and its close allies like the bin Ladens, so the story is plausible.[36]

But for the most part the Saudis remained convinced they had no serious al Qaeda problem at home. They were in denial about the growing support for bin Laden among the Saudi population. In October 2000 al Qaeda struck again, attacking a U.S. Navy destroyer at the port in Aden, Yemen. Even after the Aden attack, one on the Arabian Peninsula itself, the Saudis were still reluctant to see the enormity of the threat posed by bin Laden and his organization. Unfortunately, as we will see, so was the incoming Bush team.

During the Clinton years Washington and Riyadh cooperated on a wide range of issues, from peace diplomacy to counterterrorism. A good example of this close and intimate cooperation involved Libya. The Libyans were responsible for placing a bomb on Pan Am flight 103 on December 21, 1988, which exploded over Lockerbie, Scotland, killing all 243 passengers and sixteen crew. The United Nations imposed sanctions on Libya and demanded Tripoli turn over two Libyans suspected of involvement in the attack.

After years of stalemate the Libyans decided in 1999 to approach the United States to seek to resolve the Lockerbie incident. They asked the Saudis to set up a dialogue with Washington, and Prince Bandar approached the White House. Ambassador Martin Indyk and I then held a series of meetings with a Libyan team to discuss Libyan compliance with the UN resolutions. The dialogue was conducted at Prince Sultan's home in Geneva, Switzerland, and Bandar's home in England. In the end, the two Libyans were put on trial in The Hague, and one was convicted in 2001 of responsibility for placing the bomb on the aircraft.

It was a good example of cooperation between Washington and Riyadh to achieve a common interest, the resolution of an outstanding dispute in accordance with UN resolutions. One of those killed on Pan Am 103 was a colleague of mine from the Central Intelligence Agency. The secret diplomacy with Bandar helped bring a measure of justice and closure for his family.[37]

Not surprising, Clinton and Saudi kings Fahd and Abdallah did not always agree. The Saudis were much more determined to press their case against some of Saddam's friends from the Kuwait crisis than were the Americans. Jordan was one such case; Riyadh never really reconciled with King Hussein. Yemen was the other, and the Saudi leadership looked for every opportunity to undermine President Ali Abdallah Saleh for his support for Saddam in 1990.

In 1994 the Saudis got their chance. South Yemen, which had merged with the north only in 1990, seceded from the union. The Saudis gave their support to the southerners against Saleh, including purchasing military equipment for them. Washington was not eager to join the fray, suspecting it would become either a long-term quagmire or an outright Saleh victory. Saleh, indeed, did quickly win the 1994 civil war, leaving the Saudis without any influence in their neighbor.

The 1990s were an era of strong relations between Riyadh and Washington, perhaps the strongest ever. The Madrid and Oslo peace processes eased the recurring tensions over Israel. Iran was contained and, under Khatami, seemed less dangerous. Saddam was defeated in Kuwait and far less dangerous than before 1991. He was mostly a threat to his own people.

But by the end of Bill Clinton's eight years in office, some serious strains were under the surface in the Saudi-American relationship. The failures of Clinton's peace diplomacy in 2000 undermined the Saudis' confidence that America was truly serious about promoting final, just, and fair settlements. Saudi worries about Israel's political influence in Washington, always just below the surface, came back into play. In Riyadh, it seemed the Tel Aviv tail wagged the Washington dog. On his last day in office, Clinton gathered his NSC staff for a group picture. He turned to me and said, "You were right about Arafat." The next day Clinton called incoming Secretary of State Collin Powell and told him never to trust Arafat.

The terrorism issue was also undermining the U.S.-Saudi relationship. Both on Khobar and al Qaeda, the Saudis were convinced they knew better than America what to do and how to respond to terrorism involving Saudis. They were reluctant to trust America with sensitive information. Prince Nayef was the most reluctant, and his stonewalling against cooperation would only get worse after Clinton.

Bush

The Saudis, especially Bandar, expected that George W. Bush would come to the presidency with many of the same views of the Middle East as his father George H. W. Bush. In particular they expected him to continue his father's efforts at reaching a comprehensive Arab-Israeli peace agreement. Bush did share his father's appreciation for the importance of the American-Saudi partnership, but he had little or no interest in promoting a peace agreement between Israel and the Palestinians. In part this was because of Clinton's spectacular failures the year before. If Clinton could not get a deal, why would Bush want to try? But Bush and his team also did not believe the Palestinian issue was as crucial to regional stability as Clinton and Bush's father did. The previous presidents' experiences had taught them its centrality; Bush did not have that experience. Early in his tenure Bush hosted a small dinner for Israeli president Moshe Katsav and told one of the guests, "The Saudis thought this Texas oil guy was going to go against Israel, and I've told them you have the wrong guy."[38]

Bush's national security adviser, Condoleezza Rice, and her deputy, Stephen Hadley, asked me to stay on at my job in the White House for the first year of the Bush presidency. Rice and Hadley were smart and experienced security experts, but they had little experience in the Middle East. Both are unfailingly polite and thoughtful, and I was honored to be asked; I agreed to one last year at the National Security Council.

The Palestinian intifada that had followed the failure of peace talks at Camp David was the critical Middle East problem early in the Bush presidency. As Rice later wrote in her memoirs, "The low intensity war between Palestinians and Israelis dominated our security agenda" for the first nine months of Bush's opening year at the White House.[39] The intifada produced endless violence, including horrific suicide bombing attacks in Israeli cities by the extremist Islamic group Hamas and bloody Israeli retaliation operations in the West Bank and Gaza. The cycle of violence only got worse.

The Bush team was divided on how to handle the low-intensity war. Secretary of State Colin Powell and director of the CIA George Tenet (who had been at Camp David with Clinton) favored a balanced approach that sought to work with both sides, including Arafat, to reduce tensions. They also believed

Bush needed to articulate his own vision of a just peace to provide some incentive to end the violence. White House officials, including Vice President Richard Cheney, were more inclined to just back Israel and its new right-wing prime minister, Ariel Sharon. As Rice noted later, this division hampered decisionmaking, especially given the "ultra hawkish" staff in the vice president's office.[40]

But Bush and his entire team were united on one thing. They urgently wanted to establish a good relationship with Saudi Arabia, and to do that they wanted a meeting with Crown Prince Abdallah. Bush, Cheney, Powell, Defense Secretary Donald H. Rumsfeld, and Rice all wanted to get Abdallah to Washington for a meeting with the president.

The invitation was sent through Bandar. The answer was a firm and unequivocal no. The crown prince would not see the president until Bush took action on Palestine. He wanted Bush to take dramatic action to halt the violence between Israel and the Palestinians; he wanted Bush to see Arafat; and he wanted the Israeli occupation of the West Bank and Gaza to end. He was already framing in his mind a peace proposal that he would put forward in February 2002.

To mark the tenth anniversary of Kuwait's liberation in March 2001 Powell traveled to the region for his first engagement as secretary of state with Middle East rulers. In Saudi Arabia he invited the crown prince to Washington; Abdallah again refused and urged the secretary to do more to ease the crisis in the West Bank and East Jerusalem.

Powell tried again on June 29, 2001, in Paris where the crown prince was visiting the French leadership. As in March, I accompanied the secretary, representing the NSC. The meeting took place in the magnificent George V Hotel. A large conference room had been transformed with oriental carpets and lush Louis XIV furniture into a Saudi *diwan* with the chairs all forming a giant rectangle with the crown prince at one end and all his princes attending to hear what transpired.

After some opening pleasantries, the crown prince passed a book of photographs to the secretary. It featured dramatic pictures of Palestinian children and women killed in the intifada. The imagery was disturbing and awful. Of course, both Israelis and Palestinians were dying in the conflict, but Abdallah was focused only on the Palestinians. He told the secretary that they died at the hands of American weapons provided to Israel, that America had a moral obligation to stop the carnage, and that since Powell was a military man by profession he had a special, personal responsibility for acting to save children. Powell and Abdallah got emotional. The two exchanged comments candidly and hotly. It was clear, once again, that Abdallah was not coming to Washington.[41]

George H. W. Bush tried to use his own relationship with the crown prince on his son's behalf. The father had stayed in close contact with Abdallah after 1992 and had traveled to Riyadh in November 1998 and in January 2000.[42] After the 2000 election Bush senior went to England to see Prince Bandar at his home outside London, and the two met again in Washington the night before Bush's son was inaugurated.[43] Now he called the crown prince to assure him that the president was committed to finding peace in the region. The Saudi was duly respectful of the former president but made clear he was not budging.[44]

Prince Turki, the intelligence chief, came to Washington in July to see me and other officials. He wanted to know why Bush junior was not acting like Bush senior.[45] I met with him at his hotel suite in Tyson's Corner near Washington. It was clear to me that Turki and Bandar were in some trouble with the crown prince for not anticipating better how George W. Bush would perform in office.

The Kingdom's two preeminent American experts had given their boss predictions about Bush that had not come to pass. That fall, when Turki was removed from his position as chief of intelligence, it was perceived in the White House that his removal was a sign of Abdallah's anger at Washington.[46] Turki went on to be Abdallah's ambassador to the United Kingdom and later replaced Bandar in Washington.

The crown prince next dropped a bombshell on the White House. In August 2001 Abdallah cancelled with no notice a high-level military visit to Washington. The Saudi armed forces chief of staff, who had arrived early for the meetings, was called home abruptly.[47]

Then the crown prince sent a momentous letter to Bush. The letter crystallized the depth of Saudi anger at Washington. It "rocked the White House," as one senior National Security Council official described it later. Another characterized it as "a Saudi threat of some kind of fundamental reevaluation of the relationship unless America committed to doing something serious to stop the violence."[48]

Bandar showed the letter to Marwan Muasher, the well-plugged-in Jordanian ambassador in Washington. Muasher recalls that the letter "pointedly said it had become clear to Saudi Arabia that the U.S. administration was working against Arab interests, and in a clear reference to oil prices, he [Abdallah] wrote that Saudi Arabia would reciprocate by pursuing its own interests without consideration for American interests."[49]

Just six months into the Bush administration, the relationship was in acute crisis. This was the darkest moment in American-Saudi relations since 1973, with the first explicit threat of the oil weapon since the spring of 1974. The military relationship forged in 1990–91 was at risk, as well. The situation moved to the top of Bush's agenda.

Rice and Powell instructed William Burns, the assistant secretary of state for the Near East, and me to draft a response to the crown prince. Our instructions were to find a way to heal the breach with Abdallah and get the relationship back on track. Our draft letter was reviewed by all the top players in the Bush administration and signed by the president. The key commitment was the president's promise that the goal of American policy in the Israeli-Palestinian dispute would be the creation of an independent Palestinian state. While Clinton had implicitly been working for a two-state solution after Oslo, Bush's letter was the first overt and formal American commitment to a Palestinian state. Bush promised in the letter to announce publicly his commitment at the United Nations General Assembly meeting in New York in September.[50]

In the first days of September 2001 Bandar was invited to the White House to receive the response letter directly from the president. Bandar was optimistic it would be persuasive. He flew to Riyadh immediately. Upon his return to the United States, on September 7, 2001, Bush, Cheney, Rice, Hadley, Bandar, and I met on the Truman Balcony of the White House in the early evening. Bandar reported that the letter and the Bush commitments had resolved the crisis with the crown prince. Bush was relieved and pleased. The White House official photographer recorded the moment.[51]

On Saturday, September 8, 2001, Bandar attended a wedding celebration party for my wife and me in Old Town Alexandria. He was beaming. He said, "I'm the happiest man in town." He and Director Tenet went out to a late dinner after the party, where Bandar told the director the royal family had never been angrier with Washington than that summer.[52]

The next day, Sunday, September 9, Ahmed Shah Massoud, the Tajik leader of the opposition to the Taliban and al Qaeda in Afghanistan, was assassinated at his base in northern Afghanistan. The two assassins, who had posed as journalists, were members of al Qaeda, and the assassination of the Taliban's top enemy was the essential precursor to the attack on America that soon followed. On Monday Ambassador Muasher delivered a letter from Jordan's King Abdallah II—who had succeeded his father in February 1999—calling on Bush to stop the violence and convene a final peace agreement conference.[53]

The next morning, Tuesday, September 11, I was in the White House Situation Room with Rice when the second hijacked aircraft smashed into the World Trade Center. The events of 9/11 seemed to change everything for the Bush White House, America, and the world. It was the bloodiest day in American history since the Civil War, and we are still grappling with the impact of the 9/11 attacks more than fifteen years later.

Richard Clarke, the administration's top terrorism adviser, who had held the same job for Clinton, would later testify to the 9/11 Commission that he believed Bush, Cheney, and Rice paid insufficient attention to the warnings of an impending al Qaeda attack in the spring and summer of 2001. George Tenet, the director of central intelligence, consistently warned that an attack was imminent and that it would be far more devastating than the African or Aden attacks. (Despite the fact that I was the special assistant to the president for Near East Affairs with responsibility for Saudi issues in particular, I was never asked to testify to the commission or any official investigation of the attack— probably because I would have seconded Clarke's point.)

Bandar and I spoke often on the phone on September 11, 2001. He rapidly communicated the Kingdom's horror at the attack and sympathies for the victims. Once it became clear that Osama bin Laden and al Qaeda were behind the attacks, Tenet arranged for Bandar to get a complete briefing on the plot. Crown Prince Abdallah supported Bush's decision to invade Afghanistan and topple the Taliban government. The Saudis had long ago soured on the Taliban, especially after its leader Mullah Omar refused to hand bin Laden over to Prince Turki in 1998.

Foreign Minister Prince Saud bin Faisal meeting with President George W. Bush, September 2001. Also attending are Prince Bandar, and on the right, Secretary of State Colin Powell and the author. (Author's collection)

Bandar had to devote much of his attention after 9/11 to the mounting anger in the United States at Saudi Arabia. The media put much of the blame for the rise of al Qaeda on the Saudis and their Wahhabi faith. Even Bandar and his wife Haifa were accused of helping the hijackers.

The annual opening of the UN General Assembly was postponed until November due to the disruption in New York City. On November 10, 2001, Bush addressed the General Assembly and said the Taliban and al Qaeda "are now virtually indistinguishable." He promised their swift defeat.

Bush also said, "The American government also stands by its commitment to a just peace in the Middle East. We are working toward the day when two states—Israel and Palestine—live peacefully together with secure and recognized borders as called for by the Security Council resolutions." Bush had lived up to his commitment to Abdallah from September.[54]

Despite Bush's unprecedented public American commitment to support a Palestinian state, the violence in the region got worse. Dozens of Israelis died in horrific suicide bombings in Tel Aviv, Jerusalem, and other cities. Prime

Minister Sharon responded by sending Israeli forces back into cities that had been turned over to Palestinian hands as a result of the Oslo process. Arafat's headquarters in Ramallah on the West Bank was surrounded by the Israeli army and put under siege.

In an interview with *New York Times* columnist Tom Friedman, in February 2002, Crown Prince Abdallah revealed his own plan for a permanent peace agreement. An Arab summit in Beirut in March endorsed Abdallah's call for full Israeli withdrawal from the occupied territories, to be matched by full normalization of relations between Israel and all the Arab states. Abdallah called it "full withdrawal for full normalization."[55] Prime Minister Sharon promptly rejected the historic Saudi initiative.

Armed with Bush's General Assembly commitment and his own Arab summit-blessed peace plan, Crown Prince Abdallah made his long-awaited visit to see Bush in April. They met at Bush's home in Crawford, Texas, on April 25, 2002. The tete à tete was almost a disaster. After listening to Bush explain why he could not stop Sharon's siege of Arafat in his office in Ramallah and argue that Saddam Hussein was the biggest threat to regional peace, Abdallah gathered his advisers to leave. They told the president's Arabic translator, Gamal Helal, that the crown prince had decided to leave the summit, break off the conversation with Bush, and hold a press conference on his way home. The crown prince would say his mission to end the siege and promote his peace plan had failed due to Bush's intransigence. As Bush wrote later, "America's pivotal relationship with Saudi Arabia was about to be seriously ruptured."[56] Rice later wrote that the Saudi walkout would have been a "disaster."[57]

In their accounts of what came next, Bush and Rice both emphasize the president's decision to take the crown prince on a ride around his farm. Bush tried to calm tensions by talking about farming, but he "wasn't making much headway" when a turkey was spotted by the side of the road. Then Abdallah grabbed Bush's hand and said it was an omen: "a sign from Allah." Tensions melted. Later Bush wrote, "I had never seen a hen turkey on that part of the property before, and I haven't seen one since."[58]

Although amusing, the turkey story is obviously misleading. Translator Helal, who was the only other person on the ride, says Bush made a clear and firm commitment to Abdallah to get the siege of Arafat's headquarters in

Ramallah lifted immediately.[59] As one of Bush's aides wrote later, "Within days, on April 28, the Israeli cabinet decided to move the tanks back and free Arafat; Abdallah presumably saw an American hand at work in that decision."[60] But the relief proved temporary, and the war between Israel and the Palestinians escalated throughout the remainder of the year.

In June 2002 Bush dramatically changed the dynamics of Palestinian relations with America when he gave a speech in the Rose Garden calling on "the Palestinian people to elect new leaders, leaders not compromised by terror." He said, "I call upon them to build a practicing democracy, based on tolerance and liberty." Rice played a key role in the formulation of the new American policy of calling for Arafat's removal and replacement by a functioning democracy in an Arab country.[61]

For the Saudis it was a difficult solution to the impasse. They had no particular affection for Arafat, who they had always distrusted. But they were no fans of democracy, either. Particularly disturbing for the Saudis was the idea that democracy could be more or less imposed on an Arab state by the United States. If Washington could dump one Arab autocrat for a democratic alternative, where would it end? If democracy is the only path to stability and peace in the Middle East, where does that leave a theocratic absolute monarchy? These questions were not muttered in public, but they certainly were pondered in the palaces of Saudi Arabia and other countries.

The near disaster at Crawford illustrated how damaged the American-Saudi relationship had become by mid-2002. The Palestinian issue was the main driver in the steady deterioration. The Saudis never trusted Bush's handling of the Israeli-Palestinian conflict after 2002 and distanced themselves from American diplomacy toward the conflict. Abdallah continued to push his peace plan.

Iraq

One issue that got little Saudi attention at Crawford was Iraq. In fact, the Bush administration had already decided to make Iraq the centerpiece of its Middle East policy. Bush told Abdallah that he was determined to do more about Saddam Hussein, but he and his team were not ready to discuss their plans in any detail.

The Kurds were the first leaders in the Middle East to learn of the president's decision to remove Saddam Hussein from power as the next step in his global war on terror. In 1991 after Desert Storm, President Bush senior had created a no-fly zone in northern Iraq to protect the Iraqi Kurdish minority from Saddam's repression; this mirrored the similar zone protecting Shias in southern Iraq. In the wake of the Iran-Iraq war in 1988, Saddam had murdered thousands of Kurds, some by using poison gas. After Desert Storm the Kurds rose up in rebellion and were again attacked by Saddam's weakened but still deadly forces. Bush created Operation Provide Comfort to defend the Kurds.

By 2002 Provide Comfort had helped create an all-but-independent Kurdish state in northern Iraq ruled by two competing Kurdish parties: Masoud Barzani's Kurdish Democratic Party and Jalal Talabani's Patriotic Union of Kurdistan. Both had long ties to the CIA, but bitter experience led them to doubt American promises of help. Nixon had abandoned a Kurdish rebellion backed by the CIA in 1974; Reagan had stood by passively when Saddam gassed the Kurds in 1988; and Bush senior had been slow to stop Saddam in 1991.

But if Washington wanted good intelligence on what was going on in Iraq in 2002, it badly needed the Kurds. Only in the north could American intelligence operate on Iraqi territory. So Bush authorized Tenet to tell the Kurdish leaders that he was seriously determined to oust Saddam. In March 2002 Tenet met with both Barzani and Talabani secretly in Washington to enlist their aid in the coming campaign to overthrow Saddam by military invasion. It marked the first decisive step toward war.[62]

Talabani returned to northern Iraq via London. By March 2002 I was a member of the Royal College of Defense Studies in London. I had known Talabani for over a decade, since I had first brought him to the White House in 1992 to meet with Brent Scowcroft. I had visited him in his home in Sulaymaniyah in 1994. Over lunch at a restaurant close to Harrods in London, Talabani told me Tenet had promised that if Bush made a final decision to go to war with Iraq the goal would be to remove Saddam from power. Talabani was ecstatic, thrilled to be planning his oppressor's end.

The White House held off briefing the Saudis, suspecting they would be less thrilled with the news. The Saudis did not get their formal briefing on Bush's plans until long after the de facto decision to invade Iraq had been made. They did notice the drumbeat of war much earlier, of course, for example on August 26, 2002, when Vice President Cheney gave a high-profile speech in Nashville, Tennessee, signaling U.S. intentions about Iraq. He said, "Simply stated, there is no doubt that Saddam Hussein now has weapons of mass destruction." It was the opening public salvo in what would be a rush to war.[63]

Prince Turki had taken up his new job as ambassador to the United Kingdom, and he asked me to dinner after the Cheney speech. He expressed grave concerns about a war to topple Saddam. What would replace Saddam? Would elections be held to create a new Iraq? That would lead inevitably to a Shia-dominated state, given that the Shia are the majority of the population in Iraq. And that would give Iraq to Iran, Turki warned, upsetting the balance of power in the Middle East in general and the Gulf in particular.

Turki said much the same in public. In a visit to Washington he told the *Washington Post* that the idea that the United States could solve its problems in the region through the use of military might in Iraq was wrongheaded and downright dangerous. "A military invasion with U.S. soldiers is not going to be welcome, not by the Iraqi people, not by other people in the region. We Saudis will have to live with the consequences."[64]

The official Saudi request for Bush to explain his Iraq policy came on November 15, 2002, when Bandar called on the president in the White House. Bandar had been out of town most of the weeks since the Crawford meeting. Officially, he was ill. It was an old Bandar tactic. When the Saudis were upset with the White House, Bandar played hard to get, literally. He did not want to be the messenger of bad news for the crown prince nor convey more bad news to Bush from Riyadh. So he simply stayed out of town for months. But by November he needed to ask Bush directly what his plans were.

Bush was still not ready to tell the Saudis. So Bandar, instead, gave Bush Riyadh's view. Any move to topple Saddam had to be linked to meaningful progress on the Israeli-Palestinian issue. That was the bargain Fahd and Bush senior had made in 1990–91, and the same bargain was essential in 2002.[65]

Bandar finally got his briefing on Bush's war plans on January 11, 2003. In a deliberate repetition of August 3, 1990, Cheney invited Bandar to his office (now in the White House, not the Pentagon as in 1990), where the vice president, Secretary of Defense Rumsfeld, and Chairman of the Joint Chiefs of

Staff General Richard Myers briefed Bandar on the war plan to oust Saddam. It was detailed and specific, with a clear goal of marching all the way to Baghdad. Bandar asked if Bush was really serious about going all the way. Cheney told him Saddam would be "toast" when the war was over. Two days later Bush met with Bandar directly and told him the same bottom line. He asked for Saudi support.[66]

Bandar flew immediately to Riyadh to convey the briefing from Bush to the crown prince. Abdallah told him to keep the message absolutely secret until he decided how to respond.[67] Abdallah and the senior princes were not eager for war. They wanted Saddam removed, certainly, but they were deeply concerned about the day after. The problems Turki had laid out with me and in his interview with the *Washington Post* were on their minds. What would replace Saddam? If elections were held, it would inevitably mean a Shia-dominated Iraq, anathema to the Saudis. On the other hand, the Saudis did not want to break publicly with Washington on such a major issue. The relationship with Washington was already on the ropes over Palestine; another public blow-up on Iraq would not help. The Saudis stayed on the sidelines as the war drums beat in Washington and London.

On March 15, 2003, Bandar called on Bush again in the White House. He had a message from the crown prince. The Saudis were still eager to avoid a war, Bandar said, but if it had to happen, do it quickly. Bandar deliberately stressed the urgency part of the message, not the appeal to avoid war. The president's team noted that the ambassador was "tired, nervous and excited . . . sweating profusely" and overweight. The strain of the job was showing clearly, and Bandar was not handling the pressure well.[68]

The Saudis agreed to provide very quiet assistance to the American war effort. The Prince Sultan air base was used to support the war, and American Special Forces operated from Saudi bases along the Iraq frontier. But the bulk of the American and British invasion force came out of Kuwait. As soon as the war ended, the American forces left the air base, which reverted to exclusive Saudi use in late April 2003. American military forces were no longer present in the Kingdom for the first time since August 1990.[69]

Bandar played a complicated game during the build-up and launch of the war. Of course, he knew the Kingdom was a reluctant partner in the conflict and that Abdallah shared the doubts expressed by Turki about the wisdom of

Bush's adventure in Iraq. He also knew Abdallah was much more concerned with the Palestinian issue. But he recognized the central importance of the war for Bush and his presidency. In public he was much more supportive of the war and its goal of eliminating Saddam than any other Saudi official. When the war succeeded in removing Saddam, Bandar openly praised the removal of "a great evil from the world" and lauded Bush for his leadership.[70] When the occupation of Iraq quickly spawned an insurgency against the American and British forces and developed into a political disaster for Bush, Bandar found himself increasingly in the doghouse in Riyadh. He was losing the confidence of the crown prince.

Terror at Home

The American focus on Iraq in the spring and summer of 2002 was also noted by Osama bin Laden and al Qaeda. The American intervention in Afghanistan had toppled the Taliban Islamic Emirate, but bin Laden and most of his top lieutenants got away, fleeing into Pakistan.[71]

Before September 11, bin Laden had been careful not to carry out violent operations in his own country. Although he endorsed the attacks on American military troops in Riyadh in 1995 and in Khobar in 1996, he made clear that he had no direct involvement in either operation, and no evidence suggests he did. Perhaps he did not want to open a campaign at home prematurely, before his cadres were strong enough—or perhaps he was just eager to keep a low profile inside the Kingdom so he could continue to raise money and find recruits there. The U.S. invasion of Afghanistan led to a change in bin Laden's posture. The unexpected swiftness of the invasion and its rapid toppling of the Taliban regime were partly responsible. In 2002, after the fall of Kabul, several hundred Saudi members of al Qaeda returned to the Kingdom and worked with sleeper cells that had been operating covertly there for several years at bin Laden's direction.

In February 2003, on the eve of the Iraq war, bin Laden issued an audio message directed at Iraqis. He said he was "following with intense interest and concern the Crusaders' preparations for war to occupy one of Islam's former capitals, loot Muslims' riches and install a stooge government to follow its masters in Washington and Tel Aviv to pave the way for the establishment of a Greater Israel." He called on all Muslims to be prepared to fight the American invasion and work together to sabotage it. Bin Laden had already dispatched a key aide, Abu Musaib al Zarqawi, to organize the resistance to the American invasion and occupation.[72]

But al Qaeda had even bigger ambitions than to turn Iraq into a quagmire for America. Bin Laden's goal was to overthrow the House of Saud itself. Bin Laden previewed the insurrection in the Kingdom in a major address to the Muslim world on February 14, 2003, coinciding with the eve of the U.S.-led invasion of Iraq. Delivered on the holy day of Eid al Adha, bin Laden's statement was the first and only in which he framed his argument in the form of a sermon. He wanted to give this message special importance. The address came just a few days after his "Letter to the Iraqi People," in which he urged Iraqis to get ready to fight the invaders. Bin Laden was evidently preparing for an epic battle on two fronts simultaneously.

Bin Laden accused the House of Saud of betraying the Ottoman Empire to the British in the First World War and opening the door to Western (Crusader) and Jewish (Zionist) domination of the Muslim world (the *ummah*). Moreover, he argued that the goal of the Crusaders was to divide the Saudi Kingdom into smaller states to make it easier to control and accused the Saudi family of complicity in this endeavor. The goal of the Crusader invasion of Iraq and of the Crusader military forces in the Arabian Peninsula, bin Laden said, is to consolidate Greater Israel, which will incorporate "large parts of Iraq and Egypt within its borders, as well as Syria, Lebanon, Jordan, the whole of Palestine and a large part of Saudi Arabia."[73]

Bin Laden then called for the overthrow of all the monarchies of the Arabian Peninsula (in Kuwait, Bahrain, Qatar, Saudi Arabia, and the others), which he said were nothing but traitors or "quislings," a reference to the Norwegian Nazi who betrayed his country to Adolf Hitler. The Saudis must be overthrown for many reasons, he claimed, but above all because they have betrayed the Palestinian cause to "Jews and Americans." Bin Laden railed against Crown Prince Abdallah for his proposal at the Beirut Arab summit in March 2002 suggesting a permanent peace agreement with Israel by all the Arabs if Israel withdrew to the 1967 lines, an act he said "betrayed the *ummah*."

Bin Laden admitted that overthrowing the monarchies would not be an easy task, given America's support for the Saudis, but he reminded his listeners that no one anticipated the fall of the Soviet Union in Afghanistan. America has been defeated before, he said, in Lebanon in 1982 and in Somalia in 1993. Most important, he recalled 9/11, which he pronounced a "brave and beautiful operation, the likes of which humanity has never seen before destroying the idols of America" and striking "the very heart of the Ministry of Defense and the American economy." That operation "in Manhattan was a result of the unjust policies of the American government on the Palestinian issue," he said. He concluded that "America is a super power . . . built on a foundation of straw."

Just prior to this public declaration of war on the House of Saud, bin Laden met secretly in Pakistan with the head of al Qaeda's infrastructure inside the Kingdom. Yusuf al Ayiri, known by his nicknamed "*al battar*" or "the Sabre," was reluctant to start an insurrection in the Kingdom because he feared the al Qaeda organization was not strong enough. Bin Laden insisted and the Sabre return to the Kingdom to start the war.[74]

The first major attack came on May 12, 2003, when al Qaeda terrorists simultaneously attacked three compounds in Riyadh where foreign workers were housed. One was used by employees of the Vinnell Corporation, which trains the National Guard. Twenty-seven people died in the attacks, nine of them Americans, and more than 160 were wounded. It was the worst act of terrorism in the capital's history.[75]

Central Intelligence Agency director George Tenet immediately traveled to Riyadh to see Crown Prince Abdallah. Tenet told the crown prince that the CIA believed "your family and the end of its rule is now the objective" of bin Laden. "Al Qaeda operatives are prepared to assassinate members of the royal family and to attack key economic targets," Tenet told Abdallah. The United States would provide all the assistance it could to help defeat al Qaeda in the Kingdom.[76]

Shaken by the bombings and Tenet's assessment of al Qaeda, Abdallah decided to give operational command of the counterterrorism battle to Muhammad bin Nayef, the son of Interior Minister Prince Nayef. Educated in the United States at Lewis and Clark College in Oregon, Prince Muhammad had extensive experience with the FBI and Scotland Yard. His father distrusted the

Americans and British and had badly underestimated al Qaeda (he had famously blamed the Mossad for the 9/11 attacks rather than al Qaeda). The crown prince decided he was not the right man for defending the Kingdom.[77] Prince Nayef kept the title of minister of the interior, but his son was now in charge.[78] Tenet later credited him with winning the war that lay ahead inside the Kingdom.[79]

For the next three years the Interior ministry, with help from the National Guard, engaged in a bloody and dangerous war with al Qaeda inside the Kingdom. It was by far the most serious internal challenge to the House of Saud since the founding of the modern Kingdom by Ibn Saud. Dozens of firefights occurred in every major Saudi city as the Interior ministry tracked down members of the terrorist underground. The Sabre was killed in a confrontation with the police on May 30, 2003, and was replaced by another bin Laden appointee.

Muhammad bin Nayef provided extensive assistance to two journalists who wrote an authoritative account of the war in 2014. Using materials captured by the Interior ministry in raids on al Qaeda safe houses and the interrogations of captured terrorists, their book, *The Path of Blood*, is the prince's insider look at the war.

In November 2003 an attack on another residential compound killed seventeen and wounded more than one hundred. The next month a Saudi major general was injured in an attack. On December 17, 2003, the American Embassy in Riyadh ordered nonessential staff to leave the country. The United States evacuated most of its diplomats from the Kingdom in April 2004 and urged Americans not to travel to Saudi Arabia due to "credible and specific intelligence" of imminent attacks.[80]

One of the worst series of attacks occurred in Khobar, the Saudi town where the Saudi Hezbollah had attacked the United States Air Force barracks in 1996. On May 29 and 30, 2004, an al Qaeda team calling themselves the Jerusalem Squadron killed twenty-five people in multiple attacks on Western targets. In June an American engineer was kidnapped and then beheaded by another al Qaeda team in Riyadh. Prince Muhammad's position was elevated to the level of minister to give him more authority to command the counterterrorist forces.[81]

The American consulate in Jidda was attacked on December 6, 2004. One American female diplomat, Monica Lemieux, narrowly escaped death in the attack, but four Saudi security personnel and five local employees of the embassy died. The attackers were killed or captured by Saudi security forces.[82] At the end of the year the Ministry of the Interior headquarters in Riyadh—an iconic building shaped like an inverted pyramid—was attacked by multiple car bombs.

Gradually the Interior ministry got the upper hand. The violence of the al Qaeda attacks dried up popular support for the terrorists among most Saudis. While many were sympathetic with the jihadists when they attacked abroad, attacking Saudi targets inside the Kingdom killed many innocents. The insurgency in neighboring Iraq also siphoned off many potential recruits for al Qaeda inside the Kingdom. Hundreds of young Saudis went to Iraq to fight the American and British occupation, which was unpopular in both Iraq and Saudi Arabia.[83] U.S. officials estimated that at least 45 percent of the foreigners in Iraq fighting the occupation were Saudi citizens.[84] Saudi sources said that 5,000 Saudis had joined the insurgency by October 2003, most of them joining Zarqawi's al Qaeda in Iraq.[85]

Most important, Prince Muhammad bin Nayef led a ferocious and ruthless campaign against the al Qaeda infrastructure. Lists of the most prominent terrorists were circulated among the population, and then those on the lists were systematically hunted down until killed or captured. The Sabre had been right: the Interior ministry was too strong for al Qaeda. In December 2004 bin Laden issued another appeal to Saudis to overthrow the monarchy, but by then the tide of battle was favoring Prince Nayef. This 2004 statement criticized Fahd for ruling the country despite a debilitating stroke, arguing that "the idea that the entire length and breadth of the land is ruled in the name of a king who for a decade has no longer known what is going on is incredible." He attacked the royal family for corruption and self-indulgence, noting the King's palace in Jidda occupies more land than the entire emirate of Bahrain. Prince Bandar was singled out for bin Laden's criticism for planning the invasion of Iraq with Bush and Cheney.[86]

The Saudi clerical establishment joined the royal family in the battle. The minister of Islamic affairs, Shaykh Salih Bin Abd al Aziz al Shaykh—a descendant of Muhammad Ibn 'Abd al Wahhab—organized the clerical establishment to condemn and castigate the terrorists as enemies of Islam and of the state. Working with the Interior ministry, the clerics set up rehabilitation centers to reeducate captured terrorists and persuade them to provide intelligence on the al Qaeda leadership.

In contrast, the clerics openly favored the insurgency in Iraq as a holy war against foreign and infidel occupation. A group of three dozen clerics issued a statement publicly in December 2006 supporting the struggle against the Crusader-Safavid occupation, alleging America and Iran were secretly colluding against Iraqi Sunni Arabs. The statement said, "It is clear that their goal is to take over Iraq as a partnership between the Crusaders and the Safavid, realizing their ambitions in the region which are protecting the Jewish occupiers in Palestine, removing Sunni influence, encircling the Sunni in the whole region and creating a Shia crescent" across Iraq and Syria.[87]

The official Saudi clerical position was announced by Minister Shaykh al Shaykh in October 2007. He said only the Saudi king had the right to send Saudis abroad to fight in jihad. Thus, al Qaeda was wrong to urge young Saudis to fight in Iraq without royal blessing. In practice, however, the minister's proclamation had little effect. In a more practical move, Nayef built a double-tracked barbed wire electric fence along the Saudi border with Iraq to discourage traffic across the frontier.

The last major al Qaeda attack in Saudi Arabia occurred on February 24, 2006, when terrorists struck the Abqaiq oil refinery in the Eastern Province, the country's single most important economic target. The operation was a failure, and within days the Saudi authorities killed all involved in the planning and execution of the attack. Gun fights between al Qaeda members and Interior ministry forces would continue for several more months, but the Abqaiq attack in retrospect was the final major operation of bin Laden's war on the House of Saud.[88]

The war with al Qaeda inside the Kingdom preoccupied the country's leadership for almost four years. King Fahd passed away on August 1, 2005, and Abdallah succeeded him. Bandar departed Washington a month later, ending his two decades as the king's man in America. Prince Turki took his place as the ambassador. It was a job he did not relish taking.

After his 2004 reelection, Bush had a second meeting with Abdallah in Crawford in April 2005, but it was little more than a photo opportunity. Bush had announced two years earlier that America was determined to build democracy in Iraq and that the American agenda in the Middle East would now feature the support of democratic reforms. Bush emphasized this campaign to bring democracy and freedom to the region in his January 2004 State of the Union address.

The Saudis were appalled. In August 2004 Egyptian president Hosni Mubarak, another autocrat, visited the Kingdom. Abdallah and Mubarak called for an end to the U.S. occupation of Iraq. America's two most important allies in the Arab world were, thus, publicly on record opposing the continued American presence in Iraq. Increasingly the Saudis criticized the Iraq war for empowering their rival Iran. Foreign Minister Prince Saud al Faisal visited Washington in September 2005 and warned the White House that Iraq was disintegrating into civil war and that Iran was the major beneficiary. Prince Saud told the press, "Iraq is finished forever. It will be dismembered which will bring so many conflicts in the region that it will bring the whole region into turmoil." Worse, Saud said, the Bush decision to invade Iraq "handed the whole country over to Iran without reason." Later he added a more colorful line: Bush had given Iraq to Iran on a "golden platter."[89]

In practice, the Bush rhetoric about promoting democracy was never turned into a serious policy initiative toward the region as a whole. The only practical manifestations were in Palestine and Iraq, where the calls for democracy were manifestations of broader policy goals. Riyadh was critical of both. Instead of supporting political reform in the Palestinian Authority after Arafat's death in 2004, the Saudis encouraged the two main Palestinian parties, Fatah and Hamas, to work together. King Abdallah summoned both to Mecca in February 2007 and pressed them to unite against the Israeli occupation. The unity deal they agreed to in Mecca did not last long, but it was a sign of further stress in the partnership with Washington.

At the Arab summit in March 2007, the Saudi king urged adoption of a joint statement labeling the American presence in Iraq "an illegal foreign occupation." Prince Turki said the promotion of democracy in Iraq by the United States was a disaster. Turki said: "Democracy turned to a hateful sectarianism, justice turned to oppression, the rule of law ended up being the rule of the militias and human rights became death warrants." The White House was furious with Turki, and Abdallah declined another invitation to visit the United States.[90]

By the end of the Bush administration, the American relationship with Saudi Arabia had soured immensely. Only in the counterterrorism business was the relationship healthy. Prince Muhammad bin Nayef and the king carefully kept that essential business undamaged by the disagreements on other issues. As a sign of the tension, Prince Turki left as ambassador after only eighteen months on the job. He had found the job even more difficult than he anticipated. Bandar had tried to keep the American portfolio in his own hands even after leaving Washington in 2005 and had a habit of coming to town without telling Turki. Bandar had little credibility with the Bush team, however, after his failed last years as ambassador. The Bush team disliked Turki for his frank and honest comments about Bush's policies. What had seemed, eight years earlier, to begin as a return to the good old days of George H. W. Bush had turned into a failed partnership. Bush's successor would have to try to get things back on track.

Chapter Six

OBAMA AND TRUMP,
ABDALLAH AND SALMAN,
2009 TO 2017

Prince Saud al Faisal inherited the dignity and grace of his father, King Faisal. A graduate of Princeton and fluent in seven languages, Prince Saud served as the Kingdom's foreign minister for forty years. He represented his country at countless international meetings, always impressing his counterparts with his eloquence and command of his brief. I knew him for more than three decades. Once he entertained a delegation headed by Madeleine Albright, America's first female secretary of state, at his home in Riyadh, where we had the pleasure of meeting his wife and daughters.

In August 2008, during a visit to Washington, Prince Saud asked the Obama presidential campaign for an informal meeting with a campaign foreign policy expert to discuss the state of Saudi-U.S. relations. I had joined the campaign in the spring of 2007 at the request of Anthony Lake, my former boss at the National Security Council in 1993 and the head of Obama's foreign policy advisory team. The campaign sent me to have lunch with the prince at his suite at the Hay-Adams Hotel near Lafayette Square and the White House.

Prince Saud characterized the relationship, after almost eight years of George W. Bush, as a "train wreck." He repeated his public line that the war in Iraq had given Baghdad to the Iranians on a "golden platter." The war in Lebanon in 2006 between Israel and the Iranian-backed Hezbollah had strengthened Iran's grip on Beirut, and the Arab-Israeli peace process was in shambles. A peace conference Bush had called in Annapolis, Maryland, in 2007 had not led to any breakthroughs. The so called "Freedom Agenda" Bush had announced was rejected by America's allies in the region, including the House of Saud. The dialogue between Riyadh and Washington was poisonous, Prince Saud said, and King Abdallah was very disappointed. Only on counter-terrorism issues was there a productive conversation. He credited Prince Muhammad bin Nayef, the minister of interior, and Prince Muqrin, the chief of intelligence, with that success story.

The foreign minister hoped the next president, whether it was Senator Barack Obama or Senator John McCain, would work to put the relationship back on a stable and productive path. It was too important to both countries not to do so. He also urged Washington to look closely at King Abdallah's interfaith dialogue project, where the Saudi monarch was hosting discussions between religious leaders from all the world's faiths.

Abdallah

Barack Obama inherited a country in deep trouble. The financial markets had melted down in the fall of 2008, causing the worst recession in American history since the 1930s. Unemployment was soaring, and millions of people had lost their homes or much of their life savings; sometimes both. America was engaged in two major ground wars overseas. The war in Iraq had stabilized somewhat because of a large surge in American forces in 2007, but the insurgency had not been defeated and al Qaeda in Iraq remained a deadly foe. In Afghanistan the Taliban were resurgent, and next-door in Pakistan al Qaeda was thriving. The search for Osama bin Laden had gone cold.

Obama was determined to reset America's relationship with the Muslim world. With two large American armies occupying two large Islamic countries, it was imperative to reach out to the Islamic world and restore some measure of confidence in American leadership. Obama planned to make a major address to the Islamic world from Cairo, Egypt, in June 2009.

Before arriving in Cairo, Obama stopped first in Riyadh to meet King Abdallah; it was his first-ever visit to the Kingdom. The stop was a clear sign of the importance Obama placed on getting ties with the Kingdom back on track. Obama is the son of a Kenyan Muslim, and he spent part of his childhood in Indonesia, the world's most populous Muslim country. He billed his stop in Riyadh as a chance to come to where Islam started.

But Obama's meeting with the king went poorly. Obama had promised to shut down the notorious prison in Guantanamo Bay, Cuba, housing terrorism suspects, on the first day of his presidency. His homeland security adviser, John Brennan, had worked with the Saudi security services to persuade the Kingdom to take dozens of the Guantanamo prisoners from Yemen to Saudi Arabia to help empty the Cuban jail. Apparently the staff work on the Saudi side was incomplete; the king knew nothing about the deal and was surprised when Obama brought it up as an agreement. It was not agreed at all, the king said.[1]

Obama's main goal in Riyadh was to try to jump-start the stalled Israeli-Palestinian peace process, which had been stalemated since Bush's failed Annapolis summit. Obama was pressing Israeli prime minister Benjamin "Bibi" Netanyahu to halt all settlement activity in the occupied territories, including East Jerusalem, to set the stage for a resumed peace process with the Palestinians. Netanyahu vigorously opposed a freeze but had suggested that if Obama could deliver a major gesture from the Arab states—in particular a public meeting between Bibi and King Abdallah—he could accept a temporary freeze. When Obama made the case to the king, Abdallah turned him down. Abdallah said the Kingdom "will be the last to make peace with the Israelis" after all the other Arabs have been satisfied in their requirements.[2] It was unimaginable for a Saudi king to meet publicly with an Israeli prime minister until after a Palestinian state was created and full Israeli withdrawal was implemented. The royal family, the clerical establishment, and the general population would never have approved such a meeting. It was puzzling that Obama and his aides thought it was even possible.[3]

One reason the idea might have seemed plausible to them was the growing animosity in both Israel and Saudi Arabia toward Iran. Both Israelis and Saudis seemed more worried than ever about Iran's growing influence in the region, a byproduct of the Iraq war, and some observers suggested the Saudis might be willing to take a more flexible line on Israel to build a regional consensus against Iran, an argument strongly pressed by right-wing forces in Israel. It was in 2009, and remains today, a fantasy. The Saudis have long been willing to have discreet contacts with Israel, often via third parties, to contain regional threats. They did so in the 1960s against the meddling in Yemen by Egypt's Nasser. But they are not willing to compromise their policy toward the Israeli-Palestinian question or to meet publicly and officially with Israeli leaders. The notion of an Israel-Sunni Arab entente against Shia Iran, with the Kingdom at its center, is a mirage. The Saudis are not interested in an alliance with Israel.

The president's speech in Cairo was a public relations success that took attention away from the Riyadh disappointments. Obama acknowledged the "great tension between the United States and Muslims around the world" and called for "a new beginning based on mutual interest and mutual respect." He promised to close the Guantanamo prison, end torture of captured suspected al Qaeda prisoners, bring home all American troops from Iraq, and seek a two-state solution to the Palestinian question. He deliberately criticized Bush's push for democracy in the Arab world as discredited by its "connection to the war in Iraq," and promised America would not impose any system of government on other states. He did call for the promotion of human rights and greater tolerance in Islam, and he praised King Abdallah's "interfaith dialogue."[4]

Obama flew home from Cairo without stopping in Israel, a striking change from his predecessors, Democrats and Republicans. No president before Obama would have thought to make a formal state visit to Saudi Arabia or Egypt without a matching visit to Jerusalem.

Just as Obama arrived in the Middle East, Osama bin Laden and his Egyptian deputy, Ayman Zawahiri, each released messages from their hideouts in Pakistan. Eight years after 9/11, both were still alive and plotting more attacks. Both statements called on Muslims to shun Obama and predicted his policies would just be more of the same as his predecessor.[5] It was a stark reminder that Bush had not defeated al Qaeda and a preview of how Obama's administration would be grappling with al Qaeda and its offshoots for the next eight years.

Another dramatic illustration of al Qaeda's continued danger came in the summer of 2009. A Saudi al Qaeda operative named Abdallah al Asiri offered to defect to the Saudis and provide inside information on the al Qaeda organization in Yemen. Al Qaeda had reinvented its Saudi operation in the Arabian Peninsula in early 2009, after its defeat inside Saudi Arabia, by merging its Saudi and Yemeni wings together to create al Qaeda in the Arabian Peninsula. Asiri promised to give secret information on the merged network and induce further defections if he got a meeting with Prince Muhammad bin Nayef, the interior minister.

Prince Nayef agreed, despite having been the target of at least two previous al Qaeda assassination attempts. This turned out to be a third. Asiri's brother was a brilliant bomb maker and had hidden a bomb in al Asiri's rectum. Fortunately, when the bomb exploded, only the terrorist was killed. Prince Muhammad sustained some injury but survived. It was a close call.[6]

Obama tried hard to implement the promises he made in Cairo but with little tangible success. By November 2010 Secretary of State Hillary Clinton told a Brookings Institution forum that the president's peace initiative had broken down and would be replaced by American shuttling between the parties. Her successor, John Kerry, tried again in Obama's second term to restart negotiations and failed again. Guantanamo stayed open, albeit with fewer prisoners. Polls showed Muslim antipathy toward American policies in the region was as intense during the Obama years as in the Bush years.

Iran's pursuit of nuclear weapons and regional hegemony was a top Obama priority. In part, King Abdallah shared these concerns. The Saudis were not that worried by Iran's nuclear program per se but rather by its pursuit of regional dominance and its use of Shia subversion to accomplish that goal. Abdallah's efforts at rapprochement with Iran in the late 1990s had long since sputtered out. He was appalled that Bush's war in Iraq had strengthened Iranian influence. When Secretary of Defense Robert Gates visited Riyadh in the last year of the Bush administration, Abdallah pressed for an American military attack on Iran. Gates explained that the United States had its hands full in Iraq and Afghanistan and became irritated at the notion America should "send its sons and daughters into a war with Iran in order to protect Saudi interests as if we were mercenaries."[7] Abdallah backed off, impressed by Gates's candor, but he was still very concerned about Iran.

Obama wisely kept Gates on as secretary of defense. Both feared that if Iran got close to building a nuclear weapon, Israel would take military action to try to stop it, just as it had done to Iraq in 1981 and Syria in 2007. Gates later said, "Israel's leaders were itching to launch a military attack on Iran's nuclear infrastructure." An Israeli attack on Iran, Gates believed, would almost certainly require the United States "to be drawn in to finish the job or to deal with Iranian retaliatory attacks against Israel and our friends in the region," including the Saudis. This would provoke a regional war.[8]

Gates traveled to Riyadh again in March 2010 to see Abdallah. They met at the king's farm. Kansas-born Gates said it was like no farm he had seen before. "We had dinner inside a tent—with crystal chandeliers—that could have held the entire Ringling Brothers circus and then some." After dinner Gates and the king agreed on a massive new U.S. arms sale to the Kingdom, the largest ever. It would cost at least $60 billion and include the purchase of eighty-four new F15S fighter planes, upgrades for the seventy F15S jets the Saudis already owned, twenty-four Apache attack helicopters, and seventy-two Blackhawk helicopters. The enormous sale was intended to increase Saudi capabilities to defend against Iran, but Gates found "Abdallah was very cautious about any kind of overt military cooperation or planning with the United States that the Iranians might consider an act of war." Later, after intense discussions between Netanyahu and Gates, Israel agreed not to press its supporters in Congress to fight the sale to Riyadh, in return for a promise of twenty more F35 "stealth" aircraft from the United States.[9]

The Arab Spring

The outbreak of revolutions across the Arab world in 2010–11, which quickly became known as the Arab Spring, surprised everyone. Leon Panetta, then director of the Central Intelligence Agency, wrote later that CIA analysts for years had warned of "building pressures across the Middle East and North Africa—increasing numbers of young people unable to find work; rising income disparities; deepening anger at corruption; alienation from ossified regimes." The CIA, Panetta noted, identified the "sources of pressure long before they blew. At the same time, we did not anticipate the flash points or the speed with which events might unfold. We scrambled to keep up."[10] The CIA was not alone in being surprised and scrambling. Among the others was Saudi Arabia.

Protests and demonstrations began in Tunisia in late 2010, and President Zine al Abedine Ben Ali was toppled from power in only a few days. King Abdallah welcomed him to live in exile in Saudi Arabia immediately. (And he is still there.) The king also cut short a vacation in Morocco and returned home.

The unrest spread rapidly to Egypt, the Arab world's most populous country and a close Saudi ally since Hosni Mubarak replaced Sadat in 1981. On January 25, 2011, massive demonstrations took place in Cairo, and within three days the army was called into the streets to restore order. Mubarak's regime seemed vulnerable very quickly.

Inside the Obama administration there was a split on how to respond to the rapidly developing situation. According to Bob Gates's account, Gates, Clinton, Vice President Joe Biden, and National Security Adviser Tom Donilon counseled patience and caution. They wanted to work with Mubarak and the army to arrange a smooth transition of power over several months to a successor chosen by Mubarak, most likely intelligence chief Omar Sulaiman, who was well known in Washington. Obama's National Security Council senior advisers, Dennis McDonough and Ben Rhodes, homeland security chief John Brennan, and the vice president's top adviser, Tony Blinken, were more eager to support rapid change and press for Mubarak to go quickly.[11]

Mubarak had been a strong American ally for three decades, steadfastly maintaining the 1979 peace treaty with Israel. He had sent two divisions to help defend Saudi Arabia against Iraq in 1990. But the American message, both privately and publicly, to the Egyptian army was that American assistance to Egypt would be in danger if force and violence were used to keep Mubarak in power. The Pentagon reinforced that message directly to senior

Egyptian generals. On January 29 Mubarak fired his cabinet and made Sulaiman vice president.

Obama and Clinton then sent Frank Wisner, a former U.S. ambassador to Egypt, to Cairo in hopes of encouraging an "orderly transition" of power. Mubarak, however, refused to leave before his term in office expired in September. Obama responded publicly with a call for an orderly transition that "must begin now." Obama had sided with the activists in the White House; Mubarak had to go. The White House said: "When we said now, we meant yesterday."[12] On February 11 the Egyptian army forced Mubarak to resign, and army commander General Mohamed Hussein Tantawi took power as an interim leader pending elections.

Obama hailed the move as a sign that "the arc of history has bent toward justice once more." He likened the change in Egypt to the nonviolent movements led decades earlier by Mahatma Gandhi and Martin Luther King Jr. Obama also enthused that there is "something in our souls that cries out for freedom."[13]

King Abdallah and the other Gulf monarchs were outraged. America had just abandoned a friend and helped force him from office. If Obama could dispense with Mubarak so quickly, what future did they have if the revolutions spread to their countries?

The hypothetical became a pressing reality next door in Bahrain just as Mubarak was falling. The small island nation has a majority Shia population but a Sunni ruling family, the Khalifas. The population of the island is 1.3 million, with slightly less than 50 percent being Bahraini citizens (and 75 percent of them are Shia). The Shia majority periodically staged demonstrations and rock-throwing riots throughout the 1980s and 1990s, demanding political reforms and more development for Shia neighborhoods. Inspired by the events in Tunisia and Egypt, demonstrations quickly began in Bahrain. In February 2011 more than 100,000 people demonstrated in Manama's Pearl Circle, the city's center, demanding change.

The Khalifa rulers in Bahrain and the Saudis saw the demonstrators as pawns of Iran. Rather than accepting their legitimate demands for better treatment, they jointly determined to repress the demonstrations. For the Saudis, what happens in next-door Bahrain is an existential issue. If the Shia majority took power in Bahrain, that would inspire unrest in the Eastern Province, a longstanding area of Shia turbulence inside the Kingdom and the home of its oil wealth. In the worst case it would mean Iran acquired a foothold on the southern shore of the Persian Gulf.

King Abdallah was inclined to fear the worst case in 2011. As Secretary Clinton wrote later, the Saudis "saw the hidden hand of Iran. They worried that their large adversary across the water was fomenting unrest in order to weaken their government and improve its own strategic position."[14] Clinton called her Bahraini counterpart and urged patience and conciliation. The Bahraini crown prince began a dialogue with the protesters, aided by Clinton's diplomats.

On Friday March 4, 2011, the demonstrations grew to 200,000 people, equal to almost one-half of the country's citizens. They called for the overthrow of the king. Secretary Gates arrived in Manama a week later to try to calm the situation.

Bahrain has been an American ally for decades; the United States Navy has had an installation in Bahrain since 1947. By 2011 that base was the headquarters for the Fifth Fleet, which was responsible for operations in the Gulf and the Indian Ocean. The Navy, therefore, had a strong interest in keeping the Khalifas in power. But Gates was uneasy with America propping up indefinitely a minority government hated by so many of its people. He told King Hamad and Crown Prince Salman that "baby steps" toward reform were not enough. He predicted that if the unrest went on long enough Iran would take advantage of the situation.[15]

The Bahrainis briefed the Saudis on Gates's message. Feigning illness, King Abdallah told Gates not to come to Riyadh. He had already made his decision. He communicated to Obama that if the United States interfered in Bahrain it would provoke a rupture in Saudi-American relations. On Sunday, March 13, the demonstrators stormed Manama's financial district, taking control of the island's economy. The American defense attaché in Riyadh reported that the Saudis were preparing to use force to quell the unrest by sending troops over the causeway linking the island to the Eastern Province (the Saudis had built it with sufficiently wide lanes to allow armored vehicles to cross).[16]

The next day, March 14, 1,200 troops from the Saudi Arabian National Guard—the king's men—crossed the King Fahd causeway with armored personnel carriers to prop up the Khalifa dynasty. An additional 800 troops from the United Arab Emirates joined them. The Bahraini government had officially requested their intervention. Using helicopters and tanks, the Bahraini security forces crushed the demonstrations and cleared the financial district and Pearl Circle. At least thirty people died. Obama called Abdallah to urge restraint, and the king replied: "Saudi Arabia will never allow Shia rule in Bahrain—never."[17] When Clinton called Prince Saud, he was implacable, blaming Iran for all the island's problems.[18]

This was the first time Saudi Arabia had used force to stem the Arab Spring, and it exposed a massive break with Washington. The intervention in a close neighbor underscored the House of Saud's conclusion that the Arab Spring was an existential threat to its survival.

Abdallah also took measures to ensure there would be no demonstrations at home. In February he announced that $37 billion in new funds would be devoted to building homes, schools, and mosques across the country to stave off any unrest. In a TV broadcast in March he promised another $93 billion to build more housing and provide jobs. Public sector employees, the majority of Saudi workers, got pay bonuses. Abdallah was worried enough by the Arab Spring to spend $130 billion to keep it away. Only a few minor demonstrations took place.[19] James Smith, then American ambassador to Saudi Arabia, believes the massive aid package was the direct result of the king's fear that the revolutionary wave would hit the Kingdom sooner rather than later and needed to be bought off.[20]

The king took other steps to buy insurance. Oman and Bahrain, the two poorest Gulf Cooperation Council members, each got $10 billion in aid from the Saudis, Kuwaitis, Qataris, and Emirates in 2011 to ensure stability.[21] Prince Bandar bin Sultan bin Abdul Aziz, who had left Washington under a cloud for misinterpreting George Bush, had been given a job as national security adviser to the king. In March 2011 he was dispatched to Pakistan and China. In Pakistan Bandar asked for assurances that, if requested, Islamabad would send elite troops to the Kingdom to restore order if demonstrations got out of hand.[22] This was a repeat of King Khalid's request to Pakistani dictator Zia ul Haq in the 1980s for help after the takeover of the Grand Mosque in Mecca. Again the Pakistanis promised they would send troops if needed. More immediately they augmented the battalion of troops they had in Bahrain with a recruiting drive that hired experienced Pakistani soldiers to join the Bahrain Defense Forces, giving it more muscle to quell Shia unrest.[23]

In Beijing, where Bandar had secretly negotiated the East Wind missile deal two decades earlier, he pressed for Chinese political support for the Saudi counterrevolution. It was an easy sell since the Chinese were no fans of democracy, and Bandar could also promise that future investment and business deals would be steered toward China.[24] The trip restored Bandar's stature in the king's eyes. The next year Abdallah would promote Bandar to be chief of Saudi intelligence, a much more important job. His task would be to coordinate the clandestine counterrevolution.

Yemen, Saudi Arabia's traditional nemesis to the south, had its own version of an Arab Spring. Ali Abdullah Saleh, who had backed Iraq in 1990 and who the Saudis had tried to overthrow in 1994, faced massive demonstrations calling for an end to his decades of misrule. The opposition was deeply divided, however. Some were democracy advocates and wanted to end corruption and misrule. Others were southern separatists who wanted to restore South Yemen's independence, which Saleh had ended in 1990. In the north, the Zaydi Shia tribes that Saudi Arabia had backed in the 1960s had found a new leadership in the Houthi family, which sought to restore Zaydi dominance and flirted with Iranian support. The Saudis and Houthis had engaged in border clashes for years. Saleh fought six major military campaigns against the Houthis before 2011.

Working with the other Gulf states, a prolonged political process finally edged Saleh out of power, to be replaced by his former deputy, a southerner named Abdrabbu Mansour Hadi. The formal ceremony was held in Riyadh in November 2011 with King Abdallah presiding. Hadi then began a complex national dialogue to develop a stable government for Yemen. For the Saudis it was a tolerable outcome, though it proved to be short-lived.[25]

Revolutions in Syria and Libya provided a different choice for the Kingdom. Bashar Assad and Muammar Qaddafi were not long-standing Saudi allies. The Syrian regime had been an Iranian ally since 1980. The Saudis had pursued the Middle East peace process with Damascus in part to woo Damascus away from Tehran. They had helped resolve the Pan Am 103 case, not to help Tripoli but to ease tensions between the Arab world and the United States. Prince Bandar had been at the center of both efforts.

So when revolutions broke out in Syria and Libya, King Abdallah backed the revolutionaries. He was not hoping for democracy in either case; rather, he hoped new Sunni Arab strongmen would replace the existing tyrants but would be more inclined to accept Saudi influence. But the Saudis made clear to Washington that their assistance in getting rid of Assad and Qaddafi depended on America accepting the outcome in Bahrain.

After refusing to see Gates during the Bahrain crisis, Abdallah met him a month later when it was settled. They met at the king's palace office in Riyadh, which Gates noted was ten times larger than his own office in the Pentagon and was decorated with eight crystal chandeliers. The king had a carefully prepared message for Gates to take to Obama. Saudi Arabia and the United States had been partners in a strategic relationship for seventy years, but he said American behavior in Egypt and Bahrain had threatened that partnership. Some Arabs were saying America had treated its allies like it treated the shah when he was deposed. It was imperative for America to "listen to its friends" in the region. Finally, the king told Gates, "Iran is the source of all problems."[26]

Secretary Clinton got a similar warning from Prince Saud, the foreign minister. Saudi Arabia could help in Syria and Libya only if it was not being criticized at the same time for its occupation of Bahrain.[27] If the United States pushed a "freedom agenda" for the Arab Spring, the relationship with Riyadh would be endangered. If Washington was more pragmatic, cooperation could continue. In May 2011 Obama gave a long-awaited speech on the Arab Spring. He never once uttered the words "Saudi Arabia," but he urged pragmatism and dealing with each country based on its own circumstances.

The revolutions in Syria and Libya turned into bloody civil wars that continue today with no end in sight. The Saudis have been particularly active in Syria, where Abdallah took a personal interest in the revolution. He appointed as head of Saudi intelligence Prince Bandar, who, ironically, had a long history with the Assads. When Hafez Assad died in 2000, shortly after the failed summit with Clinton in Geneva, Bandar rushed to Damascus to persuade Syria's generals to back the young son, Bashar, to be president. By 2012 Bandar and King Abdallah had soured on Bashar al-Assad and hoped to recreate the Afghan model in Syria—that is, an insurgency armed and paid for by America and Saudi Arabia that would topple a pro-Iranian regime.[28]

The Kingdom clandestinely bought arms for the Syrian Sunni rebels, particularly in Croatia, and smuggled them to the rebels through Jordan. One study assessed that the Saudis bought arms for the Syrian rebels worth more than $1 billion from East European sources between 2012 and 2016.[29] But Obama was not very enthusiastic about the mission. U.S. support was slow in coming and limited in scale. Jordan proved a weak ally, as well. Some elements within Jordanian intelligence took some of the arms intended for the rebels and sold them on the black arms market; in the end, some even ended up in the hands of terrorists who killed two Americans in Amman in November 2015.[30]

The Saudi clerical leadership publicly urged all Muslims to support the revolution against the Iranian and Hezbollah-supported Alawite government of Assad. The grand mufti, Shaykh Abd al Aziz ibn Abdullah al Shaikh, publicly endorsed the war against Assad and his allies in May 2013. Saudis began to join the rebel camp and travel to Syria to join the fight.[31]

But Egypt was and remains the Saudis' main concern after the Arab Spring. After the fall of Mubarak, elections brought to power a government that was dominated by the Muslim Brotherhood. Although the Saudis had years of experience dealing with members of the Brotherhood, Riyadh was profoundly uneasy about a freely elected Islamic government ruling the most populous Arab state. If an Islamic democracy, however flawed, could successfully govern Egypt, it would set an example for every Muslim country. Saudi citizens would ask, if democracy worked in Egypt, why might it not work in Saudi Arabia? In short, success for the democratic process in Egypt would pose an existential threat to the Kingdom itself and would be a powerful argument for reform, if not revolution, in all the monarchies.

The new Egyptian government led by Mohammad Morsi had many enemies at home. The army was especially worried that the Brotherhood would begin to chip away at its prerogatives. Those who had benefited from the Mubarak regime wanted a restoration of a military-dominated government. The economy did not improve, and many who had demonstrated for democracy became disillusioned.

The Saudis had an important ally in the counterrevolutionary camp. General Abdel Fattah al-Sisi had been Egypt's defense attaché in Riyadh before the revolution, who was well known to Bandar and Saudi intelligence. In April 2012 he was promoted from head of Egyptian military intelligence to minister of defense. Rather than backing up Morsi, al-Sisi began plotting his ouster. The army privately encouraged demonstrations to undermine the legitimacy of the government. A year later, in July 2013, after increasingly large and disruptive demonstrations against the government of President Morsi, General al-Sisi gave the president a forty-eight-hour ultimatum to give up power. When the ultimatum expired, al-Sisi and the army took power, arrested Morsi and hundreds of Muslim Brotherhood supporters, and ruthlessly cracked down on any opposition. The Egyptian revolution was over; a counterrevolution and coup had bent "the arc of history" back to authoritarianism.

King Abdallah issued a public endorsement of the coup less than two hours after al-Sisi announced Morsi had been deposed and the constitution suspended. Saudi Arabia was the first government to back the takeover, and Abdallah followed his public statement a few hours later with a phone call to al-Sisi, which was made public. The counterrevolution had an overt foreign backer. Within a week Saudi Arabia organized a $12 billion aid package for Egypt. The Kingdom provided $5 billion, Kuwait $4 billion, and the United Arab Emirates the remaining $3 billion. The aid came with no strings attached and no requirement that al-Sisi restore democracy, ever.[32]

The clock had been turned back in Egypt. Obama and his new secretary of state, John Kerry, were unwilling to take any serious action to stop the coup and counterrevolution. Sisi was elected president in carefully controlled elections held a year after the coup. In his victory speech, al-Sisi mentioned only one foreign leader by name, King Abdallah, praising the king for the help Saudi Arabia had provided Egypt. Abdallah called al-Sisi fifteen minutes after his election to thank him for leading Egypt from the "strange chaos" of the Arab Spring.[33]

On June 20, 2014, the king did a victory lap in Cairo. It was a very unusual state visit. He flew to Cairo from Morocco, where he had been getting medical attention, but did not leave his special executive jumbo jet; instead, Sisi joined him inside for a thirty-minute meeting, then the king flew home. He spent no time in Egypt other than in his own aircraft. The ninety-year-old king was the first head of state to visit Egypt after the coup. Accompanying Abdallah was Foreign Minister Prince Saud and Chief of Intelligence Prince Bandar. Bandar's presence was highlighted in the Saudi press, a thank-you gesture from the king to the coup master.[34] The king's eldest son, Minister of National Guard

Affairs Prince Mitab, followed up the brief summit with a longer visit to Cairo later in 2014 to solidify ties with the military government.

Perhaps the major beneficiary of the failure of the Arab Spring was, ironically, al Qaeda. At first the revolutions threatened the narrative and ideology of the jihadists. When Mubarak and other dictators were toppled by mass popular movements, it appeared for a brief moment that there was a real and tangible path for democratic change in the Arab world. Twitter and social media had helped topple Mubarak, not terror. Al Qaeda suddenly seemed out of date. But not for long.

When the counterrevolution took control of Bahrain and Egypt and civil war wracked Syria and Libya, al Qaeda could argue its ideology had been upheld. Only jihad could change the Arab states. America was not a friend of change, the jihadists charged, because it did not really stand up for change at all. The ideology of Osama bin Laden was validated by the outcome of the Arab Spring in the eyes of its supporters and many others.

But bin Laden himself did not live to see the Arab Spring's failure. In May 2011 United States Navy SEAL commandoes brought justice to the mastermind of 9/11. The Central Intelligence Agency, using good analysis and sophisticated collection means, had found bin Laden hiding in a specially built house less than a mile from the Kakul Military Academy, Pakistan's equivalent of West Point or Sandhurst; he had been there at least five years. When Obama was told by the CIA that they believed bin Laden was present at this hide-out in Abbottabad, Pakistan, the president decided that no Pakistanis would be told. Obama rightly decided that Pakistan could not be trusted with the information, that it was all too likely that if the Pakistanis learned that the CIA had found bin Laden in Abbottabad, he would be alerted and flee. It was a remarkable decision given that, in the decade since 9/11, Obama and Bush together had provided over $25 billion in aid to Pakistan to fight al Qaeda.

Without bin Laden's charismatic leadership, the al Qaeda movement splintered. The most potent faction was the one in Iraq that Abu Musaib al Zarqawi had created after the American invasion. Al Qaeda in Iraq had been mauled by the surge in American troops that President Bush ordered in 2007 (and Zarqawi himself was killed in 2006), but it was not defeated. In 2014 the group's new leader broke with bin Laden's heir, the Egyptian Ayman Zawahiri, and announced that his group, the Islamic State of Iraq and al Shams (Syria) was the rightful heir to bin Laden. Abu Bakr al Baghdadi al Husseini al Hashemi al Quraishi, as he called himself, claimed to be a descendant of the Prophet Muhammad. He proclaimed himself caliph in June 2014 shortly after his group seized the Iraqi city of Mosul. At its peak, the Islamic State controlled an area across Syria and Iraq larger than Britain.

In naming himself the caliph, Ibrahim Baghdadi implicitly was announcing he was the rightful custodian of the two holy mosques in Mecca and Medina. He was quick to follow up this proclamation of a new caliphate with a call for the overthrow of the House of Saud and the end of the monarchy. The group's Internet magazine *Dabiq* showed a picture of the Kaaba in Mecca with the Islamic State flag flying over it.[35]

King Abdallah hosted an international conference in Jidda in September 2014 that formed an international coalition to fight the Islamic State. On September 22, 2014, the Royal Saudi Air Force joined the United States Air Force and other coalition allies in bombing Islamic State targets in Iraq and Syria.[36]

Abdallah's health deteriorated steadily after the Arab Spring. He continued to be a chain smoker and suffered from an assortment of illnesses. He had outlived two of his designated heirs: Prince Sultan had been crown prince from 2005 until 2011, and Prince Nayef bin Abdul Aziz was crown prince from 2011 until his death in June 2012. On Nayef's death, Abdallah's half-brother, Prince Salman bin Abdul Aziz al Saud, ascended to the office of crown prince, then on January 23, 2015, Abdallah passed away and Salman became king of Saudi Arabia.

Abdallah was a cautious reformer by Saudi standards. He had allowed a limited electorate to help choose municipal councils in the Kingdom, the first time ever Saudis were given a vote. The councils had strictly limited powers, but they represented a first step toward political reform. Abdallah also promoted female education and even appointed a woman to be deputy minister of education, the first and only time a woman had held such a high office in the Kingdom (she was ousted after Abdallah died). The king promised women would gain the right to vote in municipal elections and even run for office, a promise realized only after his death. Within the stark limits of the Kingdom's Wahhabi Islam, Abdallah was more advanced in this thinking on reform than archconservatives such as his brother Prince Nayef, who opposed any change in the status quo.

King Abdallah had ruled Saudi Arabia either de facto while Fahd was incapable or as king in his own right for two decades. A cautious and risk-averse man, Abdallah dealt with three U.S. presidents and forged the post–Desert Storm Saudi-American partnership. That partnership survived two near-death experiences on his watch: the quarrel with Bush over Palestine in 2001 and the quarrel with Obama over Egypt and Bahrain in 2011.

Salman

Salman was born on December 31, 1935, in Riyadh. His mother was Ibn Saud's favorite wife, Hassa bint Ahmad al Sudairi, which makes him a member of the Sudairi clan inside the royal family. He outlasted his two full brothers, Sultan and Nayef, to become king. Salman was appointed governor of Riyadh province by Faisal in 1963, and he would remain governor for almost a half-century. During that time the capital was transformed from a backwater town of fewer than 100,000 residents into a modern city of 7 million people, with skyscrapers, modern highways, a metro system, hospitals, and universities. He oversaw this transformation while maintaining excellent relations with the Wahhabi clerical establishment and ensuring the city retained its Islamic identity. It is the most Wahhabi city in the world.

Because most of the royal family lives in Riyadh, as governor, Salman was also the sheriff of the family. If a young prince or princess got into trouble with the law or into alcohol or drugs, it would be Salman's job to discreetly resolve the issue. The same would be true for older members of the family and their allies in business or religion. This gave him enormous power within the royal family and a reputation for being fair, pious, and efficient.

Salman was also in charge of raising funds for jihadist causes that the family supported. As noted earlier, King Faisal made him chairman of a committee to raise money to support the Palestinians after the 1967 war, and he still holds that title. King Khalid and King Fahd put him in charge of raising money for the Afghan mujahedin, and he worked closely with the senior clerics to support their cause at home and abroad. Crown Prince Abdallah sent him to Bosnia to raise support for the Bosnian Muslims in the 1990s. Again this fundraising role reinforced his position as a champion of Wahhabi causes and his close relations to the clerics.

American diplomats working in the Kingdom got to know Salman well as governor. The American embassy, like every foreign diplomatic post, was originally in Jidda, but as the capital grew it moved to Riyadh, where all foreign embassies are housed in a special diplomatic quarter. Salman oversaw their security. Especially during the troubled 1990s and early 2000s, when the Kingdom faced serious terrorist threats, Salman was an important interlocutor for American ambassadors seeking to ensure security for their staff and installations.

On Salman's accession to the throne in January 2015 Deputy Crown Prince Muqrin bin Abd al Aziz moved up to become crown prince. Muqrin, born September 15, 1945, is the last surviving acknowledged son of Ibn Saud. His mother was a concubine of Ibn Saud named Baraka al Yamanyah, a Yemeni girl. This maternal bloodline set Muqrin apart from the more "pure" Saudi siblings of Ibn Saud and was held against him by many all his life. But his father did acknowledge his son as his own and, thus, Muqrin had a claim to the line of succession.

Muqrin is a pilot who was trained at the Royal Air Force academy in Cranwell in England. In 1965 he joined the Royal Saudi Air Force as a jet pilot and he remained until 1980, when he was appointed governor of Hail province. During this time, while both were in the air force, he and Prince Bandar became close friends. In 1999 Abdallah moved him to be governor of Medina province. Abdallah was fond of his younger half-brother, whom he undoubtedly saw as another outsider from the Sudairis.[37]

In 2005 Muqrin became the head of Saudi intelligence. He was Prince Mohammad bin Nayef's partner in the war with al Qaeda, although his responsibility was external intelligence, not internal security. In interviews with key intelligence chiefs in the United States, Europe, and the Arab world during Muqrin's tenure, I was told that Muqrin was a professional, if not outstanding, chief. Bandar took the place of his friend Muqrin in July 2012, when Abdallah began grooming Muqrin to be a future crown prince. He became deputy prime minister in 2013 and formally moved to be deputy crown prince later that year.

In a shocking and unprecedented move, King Salman removed Crown Prince Muqrin from his position as the heir apparent on April 21, 2015, only three months after Abdallah died. No explanation was offered for the change, and Muqrin himself has never explained why he was removed from office. There is no reason to believe he was either unfit for the job or did not want to serve. Even before Muqrin's ouster, his friend Prince Bandar had been stripped of his remaining official positions in the government.[38]

Removing Muqrin ended the line of succession established by King Faisal upon his ascension to the throne more than a half-century earlier. No longer would succession pass among the sons of Ibn Saud, since Muqrin is the last acknowledged capable son. Instead, succession would pass to a crown prince lacking the legitimacy of being a direct heir and son of the founder of the modern Saudi Kingdom. That was, of course, inevitable, sooner or later, but Salman advanced the moment dramatically in April 2015. His move may well prove to have been a major mistake if succession quarrels damage family unity in the years ahead. Leaving Muqrin, a thoroughly qualified heir, in place would have put off the legitimacy issue for years, maybe decades.

Muqrin was replaced by Prince Muhammad bin Nayef, who is, without question, the most qualified member of his generation of Saudi princes to take up the throne. He is brave, smart, effective, and popular. He is also the epitome of the Saudi "deep state," as one commentator has written—the man who knows how to fight terrorism and suppress dissent in the Kingdom. There is little risk of political reform on his watch. Nayef controls "this deep state, now an empire of intelligence services, police agencies and emergency forces, in addition to a vast number of civil servants, judges, prison officials and Wahhabi loyalist circles."[39] There is one other important fact about Crown Prince Muhammad bin Nayef: he has no sons, only daughters.

To replace Muhammad bin Nayef as the third in line, Salman picked one of his own sons, Muhammad bin Salman. Only twenty-nine when selected to be deputy crown prince, Muhammad bin Salman is not the king's oldest or most experienced son. His elder brothers include Saudi Arabia's only astronaut, province governors, wealthy businessmen, and media moguls. But the king clearly favors this prince.

Muhammad bin Salman is different in many ways from the thousands of other Saudi princes today, while at the same time similar to a large part of the

President Barack Obama with Crown Prince Muhammad bin Nayef and Deputy Crown Prince Muhammad bin Salman at the White House, May 13, 2015. (Getty Images News/Chip Somodevilla)

overall population. He is far younger than most of his potential rivals for the throne. By picking this son, Salman has skipped a whole generation of Saudi princes. Muhammad was not educated abroad, but, instead studied at a Saudi university. He is not fluent in English, although he understands some, or believes he does. He sports a beard, unusual among the royals. His youth makes him popular with the majority of the population which, like him, is thirty or younger.[40]

The king quickly moved his favorite son into important positions of power. On Abdallah's death, Muhammad bin Salman was appointed by his father to be defense minister and chief of the Royal Court. This gave him command over the armed forces and access to the royal court and the king. Less than a hundred days later he became third in the hierarchy as deputy crown prince. He was also made chairman of an interagency committee to decide all economic and financial policy, including all issues related to petroleum policy. It is an extraordinary and unprecedented accumulation of power in the hands of one very young prince.

The first major challenge for the king and Defense Minister Muhammad bin Salman was Yemen. The political process that replaced Ali Abdallah Saleh with Abdrabbu Mansour Hadi dragged on into a prolonged national dialogue that culminated in a proposal to turn the country into a federation of six regions, four in the north and two in the south. The rebellious Houthis rejected the proposal because their region was landlocked and isolated. Saleh, who refused to go into exile, made an alliance with the Houthis against Hadi. In September 2014 the Houthis and Saleh loyalists seized control of the capital Sana'a.

By January 2015 the Houthis and Saleh had taken control of most of north Yemen, including the major port at Hodeidah. Hadi was placed under house arrest and parliament dissolved. The rebels signed an agreement with Iran to establish direct commercial flights between Tehran and Sana'a four times a day, and Iran agreed to build an electrical power plant in Yemen. Hadi fled to Riyadh, and the rebels began to march on Aden, the former capital of the south and the largest port on the Arabian Sea.

For the new king and his young defense minister, the deteriorating situation in Yemen seemed to suggest Iran was about to gain a foothold on the Arabian Peninsula in the Kingdom's backyard. The Houthis had long-time connections with Iran's Revolutionary Guards and Hezbollah. Small numbers of advisers from both the Iranian guards and Hezbollah had come to Yemen to assist the Houthis, especially with their ballistic missiles. It is estimated, as of this writing, that Iran provides $10 million to $20 million in aid to them each year.[41] Iranian newspapers trumpeted that four Arab capitals—Beirut, Damascus, Baghdad, and Sana'a—were under Iranian influence. In truth, neither Saleh nor the Houthis were Iranian pawns or even allies, but for the Saudis the situation was intolerable.

Riyadh quickly put together a coalition of its fellow Gulf monarchies (minus Oman), Egypt, Jordan, Morocco, Sudan, and some African states to restore Hadi to power. On March 25, 2015, the new coalition led by Muhammad bin Salman announced the beginning of Operation Decisive Storm, and the Saudis began bombing Saleh and Houthi forces across Yemen. The rebels responded with missile attacks on Saudi border cities and battles erupted on the Saudi-Yemeni border.

The air war was not decisive by any means. Although it imposed terrible suffering on the poorest country in the Arab world and created an enormous humanitarian crisis for Yemen's 25 million people, it did not restore Hadi to power. Instead, he moved to Aden, which became the de facto capital of his state. Backed by small contingents of Saudi and Emirati troops, Hadi gradually took control of the south.[42] The war became a bloody stalemate, with no end in sight, while tens of thousands of Yemeni civilians suffered the consequences of fighting, bombing raids, famine, and disease.

The United Nations Security Council, dominated by Saudi friends and oil customers, adopted a resolution on April 14, 2015, endorsing the Saudi position and demanding the Houthis "withdraw their forces from all areas they seized" and "immediately and unconditionally relinquish all additional arms seized from military and security installations, including missiles." Only Russia abstained on resolution 2216, arguing that it was unbalanced and unenforceable.

The hastily formed alliance was not joined by Pakistan. The Saudis had expected the Pakistanis to provide troops for the ground war in Yemen and summoned Prime Minister Nawaz Sharif to meet with the king and his ministers. The Pakistanis found the king and his court in a state of near panic. They were frightened by the Houthis' successes and determined to stop the Iranians but had no plan for how to defeat the enemy. The mood was reckless, one senior Pakistani told me later. There was no plan for an endgame, an achievable outcome at a reasonable price.

Despite Saudi assumptions, Sharif wanted no part of a war between Sunnis and Shias. His own country had a large Shia minority and a long border with Iran. He convened the Pakistani parliament to debate the Saudi request. In a stunning rejection, the parliament voted unanimously against sending any troops to Saudi Arabia. A half-century of Saudi courtship of Pakistan had failed to secure Pakistani support at a crucial moment. The Pakistani press was filled with angry articles about Saudi arrogance and recklessness.

Pakistan's rejection of Saudi troop requests raised another issue. For decades many outside observers had wondered whether Riyadh and Islamabad had a secret understanding that, in case of a dire external threat to the Kingdom, Pakistan would provide nuclear weapons to Saudi Arabia. The Saudi purchase of Chinese intermediate-range ballistic missiles in the 1980s had added meat to the question. Why would the Saudis buy missiles expressly designed to carry nuclear bombs without having nuclear warheads? Publicly, Saudi officials avoided any discussion of the question, but Prince Saud and others, in private, were more disposed to suggest that some kind of discreet understanding did exist. In 2014 the Saudis displayed their Chinese CSS2 missiles in public for the first time ever in a military parade. The guest of honor at the parade was the Pakistani army chief of staff. Saudi officials were eager to encourage observers like me to make the connection.

If there is a real connection, the Pakistan refusal to join the war in Yemen would suggest any such understanding is based on weak foundations. With Pakistan unwilling to send troops to fight the Houthis, how reliable was any vague promise to provide a nuclear warhead? The war that was designed to strengthen Saudi deterrence had, unintentionally, appeared to erode it.

Defense Minister Muhammad bin Salman was the face of the war, at least in the beginning. He was seen everywhere on Saudi television and in the newspapers meeting with the troops and chairing meetings of the generals. Saudi radio stations broadcast songs praising his leadership. Critics, on the other hand, dismissed him as the young general in over his head.

The king's promotion of his son and the war has its critics within the royal family. In 2015 several Saudi watchers, including myself, received unsolicited emails from unidentified members of the royal family harshly critical of Muqrin's demotion, Muhammad bin Salman's promotion, and the handling of Saudi policy toward Yemen. Some alleged the king was mentally unfit for office and was being used by his son. In time these letters came into the public domain and got widespread attention in the media then, gradually, they ceased to appear.[43]

The war is an expensive proposition for the Kingdom. Not only is there the military expense of a modern air war, but Riyadh also props up the Hadi government in Aden and funds the contributions of many poor allies, such as Sudan. The United Arab Emirates and Kuwait help significantly with the expenses.

Saudi Arabia has achieved significant territorial advantages from the war. The Hadi forces control Aden, the largest port and city in the south. They also control Perim Island, which sits in the middle of the strategic Bab al Mandab Strait that divides Africa and Asia at the mouth of the Red Sea. The island of

Socotra in the Indian Ocean is also in the hands of the pro-Saudi forces. In May 2016 Saudi-backed troops took control of the port city of Mukkala and the province of Hadramawt in southwest Yemen, giving Saudi Arabia a land connection directly to the Indian Ocean. Al Qaeda in the Arabian Peninsula had taken Mukkala during the confusion at the start of the war. While all of these territories remain under nominal Yemeni sovereignty, Saudi Arabia certainly has access to them and has military forces based in some of them.

The United States and United Kingdom provide crucial support for the Saudi war. Since the Royal Saudi Air Force is equipped entirely with American and British aircraft and equipment, the war could not go on without the backing of Washington and London.

When Abdallah passed away, Obama was quick to develop a dialogue with the new king. He cut short a trip to India to visit the Kingdom right after the succession occurred. He invited Salman to visit Washington for a summit with the Gulf Cooperation Council leaders. Salman instead sent Muhammad bin Nayef and Muhammad bin Salman, in what was seen by many at the time as a snub of the president. But later in 2016 the king did visit Washington for talks with the president. Muhammad bin Salman made a visit, as well, touring not only Washington but also San Francisco and New York to lay out his plans for Saudi economic reform, what is billed as Saudi Vision 2030.

Much of the discussion between the king and the president focused on Iran. The Saudis are increasingly concerned about the expansion of Iranian influence in the Arab world. In their eyes Iran is the dominant power in Iraq, Syria, and Lebanon, and it aspires to turn Yemen into a proxy. Iran also supports terrorist groups like Hezbollah and subversion in Bahrain and the Eastern Province.

Riyadh was critical of the nuclear accord negotiated between the five permanent members of the Security Council plus Germany and Iran in the spring of 2015. The deal strictly limits Iranian nuclear activity in return for lifting most of the economic sanctions on Iran imposed by the UN in the decade before 2015. The Saudis preferred keeping the sanctions in place permanently and keeping Iran isolated as a pariah nation.

Israel also strongly opposed the nuclear deal with Iran, creating an awkward overlap of interests for the Saudis, who do not want to appear to be working with Israel. King Salman kept his critique of the deal mostly behind closed doors in 2015, leveraging his silence in exchange for American and British support in Yemen.

The Saudi-Iranian rivalry has steadily escalated on Salman's watch. First there was the Yemen war. Then Saudi Arabia organized a coalition of Sunni Muslim states to form a military alliance based in Riyadh against terrorism. Three dozen states joined the entente, but Iran and Iraq were conspicuously absent. Large military maneuvers practiced repelling a mock Iranian invasion of northern Saudi Arabia from Iraq in the winter of 2015–16.

In the summer of 2015, in Lebanon, Prince Muhammad bin Nayef's security forces captured the mastermind of the 1995 Khobar Towers attack. Ahmed Ibrahim al Mughassil was just off a flight from Tehran to Beirut. The Saudis quickly took him from Lebanon to the Kingdom. It was a major coup for the prince.[44]

In January 2016 the Saudis executed several dozen alleged terrorists. Most were members of al Qaeda but one was a prominent Shia cleric, Nimr al Nimr, from the Eastern Province. Protests in Iran turned into an attack on the Saudi embassy. King Salman broke diplomatic relations with Iran in return. The Kingdom encouraged other Arab and Muslim states to do the same, and Bahrain, Sudan, and the Maldives did so. In July 2016 former intelligence chief Prince Turki al Faisal attended a conference in Paris hosted by the anti-clerical Iranian opposition group known as the Mujahedin e Khalq and called for the overthrow of the Islamic government in Iran. Iranian pilgrims were excluded from the hajj to Mecca on the grounds that without diplomatic relations they could not get the proper credentials.

The Saudi-Iranian rivalry and the Sunni-Shia sectarian war crossed the boundaries of the Middle East and helped nurture civil wars in Syria, Iraq, and Yemen. Never before has the sectarian conflict within Islam burned as fiercely as it does today.

Egypt remains at the top of Saudi concerns. In April 2016 the king paid a five-day visit to Egypt to support General Sisi. The Saudis promised $16 billion in additional investment in the economy. The Egyptians ceded control to the Saudis of two strategic uninhabited islands in the Straits of Tiran, named Tiran and Sanafir, and the king promised to build a bridge across the straits through the islands to provide a land corridor from Egypt to Saudi Arabia. The acquisition of the two islands gives Saudi Arabia nominal control over both

Israel's and Jordan's access to the Red Sea, and the Kingdom was quick to announce it would guarantee free access. Together with the acquisition of bases in Yemen, the acquisition of Tiran and Sanafir expands Saudi influence in the Red Sea. Technically the Egyptians maintained they were only returning the islands to Saudi control after Ibn Saud had asked Egypt to protect them in 1948 from Israel. However, this explanation was unpopular in Egypt, where many saw the affair as a pay-off for Saudi support for Sisi's coup.[45]

On the surface, Obama's relations with Salman were marred by some scratchy public spats. Saudi papers printed harsh indictments of Obama's policy toward Iran and, especially, his unwillingness to intervene boldly in the Syrian civil war against Bashar Assad. Obama was critical of the Saudis for not doing more to fight the Islamic State and for encouraging sectarian strife. In one interview he suggested the Saudis were "free riders" on American security, prompting a furious response from Prince Turki. Turki wrote that perhaps Obama was "petulant about the Kingdom's effort to support the Egyptian people" in the coup against Morsi. He harkened back to the good old days of George H. W. Bush and the liberation of Kuwait.[46]

Behind the public war of words, however, the Saudi-American connection remained strong in critical areas. Obama and his aides defended the Kingdom against continued accusations of being involved in the 9/11 plot, dismissing a long-classified 2002 Senate report on the alleged Saudi role as having been overtaken by later, more thorough, investigations. CIA director John Brennan stated publicly that "Saudi Arabia is among our closest counterterrorism partners" and praised Crown Prince Muhammad bin Nayef as "a very close partner."[47]

The arms relationship expanded considerably on Obama's watch. While some areas of discord remain, the military-to-military relationship is stronger than ever, if measured in arms sales between Washington and Riyadh. According to a Congressional Research Service study, the Kingdom purchased arms worth a total of $111 billion on Obama's watch.[48] A considerable portion came in the deal Defense Secretary Gates negotiated with King Abdallah, but the war in Yemen has added billions more. There has been some criticism in Congress over the wisdom of these massive arms sales, particularly by Connecticut senator Christopher Murphy, but the Obama administration defended them as crucial to maintaining the health of the special relationship with the Kingdom.

Barack Obama understood the importance of Saudi Arabia before he was elected president, and he made reaching out to its kings a high priority during his entire term in office. He was quick to offer his condolences in person when King Abdallah died and Salman ascended to the throne. Obama had at his side a genuine Saudi expert, John Brennan, who had served in the Kingdom twice while he was in the CIA. The relationship between the two countries occasionally was stormy, but it was one the president knew mattered a lot.

No president since Franklin Roosevelt courted Saudi Arabia as zealously as did Obama. He traveled to the Kingdom more than any of his predecessors and more than any other country in the region, including Israel. But by 2016 the Saudis had soured on Obama. Part of the reason was Obama's perceived desire to reduce America's role in the region. He did want to get out of Iraq and not get dragged into Syria. He also failed to deliver on his promises of an Israeli-Palestinian agreement.

But the key reason for Saudi disenchantment was the Arab Spring. Faced with a potential existential threat to the Kingdom's survival, Obama wavered on backing autocrats and monarchies. He seemed to be ready to let revolution topple American allies or at least result in major political reforms. The Saudis, instead, want any American president to stay away from awkward and difficult issues like religious freedom, freedom of the press, gender equality, and political reform. In November 2016 the Saudis got a U.S. president who would avoid such issues, Donald J. Trump.

Trump Visits Salman

Trump has courted the Kingdom even more zealously than Obama, and the Saudis reciprocated. He sent his director of the Central Intelligence Agency, Michael Pompeo, to Riyadh on his first trip abroad to see the Saudis. Pompeo awarded Crown Prince Muhammad bin Nayef the George Tenet Medal for excellence in fighting terrorism. Deputy Crown Prince Muhammad bin Salman next visited the White House and had lunch with the president and his senior team.

On May 20, 2017, Trump traveled to Riyadh as his first destination on his first trip abroad. It was a striking example of the importance Saudi Arabia holds for American national security. The Saudis rolled out the red carpet with an impressive reception at the airport and huge posters with the president's image on skyscrapers.

There were three summits in Riyadh. First, King Salman met with the president, then leaders of the six Gulf Cooperation Council states had a summit with Trump, and finally, forty Muslim leaders from around the world met with the president, who delivered a speech about Islam. Among those attending were the president of Egypt, prime minister of Pakistan, king of Jordan, and the amirs of Kuwait, Bahrain, Qatar, and the United Arab Emirates. All the key figures in the Saudi hierarchy met with the president, as well; even former crown prince Muqrin had a session with the president's daughter Ivanka.

Unlike Obama, Trump next flew to Israel for a meeting with Netanyahu. Trump told the prime minister that King Salman was ready for a comprehensive Arab-Israeli peace agreement along the lines of the Arab peace plan originally put forward by Fahd in 1981 and repeated by Abdallah in 2002.

The backdrop to the president's trip was growing scandal at home. The president had fired his first national security adviser, Michael Flynn, for misleading comments about his meetings with Russian officials, and then after the summit, Trump fired the director of the Federal Bureau of Investigation because of his investigation of the administration's connections with Moscow. The president's son-in-law was also tainted with the scandal. It was all reminiscent of Nixon's visit to the Kingdom in 1974.

The two-day visit to the Kingdom was long on ceremony and symbolism and short on substance. A major arms deal worth $110 billion was promised, but no contracts were signed and the joint statement of the two countries made no mention of any deal. A new center for countering violent extremist propaganda was inaugurated with a bizarre photo-op of the king, President Trump, and Egyptian president al-Sisi putting their hands on a glowing orb. The joint statement highlighted "the strong historical and strategic relations" between the two countries and promised cooperation on international terrorism and regional issues. The strongest language was reserved for "the need to contain Iran's malign interference in the internal affairs of other states." No specifics were addressed.[49]

There also was no mention of human rights, democracy, or political reform. The issues that had troubled Saudi-American relations under Obama were left off the table and not discussed. Trump embraced the Bahraini amir and the Egyptian president enthusiastically. Instead, the emphasis was on forging a new strategic partnership for the twenty-first century. The American-Saudi partnership, at least on paper, was stronger than ever.

In short the Saudis played Trump like a fiddle, flattering him and giving his first foreign trip a glittering start. Just like FDR and Ibn Saud in 1945, the summit was more symbol than substance. The Saudis were happy to be rid of Obama and to get an unqualified endorsement for their campaign against Iran from the American president.

Just a few weeks later the king moved to secure his favorite son's position in the hierarchy. Muhammad bin Nayef was fired on June 21, 2017, and replaced by Muhammad bin Salman. As with Muqrin, no explanation was given for the unprecedented step of removing a sitting crown prince. Nayef was also ousted from the Ministry of the Interior. The house of Saud and the house of al Shaykh were quick to endorse the change. No successor was announced immediately to be the new deputy crown prince. The Saudi media hailed it as a triumph for the younger generation in the Kingdom. Trump called and congratulated the new crown prince. The news was greeted much less enthusiastically elsewhere. The *New York Times* editorialized that the "young and brash" prince was not "ready for the top leadership post." It cited the Yemen war as a sign that the "prince acted without thinking through the consequences" of his decision.[50] *The Economist* criticized the young man as impetuous and a "callow, hot headed prince," even "dangerous."[51] But he is now the future of the Kingdom and will be the next king for presidents to deal with.

Chapter Seven

WHITHER SAUDI ARABIA

It was October 1999 and I was in Geneva, Switzerland, with Assistant Secretary of State Martin Indyk to see Ambassador Prince Bandar. Bandar was hosting a secret meeting between representatives of the United States and Libya at his father's palatial home on Lake Geneva. It was the latest in a series of secret meetings that year hosted by the Saudis to broker a deal where Libya would turn over those responsible for blowing up Pan Am 103 over Lockerbie, Scotland, for trial in The Hague in return for an easing of sanctions. President Bill Clinton and Crown Prince Abdallah had explicitly authorized this secret diplomacy.[1]

After a day of discussions with the Libyans, Bandar took us out to an unforgettable dinner. He chose La Perle du Lac, perhaps the most elegant restaurant in the city, with a fabulous wine cellar. We certainly tested it that night.

I had another issue to discuss with Bandar unrelated to Libya. Only days earlier, Pakistan's elected prime minister Nawaz Sharif had been overthrown in a coup d'état by his military chief of staff Pervez Musharraf. The origins of the coup began earlier in 1999, when Musharraf had ordered Pakistani troops to cross the so-called line of control between Pakistani-controlled Kashmir and the Indian-controlled part of Kashmir. This troop movement forced a major confrontation between the two nuclear weapons states and resulted in a bloody war in the Himalayas around a town named Kargil. In the end, Sharif came to Washington on July 4, 1999, and reluctantly but bravely agreed to pull his army back behind the line of control. The war was over but the controversy over responsibility for the debacle produced a showdown in Pakistani politics that Musharraf won and Sharif lost.

Bandar had been helpful on July 4 in resolving the crisis. I had briefed him the night before on how the Kargil war was approaching a climax and the danger Clinton believed it posed of escalating into a nuclear exchange, which would have been the first-ever war between two states with nuclear weapons. Bandar had met Sharif at Dulles Airport when his flight arrived from Islamabad and urged him to find a way out of the crisis on the ride from the airport to Blair House, where the summit with Clinton was to take place. For decades Saudi Arabia had been a major source of aid and support for Pakistan, and together with Washington the two countries had won the war against the Soviet Union in Afghanistan in the 1980s.

In Geneva I reminded the prince of his role on July 4 and asked him to help again. Clinton was worried that Musharraf would have Sharif executed for treason or some other trumped-up charge. In 1979 General Zia ul Haq had overthrown and then executed his civilian boss Zulfiqar Bhutto in a coup. The execution had poisoned Pakistani politics for decades and helped destabilize the country.

The United States had little leverage with Musharraf. Clinton had denounced the coup as a break in Pakistani democracy. Under U.S. law, Washington had immediately cut off all assistance to Pakistan, especially military aid and contacts. These sanctions were added to those imposed when Pakistan tested nuclear weapons in 1998. Musharraf was unlikely to listen to Clinton.[2]

Clinton had directed me to find a way to stop another execution. I knew the Saudis had clout with the Pakistani army and could help; if Abdallah weighed in with Musharraf and offered to take Sharif into exile in the Kingdom, the general would almost certainly have to agree. The offer of exile would provide a way out of the problem of what to do with the ousted prime minister. The Saudis could assure Musharraf that Sharif would not engage in plotting his return to power from the Kingdom. While it would not make Pakistan stable, given its enormous problems, Sharif's exile in Saudi Arabia would give the country a better chance than would the execution of another civilian leader. Moreover, Sharif had been a good friend of Saudi Arabia on many issues during his two tenures in office, and Abdallah valued that bond.

Bandar agreed to help. He urged Crown Prince Abdallah and King Fahd to offer exile to the Pakistanis. Bandar's friend, Prince Muqrin, and his father, Prince Sultan, also weighed in to help convince Musharraf to let Sharif go into exile. It took several months to work out. The White House and the Royal Court worked closely to coordinate the exile agreement. Sharif was tried on charges of terrorism but Saudi intervention finally worked. In his memoirs, Musharraf credited the Saudis with saving Sharif from being executed like Bhutto.[3]

The episode is a good example of how the Saudi-American relationship can be used to produce positive outcomes, not just for the two countries

President Donald Trump and First Lady Melania Trump opening the World Center for Countering Extremist Thought in Riyadh, Saudi Arabia, May 2017, with King Salman bin Abdul Aziz al Saud (center) and President Abdel Fattah al-Sisi of Egypt (far left). (Saudi Press Agency via AP)

themselves but for broader regional reasons. Fahd and Bandar were not particularly worried about preserving democracy in Pakistan, but they were very worried about instability in a nuclear-armed ally. Like Clinton, they worried that Nawaz Sharif would be considered a martyr if he was executed, leading to riots and perhaps even a general breakdown in law and order. With Sharif safely in the Kingdom, the Saudis would have one of Pakistan's most important politicians beholden to them for the rest of his life. It was a long-term bet that eventually paid off. In 2008 Musharraf was forced from office by popular demand, Sharif returned from exile, and today he is again prime minister of Pakistan. He later wrote to thank me for my role in his avoiding the noose.

History of Tension and Unease

Like every president since Richard Nixon, Donald Trump sought to court the Saudis as soon as he entered the Oval Office. Trump sent his director of central intelligence, Mike Pompeo, to Riyadh on his first foreign policy trip as director with a message for the royal family that the new administration wanted to "reset" American-Saudi relations on a positive basis. Pompeo gave Crown Prince Muhammad bin Nayef a medal, named after former CIA director George Tenet, for fighting terrorism; it was a symbol of American respect for the prince's work on counterterrorism. Deputy Crown Prince Muhammad bin Salman came to Washington in March 2017 to see the president and other senior officials. Trump then made the Kingdom his first foreign stop in May. The visit was widely hailed in the Kingdom as a positive signal that the two states were back on track. There were the compulsory allusions to President Franklin Roosevelt and King Ibn Saud on the USS *Quincy* in 1943, yet beneath the public signs of amity longstanding differences and tensions remain in the relationship.

The relationship between the world's last absolute monarchy, Saudi Arabia, and the world's foremost democracy, the United States, has been troubled since its birth at the summit on the *Quincy*. Saudi kings and American presidents have little in common. They share no common cultural or historical past and have no shared political heritage or practices. Absolute monarchs running a theocracy have little sense of the complexities of modern elections or the checks and balances of a complex government with hundreds of lobby groups and competing political interests. Presidents, by contrast, have little experience in the complexities of Islamic jurisprudence and governance and few insights into the mechanics of an enormous royal family that jealously guards its secrets.

Yet Roosevelt and Ibn Saud had a successful meeting, which is why it is still lionized whenever Saudi kings and U.S. presidents meet. They struck the essential bargain that remains at the core of the relationship more than seven decades later: American security guarantees for the Kingdom and Saudi guarantees of affordable oil for the world economy.

But this crucial initial meeting also came close to failure because of fundamental differences over the fate of Palestine. The president's efforts to convince the king to support the creation of a Jewish state, either in Palestine or in Libya, were completely rebuffed. No amount of presidential charm could change the king's abject rejection of the notion of Israel. If Roosevelt had continued to make the case for a Zionist state, the summit would have collapsed. The president was smart to let it go.

For the next twenty-five years Saudi Arabia was a backwater for American presidents. None visited the Kingdom even though two visited Iran (Eisenhower and Nixon). Secretary of State John Foster Dulles was the only secretary of state to visit the Kingdom during this period, and no secretary of defense did so. While American oil companies expanded their critical role in the development of the Saudi petroleum business and got support from their government for doing so, the White House, from 1945 to 1973, saw Saudi Arabia as a backward and remote corner of the world, nowhere near the top of its priority list. The United States military presence in the Kingdom at Dhahran air base was allowed to end in 1962 without much attention or fanfare.

John F. Kennedy did have an important engagement with then Crown Prince Faisal in 1962. Their meeting produced a rare presidential intervention in Saudi domestic politics and society, when Faisal agreed to several reforms at home, most notably the abolition of slavery. Kennedy succeeded in persuading Faisal to take these steps because the Kingdom was under severe threat. The Soviet and Egyptian intervention in Yemen threatened the Kingdom with a dangerous hostile neighbor in its backyard, while the internal situation in the Kingdom was imperiled due to King Saud's weak and inconsistent leadership.

The Arab world was in the midst of a revolutionary upheaval as monarchs fell in Yemen and Iraq.

Kennedy's manner was also deliberate and low-key. He did not castigate the Kingdom in public. While he believed it was badly out of date and archaic, he kept those views to himself. With Faisal he provided security assurances in public and raised his concerns about the internal health of the Kingdom only in private in the residential quarters of the White House, far from the media and even most of his own administration.

Faisal was also receptive to the advice. He understood the kingdom needed to reform. He wanted to remove his brother from the throne and take the necessary actions to save the monarchy and preserve the House of Saud.

Kennedy's successors, Lyndon Johnson and Richard Nixon, left Saudi Arabia in the backwater. Johnson tilted American diplomacy in the Middle East decisively toward Israel in 1967. Nixon ignored the region when he came into office and kept ignoring it until 1973, with the exception of Iran. Nixon made the Iranian shah America's preferred ally in the region and provided him with an enormous quantity of American arms.

King Faisal's decision to impose an oil embargo against America in November 1973, following the Arab-Israeli war, fundamentally changed the arc of Saudi-American relations. The king did more damage to the American economy than the Soviet Union was able to do during the entire Cold War. The recession that followed the oil embargo and the rise in oil prices, coupled with severe inflation, put millions of Americans out of work. The Saudis had finally gotten the attention of the White House. First, Secretary of State Henry Kissinger and then President Nixon traveled to Riyadh to implore the king to lift the embargo and to put the Saudi-American relationship back on track.

The king insisted the relationship could only get back on track if the president made securing a comprehensive Arab-Israeli peace a priority. Faisal also insisted that East Jerusalem be returned to Arab sovereignty. He grew increasingly disillusioned with Secretary Kissinger and Presidents Nixon and Gerald Ford. Had he not been assassinated in 1975, another oil embargo would have been likely.

The partnership between kings and presidents has endured despite other near-death moments since 1973. In 1978 and 1979, the conclusion of a separate Egyptian-Israeli peace deal and the collapse of the monarchy in Iran deeply shook Saudi confidence in American diplomacy and security guarantees. King Khalid, who succeeded Faisal, believed President Jimmy Carter was ignoring Saudi concerns about Jerusalem and Palestine while doing nothing to keep a fellow monarch, the shah of Iran, on his throne. Only the Soviet invasion of Afghanistan in 1979 and the start of the Iran-Iraq war in 1980 salvaged the relationship.

President Ronald Reagan's flirtation with Iran in 1986 produced another crisis in the relationship. After promising American support for Iraq and delivering critical intelligence to save Saddam Hussein from defeat, the president engaged in one of the most foolish and dangerous foreign policy adventures in American history, one that could have led to his impeachment. Reagan managed to restore a measure of Saudi confidence in America by engaging in an undeclared naval war with Iran in 1988; this step helped persuade Ayatollah Ruhollah Khomeini to end the long war with Iraq. King Fahd played a crucial behind-the-scenes role in persuading Saddam to accept a cease-fire and not seek total victory.

The 1990s were the golden age of Saudi-American relations. President George H. W. Bush's decision to send hundreds of thousands of American troops to defend the Kingdom in 1990 and then to liberate Kuwait in 1991 changed the arc of the relationship once again. The Saudis knew America had saved them from an Iraqi invasion and the partition of the Kingdom. Although the American military presence helped inspire jihadist radicalism inside the Kingdom, it was very popular among the top princes of the House of Saud royal family.

Bush's determination, after the Persian Gulf War, to pursue a comprehensive Arab-Israeli peace settlement through negotiations starting in Madrid further solidified Saudi confidence in American leadership. By making the first steps toward recognizing legitimate Palestinian aspirations, Bush promised King Fahd that his concerns about addressing the root cause of the Arab-Israel problem were shared by the American president.

Bill Clinton took the peace process and the relationship with Saudi Arabia to new levels of cooperation during his administration. King Fahd, and then Crown Prince Abdallah, supported Clinton's hands-on approach to Middle East peacemaking. The Saudis, especially Prince Bandar, became important behind-the-scenes players in encouraging Syria and the Palestinians to reach accommodation with Israel. At the same time Saudi Arabia was a robust partner with America on a wide range of issues, including the containment of Iraq and Iran; maintaining peace and stability in South Asia; resolving the issue of Libya's role in the 1988 bombing of Pan Am flight 103; and keeping world oil prices low.

But the disastrous failures of Clinton's peace diplomacy in 2000 left a damaging mark on Saudi-American relations. The relationship had another near-death moment in 2001 when Crown Prince Abdallah refused President George W. Bush's repeated requests for a summit. At the peak of the crisis, Abdallah threatened a fundamental break in the relationship and even hinted at using the oil weapon again. Only Bush's promise to support a two-state solution to the Israeli-Palestinian conflict prevented a breakdown.

The terrorist attacks in the United States on September 11, 2001, posed another fundamental danger to the Saudi-American relationship. Many Americans blamed the Kingdom for playing some role in the attacks, either through funding al Qaeda, actively conspiring in the plot, or gross negligence in fighting the terrorist group. Those concerns linger today and remain a source of friction in the relationship.

President Barack Obama had his own near-death moment with King Abdallah in 2011 as a result of the Arab Spring. Obama's support for regime change in Egypt deeply shook Abdallah's confidence in the president's judgment and reliability. The crisis in Bahrain and the Saudi intervention on the island immediately brought the danger home to the king. Obama backed off from his support for reform in the region, and the crisis passed.

On the positive side, this list of crises in the relationship underscores its fundamental importance and resiliency. Kings and presidents have surmounted difficult moments and challenging times and reaffirmed in every case the importance and benefits of working with each other. Nixon resisted hawks who wanted a military response to the oil embargo. Carter and Reagan worked closely with King Fahd to fight Soviet aggression. Bush senior and Clinton found common ground with Riyadh on a global agenda. Bush junior and Obama defended the Kingdom from accusations of involvement in 9/11 and helped it fight al Qaeda and the Islamic State at home. The importance of good ties with the Saudi kings has become bipartisan common ground in Washington even when many other foreign policy issues are hotly contested.

On the other side, the near-death moments in the partnership reflect some fundamental and deep-seated differences between kings and presidents that challenge the relationship and could endanger its survival. Despite its seven-plus decades, the relationship lacks deep roots and ballast. The two countries have shared interests but no shared values. Just as kings and presidents have little in common personally, the two countries have almost nothing in common, except, on occasion, common enemies.

In contrast, the United States and France, America's oldest ally, share a common commitment to democracy and the rule of law. They share a common history in the Western community of nations and a common faith. While their political institutions differ, their fundamental politics have many similarities. When their leaders meet and agree on common objectives or disagree on what to do, there is always a reservoir of deep understanding between the two nations to help keep temporary disputes from unraveling the long-term relationship.

The absence of similar common values and deep roots means the relationship between the United States and Saudi Arabia is a far more transactional one, based on overlapping, often temporary, interests. These interests can be compelling, like fighting the Soviet Union or Saddam's Iraq, but they are not likely to last when the immediate threat changes or evaporates.

One measure of the volatility of the relationship is the pace at which American ambassadors to Saudi Arabia are turned over. Since 1940, twenty-seven U.S. ambassadors or chargés have been accredited to the Kingdom. At first they resided in Cairo, then Jidda, and today Riyadh. On average they have spent about two-and-a-half years in the assignment. Only a handful (Herman Eilts, John West, and Wyche Fowler) spent more than three years. The turnover rate reflects the difficulty of making a strong personal connection with the princes, as well as the frequency of irritants in the dialogue. In contrast, Saudi Arabia has sent ten ambassadors to the United States.

The strongest advocates of close ties with Saudi Arabia are, of course, the oil companies, arms dealers, and financial interests that make so much of their money doing business with the Kingdom. This is a strong and powerful lobby. Faisal tried to use it in 1973 to get Nixon involved in the Arab-Israel conflict, but pro-Saudi business interests lacked the clout to get his attention. These interests can help sell the American Congress on arms sales to Saudi Arabia, but only if a president is inclined to fight for such sales over the frequent op-position of Israel and its powerful allies on Capitol Hill.

The United States is far less dependent on Saudi oil today than it was in 1973. But other countries still depend heavily on Saudi oil, including Japan, China, and much of Western Europe. Since the U.S. economy needs growth in those economies to prosper itself, the global dependence on Saudi oil makes the Kingdom as important as ever.

Three Stumbling Blocks

Three fundamental issues hamper the relationship between Saudi Arabia and the United States. On these issues kings and presidents have basic disagree-ments about core goals and objectives. Interest and mutual accommodation can overlap, but it is difficult to find them. The three issues—the Israel-Palestine conflict; the role of Wahhabi Islam in Saudi policy at home and abroad; and the pursuit of political reform in the Arab world—are likely to be disruptive factors in the relationship in the years ahead and will require cre-ative diplomacy to manage.

The question of whether Palestine should be the home of a Jewish state, which preoccupied Roosevelt and Ibn Saud in 1945, has now changed into the issue of how to create a Palestinian state that will live in peace with Israel. The change has been slow in coming and has deeply troubled the U.S.-Saudi partnership. In 1948, when President Harry Truman recognized Israel only minutes after it declared its independence, then Prince Faisal recommended to his father Ibn Saud that the Kingdom break diplomatic ties with Washington. Ibn Saud realized his poor desert state was too dependent on American secu-rity to do so, and he protested Truman's decision but took no action.

After the Arab-Israeli war in 1967, then King Faisal joined an oil embargo against the United States and United Kingdom to press Washington and London to force Israel to withdraw from the territories it had seized. The em-bargo was a failure. Six years later, after the 1973 war, Faisal imposed a much more damaging oil embargo and succeeded in compelling Richard Nixon to become a mediator in the region.

Three decades of American diplomacy followed, with repeated efforts to secure a just, lasting, and comprehensive resolution of the Arab-Israel question. Successive Saudi kings had doubts about America's commitment to a just solution for the Palestinians. King Khalid concluded President Carter had opted for a separate Egyptian-Israeli peace at Camp David in 1978, thus forsaking the Palestinians, and broke relations with Cairo. Egyptian-Saudi ties resumed only after Anwar Sadat was assassinated in 1981. King Fahd concluded President Reagan was dodging the issue in the 1980s, but their common interest in thwarting Soviet and Iranian threats became higher priorities than the peace process—until the first Palestinian uprising, or intifada, began in 1988.

George H. W. Bush and Bill Clinton devoted considerable political effort and their own direct involvements in the peace process for more than a decade. The Saudis backed the Madrid and Oslo processes behind the scenes. They undoubtedly could have done more and been more proactive, but their contribution was important in giving the processes the blessing of the wealthiest Arab state and the protector of the holy mosques.

When the Oslo process failed in 2000 and George W. Bush showed little or no interest in trying to revive it Abdallah was prepared to fundamentally shake up the relationship. Events—the 9/11 attack in the United States and the al Qaeda insurgency in Saudi Arabia—intervened and the relationship staggered ahead.

This recitation of the ups-and-downs of the impact of peace diplomacy on the American-Saudi relationship illustrates two important points. First, the saliency of the Palestinian issue is, in part, a reflection of events in the broader Arab-Israel conflict. When there are wars, the Palestinian question, obviously, is more urgent, and when there is peace or a protracted stalemate, the issue recedes but never goes away.

The history also illustrates a second point that is more germane to the Saudi-American dialogue. Much depends on the passion of the sitting Saudi king about the Palestinian cause. Faisal was especially passionate about the importance of creating a Palestinian state and restoring Arab sovereignty in Jerusalem. For him, the issue became his top priority. King Abdallah was equally passionate in his own way. For much of the 1990s he believed American diplomacy was the means to secure his end. When that failed in 2000, he was deeply distressed and eventually made his own effort to produce a peace plan.

Kings Khalid and Fahd were also passionate about the Palestinian issue, but the record demonstrates they did not assign it the same overwhelming priority. It is too soon to make a judgment about King Salman.

An open question is whether the sons and grandsons of Ibn Saud will have the same commitment as their fathers and grandfather. It is likely they will. The Palestinian cause is deeply popular in Saudi society, especially within the clerical establishment. The House of Saud has made creating a Palestinian state, with Jerusalem as its capital, a signature policy since the 1960s. Generational change is unlikely to alter that fundamental posture.

It is also important to note that, despite profound differences over the question of Palestine and Jerusalem, the Kingdom has been prepared to collude, quietly, with Israel against common foes since at least the 1960s. Faisal accepted Israeli arms aid to the Yemeni royalists because it helped weaken Egypt's Nasser. The convergence of interests was temporary, however, and never compromised the Saudi position on Palestine or Jerusalem.

Behind the scenes there is, also, private cooperation today on some security issues. Discreet sales of Israeli high-technology counterterrorism equipment via third parties have been reported.[4] The Saudis and Israelis have overlapping interests in the containment of revolutionary Iran. There is circumspect cooperation, or at least indirect collaboration, in pressing Washington to do more to confront and contain Iran and its Shia allies, Hezbollah and the Houthis. Israeli officials are quick to make these connections and speak openly about them. Saudis are much less eager.

Today, Saudi Arabia is more willing than ever before to allow a handful of its citizens to interact with Israelis in public. A few Saudis have visited Israel (not government officials), always also traveling to the Palestinian Authority in Ramallah. The Saudi government has publicly disowned these Saudi visitors to Israel, but taken no serious action against them.[5] A handful of Saudis have appeared alongside Israelis at think tanks, Prince Turki being the most prominent. He always stresses at such meetings that Israel should accept the Arab peace plan developed by Abdallah and withdraw from the West Bank and East Jerusalem. He also makes clear that there will be no recognition of

Israel and no normalization of relations with Israel until there is a full and just peace.

For American presidents it is vital to understand the centrality of the Palestinian issue in Saudi national security policy. A vibrant and effective peace process will help cement a strong relationship between king and president; a stalled or exhausted process will damage their connection. The Saudis emphasized the Palestinian issue in their public statements about Trump's meeting with Prince Muhammad bin Salman. Trump has promised he will seek a deal.

The best approach for America to take is to pursue a peace agreement between Israel and the Palestinians, with the endorsement of Saudi Arabia and the rest of the Arab world when a deal is made. Of course, history shows that success in this arena is very difficult to achieve and, therefore, unlikely. Nonetheless, working toward such a deal is the right course of action.

The second major disruptive issue in U.S.-Saudi relations is more complex and less susceptible to direct diplomacy. Saudi Arabia has a unique connection with a unique form of Islam. The Kingdom is founded on the alliance between the House of Saud and the House of al Shaykh, the descendants of Muhammad Ibn 'Abd al Wahhab. This alliance is at the center of what makes Saudi Arabia the special country it is: an absolute monarchy combined with a strongly conservative theocracy.

This alliance between the royal family and the clerical establishment has evolved over the decades. The kings have tended to push the process to ensure the survival of the state. Ibn Saud was ready to work with the United Kingdom and then the United States, two foreign Christian powers, which his predecessors would have regarded as the epitome of evil and just targets for jihad. He accepted borders for his state, something the first Saudi state in the eighteenth century would never had accepted, even from a fellow Muslim state, the Ottoman Empire. King Faisal introduced reforms, such as female education and the abolition of slavery, that were questioned by many clerics. He was assassinated for introducing television. Fahd and Abdallah were both reformers in their own ways. So the Saudi family has successfully nudged the al Shaykh establishment into a more tolerant and modern world.

But there are limits to how far and how fast change can be made, and every Saudi king is acutely aware of them. The clerics are popular. For example, the eleven most popular Twitter handles in the Kingdom are those of conservative Wahhabi clerics.[6] Saudi Arabia cannot abandon Wahhabism and survive in its current form. Nor does the royal family want to abandon its faith. King Salman built the capital city to be a symbol of the alliance with the *ulema*. Salman has devoted his life to raising funds to promote the cause of the mujahedin from Afghanistan to Palestine.

The importance of Saudi religious belief is especially critical on the question of gender equality in the Kingdom. As one Saudi expert has written, the status and place of women "are what makes Saudi Arabia unique and different from other Arab and Muslim countries."[7] The Saudi Wahhabi interpretation of Islam is founded in a large corpus of religious legal findings. An estimated 30,000 fatwas or religious decrees have been blessed by the clerics in the last half-century to regulate every aspect of female life in the Kingdom and cement its gender policies.[8] Women live segregated from the public space for the most part, and they wear black while men wear white.

Some change has occurred for Saudi women. King Abdallah promised they could vote in the municipal elections, and King Salman lived up to that promise in 2015. Women ran for office and some of them won. More women are studying in university than ever before. But very few women can aspire to jobs in the workforce, and the rate of polygamy in the Kingdom has actually gone up since the oil boom of the 1970s.[9] According to a Saudi study, over half a million Saudi men have more than one wife.[10]

The status of Saudi women is a unique phenomenon in the Muslim world. Even its neighbor Qatar, which is also a Wahhabi state, allows Qatari women to drive and provides employment for many women in public service. Saudi women live sedentary lives and spend little time outside the home. As a consequence 80 percent have a vitamin D deficiency.[11] The Saudi treatment of women is also a serious barrier to American-Saudi relations and is likely to become an even more significant complication as gender politics change in America much faster than in the Kingdom.

Saudi religious beliefs also play a role in the issue of terrorism. There is no question that Saudi Arabia is a target of Islamic radical jihadist groups like al Qaeda and the Islamic State. Saudi Arabia has been, for over a decade, a crucial partner with America in the battle against the global jihadist network of terrorist groups. In 2010 the Saudis provided critical intelligence information that foiled an al Qaeda plot to blow up a commercial delivery aircraft over Chicago. The Saudi deep state that fights any dissent at home is effective in fighting terrorism, as well. Former crown prince Muhammad bin Nayef is the epitome of the deep state and its counterterrorism successes.

But there is also no question that the lack of tolerance inherent in the Saudi Islamic faith, especially in its severe attitude toward the Shia, has played a role in the development of the extreme views of Osama bin Laden and Abu Bakr al Baghdadi. The extremist ideology and narrative of al Qaedism has a connection to some of the extremes of Wahhabism. As one senior counterterrorist expert has noted, both al Qaeda and the Islamic State are "rooted in the hate-filled religious doctrine, curriculum material and money that Saudi Arabia pumped out to the wider Muslim world to counter its Shia rival, Iran."[12]

John Brennan, President Obama's Saudi expert, characterizes the issue this way: The Saudi intelligence services "are really very close partners with us. But . . . the Saudi government and leadership today have inherited a history whereby individuals have embraced a rather fundamentalist extremism in their version of the Islamic faith." The former CIA director argues that "these very fundamentalist realms of Saudi supported organizations fully exploited them as a spring board for militancy, extremism and terrorism."[13]

The challenges posed by Saudi Arabia's unique vision of Islam for the American partnership with the Kingdom are complex and have changed over time. When Saudi Arabia was a backwater, these problems could easily be ignored. The challenges also could largely be ignored during the Cold war, when Saudi Arabia and America were allies against the Soviet Union. It is much more difficult to do so when the enemy consists of al Qaeda and other extremists who have based some of their core ideology on the official Saudi belief system that is enforced by the Kingdom's clerics.

American presidents will have to deal with these complexities in the years ahead. Obama famously said the U.S.-Saudi relationship is "complicated," which, of course, is an understatement. Differences over gender are bound to become an increasing part of any conversation between kings and presidents in the future. Differences over the causes of violent sectarian tension are becoming more apparent in the region. The Kingdom remains xenophobic in many ways, resistant to opening up to outsiders except those with special skills, and even then resists bringing them into closed zones. The Holy Cities remain closed to the vast majority of Americans who work in the Kingdom (and 99 percent of Americans in general) simply because they are for Muslims alone. The most experienced Saudi experts in the U.S. government have never visited the two cities of greatest historical and societal importance in Saudi Arabia. That is a unique aspect of a very complicated bilateral relationship.

All these issues are for diplomats and security experts. They go well beyond the standard comfort zone for most diplomats, generals, and spymasters when engaging with their counterparts. Kings and presidents will need more than a phone conversation or a few hours in the Oval Office or the Royal Palace to cope with the complexity of these matters. As Brennan puts it, "There has been explosive growth in Saudi Arabia in terms of all the trappings of modernization but yet the environment, the culture, the society and the religious traditions have not yet adapted to the twenty-first century world" that Americans live in.[14]

The third area of disharmony is newer in many ways than the long-term differences over Israel and Wahhabism. In the last decade it has become clear to many Americans and also to many Arabs that the Arab world needs fundamental political and social reforms. The revolutionary explosions that shook the Arab world in 2011, in what was called the Arab Spring, embodied the concern that the status quo in Arabia is unsustainable. Except for Tunisia, the revolutions failed, ending either in a return to autocracy or in civil war and failed states.

Saudi Arabia was the leading player in the counterrevolution. As we have seen, it sent its own troops into Bahrain to prop up a Sunni monarchy against the wishes of the Shia-majority population. They are still there. In Egypt, the Saudis helped engineer a military coup that removed a democratically elected government. They have spent billions since to keep the military in power. In Yemen they tried to keep the old regime in power but with a new leader, swapping out Ali Abdallah Saleh. As usual Yemen proved to be more difficult, and a bloody and lingering civil war followed.

At home King Abdallah spent over $100 billion to buy off potential dissent. There is no doubt that he feared the revolutionary contagion could come to the Kingdom itself. Muhammad bin Nayef's deep state has gotten larger since 2011 to ensure order and stifle any dissent. The Ministry of the Interior, in 2017, numbers close to 1 million employees.

The Kingdom does have plans for large-scale economic reforms. Muhammad bin Salman, while serving as deputy crown prince, commissioned a series of task forces to review how to reduce and even eliminate the Kingdom's dependence on oil income. The result is a plan called Saudi Vision 2030. Some of its proposals are highly visionary in the Saudi context; for example, opening up a small portion of Aramco to outside stock ownership. Others are very smart moves to better utilize existing resources, such as encouraging more religious tourism to the holy cities year-round so that the hotels and other accommodations for hajj tourists are filled more than just once a year.

Saudi Vision 2030 is only the latest in a long series of projects by the Saudi leadership to reduce a near-total dependence on oil that dates from the 1970s. None of these ideas has had any appreciable impact on reducing the government's dependence on oil income. Various schemes have also tried to encourage more Saudi participation in the labor market, which would both give more Saudis jobs and keep their wages in the Kingdom, rather than relying so heavily on foreign workers who send much of their income home to their families. This, too, has been a failure, and foreign workers today number almost 10 million, or one for every two Saudis.

Important as it could be, Saudi Vision 2030 is only an economic reform package and has no political dimension. It provides no promise of opening up the opaque political process or giving non-royals any role in decisionmaking. The plan also makes no provision for giving rights to women, including the right to drive. At a seminar at the Brookings Institution, one of the drafters of Saudi Vision 2030 said allowing women to drive was not on the agenda. Then King Salman issued a decree announcing women will be allowed to get drivers licenses after June 2018.

Inevitably the Saudi determination to maintain the old order in the Arab world will lead to more unrest, not less. The reasons the Arab world exploded into revolution in 2011 have not gone away or been resolved. Rather they have been repressed and stifled more than ever. Many Arabs may well be horrified with the results of the Arab Spring in Syria and Libya, for example, but they also do not want a return to the harsh dictatorships of Assad and Muammar Qadhafi.

Superficially, then, it appears Saudi Arabia is a force for order in the region, one that is trying to prevent chaos and disorder. But in the long run, by trying to maintain an unsustainable order enforced by a police state, the Kingdom may, in fact, be a force for chaos. If there is no movement toward political reform, opening up the political process and reining in the deep state, then another revolutionary tidal wave is all but inevitable and is likely to be more violent and disruptive.

Bahrain and Yemen are good examples. The Saudi military intervention in Bahrain in 2011 saved the Sunni monarchy from collapse, or at least from having to enact major reforms. But the Shia majority are even more angry today at the Khalifas and the Saudis than ever before. The Shia are becoming more radicalized, not less. Iran has more opportunity to meddle because more and more Bahraini Shia are desperate for reform. In Yemen the war has brought huge suffering for the majority Zaydi Shia population, with mass starvation caused by the Saudi blockade and many deaths from the Saudi bombing campaign. Whatever the eventual outcome of the war, a generation of Yemenis are certain to hate the Kingdom and want to seek revenge.

American presidents have generally preferred order in the Middle East to political reform. The Eisenhower Doctrine promised American support for regimes that resisted Nasser's call for revolution. Successive American presidents, both Democrats and Republicans, have backed military strongmen like Sadat and Mubarak and absolute monarchs like the Saudis and the Gulf shaykhdoms. Only Kennedy tried to encourage reform in the Kingdom, because he recognized that without change and reform the House of Saud would probably be swept aside like the monarchies of Iraq and Yemen. Trump already has expressed enthusiastic support for autocratic regimes, a major reason the Saudis are enthusiastic about his presidency.

A better approach would be for the president to treat Saudi Arabia as the United States has treated autocratic regimes in the past. In the 1980s, we did arms control deals and managed conflicts with the Soviet Union while also pressing our human rights agenda and meeting with dissidents. We helped give dissidents a platform to express their dissent. We have continued doing the same with Russia and China, engaging with the dictators in Moscow and Beijing on issues of mutual interest while also promoting the cause of liberty and freedom.

Promoting reform and change is in our national interest. In the long run it is also in the Saudis' interest. We should not avert our attention from the brutality of the Saudi deep state, nor should we avoid commenting on the gender inequality in the Kingdom or its fierce sectarian approach to the Shia minority. As *The Economist* wisely commented when Barack Obama visited the Kingdom after Abdallah's death, "Western leaders should maintain the ties but ditch the sycophancy. Their friendship should be more conditional on reform—specifically the taming of Saudi Arabia's savage religious judiciary."[15]

The Saudi leadership of counterrevolution in the Arab world is bound to cause tension over time between their kings and American presidents. Managing that tension will be increasingly difficult, especially if some Arab states do find a way to progress toward more democratic governments and open their political space to allow greater freedom.

The American-Saudi relationship, which has always been troubled, is likely to face more challenges in the years ahead. Presidents and kings will see more near-death moments in the partnership, not less.

Will the Kingdom Survive?

All of this raises one more question. How stable is the Kingdom itself? The best answer to that question was provided by King Abdallah in 2011. When the Arab Spring began he rushed home from vacation in Morocco and spent more than $130 billion to prevent an uprising in the Kingdom. There had already been trouble that winter in Jidda because of severe flooding and a botched government response. Abdallah decided to take no chances and he spent a fortune to ensure the Arab Spring bypassed his country.

Many of the reasons Tunisia, Egypt, Yemen, Bahrain, and Syria experienced upheaval in 2011 are common to Saudi Arabia, as well. It is a closed police state that allows for little or no dissent. The press is controlled by the government. There is no systematic mechanism for the population to participate in the political process aside from the municipal councils. Nearly everything about the senior leadership is opaque.

While it has made many royals fabulously wealthy, the economy has failed to provide a good standard of living for many Saudis. One expert has concluded that 300,000 Saudis enter the job market every year, but there are far too few jobs for them; in 2015 private employers added only 49,000.[16] Unemployment among young Saudi males between twenty and twenty-four, according to the official figures, is 40 percent, and overall unemployment is 20 percent. The private sector employs nine foreign workers at minimal wages for every Saudi employed.[17] If women were to enter the job market in significant numbers, the jobs problem would only get worse.

Saudis do not pay taxes; rather they live on handouts from the government, which gets 90 percent of its revenues from oil. One of the most experienced Saudi watchers concludes that "handouts abound: for the military, a major employer of Saudis; for the religious establishment whose support legitimizes the al Saud; for education, healthcare and social welfare; and more recently for a minimum wage and unemployment payments. The result is at least three generations of Saudis addicted to benefits they see as a right."[18]

Abdallah was able to dispense $130 billion in 2011–12 because of high oil prices. Prices have declined considerably since then. The Kingdom had $600 billion in reserves when he died in 2015. Some $100 billion was spent in King Salman's first year on the throne as he handed out big bonuses to Saudis to welcome his reign and embarked on an expensive war in Yemen.[19]

Military spending is an enormous burden for the country. In 2015 the Stockholm International Peace Research Institute, a globally respected think tank that studies arms spending, reported that Saudi Arabia spent $87.2 billion on defense, making it the third-largest defense spender nation in the world, exceeded only by the United States and China. With only 20 million citizens, Saudi Arabia spent more on its military than Russia, the United Kingdom, India, or France.[20] Per capita defense spending is over $6,900 per year. Saudi Vision 2030 plans to cut the percentage of foreign purchases of military equipment for the military from 98 percent today to 50 percent by 2030, but few if any experts believe that is possible given the lack of a major industrial base in the Kingdom. The Yemen war only increases the burden on the defense budget. There are no public Saudi figures on the cost of the conflict, but a detailed study by a British think tank concluded they are substantial.[21]

Many in the younger generation recognize the current system is unsustainable. Half the population is under twenty-five. Crown Prince Muhammad bin Salman recognizes the system needs reform, which is why he is pushing Saudi Vision 2030 so aggressively.

Saudi Arabia also has significant regional tensions that could help produce discontent. Residents of the Hijaz and Asir have never fully been reconciled to

Nejdi dominance. The Eastern Province, with its Shia-majority population, is always a source of concern. Sixty percent of the employees of Aramco are Shia. If economic problems create discontent, it could take on regional dimensions as well.

The Achilles heel of any absolute monarchy is the succession issue. For sixty years the House of Saud resolved the question by transferring it among the sons of Ibn Saud. Each enjoyed complete legitimacy because he could trace his power directly back to the founder of the modern Saudi state. Only once did the system fail, when Ibn Saud's eldest son proved incompetent for the job and was ushered out of office, during the course of a decade, by his brother Faisal. This was a brilliant system that ensured family unity for the most part, provided legitimacy to each successor, and avoided the succession infighting that doomed the second Saudi state in the nineteenth century—but it would, inherently, run out of heirs. By removing two crown princes over the course of two years, first Muqrin, then Nayef, and then installing his own son as designated heir, King Salman seems to have resolved the succession question in favor of the next generation.

Muhammad bin Salman, who could rule as king for several decades, is the foremost proponent of change in the Kingdom today. His Saudi Vision 2030 is a stark commentary that the current system is unsustainable. But he is also the architect of the war in Yemen, a reckless and impulsive decision to go to war without an endgame in mind. If the Yemen war is his long-term legacy, then he will not be fit for the tough job of managing Saudi domestic and foreign policy.

The crown prince was also the prime advocate for cutting Saudi Arabia's land border with Qatar in July 2017 allegedly to punish Qatar for sponsoring terrorism. Bahrain and the United Arab Emirates joined the blockade, as did Egypt, effectively splintering the Gulf Cooperation Council. Iran and Turkey backed Qatar. The GCC has been a key supporter of American interests in the Gulf for decades and Qatar houses the largest American military base in the region.

All of this has enormous implications for America. Saudi Arabia has been America's partner in the Middle East since 1943. Every president since Franklin Roosevelt has understood the importance of building a bond with his counterpart, the king of Saudi Arabia. The relationship has often been strained, with moments of near-death, but its importance has never been in doubt.

With the region in more chaos than ever before, due to the failure of the Arab Spring and the rise of extremist terrorists like al Qaeda and the Islamic State, Saudi Arabia's importance has only gotten greater. America's other Arab partners, like Egypt and Iraq, are weaker today than a decade ago. Other partners, like Jordan and the United Arab Emirates, are valuable but lack the clout of the Kingdom.

If there is regime change in Saudi Arabia—still very unlikely but not impossible—who would take the place of the House of Saud? Al Qaeda and other extreme groups have supporters in many Saudi cities despite Muhammad bin Nayef's years of counterterrorism operations. They, undoubtedly, have sympathizers in the clerical establishment at the grassroots level although not in the top leadership. But the extremists have lost popular support over the last decade by their acts of violence and are unlikely ever to gain power.

A more likely alternative might be the military. A succession crisis might precipitate a move by the military to restore order. The Saudi Arabian National Guard is deployed intentionally to forestall any attempt to overthrow the monarchy by rebels, whether they are Shia or Sunni extremists or the regular army. National Guard commander Prince Mitab is King Abdallah's favorite son and the only senior member of Abdallah's family to retain a powerful position of authority after his death.

At the end of the day, it is important to remember that the House of Saud is a survivor. Two previous Saudi states fell due to outside intervention and internal family quarrels, and the family was forced into exile. But it came back. It has since outlived its royal rivals, the Hashemites in Iraq and the Pahlavis in Iran. It has outlived its secular rivals, Nasser in Egypt and Saddam in Iraq. Since Faisal it has produced a succession of kings who have been effective rulers. For presidents to come, the Saudi king will likely remain a crucial if difficult partner.

In 2013 I wrote a memo for Barack Obama on the occasion of his reelection. It was titled, "Black Swan: Revolution in Riyadh" and was published by the Brooking Institution.[22] I argued the Saudis are survivors and have considerable strengths, but I also suggested revolution is no longer unthinkable in the Kingdom. I outlined all the arguments laid out in this chapter. I also suggested there is little or nothing America can do to prevent a revolution in Saudi Arabia if the circumstances make one likely. The short, four-page memo was translated into Arabic and posted on the Brookings website. The reaction in the Kingdom was astonishing. The Black Swan memo was read by tens of thousands of Saudis. It was among the most popular postings Brookings had ever posted on the Kingdom. Saudis know the relationship with America matters a great deal and that the future of the Kingdom is less certain today than at any time in the recent past. So should Americans, as well.

Appendix

THE OFFICIAL RECORD ON
SAUDI ARABIA AND 9/11

More than sixteen years after the terrorist attack of September 11, 2001, many Americans still believe Saudi Arabia had some role in the plot. Political leaders, survivors of the violence, relatives of those killed, and many average citizens suspect some Saudi hand in the attack on America. Fifteen of the nineteen terrorists were Saudis and so was the leader of al Qaeda, Osama bin Laden. But two American presidents, George Bush and Barack Obama, have both held that the Kingdom was not responsible for the attack or involved in the plot.

Part of the reason the suspicion has lingered so long despite two administrations' dismissal of the allegations involves a joint report prepared in late 2002 by the Senate and House Intelligence committees. One part of that report—which remained classified until July 2016—dealt with accusations of Saudi involvement in the attack. Because it had been kept secret, that section of the report attracted intense interest and speculation. What did the famous twenty-eight secret pages say about Saudi involvement? When it finally was released, the two opening sentences were damning: "While in the United States some of the September 11 hijackers were in contact with and received support or assistance from individuals who may be connected to the Saudi government. There is information primarily from FBI sources that at least two of these individuals were alleged by some to be Saudi intelligence officers."[1]

The 2002 report made clear, however, that its judgments were very preliminary and needed much more investigation.

The congressional report highlighted the role of three Saudis—Omar al Bayoumi, Osama Bassman, and Shaykh al Thumairy—who provided assistance to two of the al Qaeda terrorists when they first arrived in California in February 2000. The terrorists, Khalid al Mihdhar and Nawaf al Hazmi, were known to the CIA as al Qaeda operatives, but for reasons that have never been fully explained the CIA did not alert the FBI to their arrival in 2000. Al Thumairy is the most intriguing of the three Saudis because he was an accredited diplomat at the Saudi consulate in Los Angeles. He and the others allegedly provided assistance to the two terrorists as they looked for a place to stay in California. The Joint Inquiry also raised reports that Haifa bint Faisal, Prince Bandar's wife, had sent money to the wife of one of the Saudis allegedly in contact with the two terrorists.

The joint inquiry report made no connection between Saudi individuals and any of the other nineteen terrorists, nor does it claim any connection with Mihdhar and Hazmi once they left California as the plot matured. The report also found no connection to the hijackers' team captain, Muhammad al Atta, who arrived from Hamburg, Germany, later in 2000 to manage the plot. The report made clear that its conclusions as of late 2002 did not constitute a fully evaluated assessment of the information it does contain. That responsibility was given by the Joint Inquiry to later studies of the 9/11 plot.

The 911 Commission, established by the Congress in 2002, reviewed all the data available to the Joint Inquiry and concluded in its report in 2004 that there was no evidence to indicate the Saudi government or individual members of the Saudi government had any role in the plot. It dismissed the assertions of the Joint Inquiry as baseless. "The Commission staff found no evidence that the Saudi government as an institution or as individual senior officials knowingly support or supported al Qaida." The 911

Commission did find evidence of money going from individual Saudis to fund al Qaeda but no evidence that the Saudi government was involved in such financial support.[2]

The commission separately released a report on the funding of the plot, which looked at accusations about Haifa bint Faisal. It concluded, "despite persistent public speculation, there is no evidence that Princess Haifa bint Faisal provided any funds to the hijackers either directly or indirectly."[3]

In 2015 the FBI did an additional study of all the evidence available on the 9/11 plot. This included material found in bin Laden's hideout in Pakistan in 2011, additional interrogations of al Qaeda terrorists apprehended after 2004, and a further review of the material FBI sources had unearthed over the fifteen years since the first terrorists entered the United States. All additional allegations of Saudi involvement were reviewed, as well.

This FBI report was led by three outside experts on terrorism, chaired by Bruce Hoffman, a Georgetown University professor and one of the leading experts on al Qaeda in the United States. It validated the 911 Commission report, concluding that there is "no new information obtained since the 911 Commission 2004 Report that would change the 911 Commission's finding regarding responsibility for the 911 attacks."[4] The 2004 and 2015 reports are the most thorough assessments based on all the material available to the U.S. government, much of which is still classified, and they exonerate the Saudis. John Brennan, the CIA director in President Obama's second term, has said the earlier Joint Inquiry report is incorrect and that there is "no evidence to indicate that the Saudi government as an institution or senior Saudi officials individually had supported the 911 attacks."[5]

The existing evidence alleging Saudi involvement in the 9/11 plot, thus, has been reviewed carefully by the U.S. government more than once. The FBI keeps the investigation of the attacks open to evaluate any new material, but there is no smoking gun that points to any Saudi official.

Nonetheless, it is unlikely that the accusations will go away. Indeed, in the fall of 2016 Congress passed the Justice Against Sponsors of Terrorism Act, which authorizes court cases against the Kingdom and its officials for alleged involvement in 9/11. No other country has been given similar treatment. President Obama vetoed the act. The Congress overturned his veto, the only time

Congress overturned an Obama veto in his eight years as president. The Senate vote was 98 to 0. Donald Trump supported the bill. So the legal process will now have a chance to review what two independent commissions have already investigated. The families of victims of 9/11 have instigated a court proceeding in New York in 2017 to do just that. The case will almost certainly take years to resolve.

Notes

Prologue

1. Martin Indyk, *Innocent Abroad: An Intimate Account of American Peace Diplomacy in the Middle East* (New York: Simon and Schuster, 2009), p. 57.

2. Ariel Ben Solomon, "Saudi King Blamed Mossad for 9/11," *Jerusalem Post*, August 4, 2015.

3. Robert W. Jordan, *Desert Diplomat: Inside Saudi Arabia Following 9/11* (Lincoln, Neb: Potomac Books, 2015), pp. 16, 53.

Chapter One: FDR and Ibn Saud, 1744 to 1953

1. FDR's 1945 travel to Yalta and Cairo is recounted in Susan Butler, *Roosevelt and Stalin: Portrait of a Partnership* (New York: Knopf, 2015), p. 342.

2. Rick Atkinson, *The Guns at Last Light: The War in Western Europe, 1944–1945* (New York: Henry Holt, 2103), pp. 498, 520–521.

3. Madawi Al-Rasheed, *A History of Saudi Arabia* (Cambridge University Press, 2002), p. 75; Alexei Vassiliev, *King Faisal: Personality, Faith and Times* (London: Saqi Books, 2015), p. 56.

4. Thomas W. Lippman, *Arabian Knight: Colonel Bill Eddy USMC and the Rise of American Power in the Middle East* (Vista, Calif.: Selwa Press, 2008), p. 126.

5. Aaron David Miller, *Search for Security: Saudi Arabian Oil and American Foreign Policy, 1939–1949* (University of North Carolina Press, 1980), pp. 122–24.

6. Sarah Yizraeli, *The Remaking of Saudi Arabia: The Struggle between King Saud and Crown Prince Faysal, 1953–1962* (Tel Aviv University Press, 1997), p. 151.

7. Alexei Vassiliev, *King Faisal of Saudi Arabia: Personality, Faith and Times* (London: Saqi Books, 2015), p. 156.

8. The first chargé was a career diplomat named James S. Moose Jr., who is most famous for saying "Arabic is a language that opens the door to an empty room." As late as 1937 the State Department had assessed American interests in the Arab world did not merit opening an embassy in the Kingdom; only in 1939 was the American consul in Egypt also given responsibility for representing America in the Saudi Arabia from his post in Cairo.

9. Stephen E. Ambrose, *Ike's Spies: Eisenhower and the Espionage Establishment* (New York: Anchor, 2012), pp. 21–22.

10. Michael Darlow and Barbara Bray, *Ibn Saud: The Desert Warrior Who Created the Kingdom of Saudi Arabia* (New York: Skyhorse, 2012), p. 433.

11. Butler, *Roosevelt, and Stalin*, p. 423.

12. Thomas Lippman, "The Day FDR Met Saudi Arabia's Ibn Saud," *The Link*, April-May 2005, p. 8

13. Darlow and Bray, *Ibn Saud*, p. 437.

14. Ibid., p. 437.

15. Lippman, "The Day FDR Met Saudi Arabia's Ibn Saud," p. 9.

16. Darlow and Bray, *Ibn Saud*, p. 439.

17. Ibid., p. 440.

18. William Eddy, "F.D.R. meets Ibn Saud" (Washington: America-Middle East Educational and Training Services, 1954), p. 12.

19. Lippman, *Arabian Knight*, p. 150.

20. Joseph A. Kechichian, *Faysal: Saudi Arabia's King for all Seasons* (University of Florida Press, 2008), p. 46.

21. Lippman, "The Day FDR Met Saudi Arabia's Ibn Saud," p. 9.

22. Darlow and Bray, *Ibn Saud*, pp. 441–42.

23. Lippman, "The Day FDR Met Saudi Arabia's Ibn Saud," p. 11.

24. Ibid., pp. 10–11.

25. Darlow and Bray, *Ibn Saud*, pp. 444–45.

26. Lippman, *Arabian Knight*, pp. 167, 180.

27. Darlow and Bray, *Ibn Saud*, pp. 32–35; David Commins, *The Wahhabi Mission and Saudi Arabia* (London: I.B. Tauris, 2013), p. 18.

28. Ian Timberlake, "Wahhabism Centre shows Conservatism Still Central to Saudi Soul," AFP, October 18, 2015.

29. Joseph A. Kechichian, *Succession in Saudi Arabia* (New York: Palgrave, 2001), p. 79.

30. Simon Ross Valentine, *Force and Fanaticism: Wahhabism in Saudi Arabia and Beyond* (London: Hurst, 2015), pp. 33–34.

31. Michael Crawford, *Ibn 'Abd al-Wahhab* (London: Oneworld, 2014), pp. 22–26.

32. Ibid., p. 22.

33. Ibid., pp. 29, 45, 60.

34. Ibid., p. 69.

35. Alexei Vassiliev, *The History of Saudi Arabia* (London: Saqi Books, 2000). Chapter 3 is the best history of the first Saudi state.

36. Crawford, *Ibn 'Abd al-Wahhab*, pp. 17, 108–12.

37. Joseph A. Kechichian, *Faysal: Saudi Arabia's King*, p. 12.

38. Darlow and Bray, *Ibn Saud*, p. 52.

39. Toby Matthiesen, *The Other Saudis: Shiism, Dissent and Sectarianism* (Cambridge University Press, 2015), p. 10.

40. Neil Partrick, "Saudi Arabia and Jordan," in *Saudi Arabian Foreign Policy: Conflict and Cooperation*, edited by Neil Partrick (London: I.B. Tauris, 2016), p. 166.

41. Aaron David Miller, *Search for Security: Saudi Arabian Oil and American Foreign Policy, 1939–1949* (University of North Carolina Press, 1980), p. 34.

42. Al-Rasheed, *A History of Saudi Arabia*, p. 52.

43. Miller, *Search for Security*, p. 37.

44. Darlow and Bray, *Ibn Saud*, p. 371.

45. Vassiliev, *King Faisal of Saudi Arabia*, p. 153.

46. Vassiliev, *The History of Saudi Arabia*, location 9077.

47. Department of State Bulletin of October 21, 1945, p. 623.

48. Miller, *Search for Security*, p. 200

49. Darlow and Bray, *Ibn Saud*, pp. 463–65.

Chapter Two: Faisal, Kennedy, Johnson, and Nixon, 1953 to 1975

1. Ishaan Haroor, "The Saudi Origins of Belgium's Islamist Threat," *Washington Post*, March 23, 2016.

2. Joseph A. Kechichian, *Faysal: Saudi Arabia's King for All Seasons* (University of Florida Press, 2008), p. 7.

3. Chams Eddine Zaougui, "Molenbeek, Belgium's Jihad Central," *New York Times*, November 19, 2015.

4. Haroor, "The Saudi Origins of Belgium's Islamist Threat."

5. Kechichian, *Faysal*, pp. 26–27.

6. Alexei Vassiliev, *King Faisal of Saudi Arabia: Personality, Faith and Times* (London: Saqi Books, 2015), p. 60.

7. Kechichian, *Faysal*, p. 29.

8. Ibid., pp. 32–36.

9. Madawi Al-Rasheed, *A History of Saudi Arabia* (Cambridge University Press, 2002), pp. 76, 107.

10. Kechichian, *Faysal*, p. 62.

11. Sarah Yizraeli, *The Remaking of Saudi Arabia* (Tel Aviv: Moshe Dayan Center, 1998), pp. 55–56.

12. Kechichian, *Faysal*, pp. 64–65.

13. Yizraeli, *The Remaking of Saudi Arabia*, p. 68

14. Percy Cradock, *Know Your Enemy: How the Joint Intelligence Committee Saw the World* (London: John Murray, 2002), p. 206.

15. Kechichian, *Faysal*, p. 70.

16. John F. Kennedy, "Imperialism—The Enemy of Freedom," July 2, 1957, can be found on the JFK Presidential Library website.

17. Warren Bass, *Support Any Friend: Kennedy's Middle East and the Making of the U.S.-Israel Alliance* (Oxford University Press, 2003), p. 4.

18. Harold Macmillan, *At the End of the Day, 1961–1963* (London: Harper and Row, 1973), p. 266.

19. Ibid., p. 276.

20. The CIA declassified hundreds of its daily reports to the White House in the 1960s in 2015. At first these were called Presidential Intelligence Checklists (PIC); later they became the President's Daily Brief (PDB). The PDB is the most highly classified product of the CIA. The declassified PICs and PDBs are available on the CIA website in its Electronic Reading Room and can be found by the date of issue.

21. PIC, October 6, 1962.

22. PIC, October 16, 1962.

23. Jesse Ferris, *Nasser's Gamble: How Intervention in Yemen Caused the Six-Day War and the Decline of Egyptian Power* (Princeton University Press, 2013), pp. 84–95.

24. Ibid., pp. 97–98.

25. Bass, *Support Any Friend*, p. 108.

26. Nigel Ashton, *King Hussein of Jordan: A Political Life* (Yale University Press, 2009), p. 92.

27. Bass, *Support Any Friend*, p. 63.

28. Ibid., p. 104.

29. Ibid., p. 104.

30. Kechichian, *Faysal*, p. 80.

31. Ibid., p. 80.

32. Vassiliev, *King Faisal of Saudi Arabia*, p. 236.

33. Ibid., p. 238.

34. PIC, October 19, 1962.

35. Daniel Yergin, *The Prize: The Epic Quest for Oil, Money and Power* (New York: Simon and Schuster, 1991), pp. 639–40.

36. Kechichian, *Faysal*, pp. 113–14.

37. Duff Hart-Davis, *The War That Never Was: The True Story of the Men Who Fought Britain's Most Secret Battle* (London: Random House, 2011), p. 96. See also Ferris, *Nasser's Gamble*, p. 132.

38. Ronen Bergman, "The Officer Who Saw behind the Top Secret Curtain," *Ynet Magazine*, June 22, 2015.

39. Hart-Davis, *The War That Never Was*, pp. 135, 139, 156; Yossi Alpher, *Periphery: Israel's Search for Middle East Allies* (London: Rowman and Littlefield, 2015), pp. 37–38.

40. Hart-Davis, *The War That Never Was*, p. 221.

41. PIC, September 26, 1962.

42. Ferris, *Nasser's Gamble*, p. 117.

43. Bass, *Support Any Friend*, pp. 129–30.

44. Kechichian, *Faysal*, p. 88.

45. Joseph A. Kechichian, *Succession in Saudi Arabia* (New York: Palgrave, 2001), p. 44.

46. Kechichian, *Faysal*, p. 77.

47. Ibid., p. 108.

48. Ashton, *King Hussein of Jordan*, p. 102.

49. Thomas Hegghammer, *Jihad in Saudi Arabia: Violence and Pan-Islamism since 1979* (Cambridge University Press, 2010), pp. 20–22.

50. Gerald Posner, *Secrets of the Kingdom* (New York: Random House, 2005), p. 170.

51. Kechichian, *Faysal*, p. 117.

52. Stephane Lacroix "Understanding Stability and Dissent in the Kingdom: The Double Edged Role of the Jama'at in Saudi Politics," in *Saudi Arabia in Transition*, edited by Bernard Haykal, Stephane Lacroix, and Thomas Hegghammer (Cambridge University Press, 2015), p. 169.

53. Office of the Historian, U.S. State Department, Foreign Relations of the United States, 1964–1968, Volume XXI, Near East Region, Arabian Peninsula, Document 278, Memorandum from the President's Special Assistant (Rostow) to President Johnson, June 18, 1966, p. 1.

54. Office of the Historian, FRUS, Document 275, Memorandum of Conversation, June 21, 1966, p. 1.

55. Office of the Historian, FRUS, Document 283, National Intelligence Estimate, The Role of Saudi Arabia, December 8, 1966, p. 1.

56. David Robarge, "Getting It Right: CIA Analysis of the 1967 Arab-Israeli War," Studies in Intelligence, *Journal of the American Intelligence Community* 49, no. 1, 2005.

57. Al-Rasheed, *A History of Saudi Arabia*, p. 129; Samir A. Mutawi, *Jordan in the 1967 War* (Cambridge, U.K.: Cambridge Middle East Library, 1987), p. 128. The Saudi brigade deployed in Ma'an, the city formerly part of the Hejaz that Ibn Saud had ceded to Jordan.

58. Kechichian, *Faysal*, p. 130.

59. Bryan R. Gibson, *Sold Out? US Foreign Policy, Iraq, the Kurds and the Cold War* (New York: Palgrave Macmillan, 2015), p. 106.

60. Ibid., p. 109.

61. Ibid., p. 153.

62. Office of the Historian, Department of State, Foreign Relations of the United States, 1969–1972 Volume XXIV, Middle East Region and Arabian Peninsula, Document 127, Telegram from the Consulate General in Dhahran to the Department of State, February 5, 1969, pp. 399–404.

63. Robert Dallek, *Nixon and Kissinger: Partners in Power* (New York: Harper Collins, 2007), pp. 524–25.

64. Kechichian, *Faysal*, p. 135.

65. Ibid., p. 138.

66. Daniel Yergin, *The Prize*, p. 597.

67. Mohamed Heikal, *The Road to Ramadan* (New York: Quadrangle, 1975), p. 268.

68. Anwar el Sadat, *In Search of Identity: An Autobiography* (New York: Harper, 1977), p. 152.

69. Yergin, *The Prize*, p. 613.

70. Kechichian, *Faysal*, pp. 137–38.

71. Yergin, *The Prize*, pp. 591–94.

72. Ibid., p. 614.

73. Vassiliev, *King Faisal of Saudi Arabia*, p. 398.

74. Ibid., p. 400.

75. Dallek, *Nixon and Kissinger*, pp. 556–58, 562; Kechichian, *Faysal*, p. 161.

76. Richard Nixon, "Remarks of the President and King Faysal Ibn Abdul Aziz of Saudi Arabia at a State Dinner in Jidda," June 14, 1974. Online by Gerhard Peters and John T. Woolley, The American Presidency Project.

77. Ibid.

78. Kechichian, *Faysal*, pp. 168–69.

79. Andrew Scott Cooper, *The Oil Kings: How the U.S, Iran and Saudi Arabia Changed the Balance of Power in the Middle East* (New York: Simon and Schuster, 2011), pp. 233–35.

80. Yergin, *The Prize*, pp. 638–39.

81. Kechichian, *Faysal*, pp. 192–95.

82. Yergin, *The Prize*, p. 638.

Chapter Three: Khalid and Carter, 1975 to 1982

1. Office of Regional and Political Analysis, Central Intelligence Agency, "Saudi Arabia: An Assessment," RP 77-100003, January 14, 1977, in Department of State, Foreign Relations of the United States, 1977–1980, Volume XVIII, Middle East Region: Arabian Peninsula (Washington: Department of State, 2015).

2. Report Prepared by the Ambassador to Saudi Arabia (West), Jidda, August 1977, Foreign Relations of the United States.

3. Andrew Scott Cooper, *The Oil Kings: How the U.S., Iran and Saudi Arabia Changed the Balance of Power in the Middle East* (New York: Simon and Schuster, 2011), pp. 361–62.

4. Jimmy Carter, *White House Diary* (New York: Farrar, Straus and Giroux, 2010), pp. 56–57.

5. Memorandum of Conversation, Riyadh, December 14, 1977, Subject: The Secretary's Meeting with Crown Prince Fahd, Foreign Relations of the United States.

6. Carter, *White House Diary*, p. 156.

7. Ibid., p. 160.

8. Telegram from the Embassy in Saudi Arabia to the Department of State, Subject: Secretary's Meeting with Crown Prince Fahd, Jidda, February 22, 1977, Foreign Relations of the United States, Volume XVIII.

9. William Simpson, *The Prince: The Secret Story of the World's Most Intriguing Royal, Prince Bandar bin Sultan* (New York: Harper Collins, 2006), p. 53.

10. Briefing Memorandum from the Assistant Secretary of State for Near Eastern and South Asian Affairs (Saunders) to Secretary of State Muskie, Washington, December 18, 1980, Foreign Relations of the United States, Volume XVIII.

11. Carter, *White House Diary*, p. 161.

12. Ibid., pp. 137, 254, 255, 257, 262.

13. Cooper, *The Oil Kings*, p. 275.

14. Intelligence Memorandum Prepared by the Central Intelligence Agency, "The Impact of Iran on Saudi Arabia: Security Concerns and Internal Reaction," RPM 79-10053, Washington, January 26, 1979, Foreign Relations of the United States, Volume XVIII.

15. Don Oberdorfor, "Frustration Marks Saudi Ties to U.S.," *Washington Post*, May 6, 1979.

16. Patrick Seale, *Asad: The Struggle for the Middle East* (London: I.B. Tauris & Co., 1988), p. 313.

17. Joseph A. Kechichian, *Succession in Saudi Arabia* (New York: Palgrave, 2001), pp. 54–55.

18. Memorandum from Gary Sick of the National Security Council Staff to the President's Assistant for National Security Affairs (Brzezinski), Subject: Cracks in Saudi Façade, Washington, December 22, 1978, Foreign Relations of the United States, Volume XVIII.

19. Cambridge Reports National Omnibus Survey, April 1980, conducted by Cambridge Reports. Available at the Roper Center at Cornell University website.

20. Summary of Conclusions of a Presidential Review Committee Meeting, Washington, April 27, 1979, Foreign Relations of the United States, Volume XVIII.

21. Thomas Hegghammer and Stéphane Lacroix, *The Meccan Rebellion: The Story of Juhayman al Utaybi Revisited* (Bristol, U.K.: Amal Press, 2011), p. 18.

22. Yaroslav Trofimov, *The Siege of Mecca: The Forgotten Uprising in Islam's Holiest Shrine and the Birth of al-Qaeda* (New York: Doubleday, 2007). On his sources, see also Thomas W. Lippman, "A Missing Link in Terror's Chain," *Washington Post*, October 21, 2007.

23. Ziauddin Sardar, *Mecca: The Sacred City* (New York: Bloomsbury, 2014), p. 326.

24. Hegghammer and Lacroix, *The Meccan Rebellion*, p. 18.

25. Sardar, *Mecca*, pp. 328–29.

26. Trofimov, *The Siege of Mecca*, p. 52.

27. Sardar, *Mecca*, p. 330.

28. Toby Matthiesen, *The Other Saudis: Shiism, Dissent and Sectarianism* (Cambridge University Press, 2015), pp. 104–07. Between seventeen and twenty-six Shia died in the crackdown in 1979 and ten SANG soldiers.

29. Trofimov, *The Siege of Mecca*, p. 151.

30. Ibid., pp. 191–92, 209.

31. Ibid., pp. 170–72.

32. Ibid., p. 225; Hegghammer and Lacroix, *The Meccan Rebellion*, pp. 20–21.

33. Trofimov, *The Siege of Mecca*, p. 227.

34. Ibid., pp. 91, 119.

35. Telegram from the Embassy in Saudi Arabia to the Department of State and Multiple Diplomatic and Consular Posts, Jidda, November 21, 1979, Subject: Occupation of the Grand Mosque, Mecca. Foreign Relations of the United States, Volume XVIII.

36. Trofimov, *The Siege of Mecca*, p. 96.

37. Ibid., p. 139.

38. National Foreign Assessment Center, Central Intelligence Agency "Saudi Arabia: The Mecca Incident in Perspective," An Intelligence Memorandum. Approved for release November 2006, p. 1. Also cited in Trofimov, *The Siege of Mecca*, p. 243.

39. National Foreign Assessment Center, CIA, "Saudi Arabia," p. 1.

40. Ibid., p. 1.

41. Madawi Al-Rasheed, *A History of Saudi Arabia* (Cambridge University Press, 2002), p. 11.

42. Sardar, *Mecca*, pp. 337–38.

43. Basharat Peer, "Mecca Goes Mega," *New York Times*, June 12, 2016.

44. Sardar, *Mecca*, p. 339.

45. "Mecca versus Las Vegas," *The Economist*, June 26, 2010.

46. Bruce Riedel, *What We Won: America's Secret War in Afghanistan, 1979–89* (Brookings Institution Press, 2014), pp. 21–23.

47. Shuja Nawaz, *Crossed Swords: Pakistan, Its Army and the Wars Within* (Oxford University Press, 2008), p. 372.

48. Memo from Brzezinski to Carter, "Reflections on Soviet Intervention in Afghanistan," December 26, 1979, National Security Archives. See also Husain Haqqani, *Magnificent Delusions: Pakistan, the United States, and an Epic History of Misunderstanding* (New York: Public Affairs, 2015), p. 245.

49. President Carter was generous in offering me access to his private diary from his years in the White House in 2014. Parts of his diary have been published and have been previously cited. This reference is from his unpublished diary, December 28, 1979, and January 4, 1980.

50. Dennis Kux, *Disenchanted Allies: The United States and Pakistan* (Johns Hopkins University Press, 2001), p. 252.

51. Robert Gates, *From the Shadows: The Ultimate Insiders Story of Five Presidents and How They Won the Cold War* (New York: Simon and Schuster, 1996), p. 146.

52. Charles G. Cogan, "Partners in Time: The CIA and Afghanistan since 1979," *World Policy Journal* 10, no. 2 (Summer 1993), p. 79; Author interview with Cogan, August 12, 2009.

53. Carter diary, December 28, 1979.

54. Carter diary, January 4, 1980.

55. Zbigniew Brzezinski, *Power and Principles: Memoirs of the National Security Adviser, 1977–1981* (New York: Farrar, Straus and Giroux, 1983), pp. 448–49; Author interview with Brzezinski, October 16, 2013.

56. Summary of Conclusions of a Special Coordination Committee Meeting, Washington, February 6, 1980, Foreign Relations of the United States, Volume XVIII.

57. Author interview with Brzezinski, October 16, 2013.

58. Carter diary, February 6, 1980.

59. Nawaz, *Crossed Swords*, p. 386.

60. President Jimmy Carter, "The State of the Union Address Delivered before a Joint Session of the Congress," January 23, 1980.

61. Peter Tomsen, *The Wars in Afghanistan: Messianic Terrorism, Tribal Conflicts, and the Failures of Great Powers* (New York Public Affairs, 2011), p. 205

62. Mohammad Yousaf and Mark Adkin, *The Bear Trap: Afghanistan's Untold Story* (London: Leo Cooper, 1991), p. 106.

63. Tomsen, *The Wars in Afghanistan*, p. 248. Tomsen's source is CIA officer Milton Bearden.

64. The Saudis also provided considerable private financial aid to other Islamic causes. For example, Saudi Arabian private funds fueled the development of the Palestinian Islamic movement Hamas. See Ze'ev Schiff and Ehud Ya'ari, *Intifada: The Palestinian Uprising—Israel's Third Front* (New York: Simon and Schuster, 1989), p. 225.

65. Scheuer, *Osama Bin Laden* (Oxford University Press, 2011), pp. 22–29.

66. Ibid., p. 49.

67. Ibid., p. 51.

68. Ibid., pp. 62–64.

69. Ibid., p. 65.

70. Tim Wells, *444 Days: The Hostages Remember* (San Diego: Harcourt Brace Jovanovich, 1985), pp. 327, 357.

71. "Interview with Dr. Charles Cogan, August 1997," Soldiers of God Cold War Interviews, National Security Archives, George Washington University, p. 2. See also James Blight and others, *Becoming Enemies: U.S.-Iran Relations and the Iran-Iraq War, 1979–1988* (Lanham: Maryland, Rowman and Littlefield, 2012), p. 66.

72. Brzezinski, *Power and Principles*, p. 451.

73. Gates, *From the Shadows*, pp. 130–31.

74. Director of Central Intelligence Stansfield Turner, Alert Memorandum for the National Security Council, Iran-Iraq Conflict, September 17, 1980. Approved for Release January 22, 2004.

75. Carter, *White House Diary*, p. 469.

76. Mohamed Heikal, *Illusions of Triumph: An Arab View of the Gulf War* (London: HarperCollins, 1993), p. 81.

77. Summary of Conclusions of a Special Coordination Committee Meeting, Washington September 27, 1980. Foreign Relations of the United States, Volume XVIII.

78. Matthiesen, *The Other Saudis*, pp. 117–18.

79. Letter from the Ambassador to Saudi Arabia (West) to President Carter, Jidda, June 3, 1980, with a Report Prepared by the Ambassador to Saudi Arabia, Foreign Relations of the United States, Volume XVIII.

Chapter Four: Fahd, Reagan, and Bush, 1982 to 1992

1. Craig Unger, *House of Bush, House of Saud* (New York: Scribner, 2004), p. 87.

2. "Royal Flush," *Forbes* Magazine, March 4, 2002.

3. Gerald Posner, *Secrets of the Kingdom* (New York: Random House, 2005), p. 75.

4. David B. Ottaway, *The King's Messenger: Prince Bandar bin Sultan and America's Tangled Relationship with Saudi Arabia* (New York: Walker, 2008), p. 51.

5. Ze'ev Schiff and Ehud Ya'ari, *Israel's Lebanon War* (New York: Simon and Shuster, 1984), pp. 68–69. See also Posner, *Secrets of the Kingdom*, p. 180.

6. Lawrence Joffe, "Shlomo Argov," *The Guardian*, February 24, 2003. The Iraqi assassin was Colonel Nawaf al Rosan.

7. Schiff and Ya'ari, *Israel's Lebanon War*, pp. 96–100.

8. William Simpson, *The Prince: The Secret Story of the World's Most Intriguing Royal* (New York: Harper Collins, 2006), pp. 97–99.

9. Nasser Ibrahim Rashid and Esber Ibrahim Shaheen, *King Fahd and Saudi Arabia's Great Evolution* (Joplin, Mo.: International Institute of Technology, 1987), pp. 140–41.

10. James Blight, Janet Lang, Hussein Banai, Malcolm Byrne, and John Tirman, *Becoming Enemies: U.S.-Iran Relations and the Iran-Iraq War, 1979–1988* (Plymouth: Rowman and Littlefield, 2012), p. 113.

11. Memorandum for Geoffrey Kemp, Senior Staff, National Security Council From Henry Rowen Chairman, National Intelligence Council, July 20, 1982, in Blight and others, *Becoming Enemies*, pp. 311–12.

12. Memorandum for the President, Subject: An Iranian Invasion of Iraq: Considerations for U.S. Policy, July 1982, in Blight and others, *Becoming Enemies*, pp. 310–11.

13. Blight and others, *Becoming Enemies*, pp. 114–15.

14. Giandomenico Picco, *Man without a Gun: One Diplomat's Secret Struggle to Free the Hostages, Fight Terrorism and End a War* (New York: Times Books, 1999), p. 61.

15. Steven R. Ward, *Immortal: A Military History of Iran and Its Armed Forces* (Georgetown University Press, 2009), pp. 255–59.

16. Rashid and Shaheen, *King Fahd and Saudi Arabia's Great Evolution*, p. 154.

17. Ibid., p. 158.

18. Robert Gates, *From the Shadows: The Ultimate Insider's Story of Five Presidents and How They Won the Cold War* (New York: Simon and Schuster, 1996), p. 321.

19. Ibid., p. 349.

20. Ottaway, *The King's Messenger*, p. 67.

21. "Saudi Arabia: Will a Row over a British Arms Deal Affect Saudi Politics?," *The Economist*, June 11, 2007.

22. Richard Halloran, "2 Iranian Fighters Reported Downed by Saudi Air Force," *New York Times*, June 6, 1984, p. 1.

23. Ottaway, *The King's Messenger*, pp. 69–70.

24. Khalid bin Sultan with Patrick Seale, *Desert Warrior* (New York: Harper Collins, 1995), pp. 138–42.

25. Ibid., p. 143.

26. Ottaway, *The King's Messenger*, pp. 71–72.

27. Ibid., pp. 73–74.

28. Khalid bin Sultan, *Desert Warrior*, p. 141.

29. Cable from CIA Deputy Director John McMahon to CIA Director William J. Casey on Providing Intelligence to Iran, January 25, 1986, in Blight and others, *Becoming Enemies*, pp. 320–21.

30. Blight and others, *Becoming Enemies*, p. xii. Malcolm Byrne, *Iran Contra: Reagan's Scandal and the Unchecked Abuse of Presidential Power* (University of Kansas Press, 2014) is by far the best study of the scandal and the investigations that followed it.

31. E-mail message, William A. Cockell to Colin L. Powell, "Iran-Iraq," January 21, 1987, in Blight and others, *Becoming Enemies*, p. 324.

32. Toby Matthiesen, *The Other Saudis: Shiism, Dissent and Sectarianism* (Cambridge University Press, 2015), pp. 120, 134–35.

33. Ibid., pp. 136–38.

34. Blight and others, *Becoming Enemies*, pp. 205–06. See also Picco, *Man without a Gun*, pp. 94–95.

35. Mohamed Heikal, *Illusions of Triumph: An Arab View of the Gulf War* (London: HarperCollins, 1992), p. 123.

36. Ibid., p. 161.

37. Ibid., pp. 162–64.

38. Ibid., pp. 214–15.

39. Ken Pollack, *The Threatening Storm: The Case for Invading Iraq* (New York: Random House, 2002), p. 34.

40. George H. W. Bush and Brent Scowcroft, *A World Transformed* (New York: Knopf, 1998), pp. 310–13.

41. Heikal, *Illusions of Triumph*, p. 244.

42. Khalid bin Sultan, *Desert Warrior*, p. 4.

43. Interview with John Nixon, March 22, 2017.

44. Colin Powell, *My American Journey* (New York: Ballantine Books, 1995), p. 450.

45. Bush and Scowcroft, *A World Transformed*, p. 322. See also Jon Meacham, *Destiny and Power: The American Odyssey of George Herbert Walker Bush* (New York: Random House, 2015), pp. 421–22.

46. Khalid bin Sultan, *Desert Warrior*, p, 9.

47. Simpson, *The Prince*, pp. 191, 195.

48. Ibid., p. 188. Bandar was given Secret Service protection in 1990 because of the fear Iraq might try to assassinate him. This meant he had unprecedented access to the White House and other government buildings. No other ambassador received this special status.

49. Pollack, *The Threatening Storm*, p. 36.

50. Heikal, *Illusions of Triumph*, pp. 255, 277.

51. Meacham, *Destiny and Power*, p. 425.

52. Khalid bin Sultan, *Desert Warrior*, pp. 18–20.

53. Powell, *My American Journey*, p. 452.

54. Bush and Scowcroft, *A World Transformed*, p. 335.

55. Harris Poll, January 1991, Roper Center for Public Opinion Research (https://ropercenter.cornell.edu, February 11, 2016).

56. Madawi Al-Rasheed, *A History of Saudi Arabia* (Cambridge University Press, 2002), p. 166.

57. Ibid., pp. 165–66.

58. Ibid., 169–71.

59. Michael Scheuer, *Osama bin Laden* (Oxford University Press, 2011), p. 51.

60. Bruce Riedel, *The Search for Al Qaeda: Its Leadership, Ideology and Future* (Brookings Institution Press, 2008), pp. 47–49.

61. Khalid bin Sultan, *Desert Warrior*, p. 315.

62. Ibid., p. 116.

63. Heikal, *Illusions of Triumph*, p. 322.

64. Khalid bin Sultan, *Desert Warrior*, p. 324.

65. Simpson, *The Prince*, p. 220.

66. Khalid bin Sultan, *Desert Warrior*, p. 260.

67. Bush and Scowcroft, *A World Transformed*, pp. 410–11.

68. Khalid bin Sultan, *Desert Warrior*, p. 318.

69. Ibid., p. 326.

70. George N. Lewis, Steve Fetter, and Lisbeth Gronlund, *Casualties and Damage from Scud Attacks in the 1991 Gulf War* (MIT Press, 1993), p. 4.

71. Bush and Scowcroft, *A World Transformed*, p. 455.

72. Khalid bin Sultan, *Desert Warrior*, p. 350.

73. Ibid., p. 426.

74. Powell, *My American Journey*, pp. 477, 516.

75. Simpson, *The Prince*, p. 252.

Chapter Five: Abdallah, Clinton, and Bush, 1993 to 2008

1. Robert M. Gates, *Duty: Memoirs of a Secretary at War* (New York: Knopf, 2014), p. 184. Gates had lunch with the Crown Prince in the same room several years later.

2. Thomas Hegghammer, *Jihad in Saudi Arabia: Violence and Pan-Islamism since 1979* (Cambridge University Press, 2010), p. 114.

3. Martin Indyk, *Innocent Abroad: An Intimate Account of American Peace Diplomacy in the Middle East* (New York: Simon and Schuster, 2009), pp. 66–68.

4. Ibid., p. 56.

5. Efraim Halevy, *Man in the Shadows: Inside the Middle East Crisis with the Man Who Led the Mossad* (New York: St. Martin's Press, 2006), p. 116.

6. Bill Clinton, *My Life* (New York: Alfred Knopf, 2004), p. 627.

7. Indyk, *Innocent Abroad*, p. 256.

8. Ibid., p. 271.

9. Clinton, *My Life*, p. 886.

10. Indyk, *Innocent Abroad*, p. 276.

11. Clinton, *My Life*, p. 938.

12. Kenneth Pollack, *The Threatening Storm: The Case of Invading Iraq* (New York: Random House, 2002), p. 70.

13. Indyk, *Innocent Abroad*, pp. 153–55.

14. Pollack, *The Threatening Storm*, p. 92.

15. Ibid., p. 93.

16. Clinton, *My Life*, p. 582; Indyk, *Innocent Abroad*, p. 56.

17. David B. Ottaway, *The King's Messenger: Prince Bandar bin Sultan and America's Tangled Relationship with Saudi Arabia* (New York: Walker, 2008), pp. 117–18.

18. Ibid., p. 122.

19. Ibid., p. 137.

20. Joshua Teitelbaum, *Holier than Thou: Saudi Arabia's Islamic Opposition* (Washington: Washington Institute for Near East Policy, 2000), p. 90.

21. Ottaway, *The King's Messenger*, p. 120.

22. Ibid., p. 128.

23. Barbara Slavin, "Officials: U.S. Outed Iranian Spies in 1997," *USA Today*, March 29, 2004.

24. Richard Clarke, *Against All Enemies: Inside America's War on Terrorism* (New York: Free Press, 2004), pp. 120–21, 129.

25. George Tenet, *At the Center of the Storm: My Years at the CIA* (New York: Harper Collins, 2007), p. 124.

26. Suzanne Maloney, *Iran's Political Economy since the Revolution* (Cambridge University Press, 2015), p. 274.

27. Indyk, *Innocent Abroad*, pp. 224–27. Malcolm Byrne, "Secret U.S. Overture to Iran in 1999 Broke Down over Terrorism Allegations," National Security Archive, May 30, 2010, has copies of Clinton's letter and Khatami's response.

28. Ottaway, *The King's Messenger*, p. 131.

29. *United States of America v. Ahmed al Mughassil et al.*, United States District Court, Eastern District of Virginia, Alexandria Division, Criminal No: 01-228-A, Department of Justice, June 2001.

30. Bruce Lawrence, ed., *Messages to the World: The Statements of Osama bin Laden* (London: Verso, 2005), p. 9.

31. Ibid., p. 4.

32. Ibid., pp. 24–25.

33. Clinton, *My Life*, pp. 797–98.

34. Ibid., p. 799.

35. Ibid., p. 803.

36. Michael Scheuer, *Osama Bin Laden* (Oxford University Press, 2011), p. 109.

37. Ottaway, *The King's Messenger*, pp. 134–35; Ted Gup, *The Book of Honor: Covert Lives and Classified Deaths at the CIA* (New York: Doubleday, 2000), pp. 308–17.

38. Elliott Abrams, *Tested by Zion: The Bush Administration and the Israeli-Palestinian Conflict* (Cambridge University Press, 2013), p. 8.

39. Condoleezza Rice, *No Higher Honor: A Memoir of My Years in Washington* (New York: Crown, 2011), p. 50.

40. Ibid., pp. 17, 55.

41. Abrams, *Tested by Zion*, p. 14.

42. Craig Unger, *House of Bush, House of Saud* (New York: Scribner, 2004), p. 189.

43. Ibid., pp. 218, 224.

44. Abrams, *Tested by Zion*, p. 14.

45. Ottaway, *The King's Messenger*, p. 151.

46. Abrams, *Tested by Zion*, p. 8.

47. Ottaway, *The King's Messenger*, p. 149.

48. Abrams, *Tested by Zion*, p. 15.

49. Marwan Muasher, *The Arab Center: The Promise of Moderation* (Yale University Press, 2008), p. 110.

50. Abrams, *Tested by Zion*, p. 15, and Muasher, *The Arab Center*, p. 110.

51. Ottaway, *The King's Messenger*, p. 154.

52. The wedding party was also attended by the ambassadors from Algeria, Bahrain, Egypt, Israel, Lebanon, and India as well as Bandar, Tenet, and numerous friends. There were so many security personnel that the restaurant had to provide a room for them to wait. See Bandar's comment in Ottaway, *The King's Messenger*, p. 154.

53. Muasher, *The Arab Center*, p. 110.

54. "U.S. President Bush's Speech to United Nations," CNN.com, November 10, 2001.

55. Muasher, *The Arab Center*, p. 117. The full text of the Arab peace plan is at pp. 281–82.

56. George W. Bush, *Decision Points* (New York: Crown, 2010), p. 402.

57. Rice, *No Higher Honor*, p. 141.

58. Bush, *Decision Points*, p. 403.

59. Interview with Gamal Helal, June 15, 2016.

60. Abrams, *Tested by Zion*, p. 36.

61. Rice, *No Higher Honor*, p. 144.

62. Bob Woodward, *Plan of Attack* (New York: Simon and Schuster, 2004), p. 116.

63. Ibid., p. 164.

64. Ottaway, *The King's Messenger*, p. 259.

65. Woodward, *Plan of Attack*, pp. 228–30.

66. Ibid., pp. 263–67.

67. Ibid., p. 268. Abdallah said, "Mum is the word."

68. Ibid., p. 348.

69. Ottaway, *The King's Messenger*, p. 215.

70. Ibid., p. 239.

71. Yaniv Barzilai, *102 Days of War: How Osama bin Laden, Al Qaeda, and the Taliban Survived 2001* (Washington: Potomac Books, 2013), p. 2.

72. Bruce Lawrence, ed., *Messages to the World: The Statements of Osama Bin Laden* (London: Verso, 2005), p. 180.

73. The sermon is titled "Among a Band of Knights" and is translated in Lawrence, *Messages to the World*, pp. 186–206.

74. Thomas Small and Jonathan Hacker, *Path of Blood: The Story of al Qaeda's War on the House of Saud* (New York: Overlook Press, 2014), p. 70.

75. Ibid., p. 91.

76. George Tenet, *At the Center of the Storm: My Years at the CIA* (New York: Harper Collins, 2007), p. 248.

77. Nayef, who became crown prince before his death, repeatedly accused the Mossad of manipulating al Qaeda and orchestrating the 9/11 attacks.

78. Small and Hacker, *Path of Blood*, p. 100.

79. Tenet, *At the Center of the Storm*, p. 250.

80. Small and Hacker, *Path of Blood*, p. 396.

81. Ibid., pp. 396–97.

82. Ibid., pp. 310–11.

83. Ibid., pp. 163, 376.

84. Ned Parker, "The Conflict in Iraq: Saudi Role in Insurgency," *Los Angeles Times*, July 15, 2007.

85. Thomas Hegghammer, "Saudi Militants in Iraq: Backgrounds and Recruitment Patterns," Norwegian Defense Research Establishment paper, February 5, 2007.

86. Lawrence, *Messages to the World*, pp. 245–75.

87. "Saudi Religious Leaders Support Sunni Insurgency in Iraq," *Global Issues Report*, January 24, 2007.

88. Small and Hacker, *Path of Blood*, p. 399.

89. Ottaway, *The King's Messenger*, pp. 240–41.

90. Ibid., pp. 263–68.

Chapter Six: Obama and Trump, Abdallah and Salman, 2009 to 2017

1. Martin Indyk, Michael O'Hanlon, and Kenneth Lieberthal, *Bending History: Barack Obama's Foreign Policy* (Brookings Institution Press, 2012), p. 122.

2. Mark Landler, *Alter Egos: Hillary Clinton, Barack Obama, and the Twilight Struggle over American Power* (New York: Random House, 2016), p. 140.

3. Indyk, O'Hanlon, and Lieberthal, *Bending History*, pp. 120–22.

4. "Remarks by the President in Cairo on a New Beginning," June 4, 2009, Cairo University, Cairo, Egypt, White House Office of the Press Secretary, June 4, 2009.

5. Christi Parsons and Mark Silva, "Obama Starts Mideast Tour in Saudi Arabia, 'Where Islam Began,'" *Los Angeles Times*, June 4, 2009, p. 1.

6. Leon Panetta, *Worthy Fights: A Memoir of Leadership in War and Peace* (New York: Penguin, 2014), p. 244.

7. Robert Gates, *Duty: Memoirs of a Secretary at War* (New York: Knopf, 2014), p. 18.

8. Ibid., p. 387.

9. Ibid., pp. 394–97.

10. Panetta, *Worthy Fights*, p. 301.

11. Gates, *Duty*, p. 504.

12. Indyk, O'Hanlon, and Lieberthal, *Bending History*, pp. 147–48.

13. Ibid., p. 150.

14. Hillary Clinton, *Hard Choices* (New York: Simon and Schuster, 2014), pp. 355–56.

15. Indyk, O'Hanlon, and Lieberthal, *Bending History*, p. 154.

16. Clinton, *Hard Choices*, p. 357.

17. Indyk, O'Hanlon, and Lieberthal, *Bending History*, pp. 157–58.

18. Clinton, *Hard Choices*, p. 358.

19. Indyk, O'Hanlon, and Lieberthal, *Bending History*, p. 155.

20. Interview with Ambassador James B. Smith, October 22, 2012.

21. Imab K. Harb, "Oman's Needed Adjustment during the Trump Presidency," Policy Analysis Research Papers, Arab Center Washington, January 18, 2017.

22. "Pakistani Soldiers on Gulf Duty Alert," Paris Intelligence Online, March 31, 2011 (www.intelligenceonline.com).

23. Bruce Riedel, "Saudi Arabia: The Elephant in the Living Room" in Kenneth Pollack and others, *The Arab Awakening: America and the Transformation of the Middle East* (Brookings Institution Press, 2011), p. 163.

24. Ibid.

25. Ibrahim Fraihat, *Unfinished Revolutions: Yemen, Libya, and Tunisia after the Arab Spring* (Yale University Press, 2016), p. 39.

26. Gates, *Duty*, pp. 534–35.

27. Clinton, *Hard Choices*, p. 359.

28. Landler, *Alter Egos*, p. 217.

29. Ivan Angelovski, Miranda Patrucic, and Lawrence Marzouk, "Revealed: The £1bn of Weapons Flowing from Europe to Middle East," *The Guardian*, July 27, 2016.

30. Mark Mazzetti and Ali Younes, "CIA Arms for Syrian Rebels Supplied Black Market, Officials Say," *New York Times*, June 20, 2016.

31. Charles Lister, *The Syrian Jihad: Al Qaeda, the Islamic State and the Evolution of an Insurgency* (London: Hurst, 2016), pp. 106, 111, 137.

32. Rod Norland, "Saudi Arabia Promises to Aid Egyptian Regime," *New York Times*, August 19, 2013.

33. "Saudi King Abdullah Visits Egypt's Sisi," Al Jazeera.com, June 20, 2014.

34. "Saudi King Stops in Cairo to Visit Egypt's Sisi," Reuters.com, June 20, 2014.

35. Chris Zambelis, "To Topple the Throne: Islamic State Sets its Sights on Saudi Arabia," *Terrorism Monitor*, March 6, 2015.

36. Lister, *The Syrian Jihad*, pp. 284–91.

37. Simon Henderso, "Who Will Be the Next King of Saudi Arabia?" Policy Watch 2035, Washington Institute for Near East Policy, Washington, D.C., February 12, 2013.

38. Karen Elliot House, "Uneasy Lies the Head That Wears a Crown: The House of Saud Confronts Its Challenges," Belfer Center, Harvard University, March 2016. See also David Ottaway, "Bandar Out: Mohammad bin Nayef Washington's New Favorite Saudi Prince," *Viewpoints* No. 70, Wilson Center, Washington, D.C., January 2015.

39. Madawi Al-Rasheed, "Who's Next in Line for Saudi Throne? Don't Ask," Al-Monitor, July 1, 2016.

40. David Ignatius, "A 30-Year-Old Saudi Prince Could Jump Start the Kingdom or Drive It off a Cliff," *Washington Post*, June 30, 2016.

41. "Saudi Arabia Warns Trump: Iran Wants to Gain Legitimacy by Reaching Mecca," Al Arabiya, March 16, 2017. See also "Signaling Saudi Arabia: Iranian Support to Yemen's al Houthis," *Critical Threats*, October 12, 2016.

42. Fraihat, *Unfinished Revolutions*, p. 50.

43. Hugh Miles, "Saudi Royal Call for Regime Change in Riyadh," *The Guardian*, September 28, 2015, and Bel Trew, "Saudi Royals Want to Overthrow King and Embrace Democracy," *The Times*, October 1, 2015.

44. David Kirkpatrick, "Saudi Arabia Said to Arrest Suspect in 1996 Khobar Towers Bombing," *New York Times*, August 26, 2015.

45. "King Salman Talks 'Unity' at Egypt's Parliament," Al-Arabiya, April 10, 2016.

46. Prince Turki al Faisal, "Mr. Obama, We Are Not 'Free Riders,' " *Arab News*, March 14, 2016.

47. John Brennan, "CIA's Strategy in the Face of Emerging Challenges: Remarks by CIA Director John O. Brennan," Brookings Institution, July 13, 2016.

48. Christopher M. Blanchard, *Saudi Arabia: Background and U.S. Relations* (Washington: Congressional Research Service, April 22, 2016), p. 39. The $111.624 billion figure is for deals between October 2010 and November 2015.

49. Office of the Press Secretary, "Joint Statement between the Kingdom of Saudi Arabia and the United States of America," White House, May 23, 2017.

50. "The Young and Brash Saudi Crown Prince," *New York Times*, June 23, 2017.

51. "A Shake up in Riyadh: The Tasks Facing the New Saudi Crown Prince," *The Economist*, June 22, 2017.

Chapter Seven: Whither Saudi Arabia

1. Martin Indyk, "The Iraq War Did Not Force Gadaffi's Hand," *Financial Times*, March 9, 2004.

2. Saeed Shafqat, "The Kargil Conflict's Impact on Pakistani Politics and Society," in *Asymmetric Warfare in South Asia: The Causes and Consequences of the Kargil Conflict*, edited by Peter R. Lavoy (Cambridge University Press, 2009), pp. 280–308.

3. Pervez Musharraf, *In the Line of Fire: A Memoir* (New York: Free Press, 2006), pp. 268–90.

4. Jonathan Ferziger and Peter Waldman, "How Do Israel's Tech Firms Do Business in Saudi Arabia? Very Quietly," *Bloomberg Businessweek*, February 2, 2017.

5. "Saudi Government Distances Itself from Israel Visit," *Dawn*, July 28, 2016.

6. Martin Chulov, "Saudi Crown Prince's Ascendancy Gives Hope of Reform—But It May Be Premature," *The Guardian*, June 22, 2017.

7. Madawi al Rashid, "Caught Between Religion and State: Women in Saudi Arabia," in *Saudi Arabia in Transition: Insights on Social, Political, Economic and Religious Change*, edited by Bernard Haykal, Thomas Hegghammer, and Stephane Lacroix (Cambridge University Press, 2015), p. 301.

8. Ibid., p. 295.

9. Ibid., p. 299.

10. "Over Half Million Saudi Men Engaged in Polygamy, Report Shows," *Al Arabiya English*, October 27, 2016.

11. James Dorsey, "Sport, Culture and Entertainment: Driving Tricky Saudi Change," *International Policy Digest*, April 10, 2017.

12. Daniel Benjamin, "Threat Assessment," *Time*, October 6, 2014.

13. John Brennan, "CIA's Strategy in the Face of Emerging Challenges: Remarks by John Brennan," Brookings Institution, Washington, July 13, 2016, p. 10 (www.brookings.edu/wp-content/uploads/2016/06/20160713_cia_brennan_transcript.pdf).

14. Ibid.

15. "An Unholy Pact: The Accession of King Salman in Saudi Arabia," *The Economist*, January 31, 2015.

16. "Looking Forward in Anger, Briefing Arab Youth," *The Economist*, August 6, 2016.

17. David Ottaway, "Saudi Arabia's Race against Time," Middle East Program Occasional Papers Series, Summer 2012, Woodrow Wilson Center, Washington, D.C., p. 5.

18. Karen Elliot House, "Uneasy Lies the Head That Wears a Crown: The House of Saudi Confronts Its Challenges," Harvard Kennedy School Belfer Center, Senior Fellow paper, March 2016, p. 10.

19. Ibid., p. 13.

20. Ishaan Tharoor, "Saudi Arabia Passes Russia as World's Third Largest Military Spender," *Washington Post*, April 5, 2016.

21. "Quantifying a 'Taboo' Subject: Saudi Arabia Counts the Cost of the Yemen War," *Gulf States News* 40, no. 1,025 (November 3, 2016).

22. Bruce Riedel, "Revolution in Riyadh," in *Big Bets & Black Swans: A Presidential Briefing Book*, edited by Martin Indyk, Tanvi Madan, and Thomas Wrights (Brookings Institution Press, 2013), (www.brookings.edu/wp-content/uploads/2016/06/big-bets-and-black-swans-a-presidential-briefing-book-20.pdf).

Appendix

1. Report of the U.S. Senate Committee on Intelligence and U.S. House Permanent Select Committee on Intelligence, Joint Inquiry into Intelligence Community Activities Before and After the Terrorist Attacks of September 11, 2001, December 2002, p. 415.

2. Ibid.

3. National Commission on Terrorist Attacks upon the United States, Monograph on Terrorist Financing, Staff Report to the Commission, 2004.

4. Bruce Hoffman, Edwin Meese, and Timothy Roemer, The FBI: Protecting the Homeland in the 21st Century, 9/11 Review Commission, Report to the Director of the FBI, March 2015.

5. Full Transcript of Al Arabiya's Interview with CIA director John Brennan, *Al Arabiya*, June 12, 2016.

Selected Bibliography

Allen, Charles. *God's Terrorists: The Wahhabi Cult and the Hidden Roost of Modern Jihad*. London: Little, Brown, 2006.

Alpher, Yossi. *Periphery: Israel's Search for Middle East Allies*. London: Rowman and Littlefield, 2015.

Ashton, Nigel. *King Hussein of Jordan: A Political Life*. Yale University Press, 2008.

Atwan, Abdel Bari. *After Bin Laden: Al Qaeda, the Next Generation*. London: New Press, 2012.

Badeeb, Saeed. *The Saudi-Egyptian Conflict over North Yemen, 1962–1970*. Boulder, Colo.: Westview Press, 1986.

———. *Saudi-Iranian Relations, 1932–1982*. London: Centre for Arab and Iranian Studies, 1993.

Baer, Robert. *Sleeping with the Devil: How Washington Sold Our Soul for Saudi Crude*. New York: Three Rivers Press, 2003.

bin Sultan, Khalid, and Patrick Seale. *Desert Warrior: A Personal View of the Gulf War by the Joint Forces Commander.* New York: HarperCollins, 1995.

Bronson, Rachel. *Thicker than Oil: America's Uneasy Partnership with Saudi Arabia.* Oxford University Press, 2006.

Catherwood, Christopher. *Churchill's Folly: How Winston Churchill Created Modern Iraq.* New York: Basic Books, 2007.

Cigar, Norman. *Saudi Arabia and Nuclear Weapons.* London: Routledge, 2016.

Clarke, Richard. *Against All Enemies: Inside America's War on Terror.* London: Free Press, 2004.

Cole, Steve. *The Bin Ladens: An Arabian Family in the American Century.* New York: Penguin, 2008.

Commins, David. *The Wahhabi Mission and Saudi Arabia.* London: Taurus, 2006.

Cooper, Andrew Scott. *The Oil Kings: How the U.S., Iran and Saudi Arabia Changed the Balance of Power in the Middle East.* New York: Simon and Schuster, 2011.

Crawford, Michael. *Ibn 'Abd al-Wahhab.* London: Oneworld, 2014.

Darlow, Michael, and Barbara Bray. *Ibn Saud: The Desert Warrior Who Created the Kingdom of Saudi Arabia.* New York: Skyhorse, 2012.

Delang-Bas, Natana J. *Wahhabi Islam from Revival and Reform to Global Jihad.* New York: Oxford, 2004.

Djerejian, Edward P. *Danger and Opportunity: An American Ambassador's Journey through the Middle East.* New York: Simon and Schuster, 2008.

Filiu, Jean Pierre. *Apocalypse in Islam.* University of California Press, 2011.

Gibson, Bryan R. *Sold Out? US Foreign Policy, Iraq, the Kurds and the Cold War.* New York: Palgrave Macmillan, 2015.

Gold, Dore. *Hatred's Kingdom: How Saudi Arabia Supports the New Global Terrorism.* Washington: Regnery Publishing, 2003.

Hart-Davis, Duff. *The War That Never Was.* London: Arrow Books, 2011.

Haykal, Bernard, Thomas Hegghammer, and Stephane Lacroix, ed. *Saudi Arabia in Transition.* Cambridge University Press, 2015.

Hegghammer, Thomas. *Jihad in Saudi Arabia: Violence and Pan-Islamism since 1979.* Cambridge University Press, 2010.

Hegghammer, Thomas, and Stephanie Lacroix. *The Meccan Rebellion: The Story of Juhayman al Utabi Revisited.* Bristol: Amal Press, 2011.

Heikal, Mohamed. *Illusions of Triumph: An Arab View of the Gulf War.* London: HarperCollins, 1993.

————. *The Road to Ramadan*. New York: Quadrangle, 1975.

Hourani, Albert. *A History of the Arab Peoples*. Harvard University Press, 1991.

House, Karen Elliot. *On Saudi Arabia: Its People, Past, Religion, Fault Lines and Future*. New York: Knopf, 2012.

————. *Uneasy Lies the Head That Wears a Crown*. Belfer Center for Science and International Affairs, Harvard University, 2016.

Jordan, Robert W., with Steve Fiffer. *Desert Diplomat: Inside Saudi Arabia Following 9/11*. Lincoln, Neb.: Potomac Books, 2015.

Kechichian, Joseph A. *Faysal: Saudi Arabia's King for All Seasons*. University of Florida Press, 2008.

————. *Succession in Saudi Arabia*. New York: Palgrave, 2001.

Lacey, Robert. *Inside the Kingdom: Kings, Clerics, Modernists, Terrorists and the Struggle for Saudi Arabia*. London: Arrow Books, 2009.

Lippman, Thomas. *Arabian Knight: Colonel Bill Eddy, USMC and the Rise of American Power in the Middle East*. Vista, Calif.: Selwa Press, 2008.

Matthiessen, Toby. *The Other Saudis: Shiism, Dissent and Sectarianism*. Cambridge University Press, 2015.

————. *Sectarian Gulf: Bahrain, Saudi Arabia and the Arab Spring That Wasn't*. Stanford University Press, 2013.

Miller, Aaron David. *Search for Security: Saudi Arabian Oil and American Foreign Policy, 1939–1949*. University of North Carolina Press, 1980.

Muasher, Marwan. *The Arab Center: The Promise of Moderation*. Yale University Press, 2008.

Murray, Williamson, and Kevin M. Woods. *The Iran-Iraq War: A Military and Strategic History*. Cambridge University Press, 2014.

Naimi, Ali Al-. *Out of the Desert: My Journey from Nomadic Bedouin to the Heart of Global Oil*. London: Penguin, 2016.

Ochsenwald, William. *The Hijaz Railroad*. University of Virginia, 1980.

Ottaway, David B. *The King's Messenger: Prince Bandar bin Sultan and America's Tangled Relationship with Saudi Arabia*. New York: Walker, 2008.

Partrick, Neil. *Saudi Arabian Foreign Policy: Conflict and Cooperation*. London: I. B. Tauris, 2016.

Picco, Giandomenico. *Man without a Gun: One Diplomat's Secret Struggle to Free the Hostages, Fight Terrorism, and End a War*. New York: Times Books, 1999.

Posner, Gerald. *Secrets of the Kingdom: The Inside Story of the Saudi-U.S. Connection*. New York: Random House, 2005.

Quandt, William. *Camp David: Peacemaking and Politics*. Brookings Institution Press, 1986.

Rasheed, Madawi Al-. *A History of Saudi Arabia*. Cambridge University Press, 2002.

Rashid, Nasser Ibrahim, and Esber Ibrahim Shaheen. *King Fahd and Saudi Arabia's Great Evolution*. Joplin, Mo.: International Institute for Technology, 1987.

Rogan, Eugene. *The Arabs: A History*. New York: Basic Books, 2009.

———. *The Fall of the Ottomans: The Great War in the Middle East*. New York: Basic Books, 2015.

Safran, Nadav. *Saudi Arabia: The Ceaseless Quest for Security*. Cornell University Press, 1988.

Sander, Nestor. *Ibn Saud: King by Conquest*. London: Selwa Press, 2008.

Sardar, Ziauddin. *Mecca: The Sacred City*. New York: Bloomsbury, 2014.

Scheuer, Michael. *Osama bin Laden*. Oxford University Press, 2011.

Scott-Clark, Cathy, and Adrian Levy. *The Exile: The Stunning Inside Story of Osama bin Laden and al Qaeda in Flight*. New York: Bloomsbury Press, 2017.

Simpson, William. *The Prince: The Secret Story of the World's Most Intriguing Royal, Prince Bandar bin Sultan*. New York: HarperCollins, 2006.

Small, Thomas, and Jonathan Hacker. *Path of Blood: The Story of al Qaeda's War on the House of Saud*. New York: Overlook Press, 2015.

Teitelbaum, Joseph. *Holier than Thou: Saudi Arabia's Islamic Opposition*. Washington: Washington Institute for Near East Policy, 2000.

Trofimov, Yaroslav. *The Siege of Mecca: The Forgotten Uprising in Islam's Holiest Shrine and the Birth of al Qaeda*. New York: Doubleday, 2007.

Unger, Craig. *House of Bush, House of Saud: The Secret Relationship between the World's Two Most Powerful Dynasties*. New York: Scribner, 2004.

Valentine, Simon Ross. *Force and Fanaticism: Wahhabism in Saudi Arabia and Beyond*. London: Hurst, 2015.

Vassiliev, Alexei. *The History of Saudi Arabia*. London: Saqi Books, 2013.

———. *King Faisal of Saudi Arabia: Personality, Faith and Times*. London: Saqi Books, 2015.

Woods, Kevin M. *The Mother of All Battles*. Annapolis: Naval Institute Press, 2008.

Yergin, Daniel. *The Prize: The Epic Quest for Oil, Money and Politics*. New York: Simon and Schuster, 1991.

Yizraeli, Sarah. *The Remaking of Saudi Arabia: The Struggle between King Sa'ud and Crown Prince Faysal, 1953–1962*. Tel Aviv University, 1997.

Index

INSIDE
BENCHLEY

While thumbing through some old snow which had accumulated in the attic last winter, I came, quite by accident, upon ten (10) or so volumes of prose works which I had dashed off during my career as a journalist (1915—7:45 P.M.).

(Signed) ROBERT BENCHLEY

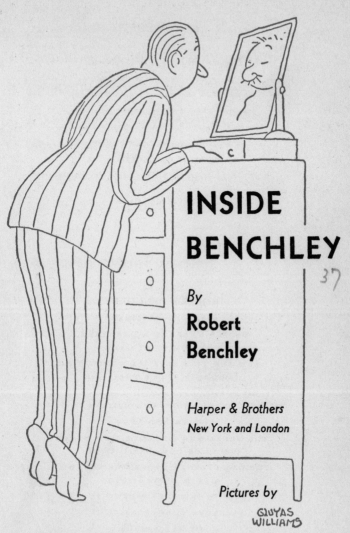

INSIDE
BENCHLEY

By
**Robert
Benchley**

Harper & Brothers
New York and London

Pictures by
GLUYAS
WILLIAMS

INSIDE BENCHLEY

Books by
ROBERT BENCHLEY

Table of Contents

vi

INSIDE
BENCHLEY

The Social Life of
the Newt

IT IS not generally known that the newt, although one of the smallest of our North American animals, has an extremely happy home-life. It
is just one of those facts which never get bruited
about.

*Since that time I have practically lived among the
newts*

I first became interested in the social phenomena
of newt life early in the spring of 1913, shortly
after I had finished my researches in sexual differentiation among ameba. Since that time I have
practically lived among newts, jotting down obser-
vations, making lantern-slides, watching them in
their work and in their play (and you may rest assured that the little rogues have their play—as who
does not?) until, from much lying in a research
posture on my stomach, over the inclosure in which
they were confined, I found myself developing
what I feared might be rudimentary creepers. And

1

so, late this autumn, I stood erect and walked into my house, where I immediately set about the compilation of the notes I had made.

So much for the non-technical introduction. The remainder of this article bids fair to be fairly scientific.

In studying the more intimate phases of newt life, one is chiefly impressed with the methods by means of which the males force their attentions upon the females, with matrimony as an object. For the newt is, after all, only a newt, and has his weaknesses just as any of the rest of us. And I, for one, would not have it different. There is little enough fun in the world as it is.

The peculiar thing about a newt's courtship is its restraint. It is carried on, at all times, with a minimum distance of fifty paces (newt measure) between the male and the female. Some of the bolder males may now and then attempt to overstep the bounds of good sportsmanship and crowd in to forty-five paces, but such tactics are frowned upon by the Rules Committee. To the eye of an uninitiated observer, the pair might be dancing a few of the more open figures of the minuet.

The means employed by the males to draw the attention and win the affection of those of the opposite sex (females) are varied and extremely strategic. Until the valuable researches by Strudlehoff in 1887 (in his *"Entwickelungsmechanik"*) no one had been able to ascertain just what it was that the male newt did to make the female see anything in

2

him worth throwing herself away on. It had been observed that the most personally unattractive newt could advance to within fifty paces of a female of his acquaintance and, by some *coup d'œil*, bring her to a point where she would, in no uncertain terms, indicate her willingness to go through with the marriage ceremony at an early date.

It was Strudlehoff who discovered, after watching several thousand courting newts under a magnifying lens (questionable taste on his part, without doubt, but all is fair in pathological love) that the male, during the courting season (the season opens on the tenth of March and extends through the following February, leaving about ten days for general overhauling and redecorating), gives forth a strange, phosphorescent glow from the center of his highly colored dorsal crest, somewhat similar in effect to the flash of a diamond scarf-pin in a red necktie. This glow, according to Strudlehoff, so fascinates the female with its air of elegance and indication of wealth, that she immediately falls a victim to its lure.

But the little creature, true to her sex-instinct, does not at once give evidence that her morale has been shattered. She affects a coyness and lack of interest, by hitching herself sideways along the bottom of the aquarium, with her head turned over her right shoulder away from the swain. A trained ear might even detect her whistling in an indifferent manner.

The male, in the meantime, is flashing his

3

gleamer frantically two blocks away and is performing all sorts of attractive feats, calculated to bring the lady newt to terms. I have seen a male, in the stress of his handicap courtship, stand on his forefeet, gesticulating in amorous fashion with his hind feet in the air. Franz Ingehalt, in his "Über Weltschmerz des Newt," recounts having observed a distinct and deliberate undulation of the body, beginning with the shoulders and ending at the filament of the tail, which might well have been the origin of what is known to-day in scientific circles as "the shimmy." The object seems to be the same, except that in the case of the newt, it is the male who is the active agent.

In order to test the power of observation in the male during these manœuvers, I carefully removed the female, for whose benefit he was undulating, and put in her place, in slow succession, another (but less charming) female, a paper-weight of bronze shaped like a newt, and, finally, a common rubber eraser. From the distance at which the courtship was being carried on, the male (who was, it must be admitted, a bit near-sighted congenitally) was unable to detect the change in personnel, and continued, even in the presence of the rubber eraser, to gyrate and undulate in a most conscientious manner, still under the impression that he was making a conquest.

At last, worn out by his exertions, and disgusted at the meagerness of the reaction on the eraser, he gave a low cry of rage and despair and staggered to a nearby pan containing barley-water, from which he proceeded to drink himself into a gross stupor.

Thus, little creature, did your romance end, and who shall say that its ending was one whit less tragic than that of Camille? Not I, for one. . . . In fact, the two cases are not at all analogous.

And now that we have seen how wonderfully Nature works in the fulfilment of her laws, even among her tiniest creatures, let us study for a minute a cross-section of the community-life of the newt. It is a life full of all kinds of exciting adventure, from weaving nests to crawling about in the sun and catching insect larvæ and crustaceans. The newt's day is practically never done, largely because the insect larvæ multiply three million times as fast as the newt can possibly catch and eat them. And it takes the closest kind of community teamwork in the newt colony to get things anywhere near cleaned up by nightfall.

It is early morning, and the workers are just appearing hurrying to the old log which is to be the scene of their labors. What a scampering! What a bustle! Ah, little scamperers! Ah, little bustlers! How lucky you are, and how wise! You work long hours, without pay, for the sheer love of working. An ideal existence, I'll tell the scientific world.

Over here on the right of the log are the Master Draggers. Of all the newt workers, they are the most futile, which is high praise indeed. Come, let us look closer and see what it is that they are doing.

The one in the lead is dragging a bit of gurry

out from the water and up over the edge into the sunlight. Following him, in single file, come the rest of the Master Draggers. They are not dragging anything, but are sort of helping the leader by crowding against him and eating little pieces out of the filament of his tail.

And now they have reached the top. The leader, by dint of much leg-work, has succeeded in dragging his prize to the ridge of the log.

The little workers, reaching the goal with their precious freight, are now giving it over to the Master Pushers, who have been waiting for them in the sun all this while. The Master Pushers' work is soon accomplished, for it consists simply in pushing the piece of gurry over the other side of the log until it falls with a splash into the water, where it is lost.

This part of their day's task finished, the tiny toilers rest, clustered together in a group, waving their heads about from side to side, as who should say: "There—that's done!" And so it *is* done, my little Master Draggers and my little Master Pushers, and *well* done, too. Would that my own work were as clean-cut and as satisfying.

And so it goes. Day in and day out, the busy army of newts go on making the world a better place in which to live. They have their little trials and tragedies, it is true, but they also have their fun, as any one can tell by looking at a logful of sleeping newts on a hot summer day.

And, after all, what more has life to offer?

"Coffee, Megg and Ilk, Please"

GIVE me any topic in current sociology, such as "The Working Classes *vs.* the Working Classes," or "Various Aspects of the Minimum Wage," and I can talk on it with considerable confidence. I have no hesitation in putting the Workingman, as such, in his place among the hewers of wood and drawers of water—a necessary adjunct to our modern life, if you will, but of little real consequence in the big events of the world.

But when I am confronted, in the flesh, by the "close up" of a workingman with any vestige of authority, however small, I immediately lose my perspective—and also my poise. I become servile, almost cringing. I feel that my modest demands on his time may, unless tactfully presented, be offensive to him and result in something, I haven't been able to analyze just what, perhaps public humiliation.

For instance, whenever I enter an elevator in a public building I am usually repeating to myself the number of the floor at which I wish to alight. The elevator man gives the impression of being a social worker, filling the job just for that day to help out the regular elevator man, and I feel that the least I can do is to show him that I know what's what. So I don't tell him my floor number as soon as I get in. Only elderly ladies do that. I keep whispering it over to myself, thinking to tell it to the world when the proper time comes. But then the big question arises—what is the proper time? If I want to get out at the eighteenth floor, should I tell him at the sixteenth or the seventeenth? I decide on the sixteenth and frame my lips to say, "Eighteen out, please." (Just why one should have to add the word "out" to the number of the floor is not clear. When you say "eighteen" the obvious construction of the phrase is that you want to get *out* at the eighteenth floor, not that you want to get *in* there or be let down through the flooring of the car at that point. However, you'll find the most sophisticated elevator riders, namely, messenger boys, always adding the word "out," and it is well to follow what the messenger boys do in such matters if you don't want to go wrong.)

So there I am, mouthing the phrase, "Eighteen out, please," as we shoot past the tenth—eleventh —twelfth—thirteenth floors. Then I begin to get panicky. Supposing that I should forget my lines! Or that I should say them too soon! Or too late! We are now at the fifteenth floor. I clear my throat. Sixteen! Hoarsely I murmur, "Eighteen out." But at the same instant a man with a cigar in his mouth bawls, "Seventeen out!" and I am not heard. The car stops at seventeen, and I step confidentially up to the elevator man and repeat, with an attempt at nonchalance, "Eighteen out, please." But just as I

8

At the same instant a man with a cigar in his mouth bawls, "Seventeen out!"

say the words the door clangs, drowning out my request, and we shoot up again. I make another attempt, but have become inarticulate and succeed only in making a noise like a man strangling. And by this time we are at the twenty-first floor with no relief in sight. Shattered, I retire to the back of the car and ride up to the roof and down again, trying to look as if I worked in the building and had to do it, however boresome it might be. On the return trip I don't care what the elevator man thinks of me, and tell him at every floor that I, personally, am going to get off at the eighteenth, no matter what any one else in the car does. I am dictatorial enough when I am riled. It is only in the opening rounds that I hug the ropes.

My timidity when dealing with minor officials strikes me first in my voice. I have any number of witnesses who will sign statements to the effect that my voice changed about twelve years ago, and that in ordinary conversation my tone, if not especially virile, is at least consistent and even. But when, for instance, I give an order at a soda fountain, if the clerk overawes me at all, my voice breaks into a yodel that makes the phrase "Coffee, egg and milk" a pretty snatch of song, but practically worthless as an order.

If the soda counter is lined with customers and the clerks so busy tearing up checks and dropping them into the toy banks that they seem to resent any call on their drink-mixing abilities, I might just as well save time and go home and shake up an egg and milk for myself, for I shall not be waited on until every one else has left the counter and they are putting the nets over the caramels for the night. I know that. I've gone through it too many times to be deceived.

For there is something about the realization that I must shout out my order ahead of some one else that absolutely inhibits my shouting powers. I will stand against the counter, fingering my ten-cent check and waiting for the clerk to come near enough for me to tell him what I want, while, in the meantime, ten or a dozen people have edged up next to me and given their orders, received their drinks and gone away. Every once in a while I catch a clerk's eye and lean forward murmuring, "Coffee"

*Placing both hands on the counter, I emit what
promises to be a perfect bellow*

—but that is as far as I get. Some one else has shoved his way in and shouted, "Coca-Cola," and I draw back to get out of the way of the vichy spray. (Incidentally, the men who push their way in and footfault on their orders always ask for "Coca-Cola." Somehow it seems like painting the lily for them to order a nerve tonic.)

I then decide that the thing for me to do is to speak up loud and act brazenly. So I clear my throat, and, placing both hands on the counter, emit what promises to be a perfect bellow: "COFFEE, MEGG AND ILK." This makes just about the impression you'd think it would, both on my neighbors and the clerk, especially as it is delivered in a tone which ranges from a rich barytone to a rather rasping tenor. At this I withdraw and go to the other end of the counter, where I can begin life over again with a clean slate.

Here, perhaps, I am suddenly confronted by an impatient clerk who is in a perfect frenzy to grab my check and tear it into bits to drop in his box. "What's yours?" he flings at me. I immediately lose my memory and forget what it was that I wanted. But here is a man who has a lot of people to wait on and who doubtless gets paid according to the volume of business he brings in. I have no right to interfere with his work. There is a big man edging his way beside me who is undoubtedly going to shout "Coca-Cola" in half a second. So I beat him to it and say, "Coca-Cola," which is probably the last drink in the store that I want to buy. But it is the only thing that I can remember at the moment, in spite of the fact that I have been thinking all morning how a coffee, egg and milk would taste. I suppose that one of the psychological principles of advertising is to so hammer the name of your product into the mind of the timid buyer that when he is confronted by a brusk demand for an order he can't think of anything else to say, whether he wants it or not.

This dread of offending the minor official or appearing at a disadvantage before a clerk extends even to my taking nourishment. I don't think that I have ever yet gone into a restaurant and ordered exactly what I wanted. If only the waiter would give me the card and let me alone for, say, fifteen minutes, as he does when I want to get him to bring me my check, I could work out a meal along the lines of what I like. But when he stands over me, with disgust clearly registered on his face, I order the thing I like least and consider myself lucky to get out of it with so little disgrace.

And yet I have no doubt that if one could see him in his family life the Workingman is just an ordinary person like the rest of us. He is probably not at all as we think of him in our dealings with him—a harsh, dictatorial, intolerant autocrat, but rather a kindly soul who likes nothing better than to sit by the fire with his children and read.

And he would probably be the first person to scoff at the idea that he could frighten me.

14

Political Parties
and Their Growth

1. *Introductory Essay*

IT WAS Taine (of "Taine Goin' to Rain No More") who said: "Democracies defeat themselves." Perhaps I haven't got that quotation right. It doesn't seem to mean much.

However, my point—and I am sure Taine's point, if he were here to make it—is that under the system of government known as a democracy, or, as it is sometimes known, the *Laissez-Faire* system (1745-1810), the ratio of increase in the population will eventually outstrip the ratio of increase in wheat production and then where will we be? Although this theory is generally credited to Malthus, I am not sure that I didn't state it before him. I certainly remember saying it when I was very young.

In writing a history of the political parties of the United States (to which this is the introductory essay and possibly the last chapter as well) one must bear constantly in mind the fact that there are two separate and distinct parties, the Republicans (a clever combination of two Latin words, *res* and *publicæ*, meaning "things of the public") and the Democrats (from the Greek *demos*, meaning something which I will look up before this goes to the

15

printer's). The trick comes in telling which is which.

During the early years of our political history the Republican Party was the Democratic Party, or, if you chose, the Democratic Party was the Republican Party. This led naturally to a lot of confusion, especially in the Democratic Party's getting the Republican Party's mail; so it was decided to call the Republicans "Democrats" and be done with it. The Federalist Party (then located at what is now the corner of Broad and Walnut streets and known as "The Swedish Nightingale") became, through the process of Natural Selection and a gradual dropping-off of its rudimentary tail, the Republican Party as we know it today. This makes, as prophesied earlier in this article, *two* parties, the Republicans and the Democrats. As a general rule, Republicans are more blonde than Democrats.

Now that we have cleared up the matter of the early confusion in names, it remains for us simply to trace the growth of the party platforms from their original sources to their present-day clearly defined and characteristic chaos. This will involve quite a bit of very dull statistical matter and talk about Inflation and Nullification, which will be enlivened by comical stories and snatches of current songs of the period. In fact, talk about Inflation and Nullification may be omitted entirely. It will also be necessary to note the rise and fall of the minor political parties, such as the Free Soil Party, the Mugwumps, the St. Louis Cardinals and Tom ("Rum-Romanism-and-Rebellion") Heflin. This

16

will not be much fun either. As a matter of fact, in outlining the subject matter of this history the thought has come to me that it shapes up as a pretty dry book and I am wondering if perhaps I haven't made a mistake in undertaking it. . . . Oh, well, we'll see.

In compiling these data and writing the book I have been aided immeasurably by the following colleagues, to whom I take this opportunity of expressing my warmest thanks (the warmest thanks on a February 9th since 1906, according to the Weather Bureau atop the Whitehall Building): B. S. Aal, Raymond Aalbue, Aalders Bros., A. C. Aalholm, Alex Aaron, the Aar-Jay Bed-Light Co., Henry W. Aarts, Theo. T. Aarup, Charles Aba, M. M. Abajian, B. Abadessa (Miss), Abbamonte & Frinchini (shoe reprng.) and Lewis Browne Zzyd.

I also wish to thank Dr. Hartmann Weydig for the loan of his interesting collection of shells, without which I would have had nothing to do when I was not writing the book. THE AUTHOR.

BIBLIOGRAPHY

"Political Parties and Their Growth, with a Key to the Calories." Robert Benchley. (Life Pub. Co.)

"Ivanhoe." Sir Walter Scott. (Ginn & Co.)

"Fifty Cocktail Recipes, with Directions for Swallowing." A. M. Herz. (Doubleday-Doran-Doubleday-Doran-Doubleday-Doran-Boom!)

"An Old-Fashioned Girl." Louisa M. Alcott. (Vir Pub. Co.)

And countless back-numbers of *Harper's Round Table*.

Call for
Mr. Kenworthy!

A GREAT many people have wondered to themselves, in print, just where the little black laundry-studs go after they have been yanked from the shirt. Others pass this by as inconsequential, but are concerned over the ultimate disposition of all the pencil stubs that are thrown away. Such futile rumination is all well enough for those who like it. As for me, give me a big, throbbing question like this: "Who are the people that one hears being paged in hotels? Are they real people or are they decoys? And if they are real people, what are they being paged for?"

Now, there's something vital to figure out. And the best of it is that it *can* be figured out by the simple process of following the page to see whether he ever finds any one.

In order that no expense should be spared, I picked out a hotel with poor service, which means that it was an expensive hotel. It was so expensive that all you could hear was the page's voice as he walked by you; his footfalls made no noise in the extra heavy Bokhara. It was just a mingling of floating voices, calling for "Mr. Bla-bla, Mr. Schwer-a-a, Mr. Twa-a-a."

Out of this wealth of experimental material I

Sometimes that was the only name he would call for mile upon mile

picked a boy with a discouraged voice like Wallace Eddinger's, who seemed to be saying "I'm calling these names—because that's my job—if I wasn't calling these—I'd be calling out cash totals in an honor system lunchery—but if any one should ever answer to one of these names—I'd have a poor spell."

Allowing about fifteen feet distance between us for appearance's sake, I followed him through the lobby. He had a bunch of slips in his hand and from these he read the names of the pagees.

"Call for Mr. Kenworthy—Mr. Shriner—Mr. Bodkin—Mr. Blevitch—Mr. Kenworthy—Mr. Bodkin—Mr. Kenworthy—Mr. Shriner—call for Mr. Kenworthy—Mr. Blevitch—Mr. Kenworthy."

Mr. Kenworthy seemed to be standing about a 20 per cent better chance of being located than any of the other contestants. Probably the boy was of a romantic temperament and liked the name. Sometimes that was the only name he would call for mile upon mile. It occurred to me that perhaps Mr. Kenworthy was the only one wanted, and that the other names were just put in to make it harder, or to give body to the thing.

But when we entered the bar the youth shifted his attack. The name of Kenworthy evidently had begun to cloy. He was fed up on romance and wanted something substantial, homely, perhaps, but substantial.

So he dropped Kenworthy and called: "Mr.

21

Blevitch. Call for Mr. Blevitch—Mr. Shriner—Mr. Bodkin—Mr. Blevitch ——"

But even this subtle change of tactics failed to net him a customer. We had gone through the main lobby, along the narrow passage lined with young men waiting on sofas for young women who would be forty minutes late, through the grill, and now had crossed the bar, and no one had raised even an eyebrow. No wonder the boy's voice sounded discouraged.

As we went through one of the lesser dining-rooms, the dining-room that seats a lot of heavy men in business suits holding cigarettes, who lean over their plates the more confidentially to converse with their blond partners, in this dining-room the plaintive call drew fire. One of the men in business suits, who was at a table with another man and two women, lifted his head when he heard the sound of names being called.

"Boy!" he said, and waved like a traffic officer signaling, "Come!"

Eagerly the page darted forward. Perhaps this was Mr. Kenworthy! Or better yet, Mr. Blevitch.

"Anything here for Studz?" said the man in the business suit, when he was sure that enough people were listening.

"No, sir," sighed the boy. "Mr. Blevitch, Mr. Kenworthy, Mr. Shriner, Mr. Bodkin?" he suggested, hopefully.

"Naw," replied the man, and turned to his asso-

"Anything here for Studz?"

ciates with an air of saying: "Rotten service here —just think of it, no call for me!"

On we went again. The boy was plainly skeptical. He read his lines without feeling. The management had led him into this; all he could do was to take it with as good grace as possible.

He slid past the coat-room girl at the exit (no small accomplishment in itself) and down a corridor, disappearing through a swinging door at the end. I was in no mood to lose out on the finish after following so far, and I dashed after him.

The door led into a little alcove and another palpitating door at the opposite end showed me where he had gone. Setting my jaw for no particular reason, I pushed my way through.

At first, like the poor olive merchant in the

23

Arabian Nights I was blinded by the glare of lights and the glitter of glass and silver. Oh, yes, and by the snowy whiteness of the napery, too. "By the napery of the neck" wouldn't be a bad line to get off a little later in the story. I'll try it.

At any rate, it was but the work of a minute for me to realize that I had entered by a service entrance into the grand dining-room of the establishment, where, if you are not in evening dress, you are left to munch bread and butter until you starve to death and are carried out with your heels dragging, like the uncouth lout that you are. It was, if I may be allowed the phrase, a galaxy of beauty, with every one dressed up like the pictures. And I had entered 'way up front, by the orchestra.

Now, mind you, I am not ashamed of my gray suit. I like it, and my wife says that I haven't had anything so becoming for a long time. But in it I didn't check up very strong against the rest of the boys in the dining-room. As a gray suit it is above reproach. As a garment in which to appear single-handed through a trapdoor before a dining-room of well dressed Middle Westerners it was a fizzle from start to finish. Add to this the items that I had to snatch a brown soft hat from my head when I found out where I was, which caused me to drop the three evening papers I had tucked under my arm, and you will see why my up-stage entrance was the signal for the impressive raising of several dozen eyebrows, and why the captain approached me just exactly as one man approaches another when he is going to throw him out.

(Blank space for insertion of "napery of neck" line, if desired. Choice optional with reader.)

I saw that anything that I might say would be used against me, and left him to read the papers I had dropped. One only lowers one's self by having words with a servitor.

Gradually I worked my way back through the swinging doors to the main corridor and rushed down to the regular entrance of the grand dining-salon, to wait there until my quarry should emerge. Suppose he should find all of his consignees in this dining-room! I could not be in at the death then, and would have to falsify my story to make any kind of ending at all. And that would never do.

Once in a while I would catch the scent, when, from the humming depths of the dining-room, I could hear a faint "Call for Mr. Kenworthy" rising above the click of the oyster shells and the soft crackling of the "potatoes Julienne" one against another. So I knew that he had not failed me, and that if I had faith and waited long enough he would come back.

And, sure enough, come back he did, and without a name lost from his list. I felt like cheering when I saw his head bobbing through the mêlée of waiters and 'bus-boys who were busy putting clean plates on the tables and then taking them off again in eight seconds to make room for more clean plates. Of all discouraging existences I can imagine none worse than that of an eternally clean plate. There can be no sense of accomplishment, no glow of duty done, in simply being placed before a man and then taken away again. It must be almost as bad as paging a man who you are sure is not in the hotel.

The futility of the thing had already got on the page's nerves, and in a savage attempt to wring a little pleasure out of the task he took to welding the names, grafting a syllable of one to a syllable of another, such as "Call for Mr. Kenbodkin—Mr. Shrineworthy—Mr. Blevitcher."

This gave us both amusement for a little while, but your combinations are limited in a thing like that, and by the time the grill was reached he was saying the names correctly and with a little more assurance.

It was in the grill that the happy event took place. Mr. Shriner, the one of whom we expected least, suddenly turned up at a table alone. He was a quiet man and not at all worked up over his unexpected honor. He signaled the boy with one hand and went on taking soup with the other, and learned, without emotion, that he was wanted on the telephone. He even made no move to leave his meal to answer the call, and when last seen he was adding pepper with one hand and taking soup with the other. I suspect that he was a "plant," or a plainclothes house detective, placed there on purpose to deceive me.

We had been to every nook of the hotel by this

time, except the writing-room, and, of course, no one would ever look there for patrons of the hotel. Seeing that the boy was about to totter, I went up and spoke to him. He continued to totter, thinking, perhaps, that I was Mr. Kenworthy, his long-lost beau-ideal. But I spoke kindly to him and offered him a piece of chocolate almond-bar, and soon, in true reporter fashion, had wormed his secret from him before he knew what I was really after.

The thing I wanted to find out was, of course, just what the average is of replies to one paging trip. So I got around it in this manner: offering him another piece of chocolate almond-bar, I said, slyly: "Just what is the average number of replies to one paging trip?"

I think that he had suspected something at first, but this question completely disarmed him, and, leaning against an elderly lady patron, he told me everything.

"Well," he said, "it's this way: sometimes I find a man, and sometimes I can go the rounds without a bite. To-night, for instance, here I've got four names and one came across. That's about the average—perhaps one in six."

I asked him why he had given Mr. Kenworthy such a handicap at the start.

A faint smile flickered across his face and then flickered back again.

"I call the names I think will be apt to hang round in the part of the hotel I'm in. Mr. Kenworthy would have to be in the dressy dining-room or in the lobby where they wait for ladies. You'd never find him in the bar or the Turkish baths. On the other hand, you'll never find a man by the name of Blevitch anywhere except in the bar. Of course, I take a chance and call every name once in so often, no matter where I am, but, on the whole, I use my own discretion."

I gave him another piece of chocolate and the address of a good bootmaker and left him. What I had heard had sobered me, and the lights and music suddenly seemed garish. It is no weak emotion to feel that you have been face to face with a mere boy whose chances of success in his work are one to six.

And I found that he had not painted the lily in too glowing terms. I followed other pages that night—some calling for "Mr. Strudel," some for "Mr. Carmickle," and one was broad-minded enough to page a "Mrs. Bemis." But they all came back with that wan look in their eyes and a break in their voices.

And each one of them was stopped by the man in the business suit in the downstairs dining-room and each time he considered it a personal affront that there wasn't a call for "Studz."

Sometime I'm going to have him paged, and when he comes out I shall untie his necktie for him.

A Romance
in Encyclopedia Land

Written After Three Hours' Browsing in a New Britannica Set

PICTURE to yourself an early spring afternoon along the banks of the river Aa, which, rising in the Teutoburger Wald, joins the Werre at Herford and is navigable as far as St. Omer.

Branching *bryophytu* spread their flat, dorsi-ventral bodies, closely applied to the sub-stratum on which they grew, and leafy carophyllaceæ twined their sepals in prodigal profusion, lending a touch of color to the scene. It was clear that nature was in preparation for her estivation.

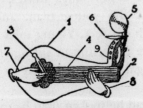

Was playing softly to himself on a double curtail or converted bass-pommer

But it was not this which attracted the eye of the young man who, walking along the phonolithic formation of the riverbank, was playing softly to

29

himself on a double curtail, or converted bass-pommer, an octave below the single curtail and therefore identical in pitch and construction with the early *fagotto* in C.

His mind was on other things.

He was evidently of Melanochronic extraction, with the pentagonal facial angle and strong orbital ridges, but he combined with this the fine lines of a full-blooded native of Coll, where, indeed, he was born, seven miles west of Caliach Point, in Mull, and in full view of the rugged gneiss.

As he swung along, there throbbed again and again through his brain the beautiful opening paragraph of Frantisek Palacky's (1798-1876) *"Zur böhmischen Geschichtschreibung"* (Prague, 1871), written just after the author had refused a portfolio in the Pillersdorf Cabinet and had also declined to take part in the preliminary diet at Kromerice.

"If *he* could believe such things, why can not I?" murmured the young man, and crushed a ginkgo beneath his feet. Young men are often so. It is due to the elaterium of spring.

"By Ereshkigal," he swore softly to himself, "I'll do it."

No sooner had he spoken than he came suddenly out of the tangle of gymnosperms through whose leaves, needle-like and destitute of oil-glands as they were, he had been making his way, and emerged to a full view of the broad sweep of the Lake of Zug, just where the Lorze enters at its northern extremity and one and a quarter miles east of where it issues again to pursue its course toward the Reuss. Zug, at this point, is 1,368 feet above sea-level, and boasted its first steamer in 1852.

"Well," he sighed, as he gazed upon the broad area of subsidence, "if I were now an exarch, whose dignity was, at one time, intermediate between the Patriarchal and the Metropoiltan and from whose name has come that of the politico-religious party, the Exarchists, I should not be here daydreaming. I should be far away in Footscray, a city of Bourke County, Victoria, Australia, pop. (1901) 18,301."

He came suddenly out of the tangle of gymnosperms

And as he said this his eyes filled with tears, and under his skin, brown as fustic, there spread a faint flush, such as is often formed by citrocyde, or by pyrochloric acid when acting on uncured leather.

Far down in the valley the natives were celebrating the birthday of Gambrinus, a mythical Flemish

31

king who is credited with the first brewing of beer. The sound of their voices set in motion longitudinal sound waves, and these, traveling through the surrounding medium, met the surface separating two media and were in part reflected, traveling back from the surface into the first medium again with the velocity with which they approached it, as depicted in Fig. 10. This caused the echo for which the Lake of Zug is justly famous.

The twilight began to deepen and from far above came the twinkling signals of, first, Böotes, then Coma Berenices, followed, awhile later, by Ursa Major and her little brother, Ursa Minor.

"The stars are clear to-night," he sighed. "I wonder if they are visible from the dacite elevation on which SHE lives."

His was an untrained mind. His only school had been the Eleatic School, the contention of which was that the true explanation of things lies in the conception of a universal unity of being, or the All-ness of One.

But he knew what he liked.

In the calm light of the stars he felt as if a uban had been lifted from his heart, 5 ubans being equal to 1 quat, 6 quats to 1 ammat and 120 ammats to 1 sos.

He was free again.

Turning, he walked swiftly down into the valley, passing returning peasants with their baa-poots, and soon came in sight of the shining lamps of the small but carefully built pooroos which lined the road.

Reaching the corner he saw the village epi peering over the tree-tops, and swarms of cicada, with the toothed famoras of their anterior legs mingling in a sleepy drone, like so many cichlids. It was all very home-like to the wanderer.

Suddenly there appeared on a neighboring eminence a party of guisards, such as, during the Saturnalia, and from the Nativity till the Epiphany were accustomed to disport themselves in odd costumes; all clad in clouting, and evidently returning from taking part in the celebration.

As they drew nearer, our hero noticed a young woman in the front rank who was playing folk-songs on a cromorne with a double-reed mouth-piece enclosed in an air-reservoir. In spite of the detritus wrought by the festival, there was something familiar about the buccinator of her face and her little mannerism of elevating her second

She turned like a frightened aardvark (male, greatly reduced)

phalanx. It struck him like the flash of a cloud highly charged by the coalescence of drops of vapor. He approached her, tenderly, reverently.

"Lange, Anne Françoise Elizabeth," he said, "I know you. You are a French actress, born in Genoa on the seventeenth of September, 1772, and you made your first appearance on the stage in *L'Ecossaise* in 1788. Your talent and your beauty gave you an enormous success in *Pamela*. It has taken me years to find you, but now we are united at last."

The girl turned like a frightened aard-vark, still

Barnaby Bernard Weenix (1777-1829)

holding the cromorne in her hand. Then she smiled.

"Weenix, Barnaby Bernard (1777-1829)," she said very slowly, "you started business as a publisher in London about 1797."

They looked at each other for a moment in silence. He was the first to speak.

"Miss Lange, Anne," he said, "let us go together to Lar—and be happy there—happy as two ais, or three-toed South American sloths."

She lowered her eyes.

"I will go with you Mr. Weenix-Barney," she said, "to the ends of the earth. But why to Lar? Why not to Wem?"

Why not to Wem? (from a contemporaneous print)

35

"Because," said the young man, "Lar is the capital of Laristan, in 27 degrees, 30 minutes N., 180 miles from Shiraz, and contains an old bazaar consisting of four arcades each 180 feet long."

Their eyes met, and she placed her hands in his.

And, from the woods, came the mellow whinnying of a herd of vip, the wool of which is highly valued for weaving.

Fascinating Crimes

1. The Odd Occurrence in the Life of Dr. Meethas

EARLY in the evening of October 14, 1879, Dr. Attemas Meethas, a physician of good repute in Elkhart, Indiana, went into the pantry of his home at 11 Elm Street, ostensibly to see if there was any of that cold roast pork left. The good doctor was given to nibbling cold roast pork when occasion offered.

As he passed through the living-room on his way to the pantry, he spoke to his housekeeper, Mrs. Omphrey, and said that, if everything turned out all right, he would be at that cold roast pork in about half a minute (Elkhart time—an hour earlier than Eastern time). "Look out for the pits," Mrs. Omphrey cautioned him, and went on with her stitching. Mrs. Omphrey, in her spare time, was a stitcher of uppers for the local shoe-factory.

This is the last that was seen of Dr. Attemas Meethas alive. It is doubtful if he ever even reached the pantry, for the cold roast pork was found untouched on a plate, and Dr. Meethas was found, three days later, hanging from the top of the flag-pole on the roof of the Masonic Lodge. The mystery was even more puzzling in that Dr. Meethas was not a Mason.

Citizens of Elkhart, on being grilled, admitted

37

The revolting death of Dr. Meethas
—Courtesy of John Held, Jr., and Life.

having seen the doctor hanging from the flag-pole
for two days, but thought that he was fooling and
would come down soon enough when he got hungry. But when, after three days, he made no sign
of descending, other than to drop off one shoe, a
committee was formed to investigate. It was found
that their fellow-citizen, far from playing a practical joke on them, had had one played on him, for
he was quite dead, with manifold and singular
abrasions. A particularly revolting feature of the

38

case was that the little gold chain which the doctor wore over his right ear, to keep his pince-nez glasses in place, was still in position. This at once disposed of the possibility of suicide.

Mrs. Omphrey and her uppers were held for examination, as it was understood that she had at one time made an attempt on the doctor's life, on the occasion of his pushing her down when they were skating together. But her story in the present affair was impregnable. After the doctor had gone through the living-room on his way to the pantry, she said that she continued stitching at her machine until nine o'clock in the evening. She thought it a little odd that Dr. Meethas did not return from the pantry, but figured it out that there was probably quite a lot of cold roast pork there and that he was still busy nibbling. At nine o'clock, however, she stopped work and started on her rounds of the house to lock up for the night. On reaching the pantry, she found that her employer was not there, and had not been there; at least that he had not touched the pork. She thought nothing of it, however, as it occurred to her that the doctor had probably remembered an engagement and had left suddenly by the pantry window in order not to worry her. So, after finishing the cold pork herself, she locked the bread-box and retired for the night. The police, on investigation, found the bread-box locked just as she had said, and so released Mrs. Omphrey.

When the news of Dr. Meethas' accident reached

La Porte, Amos W. Meethas, a brother of the victim and a respected citizen of the town, came directly to Elkhart and insisted on an investigation. He said that his brother had accumulated quite a fortune tinting postcards on the side, and was known to have this money hidden in a secret panel in the hammock which hung on the back porch. The police, guided by Mr. Amos Meethas, went to the hammock, slid the panel open and found nothing there but some old clippings telling of Dr. Meethas' confirmation in 1848. (He was a confirmed old bachelor.) This definitely established robbery as the motive for the crime. The next thing to do was to discover someone who could climb flag-poles.

Neighbors of the doctor recalled that some weeks before a young man had gone from door to door asking if anybody wanted his flag-pole climbed. He said he was working his way through college climbing flag-poles and would be grateful for any work, however small. He was remembered to have been a short youth about six feet two or three, with hair blond on one side and dark on the other. This much the neighbors agreed upon.

Working in South Bend at the time was a young man named Herman Trapp. He was apprehended by the authorities, who subsequently decided that he had no connection whatever with the tragedy.

So the strange murder of Dr. Meethas (if indeed it *was* a murder) rests to this day unsolved and forgotten, which is just as well, as it was at best a pretty dull case.

Dr. Meethas—The unfortunate victim
—Courtesy of John Held, Jr., and Life.

Christmas
Afternoon

Done in the Manner, if Not the Spirit, of Dickens

WHAT an afternoon! Mr. Gummidge said that, in his estimation, there never had *been* such an afternoon since the world began, a sentiment which was heartily endorsed by Mrs. Gummidge and all the little Gummidges, not to mention the relatives who had come over from Jersey for the day.

In the first place, there was the *ennui*. And such *ennui* as it was! A heavy, overpowering *ennui*, such as results from a participation in eight courses of steaming, gravied food, topping off with salted nuts which the little old spinster Gummidge from Oak Hill said she never knew when to stop eating— and true enough she didn't—a dragging, devitalizing *ennui*, which left its victims strewn about the living-room in various attitudes of prostration suggestive of those of the petrified occupants in a newly unearthed Pompeiian dwelling; an *ennui* which carried with it a retinue of yawns, snarls and thinly veiled insults, and which ended in ruptures in the clan spirit serious enough to last throughout the glad new year.

Then there were the toys! Three and a quarter

dozen toys to be divided among seven children. Surely enough, you or I might say, to satisfy the little tots. But that would be because we didn't know the tots. In came Baby Lester Gummidge, Lillian's boy, dragging an electric grain-elevator which happened to be the only toy in the entire collection which appealed to little Norman, five-year-old son of Luther, who lived in Rahway. In came curly-headed Effie in frantic and throaty disputation with Arthur, Jr., over the possession of an articulated zebra. In came Everett, bearing a mechanical negro which would no longer dance, owing to a previous forcible feeding by the baby of a marshmallow into its only available aperture. In came Fonlansbee, teeth buried in the hand of little Ormond, who bore a popular but battered remnant of what had once been the proud false-bosom of a hussar's uniform. In they all came, one after another, some crying, some snapping, some pulling, some pushing—all appealing to their respective parents for aid in their intra-mural warfare.

And the cigar smoke! Mrs. Gummidge said that she didn't mind the smoke from a good cigarette, but would they mind if she opened the windows for just a minute in order to clear the room of the heavy aroma of used cigars? Mr. Gummidge stoutly maintained that they were good cigars. His brother, George Gummidge, said that he, likewise, would say that they were. At which colloquial sally both the Gummidge brothers laughed testily,

What an afternoon!

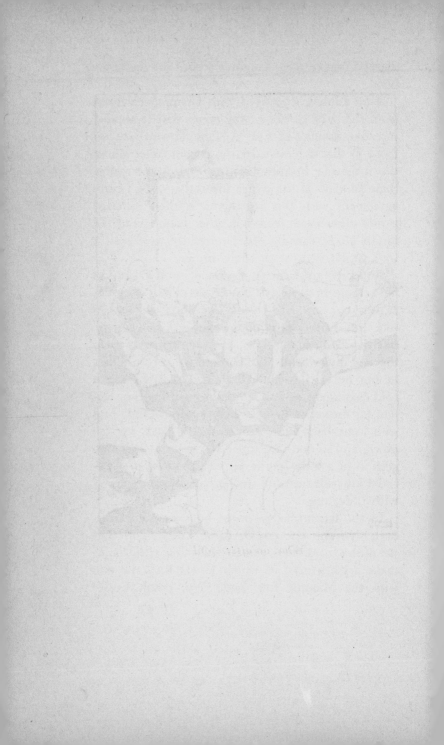

thereby breaking the laughter record for the afternoon.

Aunt Libbie, who lived with George, remarked from the dark corner of the room that it seemed just like Sunday to her. An amendment was offered to this statement by the cousin, who was in the insurance business, stating that it was worse than Sunday. Murmurings indicative of as hearty agreement with this sentiment as their lethargy would allow came from the other members of the family circle, causing Mr. Gummidge to suggest a walk in the air to settle their dinner.

And then arose such a chorus of protestations as has seldom been heard. It was too cloudy to walk. It was too raw. It looked like snow. It looked like rain. Luther Gummidge said that he must be starting along home soon, anyway, bringing forth the acid query from Mrs. Gummidge as to whether or not he was bored. Lillian said that she felt a cold coming on, and added that something they had had for dinner must have been undercooked. And so it went, back and forth, forth and back, up and down, and in and out, until Mr. Gummidge's suggestion of a walk in the air was reduced to a tattered impossibility and the entire company glowed with ill-feeling.

In the meantime, we must not forget the children. No one else could. Aunt Libbie said that she didn't think there was anything like children to make a Christmas; to which Uncle Ray, the one with the Masonic fob, said, "No, thank God!"

47

Although Christmas is supposed to be the season of good cheer, you (or I, for that matter) couldn't have told, from listening to the little ones, but what it was the children's Armageddon season, when Nature had decreed that only the fittest should survive, in order that the race might be carried on by the strongest, the most predatory and those possessing the best protective coloring. Although there were constant admonitions to Fonlansbee to "Let Ormond have that whistle now; it's his," and to Arthur, Jr., not to be selfish, but to "give the kiddie-car to Effie; she's smaller than you are," the net result was always that Fonlansbee kept the whistle and Arthur, Jr., rode in permanent, albeit disputed, possession of the kiddie-car. Oh, that we mortals should set ourselves up against the inscrutable workings of Nature!

Hallo! A great deal of commotion! That was Uncle George stumbling over the electric train, which had early in the afternoon ceased to function and which had been left directly across the threshold. A great deal of crying! That was Arthur, Jr., bewailing the destruction of his already useless train, about which he had forgotten until the present moment. A great deal of recrimination! That was Arthur, Sr., and George fixing it up. And finally a great crashing! That was Baby Lester pulling over the tree on top of himself, necessitating the bringing to bear of all of Uncle Ray's knowledge of forestry to extricate him from the wreckage.

Hallo! A great deal of commotion!

And finally Mrs. Gummidge passed the Christmas candy around. Mr. Gummidge afterward admitted that this was a tactical error on the part of his spouse. I no more believe that Mrs. Gummidge thought they wanted that Christmas candy than I believe that she thought they wanted the cold turkey which she later suggested. My opinion is that she wanted to drive them home. At any rate, that is what she succeeded in doing. Such cries as there were of "Ugh! Don't let me see another thing to eat!" and "Take it away!" Then came hurried scramblings in the coat-closet for overshoes. There were the rasping sounds made by cross parents when putting wraps on children. There were insincere exhortations to "come and see us soon" and to "get together for lunch some time." And, finally, there were slammings of doors and the silence of utter exhaustion, while Mrs. Gummidge went about picking up stray sheets of wrapping paper.

And, as Tiny Tim might say in speaking of Christmas afternoon as an institution, "God help us, every one."

The Benchley-Whittier
Correspondence

OLD scandals concerning the private life of Lord Byron have been revived with the recent publication of a collection of his letters. One of the big questions seems to be: *Did Byron send Mary Shelley's letter to Mrs. R. B. Hoppner?* Everyone seems greatly excited about it.

Lest future generations be thrown into turmoil over my correspondence after I am gone, I want right now to clear up the mystery which has puzzled literary circles for over thirty years. I need hardly add that I refer to what is known as the "Benchley-Whittier Correspondence."

The big question over which both my biographers and Whittier's might possibly come to blows is this, as I understand it: *Did John Greenleaf Whittier ever receive the letters I wrote to him in the late Fall of 1890? If he did not, who did? And under what circumstances were they written?*

I was a very young man at the time, and Mr. Whittier was, naturally, very old. There had been a meeting of the Save-Our-Song-Birds Club in old Dane Hall (now demolished) in Cambridge, Massachusetts. Members had left their coats and hats in the check-room at the foot of the stairs (now demolished).

In passing out after a rather spirited meeting, during the course of which Mr. Whittier and Dr. Van Blarcom had opposed each other rather violently over the question of Baltimore orioles, the aged poet naturally was the first to be helped into his coat. In the general mix-up (there was considerable good-natured fooling among the members as they left, relieved as they were from the strain of the meeting) Whittier was given my hat by mistake. When I came to go, there was nothing left for me but a rather seedy gray derby with a black band, containing the initials "J. G. W." As the poet was visiting in Cambridge at the time I took opportunity next day to write the following letter to him:

> Cambridge, Mass.
> November 7, 1890.

Dear Mr. Whittier:

I am afraid that in the confusion following the Save-Our-Song-Birds meeting last night, you were given my hat by mistake. I have yours and will gladly exchange it if you will let me know when I may call on you.

May I not add that I am a great admirer of your verse? Have you ever tried any musical comedy lyrics? I think that I could get you in on the ground floor in the show game, as I know a young man who has written several songs which E. E. Rice has said he would like to use in his next comic opera—provided he can get words to go with them.

But we can discuss all this at our meeting, which I hope will be soon, as your hat looks like hell on me.

> Yours respectfully,
> ROBERT C. BENCHLEY

I am quite sure that this letter was mailed, as I find an entry in my diary of that date which reads:

"Mailed a letter to J. G. Whittier. Cloudy and cooler."

Furthermore, in a death-bed confession, some ten years later, one Mary F. Rourke, a servant employed in the house of Dr. Agassiz, with whom Whittier was bunking at the time, admitted that she herself had taken a letter, bearing my name in the corner of the envelope, to the poet at his breakfast on the following morning.

But whatever became of it after it fell into his hands, I received no reply. I waited five days, during which time I stayed in the house rather than go out wearing the Whittier gray derby. On the sixth day I wrote him again, as follows:

Cambridge, Mass.
Nov. 14, 1890.

Dear Mr. Whittier:
How about that hat of mine?
Yours respectfully,
ROBERT C. BENCHLEY

I received no answer to this letter either. Concluding that the good gray poet was either too busy or too gosh-darned mean to bother with the thing, I myself adopted an attitude of supercilious unconcern and closed the correspondence with the following terse message:

53

Dear Mr. Whittier:

It is my earnest wish that the hat of mine which you are keeping will slip down over your eyes some day, interfering with your vision to such an extent that you will walk off the sidewalk into the gutter and receive painful, albeit superficial, injuries.

Your young friend,

ROBERT C. BENCHLEY

Here the matter ended so far as I was concerned, and I trust that biographers in the future will not let any confusion of motives or misunderstanding of dates enter into a clear and unbiased statement of the whole affair. We must not have another Shelley-Byron scandal.

A Christmas
Spectacle

For Use in Christmas Eve Entertainments in the Vestry

A T THE opening of the entertainment the Superintendent will step into the footlights, recover his balance apologetically, and say:

"Boys and girls of the Intermediate Department, parents and friends: I suppose you all know why we are here tonight. (At this point the audience will titter apprehensively.) Mrs. Drury and her class of little girls have been working very hard to make this entertainment a success, and I am sure that everyone here tonight is going to have what I overheard one of my boys the other day calling 'some good time.' (Indulgent laughter from the little boys.) And may I add before the curtain goes up that immediately after the entertainment we want you all to file out into the Christian Endeavor room, where there will be a Christmas tree, 'with all the fixin's,' as the boys say." (Shrill whistling from the little boys and immoderate applause from everyone.)

There will then be a wait of twenty-five minutes, while sounds of hammering and dropping may be heard from behind the curtains. The Boys' Club orchestra will render the "Poet and Peasant Overture" four times in succession, each time differently.

55

At last one side of the curtains will be drawn back; the other will catch on something and have to be released by hand; someone will whisper loudly, "Put out the lights," following which the entire house will be plunged into darkness. Amid catcalls from the little boys, the footlights will at last go on, disclosing:

The windows in the rear of the vestry rather ineffectively concealed by a group of small fir trees on standards, one of which has already fallen over, leaving exposed a corner of the map of Palestine and the list of gold-star classes for November. In the center of the stage is a larger tree, undecorated, while at the extreme left, invisible to everyone in the audience except those sitting at the extreme right, is an imitation fireplace, leaning against the wall.

Twenty-five seconds too early little Flora Rochester will prance out from the wings, uttering the first shrill notes of a song, and will have to be grabbed by eager hands and pulled back. Twenty-four seconds later the piano will begin "The Return of the Reindeer" with a powerful accent on the first note of each bar, and Flora Rochester, Lillian Mc-Nulty, Gertrude Hamingham and Martha Wrist will swirl on, dressed in white, and advance heavily into the footlights, which will go out.

There will then be an interlude while Mr. Neff, the sexton, adjusts the connection, during which the four little girls stand undecided whether to brave it out or cry. As a compromise they giggle and are herded back into the wings by Mrs. Drury, amid applause. When the lights go on again, the applause becomes deafening, and as Mr. Neff walks triumphantly away, the little boys in the audience will whistle: "There she goes, there she goes, all dressed up in her Sunday clothes!"

"The Return of the Reindeer" will be started again and the show-girls will reappear, this time more gingerly and somewhat dispirited. They will, however, sing the following, to the music of the "Ballet Pizzicato" from "Sylvia":

> *"We greet you, we greet you,*
> *On this Christmas Eve so fine.*
> *We greet you, we greet you,*
> *And wish you a good time."*

They will then turn toward the tree and Flora Rochester will advance, hanging a silver star on one of the branches, meanwhile reciting a verse, the only distinguishable words of which are: *"I am Faith so strong and pure ——"*

At the conclusion of her recitation, the star will fall off.

Lillian McNulty will then step forward and hang her star on a branch, reading her lines in clear tones:

> *"And I am Hope, a virtue great,*
> *My gift to Christmas now I make,*
> *That children and grown-ups may hope today*
> *That tomorrow will be a merry Christmas Day."*

57

The hanging of the third star will be consummated by Gertrude Hamingham, who will get as far as *"Sweet Charity I bring to place upon the tree—"* at which point the strain will become too great and she will forget the remainder. After several frantic glances toward the wings, from which Mrs. Drury is sending out whispered messages to the effect that the next line begins, *"My message bright—"* Gertrude will disappear, crying softly.

After the morale of the cast has been in some measure restored by the pianist, who, with great presence of mind, plays a few bars of "Will There Be Any Stars In My Crown?" to cover up Gertrude's exit, Martha Wrist will unleash a rope of silver tinsel from the foot of the tree, and, stringing it over the boughs as she skips around in a circle, will say, with great assurance:

> *" 'Round and 'round the tree I go,*
> *Through the holly and the snow*
> *Bringing love and Christmas cheer*
> *Through the happy year to come."*

At this point there will be a great commotion and jangling of sleigh-bells off-stage, and Mr. Creamer, rather poorly disguised as Santa Claus, will emerge from the opening in the imitation fireplace. A great popular demonstration for Mr. Creamer will follow. He will then advance to the footlights, and, rubbing his pillow and ducking his knees to denote joviality, will say thickly through his false beard:

"Well, well, well, what have we here? A lot of bad little boys and girls who aren't going to get any Christmas presents this year? (Nervous laughter from the little boys and girls.) Let me see, let me see! I have a note here from Dr. Whidden. Let's see what it says. (Reads from a paper on which there is obviously nothing written.) 'If you and the young people of the Intermediate Department will come into the Christian Endeavor room, I think we may have a little surprise for you. . . .' Well, well, well! What do you suppose it can be? (Cries of 'I know, I know!' from sophisticated ones in the audience.) Maybe it is a bottle of castor-oil! (Raucous jeers from the little boys and elaborately simulated disgust on the part of the little girls.) Well, anyway, suppose we go out and see? Now if Miss Liftnagle will oblige us with a little march on the piano, we will all form in single file ——"

At this point there will ensue a stampede toward the Christian Endeavor room, in which chairs will be broken, decorations demolished, and the protesting Mr. Creamer badly hurt.

This will bring to a close the first part of the entertainment.

"Roll
Your Own"

Inside Points on Building and Maintaining a Private
Tennis Court

ONE really ought to have a tennis-court of
one's own. Those at the Club are always so
full that on Saturdays and Sundays the people
waiting to play look like the gallery at a Davis Cup
match, and even when you do get located you have
two sets of balls to chase, yours and those of the
people in the next court.

The first thing is to decide among yourselves just
what kind of court it is to be. There are three
kinds: grass, clay, and corn-meal. In Maine, gravel
courts are also very popular. Father will usually
hold out for a grass court because it gives a slower
bounce to the ball and Father isn't so quick on the
bounce as he used to be. All Mother insists on is
plenty of headroom. Junior and Myrtis will want a
clay one because you can dance on a clay one in
the evening. The court as finished will be a combination grass and dirt, with a little goldenrod
late in August.

A little study will be necessary before laying out
the court. I mean you can't just go out and mark
a court by guess-work. You must first learn what

the dimensions are supposed to be and get as near to them as is humanly possible. Whereas there might be a slight margin for error in some measurements, it is absolutely essential that both sides are the same length, otherwise you might end up by lobbing back to yourself if you got very excited.

The worst place to get the dope on how to arrange a tennis-court is in the Encyclopædia Britannica. The article on TENNIS was evidently written by the Archbishop of Canterbury. It begins by explaining that in America tennis is called "court tennis." The only answer to that is, "You're a cock-eyed liar!" The whole article is like this.

The name "tennis," it says, probably comes from the French *"Tenez!"* meaning "Take it! Play!" More likely, in my opinion, it is derived from the Polish *"Tinith!"* meaning "Go on, that was *not* outside!"

During the Fourteenth Century the game was played by the highest people in France. Louis X died from a chill contracted after playing. Charles V was devoted to it, although he tried in vain to stop it as a pastime for the lower classes (the origin of the country-club); Charles VI watched it being played from the room where he was confined during his attack of insanity and Du Guesclin amused himself with it during the siege of Dinan. And, although it doesn't say so in the Encyclopædia, Robert C. Benchley, after playing for the first time in the season of 1922, was so lame under the right

61

shoulder-blade that he couldn't lift a glass to his mouth.

This fascinating historical survey of tennis goes on to say that in the reign of Henri IV the game was so popular that it was said that "there were more tennis-players in Paris than drunkards in England." The drunkards of England were so upset by this boast that they immediately started a drive for membership with the slogan, "Five thousand more drunkards by April 15, and to Hell with France!" One thing led to another until war was declared.

The net does not appear until the 17th century. Up until that time a rope, either fringed or tasseled, was stretched across the court. This probably had to be abandoned because it was so easy to crawl under it and chase your opponent. There might also have been ample opportunity for the person playing at the net or at the "rope," to catch the eye of the player directly opposite by waving his racquet high in the air and then to kick him under the rope, knocking him for a loop while the ball was being put into play in his territory. You have to watch these Frenchmen every minute.

The Encyclopædia Britannica gives fifteen lines to "Tennis in America." It says that "few tennis courts existed in America before 1880, but that now there are courts in Boston, New York, Chicago, Tuxedo and Lakewood and several other places." Everyone try hard to think now just where those other places are!

Which reminds us that one of them is going to be in your side yard where the garden used to be. After you have got the dimensions from the Encyclopædia, call up a professional tennis-court maker and get him to do the job for you. Just tell him that you want "a tennis-court."

Once it is built the fun begins. According to the arrangement, each member of the family is to have certain hours during which it belongs to them and no one else. Thus the children can play before breakfast and after breakfast until the sun gets around so that the west court is shady. Then Daddy and Mother and sprightly friends may take it over. Later in the afternoon the children have it again, and if there is any light left after dinner Daddy can take a whirl at the ball.

What actually will happen is this: Right after breakfast Roger Beeman, who lives across the street and who is home for the summer with a couple of college friends who are just dandy looking, will come over and ask if they may use the court until someone wants it. They will let Myrtis play with them and perhaps Myrtis' girl-chum from Westover. They will play five sets, running into scores like 19-17, and at lunch time will make plans for a ride into the country for the afternoon. Daddy will stick around in the offing all dressed up in his tennis-clothes waiting to play with Uncle Ted, but somehow or other every time he approaches the court the young people will be in the middle of a set.

After lunch, Lillian Nieman, who lives three houses down the street, will come up and ask if she may bring her cousin (just on from the West) to play a set until someone wants the court. Lillian's cousin has never played tennis before but she has done a lot of croquet and thinks she ought to pick tennis up rather easily. For three hours there is a great deal of screaming, with Lillian and her cousin hitting the ball an aggregate of eleven times, while Daddy patters up and down the side-lines, all dressed up in white, practising shots against the netting.

Finally, the girls will ask him to play with them, and he will thank them and say that he has to go in the house now as he is all perspiration and is afraid of catching cold.

After dinner there is dancing on the court by the young people. Anyway, Daddy is getting pretty old for tennis.

Opera Synopses

*Some Sample Outlines of Grand Opera Plots For Home
Study*

I

DIE MEISTER-GENOSSENSCHAFT

SCENE: *The Forests of Germany.*
TIME: *Antiquity.*

CAST

STRUDEL, *God of Rain*....................Basso
SCHMALZ, *God of Slight Drizzle*...........Tenor
IMMERGLÜCK, *Goddess of the Six Primary
    Colors* ....Soprano
LUDWIG DAS EIWEISS, *the Knight of the Iron
    Duck* ....Baritone
THE WOODPECKER.....................Soprano

ARGUMENT

The basis of "Die Meister-Genossenschaft" is
an old legend of Germany which tells how the
Whale got his Stomach.

ACT 1

*The Rhine at Low Tide Just Below Weld-
schnoffen.*—Immerglück has grown weary of always
sitting on the same rock with the same fishes swimming by every day, and sends for Schwül to suggest

something to do. Schwül asks her how she would like to have pass before her all the wonders of the world fashioned by the hand of man. She says, rotten. He then suggests that Ringblattz, son of Pflucht, be made to appear before her and fight a mortal combat with the Iron Duck. This pleases Immerglück and she summons to her the four dwarfs: Hot Water, Cold Water, Cool, and Cloudy. She bids them bring Ringblattz to her. They refuse, because Pflucht has at one time rescued them from being buried alive by acorns, and, in a rage, Immerglück strikes them all dead with a thunderbolt.

Act 2

A Mountain Pass.—Repenting of her deed, Immerglück has sought advice of the giants, Offen and Besitz, and they tell her that she must procure the magic zither which confers upon its owner the power to go to sleep while apparently carrying on a conversation. This magic zither has been hidden for three hundred centuries in an old bureau drawer, guarded by the Iron Duck, and, although many have attempted to rescue it, all have died of a strange ailment just as success was within their grasp.

But Immerglück calls to her side Dampfboot, the tinsmith of the gods, and bids him make for her a tarnhelm or invisible cap which will enable her to talk to people without their understanding a word she says. For a dollar and a half extra Dampf-boot throws in a magic ring which renders its wearer insensible. Thus armed, Immerglück starts out for Walhalla, humming to herself.

Act 3

The Forest Before the Iron Duck's Bureau Drawer.—Merglitz, who has up till this time held his peace, now descends from a balloon and demands the release of Betty. It has been the will of Wotan that Merglitz and Betty should meet on earth and hate each other like poison, but Zwei-back, the druggist of the gods, has disobeyed and concocted a love-potion which has rendered the young couple very unpleasant company. Wotan, enraged, destroys them with a protracted heat spell.

Encouraged by this sudden turn of affairs, Immerglück comes to earth in a boat drawn by four white Holsteins, and, seated alone on a rock, remembers aloud to herself the days when she was a girl. Pilgrims from Augenblick, on their way to worship at the shrine of Schmürr, hear the sound of reminiscence coming from the rock and stop in their march to sing a hymn of praise for the drying up of the crops. They do not recognize Immerglück, as she has her hair done differently, and think that she is a beggar girl selling pencils.

In the meantime, Ragel, the papercutter of the gods, has fashioned himself a sword on the forge of Schmalz, and has called the weapon "Assistance-in-Emergency." Armed with Assistance-in-Emergency" he comes to earth, determined to slay the Iron Duck and carry off the beautiful Irma.

But Frimsel overhears the plan and has a drink brewed which is given to Ragel in a golden goblet and which, when drunk, makes him forget his past and causes him to believe that he is Schnorr, the God of Fun. While laboring under this spell, Ragel has a funeral pyre built on the summit of a high mountain and, after lighting it, climbs on top of it with a mandolin which he plays until he is consumed.

Immerglück never marries.

II

IL MINNESTRONE
(Peasant Love)

Scene: *Venice and Old Point Comfort.*
Time: *Early 16th Century.*

Cast

Alfonso, *Duke of Minnestrone* . . . . Baritone
Partola, *a Peasant Girl* . . . . *Soprano*
Cleanso ⎱   ⎧ Tenor
Turino ⎬ *Young Noblemen of Venice.* ⎨ Tenor
Bombo ⎭   ⎩ Basso
Ludovico ⎱ *Assassins in the service of* ⎧Basso
Astolfo ⎭   *Cafeteria Rusticana*   ⎨Methodist
      Townspeople, Cabbies and Sparrows

Argument

"Il Minnestrone" is an allegory of the two sides of a man's nature (good and bad), ending at last in an awfully comical mess with everyone dead.

Act 1

A Public Square, Ferrara.—During a peasant festival held to celebrate the sixth consecutive day of rain, Rudolpho, a young nobleman, sees Lilliano, daughter of the village bell-ringer, dancing along throwing artificial roses at herself. He asks of his secretary who the young woman is, and his secretary, in order to confuse Rudolpho and thereby win the hand of his ward, tells him that it is his (Rudolpho's) own mother, disguised for the festival. Rudolpho is astounded. He orders her arrest.

Act 2

Banquet Hall in Gorgio's Palace.—Lilliano has not forgotten Breda, her old nurse, in spite of her troubles, and determines to avenge herself for the many insults she received in her youth by poisoning her (Breda). She therefore invites the old nurse to a banquet and poisons her. Presently a knock is heard. It is Ugolfo. He has come to carry away the body of Michelo and to leave an extra quart of pasteurized. Lilliano tells him that she no longer loves him, at which he goes away, dragging his feet sulkily.

ACT 3

In Front of Emilo's House.—Still thinking of the
old man's curse, Borsa has an interview with
Cleanso, believing him to be the Duke's wife. He
tells him things can't go on as they are, and Cleanso
stabs him. Just at this moment Betty comes rushing in from school and falls in a faint. Her worst
fears have been realized. She has been insulted by
Sigmundo, and presently dies of old age. In a
fury, Ugolfo rushes out to kill Sigmundo and, as he
does so, the dying Rosenblatt rises on one elbow
and curses his mother.

III

LUCY DE LIMA

SCENE: *Wales.*
TIME: *1700 (Greenwich).*

CAST

WILLIAM WONT, *Lord of Glennnn* . . . . Basso
LUCY WAGSTAFF, *his daughter* . . . . Soprano
BERTRAM, *her lover* . . . . Tenor
LORD ROGER, *friend of Bertram* . . . . Soprano
IRMA, *attendant to Lucy* . . . . Basso
*Friends, Retainers and Members of the local
Lodge of Elks.*

ARGUMENT

"Lucy de Lima," is founded on the well-known
story by Boccaccio of the same name and address.

70

ACT 1

Gypsy Camp Near Waterbury.—The gypsies, led by Edith, go singing through the camp on the way to the fair. Following them comes Despard, the gypsy leader, carrying Ethel, whom he has just kidnapped from her father, who had previously just kidnapped her from her mother. Despard places Ethel on the ground and tells Mona, the old hag, to watch over her. Mona nurses a secret grudge against Despard for having once cut off her leg and decides to change Ethel for Nettie, another kidnapped child. Ethel pleads with Mona to let her stay with Despard, for she has fallen in love with him on the ride over. But Mona is obdurate.

ACT 2

The Fair.—A crowd of sightseers and villagers is present. Roger appears, looking for Laura. He can not find her. Laura appears, looking for Roger. She can not find him. The gypsy queen approaches Roger and thrusts into his hand the locket stolen from Lord Brym. Roger looks at it and is frozen with astonishment, for it contains the portrait of his mother when she was in high school. He then realizes that Laura must be his sister, and starts out to find her.

ACT 3

Hall in the Castle.—Lucy is seen surrounded by every luxury, but her heart is sad. She has just been shown a forged letter from Stewart saying that he no longer loves her, and she remembers her old free life in the mountains and longs for another romp with Ravensbane and Wolfshead, her old pair of rompers. The guests begin to assemble for the wedding, each bringing a roast ox. They chide Lucy for not having her dress changed. Just at this moment the gypsy band bursts in and Cleon tells the wedding party that Elsie and not Edith is the child who was stolen from the summer-house, showing the blood-stained derby as proof. At this, Lord Brym repents and gives his blessing on the pair, while the fishermen and their wives celebrate in the courtyard.

The Tooth, the Whole Tooth, and Nothing but the Tooth

SOME well-known saying (it doesn't make much difference what) is proved by the fact that everyone likes to talk about his experiences at the dentist's. For years and years little articles like this have been written on the subject, little jokes like some that I shall presently make have been made, and people in general have been telling other people just what emotions they experience when they crawl into the old red plush guillotine.

They like to explain to each other how they feel when the dentist puts "that buzzer thing" against their bicuspids, and, if sufficiently pressed, they will describe their sensations on mouthing a rubber dam.

"I'll tell you what I hate," they will say with great relish, "when he takes that little nut-pick and begins to scrape. Ugh!"

"Oh, I'll tell you what's worse than that," says the friend, not to be outdone, "when he is poking around careless-like, and strikes a nerve. Wow!"

And if there are more than two people at the experience-meeting, everyone will chip in and tell what he or she considers to be the worst phase of the dentist's work, all present enjoying the narration hugely and none so much as the narrator who has suffered so.

73

This sort of thing has been going on ever since the first mammoth gold tooth was hung out as a bait to folks in search of a good time. (By the way, when *did* the present obnoxious system of dentistry begin? It can't be so very long ago that the electric auger was invented, and where would a dentist be without an electric auger? Yet you never hear of Amalgam Filling Day, or any other anniversary in the dental year. There must be a conspiracy of silence on the part of the trade to keep hidden the names of the men who are responsible for all this.)

However many years it may be that dentists have been plying their trade, in all that time people have never tired of talking about their teeth. This is probably due to the inscrutable workings of Nature who is always supplying new teeth to talk about.

As a matter of fact, the actual time and suffering in the chair is only a fraction of the gross expenditure connected with the affair. The preliminary period, about which nobody talks, is much the worse. This dates from the discovery of the wayward tooth and extends to the moment when the dentist places his foot on the automatic hoist which jacks you up into range. Giving gas for tooth-extraction is all very humane in its way, but the time for anaesthetics is when the patient first decides that he must go to the dentist. From then on, until the first excavation is started, should be shrouded in oblivion.

There is probably no moment more appalling

74

than that in which the tongue, running idly over the teeth in a moment of care-free play, comes suddenly upon the ragged edge of a space from which the old familiar filling has disappeared. The world stops and you look meditatively up to the corner of the ceiling. Then quickly you draw your tongue away, and try to laugh the affair off, saying to yourself:

"Stuff and nonsense, my good fellow! There is nothing the matter with your tooth. Your nerves are upset after a hard day's work, that's all."

Having decided this to your satisfaction, you slyly, and with a poor attempt at being casual, slide the tongue back along the line of adjacent teeth, hoping against hope that it will reach the end without mishap.

But there it is! There can be no doubt about it this time. The tooth simply has got to be filled by someone, and the only person who can fill it with anything permanent is a dentist. You wonder if you might not be able to patch it up yourself for the time being,—a year or so—perhaps with a little spruce-gum and a coating of new-skin. It is fairly far back, and wouldn't have to be a very sightly job.

But this has an impracticable sound, even to you. You might want to eat some peanut-brittle (you never can tell when someone might offer you peanut-brittle these days), and the new-skin, while serviceable enough in the case of cream soups and custards, couldn't be expected to stand up under heavy crunching.

So you admit that, since the thing has got to be filled, it might as well be a dentist who does the job.

This much decided, all that is necessary is to call him up and make an appointment.

Let us say that this resolve is made on Tuesday. That afternoon you start to look up the dentist's number in the telephone-book. A great wave of relief sweeps over you when you discover that it isn't there. How can you be expected to make an appointment with a man who hasn't got a telephone? And how can you have a tooth filled without making an appointment? The whole thing is impossible, and that's all there is to it. God knows you did your best.

On Wednesday there is a slightly more insistent twinge, owing to bad management of a sip of ice-water. You decide that you simply must get in touch with that dentist when you get back from lunch. But you know how those things are. First one thing and then another came up, and a man came in from Providence who had to be shown around the office, and by the time you had a minute to yourself it was five o'clock. And, anyway, the tooth didn't bother you again. You wouldn't be surprised if, by being careful, you could get along with it as it is until the end of the week when you will have more time. A man has to think of his business, after all, and what is a little personal discomfort in the shape of an unfilled tooth to the satisfaction of work well done in the office?

By Saturday morning you are fairly reconciled to going ahead, but it is only a half day and probably he has no appointments left, anyway. Monday is really the time. You can begin the week afresh. After all, Monday is really the logical day to start in going to the dentist.

Bright and early Monday morning you make another try at the telephone-book, and find, to your horror, that some time between now and last Tuesday the dentist's name and number have been inserted into the directory. There it is. There is no getting around it: "Burgess, Jas. Kendal, DDS. . . . Courtland—2654." There is really nothing left to do but to call him up. Fortunately the line is busy, which gives you a perfectly good excuse for putting it over until Tuesday. But on Tuesday luck is against you and you get a clear connection with the doctor himself. An appointment is arranged for Thursday afternoon at 3:30.

Thursday afternoon, and here it is only Tuesday morning! Almost anything may happen between now and then. We might declare war on Mexico, and off you'd have to go, dentist appointment or no dentist appointment. Surely a man couldn't let a date to have a tooth filled stand in the way of his doing his duty to his country. Or the social revolution might start on Wednesday, and by Thursday the whole town might be in ashes. You can picture yourself standing, Thursday afternoon at 3:30, on the ruins of the City Hall, fighting off marauding bands of reds, and saying to yourself, with a sigh of relief: "Only to think! At this time I was to have been climbing into the dentist's chair!" You never can tell when your luck will turn in a thing like that.

But Wednesday goes by and nothing happens. And Thursday morning dawns without even a word from the dentist saying that he has been called suddenly out of town to lecture before the Incisor Club. Apparently, everything is working against you.

By this time, your tongue has taken up a permanent resting-place in the vacant tooth, and is causing you to talk indistinctly and incoherently. Somehow you feel that if the dentist opens your mouth and finds the tip of your tongue in the tooth, he will be deceived and go away without doing anything.

The only thing left is for you to call him up and say that you have just killed a man and are being arrested and can't possibly keep your appointment. But any dentist would see through that. He would laugh right into his transmitter at you. There is probably no excuse which it would be possible to invent which a dentist has not already heard eighty or ninety times. No, you might as well see the thing through now.

Luncheon is a ghastly rite. The whole left side of your jaw has suddenly developed an acute sensitiveness and the disaffection has spread to the four teeth on either side of the original one. You doubt if it will be possible for him to touch it at all. Perhaps·all he intends to do this time is to look at it anyway. You might even suggest that to him. You could very easily come in again soon and have him do the actual work.

Three-thirty draws near. A horrible time of day at best. Just when a man's vitality is lowest. Before stepping in out of the sunlight into the building in which the dental parlor is, you take one look about you at the happy people scurrying by in the street. Carefree children that they are! What do they know of Life? Probably that man in the silly-looking hat never had trouble with so much as his baby-teeth. There they go, pushing and jostling each other, just as if within ten feet of them there was not a man who stands on the brink of the Great Misadventure. Ah well! Life is like that!

Into the elevator. The last hope is gone. The door clangs and you look hopelessly about you at the stupid faces of your fellow passengers. How can people be so clownish? Of course, there is always the chance that the elevator will fall and that you will all be terribly hurt. But that is too much to expect. You dismiss it from your thoughts as too impractical, too visionary. Things don't work out as happily as that in real life.

You feel a certain glow of heroic pride when you tell the operator the right floor number. You might just as easily have told him a floor too high or too low, and that would, at least, have caused delay. But after all, a man must prove himself a man and the least you can do is to meet Fate with an unflinching eye and give the right floor number.

Too often has the scene in the dentist's waiting-room been described for me to try to do it again here. They are all alike. The antiseptic smell, the ominous hum from the operating-rooms, the ancient *Digests*, and the silent, sullen group of waiting patients, each trying to look unconcerned and cordially disliking everyone else in the room, —all these have been sung by poets of far greater lyric powers than mine. (Not that I really think that they *are* greater than mine, but that's the customary form of excuse for not writing something you haven't got time or space to do. As a matter of fact, I think I could do it much better than it has ever been done before).

I can only say that, as you sit looking, with unseeing eyes, through a large book entitled, "The War in Pictures," you would gladly change places with the most lowly of God's creatures. It is inconceivable that there should be anyone worse off than you, unless perhaps it is some of the poor wretches who are waiting with you.

That one over in the arm-chair, nervously tearing to shreds a copy of "The Dental Review and Practical Inlay Worker." She may have something frightful the trouble with her. She couldn't possibly look more worried. Perhaps it is very, very painful. This thought cheers you up considerably. What cowards women are in times like these!

And then there comes the sound of voices from the next room.

"All right, Doctor, and if it gives me any more pain shall I call you up? . . . Do you think that it will bleed much more? . . . Saturday morning, then, at eleven. . . . Good bye, Doctor."

And a middle-aged woman emerges (all women are middle-aged when emerging from the dentist's office) looking as if she were playing the big emotional scene in "John Ferguson." A wisp of hair waves dissolutely across her forehead between her eyes. Her face is pale, except for a slight inflammation at the corners of her mouth, and in her eyes is that far-away look of one who has been face to face with Life. But she is through. She should care how she looks.

The nurse appears, and looks inquiringly at each one in the room. Each one in the room evades the nurse's glance in one last, futile attempt to fool someone and get away without seeing the dentist. But she spots you and nods pleasantly. God, how pleasantly she nods! There ought to be a law against people being as pleasant as that.

"The doctor will see you now," she says.

The English language may hold a more disagreeable combination of words than "The doctor will see you now." I am willing to concede something to the phrase "Have you anything to say before the current is turned on." That may be worse for the

81

moment, but it doesn't last so long. For continued, unmitigating depression, I know nothing to equal "The doctor will see you now." But I'm not narrow-minded about it. I'm willing to consider other possibilities.

Smiling feebly, you trip over the extended feet of the man next to you, and stagger into the delivery-room, where amid a ghastly array of death-masks of teeth, blue flames waving eerily from Bunsen burners, and the drowning sound of perpetually running water which chokes and gurgles at intervals, you sink into the chair and close your eyes.

．　．　．　．　．　．

But now let us consider the spiritual exaltation that comes when you are at last let down and turned loose. It is all over, and what did it amount to? Why, nothing at all. A-ha-ha-ha-ha-ha! Nothing at all.

You suddenly develop a particular friendship for the dentist. A splendid fellow, really. You ask him questions about his instruments. What does he use this thing for, for instance? Well, well, to think of a little thing like that making all that trouble. A-ha-ha-ha-ha-ha! . . . And the dentist's family, how are they? Isn't that fine!

Gaily you shake hands with him and straighten your tie. Forgotten is the fact that you have another appointment with him for Monday. There is no such thing as Monday. You are through for today, and all's right with the world.

As you pass out through the waiting-room, you leer at the others unpleasantly. The poor fishes! Why can't they take their medicine like grown people and not sit there moping as if they were going to be shot?

Heigh-ho! Here's the elevator-man! A charming fellow! You wonder if he knows that you have just had a tooth filled. You feel tempted to tell him and slap him on the back. You feel tempted to tell everyone out in the bright, cheery street. And what a wonderful street it is too! All full of nice, black snow and water. After all, Life is sweet!

And then you go and find the first person whom you can accost without being arrested and explain to him just what it was that the dentist did to you, and how you felt, and what you have got to have done next time.

Which brings us right back to where we were in the beginning, and perhaps accounts for everyone's liking to divulge their dental secrets to others. It may be a sort of hysterical relief that, for the time being, it is all over with.

Literary Lost and Found Department

With Scant Apology to the Book Section of the *New York Times*

"OLD BLACK TILLIE"

H.G.L.—When I was a little girl, my nurse used to recite a poem something like the following (as near as I can remember). I wonder if anyone can give me the missing lines?

> *"Old Black Tillie lived in the dell,*
> *Heigh-ho with a rum-tum-tum!*
> *Something, something, something like a lot of hell,*
> *Heigh-ho with a rum-tum-tum!*
> *She wasn't very something and she wasn't very fat*
> *But ——"*

"VICTOR HUGO'S DEATH"

M.K.C.—Is it true that Victor Hugo did not die but is still living in a little shack in Colorado?

"I'M SORRY THAT I SPELT THE WORD"

J.R.A.—Can anyone help me out by furnishing the last three words to the following stanza which I learned in school and of which I have forgotten the last three words, thereby driving myself crazy?

> "'I'm sorry that I spelt the word,
> I hate to go above you,
> Because—' the brown eyes lower fell,
> 'Because, you see, — — —.'"

"God's in His Heaven"

J.A.E.—Where did Mark Twain write the following?

> "God's in his heaven:
> All's right with the world."

"She Dwelt Beside"

N.K.Y.—Can someone locate this for me and tell the author?

> "She dwelt among untrodden ways,
> Beside the springs of Dove,
> To me she gave sweet Charity,
> But greater far is Love."

"The Golden Wedding"

K.L.F.—Who wrote the following and what does it mean?

> "Oh, de golden wedding,
> Oh, de golden wedding,
> Oh, de golden wedding,
> De golden, golden wedding!"

85

ANSWERS

"When Grandma Was a Girl"

LUTHER F. NEAM, Flushing, L. I.—The poem asked for by "E.J.K." was recited at a Free Soil riot in Ashburg, Kansas, in July, 1850. It was entitled, "And That's the Way They Did It When Grandma Was a Girl," and was written by Bishop Leander B. Rizzard. The last line runs:

"And that's the way they did it, when Grandma was a girl."

Others who answered this query were: Lillian W. East, of Albany; Martin B. Forsch, New York City, and Henry Cabot Lodge, Nahant.

"Let Us Then Be Up and Doing"

ROGER F. NILKETTE, Presto, N. J.—Replying to the query in your last issue concerning the origin of the lines:

"Let us then be up and doing,
With a heart for any fate.
Still achieving, still pursuing,
Learn to labor and to wait."

I remember hearing these lines read at a gathering in the Second Baptist Church of Presto, N. J., when I was a young man, by the Reverend Harley N. Ankle. It was said at the time among his parishioners that he himself wrote them and on being questioned on the matter he did not deny it, simply smiling and saying, "I'm glad if you liked them." They were henceforth known in Presto as "Dr. Ankle's verse" and were set to music and sung at his funeral.

"The December Bride, or Old Robin"

CHARLES B. RENNIT, Boston, N. H.—The whole poem wanted by "H.J.O." is as follows, and appeared in *Hostetter's Annual* in 1843.

1

" 'Twas in the bleak December that I took her for my
 bride;
How well do I remember how she fluttered by my
 side;
My Nellie dear, it was not long before you up and
 died,
And they buried her at eight-thirty in the morning.

2

"Oh, do not tell me of the charms of maidens far and
 near,
Their charming ways and manners I do not care to
 hear,
For Lucy dear was to me so very, very dear,
And they buried her at eight-thirty in the morning.

3

"Then it's merrily, merrily, merrily, whoa!
To the old gray church they come and go,

Some to be married and some to be buried,
And old Robin has gone for the mail."

"The Old King's Joke"

F. J. Bruff, Hammick, Conn.—In a recent issue
of your paper, Lillian F. Grothman asked for the
remainder of a poem which began: *"The King of*
Sweden made a joke, ha, ha!"

I can furnish all of this poem, having written it
myself, for which I was expelled from St. Domino's
School in 1895. If Miss Grothman will meet me in
the green room at the Biltmore for tea on Wednesday next at 4:30, she will be supplied with the
missing words.

Trout
Fishing

I NEVER knew very much about trout-fishing anyway, and I certainly had no inkling that a trout-fisher had to be so deceitful until I read "Trout-Fishing in Brooks," by G. Garrow-Green. The thing is appalling. Evidently the sport is nothing but a constant series of compromises with one's better nature, what with sneaking about pretending to be something that one is not, trying to fool the fish into thinking one thing when just the reverse is true, and in general behaving in an underhanded and tricky manner throughout the day.

The very first and evidently the most important exhortation in the book is, "Whatever you do, keep out of sight of the fish." Is that open and above-board? Is it honorable?

"Trout invariably lie in running water with their noses pointed against the current, and therefore whatever general chance of concealment there may be rests in fishing from behind them. The moral is that the brook-angler must both walk and fish upstream."

It seems as if a lot of trouble might be saved the fisherman, in case he really didn't want to walk upstream but had to get to some point downstream before 6 o'clock, to adopt some disguise which would deceive the fish into thinking that he had no intention of catching them anyway. A pair of blue glasses and a cane would give the effect of the wearer being blind and harmless, and could be thrown aside very quickly when the time came to show one's self in one's true colors to the fish. If there were two anglers they might talk in loud tones about their dislike for fish in any form, and then, when the trout were quite reassured and swimming close to the bank they could suddenly be shot with a pistol.

But a little further on comes a suggestion for a much more elaborate bit of subterfuge.

The author says that in the early season trout are often engaged with larvæ at the bottom and do not show on the surface. It is then a good plan, he says, to sink the flies well, moving in short jerks to imitate nymphs.

You can see that imitating a nymph will call for a lot of rehearsing, but I doubt very much if moving in short jerks is the way in which to go about it. I have never actually seen a nymph, though if I had I should not be likely to admit it, and I can think of no possible way in which I could give an adequate illusion of being one myself. Even the most stupid of trout could easily divine that I was masquerading, and then the question would immediately arise in his mind: "If he is not a nymph, then what is his object in going about like that try-

ing to imitate one? He is up to no good, I'll be
bound."

And crash! away would go the trout before I
could put my clothes back on.

There is an interesting note on the care and feeding of worms on page 67. One hundred and fifty
worms are placed in a tin and allowed to work
their way down into packed moss.

"A little fresh milk poured in occasionally is
sufficient food," writes Mr. Garrow-Green, in the
style of Dr. Holt. "So disposed, the worms soon
become bright, lively and tough."

It is easy to understand why one should want
to have bright worms, so long as they don't know
that they are bright and try to show off before company, but why deliberately set out to make them
tough? Good manners they may not be expected to
acquire, but a worm with a cultivated vulgarity
sounds intolerable. Imagine 150 very tough worms
all crowded together in one tin! "Canaille" is the
only word to describe it.

I suppose that it is my ignorance of fishing par-
lance which makes the following sentence a bit
hazy:

"Much has been written about bringing a fish
downstream to help drown it, as no doubt it does;
still, this is often impracticable."

I can think of nothing more impracticable than
trying to drown a fish under any conditions, up-

stream or down, but I suppose that Mr. Garrow-Green knows what he is talking about.

And in at least one of his passages I follow him perfectly. In speaking of the time of day for fly-fishing in the spring he says:

" 'Carpe diem' is a good watchword when trout are in the humor." At least, I know a good pun when I see one.

Fascinating Crimes

2. The Wallack Disappearances

SHORTLY after the Civil War the residents of Wallack, Connecticut, were awakened by the barking of a dog belonging to James Lenn, a visiting farmer. The dog was an old one, so they thought nothing of it, and went back to sleep again.

Later it was discovered that James Lenn was missing, and that the dog also had disappeared, but in the opposite direction. A search of the countryside was instituted which resulted in the finding of twenty-five empty tins, several old brooms, enough newspapers to make a fair-sized bale, and one old buggy-top. None of these seemed to have any value as clews in the mysterious disappearance of James Lenn. Some importance was attached to the discovery of the buggy-top until it was found that the missing farmer was not hiding under it.

The police, however, were not satisfied. There had been several violations of the State Fishing and Gaming ordinances in and around Wallack and public censure of the police was at its height. Chief of Police Walter M. Turbot determined to carry this case through to a finish. Thus it was that the search for Farmer James Lenn was begun afresh, a search which was destined to end in Innsbruck, Austria.

93

In the little town of Innsbruck there had been living an old garbler named Leon Nabgratz, a sort of town character, if such a thing were possible. Nabgratz had never been to America, but his young nephew, Gurling Nabgratz, son of Leon's brother

The principals in the famous Wallack disappearances
—Courtesy of John Held, Jr., and Life.

Meff, was born in that country and had lived there all his life. Late in December, 1867, he had moved to Wallack, Connecticut, where he was sold as a slave to one James Lenn.

One day, while reading the newspaper, Gurling Nabgratz came across an item indicating that slavery had been abolished four years previously and figured out that he was just a sap to be working for James Lenn for nothing. He mentioned the matter to his master, but Lenn maintained that it was only the Negro slaves who had been freed, and that Lincoln was no longer President anyway.

Nabgratz went away grumbling but did his chores that day as usual. He was seen late in the evening of April 17 in the poolroom of the village, where he is said to have made *sotto-voce* remarks and sung several slave songs of the ante-bellum South with such inflammatory refrains as "We'se all gwine ter be free!"

That night Gurling Nabgratz disappeared and was never seen again in Wallack.

This having preceded the disappearance of James Lenn by about two years, nothing was thought of it at the time. During the search for Lenn, however, the incident was recalled, and a search for Nabgratz was instituted. This made two searches going on at once in the little town of Wallack, and resulted in considerable hard feeling between the rival searching-parties. The town was divided into two camps, the "Find Lenn" faction and the "Find Nabgratz" faction, and on at least one occasion shots were exchanged.

In the meantime, in Innsbruck, Austria, Leon Nabgratz, the old garbler, was quietly pursuing his way, quite unconscious of the stir that he was causing four thousand miles away. His brother Meff had written him about Gurling's disappearance, but, as the old man never bothered to read his brother's letters, he was just as much in the dark as he had been before. More so, in fact, because he was older.

His surprise can well be imagined, therefore, when one day in the spring of 1869 the police entered his house in the Schmalzgasse and began a search for James Lenn of Wallack, Connecticut, U. S. A. In vain Nabgratz protested that he had never heard the name of Lenn and that, even if he had, it was not interesting to him. The arm of the law reaching across the Atlantic was inexorable. Leon Nabgratz's house was searched and in it was found an old trunk of suspiciously large proportions. In spite of the fact that this trunk was labeled *"Weihnachtsgeschenke"* ("Christmas presents") it was opened, and in it were found James Lenn *and* Gurling Nabgratz, together with a copy of the New York *Times* of October 12, 1868.

The mysterious Wallack disappearances were thus explained, and Leon Nabgratz was arrested for having in his possession a trunk with a misleading label on it.

Art is long and time is fleeting.

Kiddie-Kar
Travel

IN AMERICA there are two classes of travel—
first class, and with children. Traveling with
children corresponds roughly to traveling third-
class in Bulgaria. They tell me there is nothing
lower in the world than third-class Bulgarian travel.

The actual physical discomfort of traveling with
the Kiddies is not so great, although you do emerge
from it looking as if you had just moved the piano
upstairs single-handed. It is the mental wear-and-
tear that tells and for a sensitive man there is only
one thing worse, and that is a church wedding in
which he is playing the leading comedy rôle.

There are several branches of the ordeal of Going
on Choo-Choo, and it is difficult to tell which is the
roughest. Those who have taken a very small baby
on a train maintain that this ranks as pleasure
along with having a nerve killed. On the other
hand, those whose wee companions are in the romping stage, simply laugh at the claims of the first
group. Sometimes you will find a man who has
both an infant *and* a romper with him. Such a citizen should receive a salute of twenty-one guns every
time he enters the city and should be allowed to
wear the insignia of the Pater Dolorosa, giving him
the right to solicit alms on the cathedral steps.

There is much to be said for those who maintain that rather should the race be allowed to die out than that babies should be taken from place to place along our national arteries of traffic. On the other hand, there *are* moments when babies are asleep. (Oh, yes, there are. There *must* be.) But it is practically a straight run of ten or a dozen hours for your child of four. You may have a little trouble in getting the infant to doze off, especially as the train newsboy waits crouching in the vestibule until he sees signs of slumber on the child's face and then rushes in to yell, "Cop of *Life*, out today!" right by its pink, shell-like ear. But after it *is* asleep, your troubles are over except for wondering how you can shift your ossifying arm to a new position without disturbing its precious burden.

If the child is of an age which denies the existence of sleep, however, preferring to run up and down the aisle of the car rather than sit in its chair (at least a baby can't get out of its chair unless it falls out and even then it can't go far), then every minute of the trip is full of fun. On the whole, having traveled with children of all the popular ages, I would be inclined to award the Hair-Shirt to the man who successfully completes the ride with a boy of, let us say, three.

In the first place, you start with the pronounced ill-will of two-thirds of the rest of the occupants of the car. You see them as they come in, before the train starts, glancing at you and yours with little or no attempt to conceal the fact that they wish

You start with the pronounced ill-will of the rest of the occupants

they had waited for the four o'clock. Across from you is perhaps a large man who, in his home town, has a reputation for eating little children. He wears a heavy gold watch chain and wants to read through a lot of reports on the trip. He is just about as glad to be opposite a small boy as he would be if it were a hurdy-gurdy.

In back of you is a lady in a black silk dress who doesn't like the porter. Ladies in black silk dresses always seem to board the train with an aversion to the porter. The fact that the porter has to be in the same car with her makes her fussy to start with, and when she discovers that in front of her is a child of three who is already eating (you simply have to give him a lemon-drop to keep him quiet at least until the train starts), she decides that the best thing to do is simply to ignore him and not give him the slightest encouragement to become friendly. The child therefore picks her out immediately to be his buddy.

For a time after things get to going all you have to do is answer questions about the scenery. This is only what you must expect when you have children, and it happens no matter where you are. You can always say that you don't know who lives in that house or what that cow is doing. Sometimes you don't even have to look up when you say that you don't know. This part is comparatively easy.

It is when the migratory fit comes on that you will be put to the test. Suddenly you look and find the boy staggering down the aisle, peering into the faces of people as he passes them. "Here! Come back here, Roger!" you cry, lurching after him and landing across the knees of the young lady two seats down. Roger takes this as a signal for a game and starts to run, screaming with laughter. After four steps he falls and starts to cry.

On being carried kicking back to his seat, he is told that he mustn't run down the aisle again. This strikes even Roger as funny, because it is such a flat thing to say. Of course he is going to run down the aisle again and he knows it as well as you do.

In the meantime, however, he is perfectly willing to spend a little time with the lady in the black silk dress.

"Here, Roger," you say, "don't bother the lady."

"Hello, little boy," the lady says, nervously, and tries to go back to her book. The interview is over as far as she is concerned. Roger, however, thinks that it would be just dandy to get up in her lap. This has to be stopped, and Roger has to be whispered to.

He then announces that it is about time that he went to the wash-room. You march down the car, steering him by the shoulders and both lurching together as the train takes the curves and attracting wide attention to your very obvious excursion. Several kindly people smile knowingly at you as you pass and try to pat the boy on the head, but their advances are repelled, it being a rule of all children to look with disfavor on any attentions from strangers. The only people they want to play with are those who hate children.

On reaching the wash-room you discover that the porter has just locked it and taken the key with him, simply to be nasty. This raises quite a problem. You explain the situation as well as possible, which turns out to be not well enough. There is every indication of loud crying and perhaps worse. You call attention to the Burrows Rustless Screen sign which you are just passing and stand in the passage-way by the drinking-cups, feverishly trying to find things in the landscape as it whirls by which will serve to take the mind off the tragedy of the moment. You become so engrossed in this important task that it is some time before you discover that you are completely blocking the passage-way

Before you discover that you are completely blocking the passageway

and the progress of some fifteen people who want to get off at Utica. There is nothing for you to do but head the procession and get off first.

Once out in the open, the pride and prop of your old age decides that the thing to do is pay the engineer a visit, and starts off up the platform at a terrific rate. This amuses the onlookers and gives you a little exercise after being cramped up in that old car all the morning. The imminent danger of the train's starting without you only adds to the fun. At that, there might be worse things than being left in Utica. One of them is getting back on the train again to face the old gentleman with the large watch chain.

The final phase of the ordeal, however, is still in store for you when you make your way (and Roger's way) into the diner. Here the plunging march down the aisle of the car is multiplied by six (the diner is never any nearer than six cars and usually is part of another train). On the way, Roger sees a box of animal crackers belonging to a little girl and commandeers it. The little girl, putting up a fight, is promptly pushed over, starting what promises to be a free-for-all fight between the two families. Lurching along after the apologies have been made, it is just a series of unwarranted attacks by Roger on sleeping travelers and equally unwarranted evasions by Roger of the kindly advances of very nice people who love children.

In the diner, it turns out that the nearest thing they have suited to Roger's customary diet is veal cutlets, and you hardly think that his mother would approve of those. Everything else has peppers or sardines in it. A curry of lamb across the way strikes the boy's fancy and he demands some of that. On being told that he has not the slightest chance in the world of getting it but how would he like a little crackers-and-milk, he becomes quite upset and threatens to throw a fork at the Episcopal clergyman sitting opposite. Pieces of toast are waved alluringly in front of him and he is asked to consider the advantages of preserved figs and cream, but it is curry of lamb or he gets off the train. He doesn't act like this at home. In fact, he is noted for his tractability. There seems to be something about the train that brings out all the worst that is in him, all the hidden traits that he has inherited from his mother's side of the family. There is nothing else to do but say firmly: "Very well, then, Roger. We'll go back *without* any nice dinner," and carry him protesting from the diner, apologizing to the head steward for the scene and considering dropping him overboard as you pass through each vestibule.

In fact, I had a cousin once who had to take three of his little ones on an all-day trip from Philadelphia to Boston. It was the hottest day of the year and my cousin had on a woolen suit. By the time he reached Hartford, people in the car noticed that he had only two children with him. At Worcester he had only one. No one knew what had become of the others and no one asked. It seemed better not to ask. He reached Boston alone and never explained what had become of the tiny tots. Anyone who has ever traveled with tiny tots of his own, however, can guess.

The
Last Day

WHEN, during the long winter evenings, you sit around the snap-shot album and recall the merry, merry times you had on your vacation, there is one day which your memory mercifully overlooks. It is the day you packed up and left the summer resort to go home.

This Ultimate Day really begins the night before, when you sit up until one o'clock trying to get things into the trunks and bags. This is when you discover the well-known fact that summer air swells articles to twice or three times their original size; so that the sneakers which in June fitted in between the phonograph and the book (which you have never opened), in September are found to require a whole tray for themselves and even then one of them will probably have to be carried in the hand.

Along about midnight, the discouraging process begins to get on your nerves and you snap at your wife and she snaps at you every time it is found that something won't fit in the suitcase. As you have both gradually dispensed with the more attractive articles of clothing under stress of the heat and the excitement, these little word passages taken on the sordid nature of a squabble in an East Side tenement, and all that is needed is for one of the children to wake up and start whimpering. This it does.

It is finally decided that there is no sense in trying to finish the job that night. General nervousness, combined with a specific fear of oversleeping, results in a troubled tossing of perhaps three hours in bed, and ushers in the dawn of the last day on just about as irritable and bleary-eyed a little family as you will find outside an institution.

The trouble starts right away with the process of getting dressed in traveling clothes which haven't been worn since the trip up. Junior's shoulders are still tender, and he decides that it will be impossible for him to wear his starched blouse. One of Philip's good shoes, finding that there has been no call for it during the summer, has become hurt and has disappeared; so Philip has to wear a pair of Daddy's old bathing shoes which had been thrown away. (After everything has been locked and taken out of the room, the good shoe is found in the closet and left for dead.)

You, yourself, aren't any too successful in reverting to city clothes. Several weeks of soft collars and rubber-soled shoes have softened you to a point where the old "Deroy-14½" feels like a napkin-ring around your neck, and your natty brogans are so heavy that you lose your balance and topple over forward if you step out suddenly. The whole effect of your civilian costume when surveyed in a mirror is that of a Maine guide all dressed up for an outing "up to Bangor."

Incidentally, it shapes up as one of the hottest days of the season—or any other season.

"Oh, look how funny Daddy looks in his straw hat!"

"I never realized before, Fred, how much too high the crown is for the length of your face. Are you sure it's your hat?"

"It's my hat, all right," is the proper reply, "but maybe the face belongs to somebody else."

This silences them for a while, but on and off during the day a lot of good-natured fun is had in calling the attention of outsiders to the spectacle presented by Daddy in his "store" clothes.

Once everyone is dressed, there must be an excursion to take one last look at the ocean, or lake, or whatever particular prank of Nature it may have been which has served as an inducement to you to leave the city. This must be done before breakfast. So down to the beach you go, getting your shoes full of sand, and wait while Sister, in a sentimental attempt to feel the water for the last time, has tripped and fallen in, soaking herself to the garters. There being no dry clothes left out, she has to go in the kitchen and stand in front of the stove until at least one side of her is dry.

Breakfast bears no resemblance to any other meal eaten in the place. There is a poorly-suppressed feeling that you must hurry, coupled with the stiff collar and tight clothes, which makes it practically impossible to get any food down past the upper chest.

Then follows one of the worst features of the worst of all vacation days—the goodbyes. It isn't that you hate to part company with these people. They too, as they stand there in their summer clothes, seem to have undergone some process whereby you see them as they really are and not as they seemed when you were all together up to your necks in water or worrying a tennis ball back and forth over a net. And you may be sure that you, in your town clothes, seem doubly unattractive to them.

Here is Mrs. Tremble, who lives in Montclair, N. J., in the winter. That really is a terrible hat of hers, now that you get a good look at it. "Well, goodbye, Mrs. Tremble. Be sure to look us up if you ever get out our way. We are right in the telephone book, and we'll have a regular get-together meeting. . . . Goodbye, Marian. Think of us tonight in the hot city, and be sure to let us know when you are going through . . . Well, so long, Mr. Prothero; look out for those girls up at the post office. Don't let any of them marry you . . . Well, we're off, Mrs. Rostetter. Yes, we're leaving today. On the 10-45. We have to be back for Junior's school. It begins on the 11th. *Good*bye!"

It is then found that there is about an hour to wait before the machine comes to take you to the station; so all these goodbyes have been wasted and have to be gone through with again.

In the meantime, Mother decides that she must run over to the Bide-a-Wee cottage and say goodbye

Sister has tripped and fallen in, soaking herself to the garters

to the Sisbys. The children feel that they are about due for another last look at the ocean. And Daddy remembers that he hasn't been able to shut the big suitcase yet. So the family disperses in various directions and each unit gets lost. Mother, rushing out from the Sisbys' in a panic thinking that she hears the automobile, is unable to find the others. Little Mildred, having taken it upon herself to look out for the other children while they are gazing on the ocean, has felt it incumbent on her to spank Philip for trying to build one last tunnel in the sand, resulting in a bitter physical encounter in which Philip easily batters his sister into a state of hysteria. Daddy, having wilted his collar and put his knee through his straw hat in an attempt to jam the suitcase together, finds that the thing can't be done and takes out the box of sea-shells that Junior had planned to take home for his cabinet, and hides them under the bed.

The suitcase at last having been squeezed shut and placed with the rest of the bags in the hall, the maid comes running up with five damp bathing suits which she has found hanging on the line and wants to know if they belong here. Daddy looks cautiously down the hall and whispers: "No!"

At last the automobile arrives and stands honking by the roadside. "Come, Junior, quick, put your coat on! . . . Have you got the bag with the thermos? . . . Hurry, Philip! . . . Where's Sister? . . . Come, Sister! . . . Well, it's too late now. You'll have to wait till we get on the train . . .

Looks cautiously down the hall and whispers: "No!"

Goodbye, Mrs. Tremble . . . Be sure to look us up . . . Goodbye, everybody! . . . Here, Junior! Put that down! You can't take that with you. No, no! That belongs to that other little boy . . . *Junior!* . . . Goodbye, Marian! . . . Goodbye, Mrs. McNerdle! . . . Philip, say goodbye to Mrs. McNerdle, she's been so good to you, don't you remember? . . . Goodbye, Mrs. McNerdle, that's right. . . . *Goodbye!"*

And with that the automobile starts, the friends

on the porch wave and call out indistinguishable pleasantries, Junior begins to cry, and it is found that Ed has no hat.

The trip home in the heat and cinders is enlivened by longing reminiscences: "Well, it's eleven o'clock. I suppose they're all getting into their bathing suits now. How'd you like to jump into that old ocean right this minute, eh?" (As a matter of fact, the speaker has probably not been induced to go into "that old ocean" more than three times during the whole summer.)

The fact that they reach home too late to get a regular dinner and have to go to bed hungry, and the more poignant impressions in the process of opening a house which has been closed all summer, have all been treated of before in an article called "The Entrance Into the Tomb." And so we will leave our buoyant little family, their vacation ended, all ready to jump into the swing of their work, refreshed, invigorated, and clear-eyed.

Family Life in America

PART 1

The naturalistic literature of this country has reached such a state that no family of characters is considered true to life which does not include at least two hypochondriacs, one sadist, and one old man who spills food down the front of his vest. If this school progresses, the following is what we may expect in our national literature in a year or so.

THE living-room in the Twillys' house was so damp that thick, soppy moss grew all over the walls. It dripped on the picture of Grandfather Twilly that hung over the melodeon, making streaks down the dirty glass like sweat on the old man's face. It was a mean face. Grandfather Twilly had been a mean man and had little spots of soup on the lapel of his coat. All his children were mean and had soup spots on their clothes.

Grandma Twilly sat in the rocker over by the window, and as she rocked the chair snapped. It sounded like Grandma Twilly's knees snapping as they did whenever she stooped over to pull the wings off a fly. She was a mean old thing. Her knuckles were grimy and she chewed crumbs that she found in the bottom of her reticule. You would have hated her. She hated herself. But most of all she hated Grandfather Twilly.

114

"I certainly hope you're frying good," she muttered as she looked up at his picture.

"Hasn't the undertaker come yet, Ma?" asked young Mrs. Wilbur Twilly petulantly. She was boiling water on the oil-heater and every now and again would spill a little of the steaming liquid on the baby who was playing on the floor. She hated the baby because it looked like her father. The hot water raised little white blisters on the baby's red neck and Mabel Twilly felt short, sharp twinges of pleasure at the sight. It was the only pleasure she had had for four months.

"Why don't you kill yourself, Ma?" she continued. "You're only in the way here and you know it. It's just because you're a mean old woman and want to make trouble for us that you hang on."

Grandma Twilly shot a dirty look at her daughter-in-law. She had always hated her. Stringy hair, Mabel had. Dank, stringy hair. Grandma Twilly thought how it would look hanging at an Indian's belt. But all that she did was to place her tongue against her two front teeth and make a noise like the bath-room faucet.

Wilbur Twilly was reading the paper by the oil lamp. Wilbur had watery blue eyes and cigar ashes all over his knees. The third and fourth buttons of his vest were undone. It was too hideous.

He was conscious of his family seated in chairs about him. His mother, chewing crumbs. His wife Mabel, with her stringy hair, reading. His sister Bernice, with projecting front teeth, who sat think-

ing of the man who came every day to take away
the waste paper. Bernice was wondering how long
it would be before her family would discover that
she had been married to this man for three years.

How Wilbur hated them all. It didn't seem as
if he could stand it any longer. He wanted to
scream and stick pins into every one of them and
then rush out and see the girl who worked in his
office snapping rubber-bands all day. He hated her
too, but she wore side-combs.

PART 2

The street was covered with slimy mud. It oozed
out from under Bernice's rubbers in unpleasant
bubbles until it seemed to her as if she must kill
herself. Hot air coming out from a steam laundry.
Hot, stifling air. Bernice didn't work in the laundry
but she wished that she did so that the hot air
would kill her. She wanted to be stifled. She
needed torture to be happy. She also needed a good
swift clout on the side of the face.

A drunken man lurched out from a door-way and
flung his arms about her. It was only her husband.
She loved her husband. She loved him so much
that, as she pushed him away and into the gutter,
she stuck her little finger into his eye. She also
untied his neck-tie. It was a bow neck-tie, with
white, dirty spots on it and it was wet with gin. It
didn't seem as if Bernice could stand it any longer.
All the repressions of nineteen sordid years behind
protruding teeth surged through her untidy soul.

She wanted love. But it was not her husband that she loved so fiercely. It was old Grandfather Twilly. And he was too dead.

PART 3

In the dining-room of the Twilly's house everything was very quiet. Even the vinegar-cruet which was covered with fly-specks. Grandma Twilly lay with her head in the baked potatoes, poisoned by Mabel, who, in her turn had been poisoned by her husband and sprawled in an odd posture over the china-closet. Wilbur and his sister Bernice had just finished choking each other to death and between them completely covered the carpet in that corner of the room where the worn spot showed the bare boards beneath, like ribs on a chicken carcass.

Only the baby survived. She had a mean face and had great spillings of Imperial Granum down her bib. As she looked about her at her family, a great hate surged through her tiny body and her eyes snapped viciously. She wanted to get down from her high-chair and show them all how much she hated them.

Bernice's husband, the man who came after the waste paper, staggered into the room. The tips were off both his shoe-lacings. The baby experienced a voluptuous sense of futility at the sight of the tipless-lacings and leered suggestively at her uncle-in-law.

"We must get the roof fixed," said the man, very quietly. "It lets the sun in."

The Romance of Digestion

W HEN you take a bite of that delicious cookie, or swallow a morsel of that nourishing bread, do you stop to think of the marvelous and intricate process by means of which Mother Nature is going to convert it into bone and sinew and roses for those pretty cheeks? Probably not, and it is just as well. For if you did stop to think of it at that time, you would unquestionably not be able to digest that cookie—or that nourishing bread.

But whether you think of it or not this exciting process of digestion is going on, day in and day out, sometimes pretty badly but always with a great show of efficiency. It is, on the whole, probably one of the worst-done jobs in the world.

First you must know that those hard, white edges of bone which you must have noticed hundreds of times along the front of your mouth, are "teeth," and are put there for a very definite purpose. They are the ivory gates to the body. They are Nature's tiny sentinels, and if you have ever bitten yourself, you will know how sharp they can be, and what efficient little watchmen they are. Just you try to slip your finger into your mouth without your teeth's permission, and see how far you get. Or try to get it out, once they have captured it.

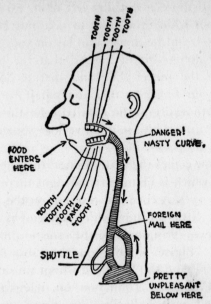

*Cross section of human food duct, showing ludicrous
process of self-styled "Digestion"*

Now these thousands of brave little soldiers, the
teeth, which we have in our mouths, take the food
as it comes through the air (in case you are snapping at a butterfly) or from the fork, and separate
it into its component parts (air, land and water).
In this process, the teeth are aided by the tongue,
which is that awful-looking thing right back of
your teeth. Don't look at it!

The tongue (which we may call the escalator of
the mouth or Nature's nobleman for short), and
the teeth toss the food back and forth between

119

them until there is nothing left of it, except the
little bones which you have to take out between
your thumb and forefinger and lay on your butter-
plate. In doing this be careful that the bone is
really on the butter-plate and that it does not
stick to your finger so that you put it back into
your mouth again on the next trip, for this would
make the little white sentries very angry and they
might all drop out.

And now comes the really wonderful part of the
romance which is being enacted right there under
your very eyes. A chemical reaction on the tongue
presses a little button which telegraphs down,
down, down, 'way down to the cross old Stomach
and says: "Please, sir, do you want this food or
don't you?" And the Stomach, whom we shall call
"Prince Charming" from now on, telegraphs (or
more likely writes) back: "Yes, dear!" or "You
can do what you like with it for all of me." Just as
he happens to feel at the time.

And then, such a hurry and bustle as goes on in
the mouth! "Foodie's going to visit Stomach!" all
the little teeth cry, and rush about for all the world
as if they were going themselves. "All aboard, all
aboard!" calls out the tongue, and there is a great
ringing of bells and blowing of whistles and bumping of porters and in the midst of it all, the rem-
nants of that delicious cookie seated nervously on
the tongue, ready to be taken down on its first
journey alone, down to see Prince Charming. For
all the joyousness of the occasion, it is a little sad,

too. For that bit of cookie is going to get some terribly tough treatment before it is through.

The food is then placed on a conveyor, by means of which it is taken to the Drying Room, situated on the third floor, where it is taken apart and washed and dried, preparatory to going through the pressing machines. These pressing machines are operated by one man, who stands by the conveyor as it brings the food along and tosses it into the vats. Here all rocks and moss are drawn off by mechanical pickers and the food subjected to treatment in a solution of sulphite, a secret process which is jealously guarded. From here the food is taken to the Playroom where it plays around awhile with the other children until it is time for it to be folded by the girls in the bindery, packed into neat stacks, and wrapped for shipment in bundles of fifty. Some of these bundles, the proteins, are shipped to the bones of the body, others, the hydrates, go to making muscle, while a third class, the sophomores, contribute to making fatty tissue which nobody wants, that is, not if he has any pride at all about his appearance. The byproducts are made into milk-bottle caps, emery wheels, and insurance calendars, and are sold at cost.

Thus we see how wonderfully Nature takes care of us and our little troubles, aided only by soda-mint and bicarbonate.

"Ask that Man"

THIS is written for those men who have wives who are constantly insisting on their asking questions of officials.

For years I was troubled with the following complaint: Just as soon as we started out on a trip of any kind, even if it were only to the corner of the street, Doris began forcing me to ask questions of people. If we weren't quite sure of the way: "Why don't you ask that man? He could tell you." If there was any doubt as to the best place to go to get chocolate ice-cream, she would say: "Why don't you ask that boy in uniform? He would be likely to know."

I can't quite define my aversion to asking questions of strangers. From snatches of family battles which I have heard drifting up from railway stations and street corners, I gather that there are a great many men who share my dislike for it, as well as an equal number of women who, like Doris, believe it to be the solution of most of this world's problems. The man's dread is probably that of making himself appear a pest or ridiculously uninformed. The woman's insistence is based probably on experience which has taught her that *any* one, no matter who, knows more about things in general than her husband.

Furthermore, I never know exactly how to begin

*I gather that there are a great many men who share my
dislike for it*

a request for information. If I preface it with, "I beg your pardon!" the stranger is likely not to hear, especially if he happens to be facing in another direction, for my voice isn't very reliable in

My voice isn't very reliable in crises

crises and sometimes makes no intelligible sound at all until I have been talking for fully a minute. Often I say, "I beg your pardon!" and he turns quickly and says, "What did you say?" Then I have to repeat, "I beg your pardon!" and he asks, quite naturally, "What for?" Then I am stuck. Here I am, begging a perfect stranger's pardon, and for no apparent reason under the sun. The wonder is that I am not knocked down oftener.

It was to avoid going through life under this pressure that I evolved the little scheme detailed herewith. It cost me several thousand dollars, but Doris is through with asking questions of outsiders.

We had started on a little trip to Boston. I could have found out where the Boston train was in a few minutes had I been left to myself. But Doris never relies on the signs. Someone must be asked, too, just to make sure. Confronted once by a buckboard literally swathed in banners which screamed in red letters, "This bus goes to the State Fair Grounds," I had to go up to the driver (who had on his cap a flag reading "To the State Fair Grounds") and ask him if this bus surely went to the State Fair Grounds. He didn't even answer me.

So when Doris said: "Go and ask that man where the Boston train leaves from," I gritted my teeth and decided that the time had come. Simulating conversation with him, I really asked him nothing, and returned to Doris, saying, "Come on. He says it goes from Track 10."

Eight months later we returned home. The train that left on Track 10 was the Chicago Limited, which I had taken deliberately. In Chicago I again falsified what "the man" told me, and instead of getting on the train back to New York we went to Little Rock, Arkansas. Every time I had to ask where the best hotel was, I made up information which brought us out into the suburbs, cold and hungry. Many nights we spent wandering through the fields looking for some place that never existed, or else in the worst hotel in town acting on what I said was the advice of "that kind-looking man in uniform."

From Arkansas, we went into Mexico, and once, guided by what I told her had been the directions given me by the man at the news-stand in Vera Cruz, we made a sally into the swamps of Central America, in whatever that first republic is on the way south. After that, Doris began to lose faith in what strange men could tell us. One day, at a little station in Mavicos, I said: "Wait a minute, till I ask that man what is the best way to get back into America," and she said, sobbing: "Don't ask anybody. Just do what you think is best." Then I knew that the fight was over. In ten days I had her limp form back in New York and from that day to this she hasn't once suggested that I ask questions of a stranger.

The funny part of it is, I constantly find myself asking them. I guess the humiliation came in being told to ask.

Cell-formations and Their Work

IT IS only recently that science has found out the exact structure of the tiny cell-formations which go to make up life. Only yesterday, in fact.

Every higher animal starts life as a single cell. This much is obvious. Look at the rainbow. Look at the formation of frost on the window-pane. Don't look now. Wait a minute. . . . Now look.

This cell measures no more than 1/125 of an inch in diameter at first, but you mustn't be discouraged. It looks like nothing at all, even under the strongest microscope, and, before we knew just how important they were, they were often thrown away. We now know that if it were not for these tiny, tiny cells, we should none of us be here today. This may or may not be a recommendation for the cells. *Quien sabe?*

Shortly after the cell decides to go ahead with the thing, it gets lonely and divides itself up into three similar cells, just for company's sake and to have someone to talk to. They soon find out that they aren't particularly congenial, so they keep on dividing themselves up into other cells until there is a regular mob of them. Then they elect an entertainment committee and give a show.

After the show, there is a fight, and the thing

breaks up into different cliques or groups. One group think they are white corpuscles or *phagocytes*. Others go around saying that they are *red* corpuscles and to hell with the white.

The other groups of cells devote themselves to music, æsthetic dancing, and the formation of starch which goes into dress-shirts. They are all very happy and very busy, and it's nobody's business *what* they do when they aren't working. We certainly are not going to snoop into that here.

We must take up, however, the work of the brain-cells, as it is in the brain that the average man of today does his thinking. (Aha-ha-ha-ha-ha-ha!)

Oh, let's *not* take up the brain-cells. You know as much about them as anybody does, and what's the use anyway? Suppose you *do* learn something today. You're likely to die tomorrow, and there you are.

And we *must* go into the question of the size of these cells. That really is important. In about 1/150000 of a cubic inch of blood there are some five million cells afloat. This is, as you will see, about the population of the City of London, except that the cells don't wear any hats. Thus, in our whole body, there are perhaps (six times seven is forty-two, five times eight is forty, put down naught and carry your four, eight times nine is seventy-two and four is seventy-six, put down six and carry your seven and then, adding, six, four, three, one, six, naught, naught, naught), oh, about a billion or so

of these red corpuscles alone, not counting overhead and breakage. In the course of time, that runs
into figures.

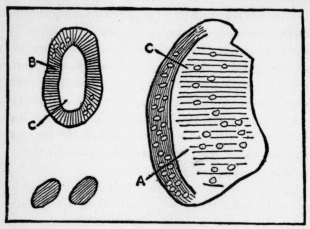

*Differentiation of cells in the lens of an eye. Doesn't
mean a thing*

Now when it comes to reproduction, you have
to look out. In the cuttlefish, for example, there is
what is known as "greesion" or budding. The or-
ganism as a whole remains unaltered, except that
one small portion of it breaks off and goes into
business for itself. This, of course, makes a very
pretty picture, but gets nowhere. In the case of
multicellular animals, like the orange, it results
in a frightful confusion.

We should have said that there are two classes
of animals, unicellular and multicellular. From the
unicellular group we get our coal, iron, wheat and

ice, and from the multicellular our salt, pepper, chutney and that beautiful silk dress which milady wears so proudly. Woolen and leather goods we import.

You will see then that by grafting a piece of one species on another species, you can mix the cells and have all kinds of fun. Winkler, in 1902, grafted a piece of Solanum (the genus to which the potato belongs) onto a stock of another kind, and then, after the union had been established, cut the stem across, just at the point of junction. The bud was formed of the intermingled tissues of the two species and was most peculiar-looking.

Winkler was arrested.

Editha's
Christmas Burglar

I T WAS the night before Christmas, and Editha was all agog. It was all so exciting, so exciting! From her little bed up in the nursery she could hear Mumsey and Daddy down-stairs putting the things on the tree and jamming her stocking full of broken candy and oranges.

"Hush!" Daddy was speaking. "Eva," he was saying to Mumsey, "it seems kind of silly to put this ten-dollar gold-piece that Aunt Issac sent to Editha into her stocking. She is too young to know the value of money. It would just be a bauble to her. How about putting it in with the household money for this month? Editha would then get some of the food that was bought with it and we would be ten dollars in."

Dear old Daddy! Always thinking of someone else! Editha wanted to jump out of bed right then and there and run down and throw her arms about his neck, perhaps shutting off his wind.

"You are right, as usual, Hal," said Mumsey. "Give me the gold-piece and I will put it in with the house funds."

"In a pig's eye I will give you the gold-piece," replied Daddy. "You would nest it away some-where until after Christmas and then go out and

132

buy yourself a muff with it. I know you, you old grafter." And from the sound which followed, Editha knew that Mumsey was kissing Daddy. Did ever a little girl have two such darling parents? And, hugging her Teddy-bear close to her, Editha rolled over and went to sleep.

·　·　·　·　·

She awoke suddenly with the feeling that someone was downstairs. It was quite dark and the radiolite traveling-clock which stood by her bedside said eight o'clock, but, as the radiolite traveling-clock hadn't been running since Easter, she knew that that couldn't be the right time. She knew that it must be somewhere between three and four in the morning, however, because the blanket had slipped off her bed, and the blanket always slipped off her bed between three and four in the morning.

And now to take up the question of who it was downstairs. At first she thought it might be Daddy. Often Daddy sat up very late working on a case of Scotch and at such times she would hear him downstairs counting to himself. But whoever was there now was being very quiet. It was only when he jammed against the china-cabinet or joggled the dinner-gong that she could tell that anyone was there at all. It was evidently a stranger.

Of course, it might be that the old folks had been right all along and that there really was a Santa Claus after all, but Editha dismissed this supposition at once. The old folks had never been right before and what chance was there of their starting in to be right now, at their age? None at all. It couldn't be Santa, the jolly old soul!

It must be a burglar then! Why, to be sure! Burglars always come around on Christmas Eve and little yellow-haired girls always get up and go down in their nighties and convert them. Of course! How silly of Editha not to have thought of it before!

With a bound the child was out on the cold floor, and with another bound she was back in bed again. It was too cold to be fooling around without slippers on. Reaching down by the bedside, she pulled in her little fur foot-pieces which Cousin Mabel had left behind by mistake the last time she visited Editha, and drew them on her tiny feet. Then out she got and started on tip-toe for the stairway.

She did hope that he would be a good-looking burglar and easily converted, because it was pretty gosh-darned cold, even with slippers on, and she wished to save time.

As she reached the head of the stairs, she could look down into the living-room where the shadow of the tree stood out black against the gray light outside. In the doorway leading into the dining room stood a man's figure, silhouetted against the glare of an old-fashioned burglar's lantern which was on the floor. He was rattling silverware. Very quietly, Editha descended the stairs until she stood quite close to him.

"Hello, Mr. Man!" she said.

"Hello, Mr. Man!" she said

The burglar looked up quickly and reached for his gun.

"Who the hell do you think you are?" he asked.

"I'se Editha," replied the little girl in the sweetest voice she could summon, which wasn't particularly sweet at that as Editha hadn't a very pretty voice.

"You's Editha, is youse?" replied the burglar. "Well, come on down here. Grandpa wants to speak to you."

"Youse is not my Drandpa," said the tot getting her baby and tough talk slightly mixed. "Youse is a dreat, bid burglar."

"All right, kiddy," replied the man. "Have it your own way. But come on down. I want ter show yer how yer kin make smoke come outer yer eyes. It's a Christmas game."

"This guy is as good as converted already," thought Editha to herself. "Right away he starts wanting to teach me games. Next he'll be telling me I remind him of his little girl at home."

So with a light heart she came the rest of the way downstairs, and stood facing the burly stranger.

"Sit down, Editha," he said, and gave her a hearty push which sent her down heavily on the floor. "And stay there, or I'll mash you one on that baby nose of yours."

This was not in the schedule as Editha had read it in the books, but it doubtless was this particular burglar's way of having a little fun. He *did* have nice eyes, too.

"Dat's naughty to do," she said, scoldingly.

"Yeah?" said the burglar, and sent her spinning against the wall. "I guess you need attention, kid. You can't be trusted." Whereupon he slapped the little girl. Then he took a piece of rope out of his bag and tied her up good and tight, with a nice bright bandana handkerchief around her mouth, and trussed her up on the chandelier.

"Now hang there," he said, "and make believe you're a Christmas present, and if you open yer yap, I'll set fire to yer."

Then, filling his bag with the silverware and Daddy's imitation sherry, Editha's burglar tip-toed out by the door. As he left, he turned and smiled. "A Merry Christmas to all and to all a Good Night," he whispered, and was gone.

"A Merry Christmas to all and to all a Good Night!"

And when Mumsey and Daddy came down in the morning, there was Editha up on the chandelier, sore as a crab. So they took her down and spanked her for getting out of bed without permission.

A Short History of American Politics

THOSE of you who get around to reading a lot will remember that a history of American politics was begun by me several chapters back—or rather, an introduction to such a history was written. Then came the Great War . . . brother was turned against brother, father against father; the cobblestones of the Tuileries were spattered with the blood of the royalists, and such minor matters as histories were cast aside for the musket and ploughshare. In crises such as that of March, 1928, the savants must give way to the men of action.

Now that the tumult and the shouting have died, however, the history of American politics can be written. The only trouble at present is that I have lost the introduction I wrote several months ago. It must have fallen down behind the bureau and the wall of the Kremlin.

To write another introductory preface would be silly, and that is the reason I have decided to write one. The other one was probably not much good, anyway. So while you all go ahead and read the other pages of this volume, I will write another introduction to a history of American politics. (That is, I will if I can get this stuff off the keys of my typewriter. Either somebody has rubbed candy over each key while I have been dozing here or the typewriter itself has a strain of maple in it and is giving off sap. I have never run across anything like it in all my experience with typewriters. The "j" key looks so sticky that I am actually afraid to touch it. Ugh!)

Well, anyway ——

A History of American Politics

(2 vol., 695 pp. 8vo................100 to 1 to show.)

INTRODUCTION

The theory of political procedure in those countries in which a democratic form of government obtains is based on the assumption that the average citizen knows enough to vote. (*Time out for prolonged laughter.*)

The Ideal State of Plato, as you will remember (you liar!), was founded on quite a different principle, but, if you will look at Greece today you will see that something was wrong in that principle, too. Plato felt—and quite rightly—that Truth is the Ultimate Good and that the Ultimate Good is Truth—or the Idea. (Check one of these three.) *Now*—in the Ideal State, granted that the citizens keep away from the polls and mind their own business, we have an oligarchy or combination of hydrogen atoms so arranged as to form Truth in the Abstract. Of course, Plato wrote only what he had learned from Socrates, and Socrates, like the wise old owl that he was, never signed his name to anything. So that left Plato holding the bag for an unworkable political theory which has been carried down to the present day.

Aristotle followed Plato with some new theories, but as he dealt mostly with the Drama and Mathematics, with side excursions into Bird Raising and Exercises for the Eye, we don't have to bother with his ideas on Government. I don't remember what they were, in the first place.

This brings us up to 1785, when the United States began to have its first political prickly-heat. It may have been a little before 1785 (I am working entirely without notes or reference books in this history), but 1785 is near enough, for the Revolution didn't end until around 1782, or 1780, and that would leave a couple of years for George Washington to begin his two terms as President and get things good and balled up. So we will say 1785.

Here we are, then, a new country, faced with an experiment in government and working on nothing sounder than a belief that the average voter is entitled to have a hand in the running of the State. The wonder is that we have got as far as we have —or *have* we?

Now, in this introduction I have tried to outline the main influences in political thought which culminated in the foundation of our form of government. I have omitted any reference to Lebœuf and

140

Froissart, because, so far as I know, Lebœuf and Froissart never had any ideas on the subject; at any rate, not the Lebœuf that I knew. I have not gone into the Hanseatic League or the Guild System, not through any pique on my part, but because, after all, they involved a quite different approach to the question of democratic government and I couldn't find any pictures which would illustrate them interestingly. If, however, any of my readers are anxious to look up the Hanseatic League, I can refer them to a very good book on the subject called "The Hanseatic League."

The Lost Language

A T THE meeting of the International Philologists' Association in Lucerne last April (1923-1925), something in the nature of a bombshell was thrown by Professor Eric Nunsen of the University of Ulholm. Professor Nunsen, in a paper entitled, "Aryan Languages: The Funny Old Things," declared that in between the Hamitic group of languages and the Ural-Altaic group there should by rights come another and hitherto uncharted group, to be known as the Semi-Huinty group. Professor Nunsen's paper followed a number on the program called "Al Holtz and His Six Musical Skaters."

According to this eminent philologist, too much attention has been paid in the past to root words. By "root words" we mean those words which look like roots of some kind or other when you draw pictures of them. These words recur in similar form in all the languages which comprise a certain group. Thus, in the Aryan group, compare, for example, the English *dish-towel,* Gothic *dersh-terl,* German *tish-döl,* Latin *dec-tola,* French *dis-toil,* Armenian *dash-taller,* Sanskrit *dit-toll* and Dutch *dösh-tööller.* In all of these words you will note the same absurdity.

In the same manner it is easy to trace the simi-

142

larity between languages of the same group by noting, as in the Semitic group, that the fundamental *f* in Arabic becomes *w* in Assyrian, and the capital *G* in Phœnician becomes a small *g* in Abyssinian. This makes it hard for Assyrian traveling salesmen, as they have no place to leave their grips.

In his interesting work, "The Mutations of the Syllable *Bib* Between 2000 and 500 B. C.," Landoc Downs traces the use of the letter *h* down through Western Asia with the Caucasian migration into Central Europe, and there loses it. For perhaps two thousand years we have no record of the letter *h* being used by Nordics. This is perhaps not strange, as the Nordics at that time didn't use much of anything. And then suddenly, in about 1200 B. C., the letter *h* shows up again in Northern Ohio, this time under the alias of *m* and clean-shaven. There is no question, however, but that it is the old Bantu *h* in disguise, and we are thus able to tell that the two peoples (the Swiss and that other one) are really of the same basic stock. Any one could tell that; so don't be silly.

Now, says Professor Nunsen, it is quite probable that this change in root words, effected by the passage of the Aryan-speaking peoples north of the Danube, Dneiper and Don (the "D" in Danube is silent, making the word pronounced "Anube"), so irritated the Hamitic group (which included ancient Egyptian, Coptic, Berber and Otto H. Kahn) that they began dropping the final *g* just out of spite. This, in the course of several centuries, re-

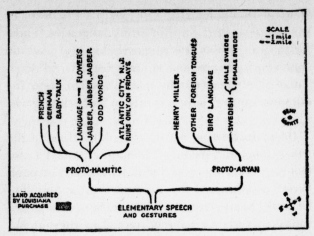

*Chart showing relation of lost language (semi-Huinty)
to other Language groups and to itself*

sulted in the formation of a quite distinct group,
the one which Professor Nunsen calls the "Semi-
Huinty." It is not *entirely* Huinty, for there still
remain traces of the old Hamitic. Just *semi*-
Huinty. Even *semi* is quite a lot.

This, of course, takes no notice of the Ural-Altaic
group. That is quite all right. No one ever does.
This group includes the Lappish, Samoyed, Mag-
yar and Tartar, and, as Dr. Kneeland Renfrew says
in his "Useless Languages: Their Origin and Excuse": "There is no sense in bothering with the
Ural-Altaic group."

So Professor Nunsen has some authority for dis-
regarding the question of grammatical gender, and

it is on this point that he bases his discovery of the existence of the Semi-Huinty languages. These languages, he says, are monosyllabic and have no inflections, the tone used in uttering a word determining its meaning. In this it is similar to the Chinese tongue, which is one of the reasons why China is so far away from the European continent.

Thus the word *reezyl*, uttered in one tone, means "Here comes the postman" in another tone, "There is a button off this pair," and, in still a third tone, "you" (diminutive).

It will be seen from this how difficult it is for the philologist to do anything more than guess at just what the lost languages were really like. He is not sure that they are even lost. If they were *not* really lost, then the joke is on Professor Nunsen for having gone to all this trouble for nothing.

Museum
Feet

A Complaint Contracted by Over-zealous Parents

THERE is one big danger in the approach of Autumn, and that is that the snappy weather may excite us into making plans for doing things we ought to have done long ago. Those of us who are parents are likely to decide that we haven't been paying enough attention to the children, that we ought to take them out more to places of interest and instruction. More of a pal than a father, is what we feel we ought to be, and yet withal an instructor, steering them into enlightening byways and taking them on educational trips to fisheries and jute manufactories, etc.

Now this is just a manifestation of Fall Fever, and will die down, so don't give in to it. Let the children educate themselves. You haven't done such a swell job with yourself that you should undertake to show someone else how to do it. And, above all, never take the kiddies to a natural history museum. Taking them to a natural history museum is one of the things a parent first feels coming on when the crisp Autumn days send the blood tingling through his veins, and it's one of the last things he should do.

146

I, myself, in a burst of parental obligation last Fall, decided to take the boys through the Smithsonian Institution in Washington. I would have picked a *bigger* place if there had been one in the country, but the Smithsonian was the biggest I could get. As a result I contracted a bad case of what is known in medical circles as "Smithsonian feet," that is, a complete paralysis of the feet from the ankles down, due to standing on first one foot and then the other in front of exhibition cases and walking miles upon miles up and down the tessellated corridors of the museum. The boys suffered no ill effects from the trip at all.

The sad thing about a trip through a museum with the children is that you start out with so much vigor and zip. On entering the main entrance lobby, you call back Herbert who takes a running slide across the smooth floor, and tell him that he must stay close to Daddy and that Daddy will show him everything and explain everything. And what a sap that makes Daddy before the day is done!

In your care not to miss anything, you stop and examine carefully the very first tablet in the entrance lobby, deciding to work to the left and look at everything on the left side of the building, and then take up the right side.

"Look, boys," you say, "it says here that this building was built by the Natural History Society of America in 1876—Oh, well, I guess that isn't very important." And you ask the attendant at the door which is the most satisfactory way to see the museum, a foolish question at best. He tells you to begin with the Glacier Hall over there at the right. This upsets your plans a little, but what difference does it make whether you see the right or left side first?

"Come on, boys," you call to both of them who are now sliding back and forth on the floor. "Here is the room where the glaciers are. Come on and look at the glaciers."

The boys by this time are very hot and sweaty, and probably less interested in glaciers than in anything else in the world. You, yourself, find nothing particularly thrilling about the rocks which are lined up for inspection in the room as you enter. However, it is a pretty important thing, this matter of glacial deposits, and both you and the boys would be better off for knowing a little something about them.

"Look, Herbert," you say. "Look, Arthur! See here where the glacier went right over this rock and left these big marks."

But Herbert is already in the next hall, which for some mysterious reason is devoted to stuffed rats demonstrating the Malthusian Doctrine—and Arthur has disappeared entirely.

"Where's Arthur, Herbert?" you yell.

"Look, Daddy," replies Herbert from across the hall. "Come here quick! Quick, Daddy!" There evidently is some danger that the stuffed rats are going to get away before you arrive, and you have to run to hush Herbert up, although you had much

*Arthur has by this time appeared several miles down
the building*

rather not look at stuffed rats, Malthusian Doctrine or no Malthusian Doctrine.

Arthur has, by this time, appeared several miles down the building in the Early American Indian Room and screams:

"Come quick, Daddy! Look! Indians!"

So you and Herbert set off on a dog trot to the Early American Indian Room.

"You boys *must not* yell so in here," you warn. "And stop running, Arthur! We've got all day (God forbid!)."

"Where did these Indians live, Daddy?" asks Herbert.

"Oh, around Massachusetts," you explain. "They fought the Pilgrims."

"It says here they lived in Arizona," reads Arthur. (Whoever taught that boy to read, anyway?)

"Well, Arizona *too*," you crawl. "They lived all over."

"What are these, Daddy?"

"Those? Those are hatchet-heads. They used them for heads to their hatchets."

"It says here they are flint stones that they struck fire on."

"Flint stones, eh? Well, they're funny-looking flint stones. They must have used them for hatchet-heads, too."

"What did they use these for, Daddy?"

"If you can read so well, why don't you read what it says and not ask me so much? Where's Herbert?"

Herbert is now on the point of pushing over a little case of Etruscan bowls in an attempt to get at the figure of a Bœotian horse in the case behind it.

"Here, Herbert, don't push that like that! Do you want to break it?"

"Yes," replies Herbert, giving you a short answer.

"Well, we'll go right straight home if you are going to act that way." (Here a good idea strikes you: Why *not* go right straight home and blame it on Herbert?)

The first evidences of "Smithsonian feet" are beginning to make themselves felt. You try walking on your ankles to favor the soles of your feet, but that doesn't help. And you haven't even struck the second floor yet.

By actual count, the word "look" has been called out eighty-two times, and each time you have looked. Forty-three questions have been asked, forty of which you have answered incorrectly and thirty-four of which you have been caught answering incorrectly. It is high time that you did go home.

But the boys are just beginning. They spot another room at the end of the wing and rush to it. You trail after them, all your old fire gone. It turns out to be Glacier Hall again.

"We've been in here before," you say, hoping that this will discourage them. "There's the door to the street over there. How about going home and coming again tomorrow?"

You trail after them, all the old fire gone

This suggestion is not even heard, for the boys are on their way up the big flight of stairs leading to the second floor. If you can make half the flight you will be doing well. By the time you reach the first landing, you are in a state of collapse.

"Look, Daddy!" you hear the little voices calling from above. "Come quick, Daddy! Skeletons!"

And skeletons they are, sure enough. Mastodon skeletons. Herbert, turning the corner hurriedly, comes suddenly on one and is thrown into a panic. Not a bad idea! Perhaps they might both be frightened into wanting to go home. But Nature herself comes to your rescue. At the end of the mastodon room Herbert comes and whispers to you.

"I don't know," you reply hopefully. "Perhaps we had better go home."

"No," screams Herbert. "I want to stay here."

"Well, come along with me then, and we'll see if we can find it. Come on, Arthur. Come with Herbert and Daddy."

So, on the pretext of locating the section of the building in question you lead the boys down stairs and out the back way.

"Over here, I guess," you say. "No, I guess over there."

By this time, you are at the street and within hailing distance of a taxi. It is but the work of a minute to hit Herbert over the head until he is quiet and to yank Arthur into the cab along with you.

"Drive quickly to 468 Elm avenue," you say to the driver.

That would be your home address.

Traveling
in Peace

EVEN in an off year, the conversational voltage is very high on the trans-Atlantic greyhounds (ocean liners). There is something in the sea air which seems to bring a sort of kelp to the surface even in the most reticent of passengers, and before the ship has passed Fire Island you will have heard as much dull talk as you would get at a dozen Kiwanis meetings at home. And the chances are that you, yourself, will have done nothing that you can be particularly proud of as a raconteur. They tell me that there is something that comes up from the bilge which makes people like that on shipboard.

I myself solved the problem of shipboard conversation by traveling alone and pretending to be a deaf-mute. I recommend this ruse to other irritable souls.

There is no sense in trying to effect it if you have the family along. There is no sense in trying to effect *anything* if you have the family along. But there is something about a family man which seems to attract prospective talkers. Either the Little Woman scrapes up acquaintances who have to have their chairs moved next to yours and tell you all

155

about how rainy it was all spring in East Orange, or the children stop people on the deck and drag them up to you to have you show them how to make four squares out of six matches, and once you have established these contacts, you might as well stay in your stateroom for the rest of the voyage.

Once you are alone, you can then start in on the deaf-mute game. When you go down to dinner, write out your order to the steward and pretty soon the rest of the people at your table will catch on to the fact that something is wrong. You can do a few pleasant passes of sign language if the thing seems to be getting over too slowly. As a matter of fact, once you have taken your seat without remarking on the condition of the ocean to your right-hand neighbor, you will have established yourself as sufficiently queer to be known as "that man at our table who can't talk." Then you probably will be left severely alone.

Once you are out on deck, stand against the rail and look off at the horizon. This is an invitation which few ocean-talkers can resist. Once they see anyone who looks as if he wanted to be alone, they immediately are rarin' to go. One of them will come up to you and look at the horizon with you for a minute, and then will say:

"Isn't that a porpoise off there?"

If you are not very careful you will slip and say: "Where?" This is fatal. What you should do is turn and smile very sweetly and nod your head as if to say: "Don't waste your time, neighbor. I can't

What you should do is turn and smile very sweetly

hear a word you say." Of course, there is no porpoise and the man never thought there was; so he will immediately drop that subject and ask you if you are deaf. Here is where you may pull another bone. You may answer: "Yes, very." That will get you nowhere, for if he thinks that he can make you hear by shouting, he will shout. It doesn't make any difference to him what he has to do to engage you in conversation. He will do it. He would spell words out to you with alphabet blocks if he thought he could get you to pay any attention to his story of why he left Dallas and what he is going to do when he gets to Paris.

So keep your wits about you and be just the deafest man that ever stepped foot on a ship. Pretty soon he will get discouraged and will pass on to the next person he sees leaning over the rail and ask *him* if that isn't a "porpoise 'way off there." You will hear the poor sucker say, "Where?" and then the dam will break. As they walk off together you will hear them telling each other how many miles they get to a gallon and checking up on the comparative sizes of the big department stores in their respective towns.

After a tour of the smoking-room and writing-room making deaf-and-dumb signs to the various stewards, you will have pretty well advertised yourself as a hopeless prospect conversationally. You may then do very much as you like.

Perhaps not quite as you like. There may be one or two slight disadvantages to this plan. There may be one or two people on board to whom you *want* to speak. Suppose, for instance, that you are sitting at one of those chummy writing desks where you look right into the eyes of the person using the other half. And suppose that those eyes turn out to be something elegant; suppose they turn out to be very elegant indeed. What price being dumb then?

Your first inclination, of course, is to lean across

Suppose those eyes turn out to be something elegant

the top of the desk and say: "I beg your pardon, but is this your pen that I am using?" or even more exciting: "I beg your pardon, but is this your letter that I am writing?" Having been posing as a deaf-mute up until now, this recourse is denied you, and you will have to use some other artifice.

There is always the old Roman method of writing notes. If you decide on this, just scribble out the following on a bit of ship's stationery: "I may be deaf and I may be dumb, but if you think that makes any difference in the long run, you're crazy." This is sure to attract the lady's attention and give her some indication that you are favorably impressed with her. She may write a note back to you. She may even write a note to the management of the steamship line.

Another good way to call yourself to her attention would be to upset the writing desk. In the general laughter and confusion which would follow, you could grab her and carry her up on deck where you could tell her confidentially that you really were not deaf and dumb but that you were just pretending to be that way in order to avoid talking to people who did not interest you. The fact that you were talking to her, you could point out, was a sure sign that she, alone, among all the people on the ship, *did* interest you; a rather pretty compliment to her, in a way. You could then say that, as it was essential that none of the other passengers should know that you could talk, it would be necessary for her to hold conversations with you clandestinely, up on the boat deck, or better yet, in one of the boats. The excitement of this would be sure to appeal to her, and you would unquestionably become fast friends.

There is one other method by which you could catch her favor as you sat looking at her over the top of the desk, a method which is the right of every man whether he be deaf, dumb or bow-legged. You might wink one eye very slowly at her. It wouldn't be long then before you could tell whether or not it would be worth your while to talk.

However it worked out, you would have had a comparatively peaceful voyage.

The Future of the Class of 1926—
North Central Grammar School

Class Prophecy by William N. Crandle, '26

THE other night I had a dream in which I saw all that was going to happen to the Class of 1926 of the North Central Grammar School in the future, and when, much to my surprise, I was elected to be Class Prophet, it occurred to me that it might be a good idea to write down the things I saw in that dream and tell you something of what is going to happen in 1950 to the members of the Class of 1926.

In this dream I happened to be walking down the street when suddenly I saw a familiar face standing on a soap-box at the corner, and in a minute I recognized Harry Washburn, our Class President, who was evidently making some sort of a speech to the assembled multitude, among whom I recognized Edna Gleen, Harriet Mastom and Lillian MacArdle. "Well," I said to myself, "I always knew that those girls were crazy about Harry, and I guess they still are." Harry was making some sort of a speech and I gathered that he was running for President of the United States, which didn't surprise me at all as Harry always was a politician in grammar school days.

A little further along I heard someone making a speech on another corner, and I looked a little closer and saw that it was Beatrice Franley, who was making a speech against the use of face-powder by girls. It seemed that Prohibition had been done away with but that Beatrice was trying to get an amendment to the Constitution preventing girls from using face-powder. "Well," I said to myself, "back in North Central, Beatrice was always rabid on the subject of girls using face-powder and she doesn't seem to have lost it even in 1950." Listening to Beatrice were George Delmot, Bertram Posner and Mary Alley.

A little further along I came to a big sign which said: "William Nevin and Gertrude Dolby, Ice-Cream Parlor," and I remembered that when they were in school William and Gertrude were always eating ice-cream at recess together, so I wasn't much surprised to find that they had gone into the ice-cream business, and it occurred to me that they probably ate more ice-cream than they sold.

Pretty soon I came to a big crowd which was watching a couple of prizefighters fighting, and imagine my surprise to find out that the prizefighters were Louis Wrentham and George DuGrasse, who had evidently gone in for prizefighting. The referee was Mr. Ranser, our old algebra teacher, and I guessed that he would give the decision to George, as George always was a favorite of his and probably still was.

In a little while I found myself in England, and

163

there I was told that Walter Dodd had been made King of England because he always dressed like a dude in school, and that he had married Miriam Friedburg and had made her Queen of England. The Prince of Wales had fallen off his horse so often that the English people had elected Philip Wasserman to be Prince because he was so good at using ponies in high-school Latin.

In France I found that George Disch, Harry Petro, John Walters, Robert Dimmock, Edwin Le-Favre and Eddie Matsdorf were working in a café together and that Mary Duggan, Louise Creamer, Margaret Penny and Freda Bertel were constant customers. In Germany, Albert Vogle had been chosen Kaiser because he was so bossy.

On the boat coming back I saw William Debney, Stella Blum, Arthur Crandall, Noble MacOnson and Henry Bostwick, all looking older than they did in North Central, but evidently prosperous, and just as I landed in America I woke up and realized that it had all been nothing but a dream.

Fascinating Crimes

3. The Missing Floor

IT HAS often been pointed out that murderers are given to revisiting the scene of their crimes. The case of Edny Pastelle is the only one on record where the scene of the crime revisited the murderer.

Edny Pastelle was a Basque elevator woman who ran one of the first elevators installed in the old Fifth Avenue Hotel, which stood at the corner of Twenty-third Street and Fifth Avenue, New York City. The elevator was of the surrey type, and was pushed from floor to floor by the operator, who was underneath climbing on a ladder. It was Mlle. Pastelle's daily task to hoist such personages as Chauncey M. Depew, Boss Tweed and Harriet Beecher Stowe up to their rooms in the Fifth Avenue Hotel. In fact, she is said to have been Miss Stowe's model for *Uncle Tom* in the novel of that name (with the word "Cabin" added to it).

In the evenings, when Edny Pastelle was not on duty, she carried Punch and Judy shows about town for whoever wanted them. As not many people wanted them, Edny's evenings were pretty much her own.

The evening of July 7, 1891, however, is on record as being not Edny's, but Max Sorgossen's.

Max Sorgossen worked in the Eden Musée, which was situated on Twenty-third Street just below the Fifth Avenue Hotel. His job was to put fresh cuffs on the wax figure of Chester A. Arthur in the Presidential Group. At five o'clock every afternoon he also took "Ajeeb," the mechanical chess player, out in the back yard for his exercise.

At five-thirty on the afternoon in question Max Sorgossen had just knocked off work and was strolling up Twenty-third Street in search of diversion. In the back of his mind was an idea that perhaps he might find another mechanical chess player for "Ajeeb" and a girl for himself and that the four of them might go down to Coney Island for the evening, as the weather was warm. As he passed the service entrance of the Fifth Avenue Hotel he met Edny Pastelle, who was likewise calling it a day. (She called it a *jour*, but that is the Basque of it.)

Edny and Max had known each other in finishing school, and so there seemed no impropriety in his speaking to her and asking her if she knew of a mechanical chess player for "Ajeeb" and if she would look with favor on an evening at Coney.

The two were seen entering a restaurant on Twenty-first Street to talk it over at 6:10. At 9:20 the next morning guests of the hotel, on trying to descend in the elevator, found it stuck between the first and third floors. When the car was finally dislodged, it was found to contain the body of Max Sorgossen. Furthermore, *the second floor, where the elevator should have stopped, was gone!*

—Courtesy of John Held, Jr., and Life.

Edny Pastelle and Max Sorgossen in the gallery of human fiends and their victims

Edny was arrested and the trial took place in the Court of Domestic Relations, since she was a domestic and there had evidently been relations, albeit unfriendly. The prosecuting attorney was a young lawyer named William T. Jerome, later William Travers Jerome. Following is a transcript of the cross-examination:

Q. What did you do after Sorgossen spoke to you on Twenty-third Street?
A. Pardon.
Q. What did you do after Sorgossen spoke to you on Twenty-third Street?
A. Plenty.
Q. Very good, Mr. Bones. And now tell me, why *is* a man with a silk hat on like Mary Queen of Scots?
A. What Scots?
Q. I'm asking *you.*
A. Animal, vegetable or mineral?
Q. Mineral.
A. The tidy on the back of that chair?
Q. No.
A. Cyrus W. Field?
Q. Give up?
A. Three spades.
Q. Double three spades.

At this point, counsel for the defense objected and the case was thrown out into a higher court, where Edny Pastelle was acquitted, or whatever you call it.

It was some thirty years later that the missing second floor of the old Fifth Avenue Hotel was discovered. A workman laying wagers on the sixteenth floor of the Fifth Avenue Building (erected on the site of the old Fifth Avenue Hotel) came across a floor which was neither the fifteenth, sixteenth nor seventeenth. The police were called in and, after several weeks of investigation and grilling, it was identified as the missing floor of the old hotel, the floor at which the little romance of Edny Pastelle had come to such an abrupt end. How it came to be on the sixteenth floor of the Fifth Avenue Building nobody knows. Perhaps Max Sorgossen could tell.

"Howdy, Neighbor!"

AMONG the inhabitants of North America there is a queer tribal custom which persists in spite of being universally unpopular. Its technical name is "paying a call." The women of the tribe are its chief priests, but once in a while the men are roped in on it and it is then that the lamentations and groans may be heard even in the surrounding villages.

Among the women-folk the procedure is as follows: The one who is to "pay a call" puts on what she considers her most effective regalia, collects ten or a dozen engraved cards bearing her name and twice that number bearing her husband's (he doesn't even know that he *has* any cards, let alone that they are being thrown around the neighborhood every Wednesday afternoon), and sets out with the bit between her teeth.

The idea is to call on as many other women as she thinks will not be at home. Ringing the doorbell at each house on her list, she inquires of the maid if her mistress is in. On receiving a favorable answer ("No") she drops the required number of cards and runs down the street to her car or bicycle or whatever she came in, and rushes off at top speed lest the maid should suddenly discover that her mistress is at home after all. The chances are, however, that the maid has had instructions to say "no" from the lady of the house herself, who is at that moment standing at the head of the stairs waiting for the door to shut.

The social amenities having been satisfied in this manner at perhaps ten other houses, the caller returns home, where she sinks into a chair, pulls off her gloves, and sighs: "Thank Heaven, *that's* done!"

It is on those rare occasions when the men of the tribe are impressed into service in this paying of calls that the thing assumes its most horrible aspect. Let us take a peek into a typical celebration of the rite.

The man returns home from the office at night, all set for an evening with a motor-boat catalog in front of the fire.

"I thought we might run up and call on the Grimsers tonight. We've owed them a call for a long time now."

"The Grimsers?" queries the husband.

"Yes, you know them. He's the little short man we saw in the drug-store the other night. She is quite pleasant, but rather fast, I understand. She told me that her husband was very anxious to know you better."

"What is he—in the insurance business?"

"No, he isn't. He's a very nice man. And *she* is just mad about you. 'Mrs. Tomlin,' she said to me, 'you don't mean to tell me that that nice-looking

On receiving a favorable answer one drops the required number of cards

husband of yours is forty years old! He looks about twenty-five. And such nice hair!' "

"Well," says the husband, not unmoved by this bit of strategy, "I suppose if we must, we must. Do I have to get dressed up?"

And so they start out for a call on the Grimsers, with whom they have no more in common than the same milkman.

Their reception is more or less formal in tone, as the Grimsers had planned on going to bed early, Mr. Grimser even having gone so far as his dressing-gown.

"Do sit over here," urges Mrs. Grimser, indicating her husband's favorite cavity in the corner of the divan, "that rocker is so uncomfortable."

"It just suits me," lies Mrs. Tomlin. "Ed says that he is glad that I like chairs like this, as it leaves all the comfortable ones in the house for him."

Everyone looks at Ed as the author of this pleasantry, and there is general, albeit extremely moderate laughter.

"Well, did you ever see such weather?" This might come from anybody. In fact, two or three are likely to say it at once. This leads to an account on the part of Mrs. Grimser of what the dampness has done to her jelly in the cellar, and a story by Mrs. Tomlin illustrating how hard it is to keep a maid contented during a rainy spell. Mr. Tomlin leads off with one he heard at the club about the farmer who prayed for rain, but noticing a sudden tightening of his wife's lips accompanied by a warn-

175

ing tapping of her right foot, he gathers that probably Mrs. Grimser's father was a clergyman or something, and trails his story off into a miserable series of noises.

Trails his story off into a miserable series of noises

This is a signal for Mrs. Grimser to say: "I just know that you men are dying to get off in a corner and talk to each other. Harry, why don't you show Mr. Grimser the plans for the new garage?"

The two men are then isolated on a window-seat, where they smoke and try to think up something to say next. Mr. Tomlin, knowing nothing about blueprints and caring less about the Grimsers' garage, its forced to bend over the sheets and ask unintelligent questions, cooing appreciatively now and then to show that he is getting it. They finally are reduced to checking up on mutual acquaintances in the automobile business, summarizing each new find with: "Yes, sir, George is a great old scout," or "Yes, sir, Nick is a great old scout." Everyone possible having been classified as a great old scout, they just sit and puff in silence, frankly talked out.

They just sit and puff in silence, frankly talked out

The ladies, in the meantime, have been carrying on much the same sort of line, except that each has her eye out for details outside the conversation. Mrs. Grimser is trying to make out just how Mrs.

177

Tomlin's transformation is tied on, and Mrs. Tomlin is making mental notes of the material in Mrs. Grimser's under-curtains. Given nothing to talk about, women can make a much more convincing stab at it than men. To hear them from a distance, you might almost think that they were really saying something.

When all the contestants are completely worn out and the two men reduced to a state of mental inertia bordering on death, Mrs. Tomlin brightens up and says that they must be going. This throws a great wave of relief over the company, and Mr. Tomlin jumps to his feet and says that he'll run ahead and see if the engine is working all right. The Grimsers very cautiously suggest that it is early yet, but unless the Tomlins are listening very carefully (which they are not) they will not hear it.

Then, all the way home, Mrs. Tomlin suggests that Mr. T. might be a little more agreeable to her friends when they go out of an evening, and Mr. Tomlin wants to know what the hell he did that was wrong.

"You know very well what you did that was wrong, and besides, what a story to start telling in front of Mrs. Grimser!"

"What story?"

"The one about the farmer who prayed for rain."

"What's the matter with that story?"

"You know very well what's the matter with it. You seem to think when you are out with my friends that you are down in the locker-room with George Herbert."

"I wish to God I *was* down in the locker-room with George Herbert."

"Oh, you make me sick."

The rest of the ride home is given over to a stolid listening to the chains clanking on the pavement as the wheels go round.

This is known in the tribe life of North America as being "neighborly," and a whole system has been built up on the tradition. Some day a prophet is going to arise out of some humble family and say, "What's the use?" and the whole thing is going to topple over with a crash and everyone is going to be a lot happier.

A Talk
to Young Men

Graduation Address on "The Decline of Sex"

TO YOU young men who only recently were graduated from our various institutions of learning (laughter), I would bring a message, a message of warning and yet, at the same time, a message of good cheer. Having been out in the world a whole month, it is high time that you learned something about the Facts of Life, something about how wonderfully Nature takes care of the thousand and one things which go to make up what some people jokingly call our "sex" life. I hardly know how to begin. Perhaps "Dear Harry" would be as good a way as any.

You all have doubtless seen, during your walks in the country, how the butterflies and bees carry pollen from one flower to another? It is very dull and you should be very glad that you are not a bee or a butterfly, for where the fun comes in *that* I can't see. However, they think that they are having a good time, which is all that is necessary, I suppose. Some day a bee is going to get hold of a real book on the subject, and from then on there will be mighty little pollen-toting done or I don't know my bees.

Well, anyway, if you have noticed carefully how

180

the bees carry pollen from one flower to another (and there is no reason why you should have noticed carefully as there is nothing to see), you will have wondered what connection there is between this process and that of animal reproduction. I may as well tell you right now that there is no connection at all, and so your whole morning of bee-stalking has been wasted.

We now come to the animal world. Or rather, first we come to One Hundred and Twenty-fifth Street, but you don't get off there. The animal world is next, and off you get. And what a sight meets your eyes! My, my! It just seems as if the whole world were topsy-turvy.

The next time you are at your grocer's buying gin, take a look at his eggs. They really are some hen's eggs, but they belong to the grocer now, as he has bought them and is entitled to sell them. So they really *are* his eggs, funny as it may sound to anyone who doesn't know. If you will look at these eggs, you will see that each one is *almost* round, but not *quite*. They are more of an "egg-shape." This may strike you as odd at first, until you learn that this is Nature's way of distinguishing eggs from large golf balls. You see, Mother Nature takes no chances. She used to, but she learned her lesson. And that is a lesson that all of you must learn as well. It is called Old Mother Nature's Lesson, and begins on page 145.

Now, these eggs have not always been like this. That stands to reason. They once had something to do with a hen or they wouldn't be called hen's eggs.

If they are called duck's eggs, that means that they had something to do with a duck. Who can tell me what it means if they are called "ostrich's eggs"? . . . That's right.

But the egg is not the only thing that had something to do with a hen. Who knows what else there was? . . . That's right.

Now the rooster is an entirely different sort of bird from the hen. It is very proud and has a red crest on the top of his head. This red crest is put there by Nature so that the hen can see the rooster coming in a crowd and can hop into a taxi or make a previous engagement if she wants to. A favorite dodge of a lot of hens when they see the red crest of the rooster making in their direction across the barnyard is to work up a sick headache. One of the happiest and most contented roosters I ever saw was one who had had his red crest chewed off in a fight with a dog. He also wore sneakers.

But before we take up this phase of the question (for it is a question), let us go back to the fish kingdom. Fish are probably the worst example that you can find; in the first place, because they work under water, and in the second, because they don't know anything. You won't find one fish in a million that has enough sense to come in when it rains. They are just stupid, that's all, and nowhere is their stupidity more evident than in their sex life.

Take, for example, the carp. The carp is one of the least promising of all the fish. He has practically no forehead and brings nothing at all to a conversation. Now the mother carp is swimming around some fine spring day when suddenly she decides that it would be nice to have some children. So she makes out a deposit slip and deposits a couple million eggs on a rock (all this goes on *under* water, mind you, of all places). This done, she adjusts her hat, powders her nose, and swims away, a woman with a past.

It is not until all this is over and done with that papa enters the picture, and then only in an official capacity. Papa's job is very casual. He swims over the couple of million eggs and takes a chance that by sheer force of personality he can induce half a dozen of them to hatch out. The remainder either go to waste or are blacked up to represent caviar.

So you will see that the sex life of a fish is nothing much to brag about. It never would present a problem in a fish community as it does in ours. No committees ever have to be formed to regulate it, and about the only way in which a fish can go wrong is through drink or stealing. This makes a fish's life highly unattractive, you will agree, for, after a time, one would get very tired of drinking and stealing.

We have now covered the various agencies of Nature for populating the earth with the lesser forms of life. We have purposely omitted any reference to the reproduction of those unicellular organisms which reproduce by dividing themselves up into two, four, eight, etc., parts without any outside assistance at all. This method is too silly even to discuss.

We now come to colors. You all know that if you mix yellow with blue you get green. You also get green if you mix cherries and milk. (Just kidding. Don't pay any attention.) The derivation of one color from the mixture of two other colors is not generally considered a sexual phenomenon, but that is because the psychoanalysts haven't got around to it yet. By next season it won't be safe to admit that you like to paint, or you will be giving yourself away as an inhibited old uncle-lover and debauchee. The only thing that the sex-psychologists can't read a sexual significance into is trap-shooting, and they are working on that now.

All of which brings us to the point of wondering if it *all* isn't a gigantic hoax. If the specialists fall down on trap-shooting, they are going to begin to doubt the whole structure which they have erected, and before long there is going to be a reaction which will take the form of an absolute negation of sex. An Austrian scientist has already come out with the announcement that there is no such thing as a hundred per cent male or a hundred per cent female. If this is true, it is really a big step forward. It is going to throw a lot of people out of work, but think of the money that will be saved!

And so, young men, my message to you is this: Think the thing over very carefully and examine the evidence with fair-minded detachment. And if you decide that, within the next ten years, sex is going out of style, make your plans accordingly. Why not be pioneers in the new movement?

Biography
by Inches

(Such as has recently been done for Keats)

A LIFE OF WILLIAM BODNEY

*Together with an Examination of His Poetry and
Punctuation*

I

GENESIS

THE weather report submitted by the Suffix
Weather Bureau on May 11, 1837, states that
shortly after three in the afternoon there was a
light rain, a precipitation of some .005 inches.
There is a certain sad significance in this technical
statement of the Weather Bureau, for during that
light rain, George and Edna Bodney were married
in the south vestry of Queen's Church.

We know that it was the south vestry because of
a letter written the next day by the Rev. Dr. Morbeling, the rector, to his sister, Mrs. Wrethnam.
"Such a mess, such a mess!" writes Dr. Morbeling.
"The north vestry has been torn up by plumbers
and plasterers for over a week now, throwing all
the business into that dark, damp old south vestry
which is very difficult to work in owing to the

danger of tripping over the litter of kindergarten chairs."

North or south vestry, however, it is certain (and essential) that George and Edna Bodney were married on May 11, 1837, for on May 13, 1837, William Bodney was born.

II

BROOK AND RIVER

Of the boyhood of William Bodney we know but little. He was brought up as most of the boys in Suffix were brought up, except for the fact that he did not go out of doors until he was eleven, and then only to strike at the postman. He was kept in the house so much because of an old prejudice of Edna Bodney's against fireflies.

We catch a glimpse of Bodney's school life, however, in a letter written by Charles Cod, a fellow student at Wimperis School (From the Danker Collection):

"There are lots of fellows here in school," writes Cod; "among them Henry Mamsley, Ralph Dyke, Luther Fennchurch, William Bodney, Philip Massteter and Norman Walsh."

Cod is no doubt accurate in his letter, although a note of personal prejudice which creeps in now and again makes it a little hard to rely on his judgment.

No more trustworthy is Norman Rully, writing to Ashman in 1845 (Arthur's Collection) when he says that Bodney paid "three shillings for a pair of skates." This is unquestionably an error on Rully's part, for skates at that time cost five shillings if they cost a nickel.

III

EARLY POETRY

We first find Bodney displaying his genius on the occasion of the presentaton to him of a knitted necktie by Laura Pensick, the sister of his friend Alan Pensick. The tie was given to him early in the afternoon and by evening the young man had composed the following sonnet in honor of its fair donor:

LINES ON OPENING A LETTER AND FINDING SAND IN IT

When hours of sorry death have thundered by
   And with them open windows to the sea
   Lycurgus from his moss-bedowered tree
Brings asphodel to deck the starry sky.
The winter-scarred olympids homeward fly
   And softly spread their wolden heraldry
   Yet Lacedemon does not wake in fantasy
Nor Thetis sing her songs to such as I.

So, Laura, how shall Eros take his due
   Or crafty Xerxes leave his tent at night
If, dropping down from his cerulean blue,
   He brings not gold with him wherewith to fight?
The ploughman homeward plods his weary way
   And, what is more, you'll be a man, my son.

• • • • •

187

The boy in Bodney is fading and giving place to the man. This sonnet, while not perfect, shows what was going on in the youth's mind. Of course, "moss-bedowered tree" is bad, and Lacedemon was the name of a country, not a person, but "winter-scarred olympids" makes up for a great deal, and the picture of decking "the starry sky" with asphodel comes doubtless from Bodney's vacation days in Polpero where there are a lot of rocks and seaweed. Henry Willers, in a most interesting paper on *Bodney's Relation to Open Windows*, points out that the "open windows to the sea" probably refers to an old window of his aunt's which she kept upstairs in the house at Ragley. Mr. Willers is probably right also in believing that in line six, the word "their" comes from a remark make by Remson to Bodney concerning some plovers sent him (Remson) after a hunting trip. "I am using *their* feathers," Remson is reported to have said, "to make a watch fob with."

These are fascinating speculations, but we must not linger too long with them. Even as we speculate, the boy Bodney is turning into the man Bodney, and is looking searchingly at the life about him. Poor Bodney! We know now that he looked once too often.

IV

SHOPPING IN LONDON

The first big adventure in William Bodney's life was a trip up to London to buy shoes. The shoes which he had been wearing in Suffix, we learn from the Town Clerk's record, were "good enough," but "good enough" was never a thing to satisfy William Bodney. The fashion at the time was to wear shoes only to parties and coronations, but Bodney was never one to stick to the fashion.

So bright and early on the morning of April 9, 1855, the young man set out for the city, full of the vigor of living. Did he go by coach or by foot? We do not know. On the coach records of April 9, there is a passenger listed as "Enoch Reese," but this was probably not William Bodney. There is no reason why he should have traveled under the name of "Enoch Reese." But whether he went by coach or over the road, we do know that he must have passed through Weeming-on-Downs, as there was no way of getting to London from Suffix without passing through Weeming-on-Downs. And as Bodney went through this little town, probably bright in the sunlight of the early April morning, is it not possible that he stopped at the pump in the square to wet his wrists against the long, hot journey ahead? It is not only possible. It is more than likely. And, stopping at the pump, did he know that in the third house on the left as you leave the pump Londonwards, was Mary Wassermann? Or, did Mary Wassermann know that Bodney was just outside her door? The speculation is futile, for Mary Wassermann moved from Weeming-on-Downs the next week and was never heard from again. But I anticipate.

Of Bodney's stay in London we know but little.

We know that he reached London, for he sent a postcard to his mother from there saying that he had arrived "safe and sound." We know that he left London, because he died fifteen years later in Suffix. What happened in between we can only conjecture at, but we may be sure that he was very sensitive to whatever beauty there may have been in London at that time. In the sonnet *On Looking Into a Stereoscope for the First Time,* written when he had grown into full manhood, we find reference to this visit to the city:

> And, with its regicidal note in tune,
> Brings succor to the waiting stream.

If this isn't a reference to the London trip, what is it a reference to?

v

PROGRESS AND REGRESS

We have seen Bodney standing on the threshold of the Great Experience. How did he meet it? Very well indeed.

For the first time we find him definitely determined to create. "I am definitely determined to create," he wrote to the Tax Collector of Suffix (Author's Collection). And with the spring of 1860 came, in succession, *To Some Ladies Who Have Been Very Nice To Me, Ode to Hester, Rumpty:*

A Fragment, and *To Arthur Hosstetter MacMonigal.* Later in the same year came *I wonder when, if I should go, there'd be.*

It is in *I wonder when, if I should go, there'd be* that Bodney for the first time strikes the intimate note.

> I sometimes think that open fires are best,
> Before drab autumn swings its postern shut . . .

"Open fires" is a delightful thought, carrying with it the picture of a large house, situated on a hill with poplars, the sun sinking charmingly behind the town in the distance and, inside, the big hall, hung with banners, red and gold, and a long table laden with rich food, nuts, raisins, salt (plenty of salt, for Bodney was a great hand to put salt on his food and undoubtedly had salt in mind), and over all the presence of the king and his knights, tall, vigorous blond knights swearing allegiance to their lord. Or perhaps in the phrase Bodney had in mind, a small room with nobody in it. Who can tell? At any rate, we have the words "open fires" and we are able to reconstruct what went on in the poet's mind if we have a liking for that sort of thing. And, although he does not say so in so many words, there is little doubt but that in using "fires" in conjunction with the word "open" he meant Lillian Walf and what was to come later.

MIRAGE

From *I wonder when, if I should go, there'd be* to *On Meeting Roger H. Clafflin for the Second Time* is a far cry—and a merry one. *On Meeting Roger H. Clafflin for the Second Time* is hepta-syllabic and, not only that, but trochaic. Here, after years of suffering and disillusion, after dis-covering false friends and vain loves, we find Bod-ney resorting to the trochee. His letter to his sister at the time shows the state of mind the young poet was in (Rast Collection):

Somehow today I feel that things are closing in on me. Life is closing in on me. I have a good mind to employ the trochee and see what that will do. I have no fault to find with the spondee. Some of my best work is spondaic. But I guess there just comes a time in every-one's life when the spondee falls away of its own accord and the trochee takes its place. It is Nature's way. Ah, Nature! How I love Nature! I love the birds and the flowers and Beauty of all kinds. I don't see how any-one can hate Beauty, it is so wonderful. . . . Well, there goes the bell, so I must close now and employ a spondee.

Seven days later Bodney met Lillian Walf.

VII

FINIS ORIGINE PENDET

We do not know whether it was at four o'clock or a quarter past four on October 17, 1874, that

Henry Ryan said to Bodney: "Bodney, I want that you should meet my friend Miss Walf. . . . Miss Walf, Mr. Bodney." The British War Office has no record of the exact hour and Mr. Ryan was blotto at the time and so does not remember. However, it was in or around four o'clock.

Lillian Walf was three years older than Bodney, but had the mind of a child of eight. This she retained all her life. Commentators have referred to her as feeble minded, but she was not feeble minded. Her mind was vigorous. It was the mind of a vigorous child of eight. The fact that she was actually in her thirties has no bearing on the question that I can see. Writing to Remson three years after her marriage to Bodney, Lillian says:

We have a canary which sings something terrible all day. I think I'll shoot it Tuesday.

If that is the product of a feeble mind, then who of us can lay claim to a sound mentality?

The wedding of Bodney to Lillian Walf took place quietly except for the banging of the church radiator. The parson, Rev. Dr. Padderson, estimated that the temperature of the room was about 78° at the time, too hot for comfort. However, the young couple were soon on their way to Bayswater where they settled down and lived a most uneventful life from then on. Bodney must have been quite happy in his new existence, for he gave up writing poetry and took to collecting pewter. We have no record of his ever writing anything after his marriage, except a sonnet for the yearbook of the Bayswater School for Girls. This sonnet (*On Looking into William Ewart Gladstone*) beginning:

O Lesbos! When thy fêted songs shall ring . . .

is too well known to quote here in full, but we cannot help calling attention to the reference to Bayswater. For it was in Bayswater that Bodney really belonged and it was there that he died in 1876. His funeral was a Masonic one and lasted three hours and twenty minutes. (Author's Collection).

Paul Revere's Ride

*How a Modest Go-Getter Did His Bit for the Juno
Acid Bath Corporation*

FOLLOWING are the salesman's report sheets
sent into the home office in New York by
Thaddeus Olin, agent for the Juno Acid Bath Corporation. Mr. Olin had the New England territory
during the spring of 1775 and these report sheets
are dated April 16, 17, 18, and 19, of that year.

> *April 16, 1775.*
> *Boston.*

Called on the following engravers this a. m.:
Boston Engraving Co., E. H. Hosstetter, Theodore
Platney, Paul Revere, Benjamin B. Ashley and
Roger Durgin.

Boston Engraving Co. are all taken care of for
their acid.

E. H. Hosstetter took three tins of acid No. 4
on trial and renewed his old order of 7 Queen-
Biters.

Theodore Platney has gone out of business since
my last trip.

Paul Revere was not in. The man in his shop
said that he was busy with some sort of local shin-
dig. Said I might catch him in tomorrow morning.

The Benjamin Ashley people said they were satisfied with their present product and contemplated no change.

Roger Durgin died last March.

Things are pretty quiet in Boston right now.

April 17.

Called on Boston Engraving people again to see if they might not want to try some Daisy No. 3. Mr. Lithgo was interested and said to come in to-morrow when Mr. Lithgo, Senior, would be there.

Paul Revere was not in. He had been in for a few minutes before the shop opened and had left word that he would be up at Sam Adams' in case anyone wanted him. Went up to the Adams place, but the girl there said that Mr. Revere and Mr. Adams had gone over to Mr. Dawes' place on Milk Street. Went to Dawes' place, but the man there said Dawes and Adams and Revere were in conference. There seems to be some sort of parade or something they are getting up, something to do with the opening of the new foot-bridge to Cambridge, I believe.

Things are pretty quiet here in Boston, except for the trade from the British fleet which is out in the harbour.

Spent the evening looking around in the coffee houses. Everyone here is cribbage-crazy. All they seem to think of is cribbage, cribbage, cribbage.

April 18.

To the Boston Engraving Company and saw Mr.

Lithgo, Senior. He seemed interested in the Daisy No. 3 acid and said to drop in again later in the week.

Paul Revere was out. His assistant said that he knew that Mr. Revere was in need of a new batch of acid and had spoken to him about our Vulcan No. 2 and said he might try some. I would have to see Mr. Revere personally, he said, as Mr. Revere makes all purchases himself. He said that he thought I could catch him over at the Dawes' place.

Tried the Dawes' place but they said that he and Mr. Revere had gone over to the livery stable on State Street.

Went to the livery stable but Revere had gone. They said he had engaged a horse for tonight for some sort of entertainment he was taking part in. The hostler said he heard Mr. Revere say to Mr. Dawes that they might as well go up to the North Church and see if everything was all set; so I gather it is a church entertainment.

Followed them up to the North Church, but there was nobody there except the caretaker, who said that he thought I could catch Mr. Revere over at Charlestown late that night. He described him to me so that I would know him and said that he probably would be on horseback. As it seemed to me to be pretty important that we land the Revere order for Vulcan No. 2, I figured out that whatever inconvenience it might cause me to go over to Charlestown or whatever added expense to the firm, would be justified.

Spent the afternoon visiting several printing establishments, but none of them do any engraving.

Things are pretty quiet here in Boston.

Went over to Charlestown after supper and hung around "The Bell in Hand" tavern looking for Mr. Revere. Met a man there who used to live in Peapack, N. J., and we got to talking about what a funny name for a town that was. Another man said that in Massachusetts there was actually a place called Podunk, up near Worcester. We had some very good cheese and talked over names of towns for a while. Then the second man, the one who knew about Podunk, said he had to go as he had a date with a man. After he had left I happened to bring the conversation around to the fact that I was waiting for a Mr. Paul Revere, and the first man told me that I had been talking to him for half an hour and that he had just gone.

I rushed out to the corner, but the man who keeps the watering-trough there said that someone answering Mr. Revere's description had just galloped off on a horse in the direction of Medford. Well, this just made me determined to land that order for Juno Acid Bath Corporation or die in the attempt. So I hired a horse at the Tavern stable and started off toward Medford.

Just before I hit Medford I saw a man standing out in his night-shirt in front of his house looking up the road. I asked him if he had seen anybody who looked like Mr. Revere. He seemed pretty sore and said that some crazy coot had just ridden by and knocked at his door and yelled something that he couldn't understand and that if he caught him he'd break his back. From his description of the horse I gathered that Mr. Revere was the man; so I galloped on.

A lot of people in Medford Town were up and standing in front of their houses, cursing like the one I had just seen. It seems that Mr. Revere had gone along the road-side, knocking on doors and yelling something which nobody understood, and then galloping on again.

"Some god-dam drunk," said one of the Medfordites, and they all went back to bed.

I wasn't going to be cheated out of my order now, no matter what happened, and I don't think that Mr. Revere could have been drunk, because while he was with us at "The Bell in Hand," he had only four short ales. He had a lot of cheese, though.

Something seemed to have been the matter with him, however, because in every town that I rode through I found people just going back to bed after having been aroused up out of their sleep by a mysterious rider. I didn't tell them that it was Mr. Revere, or that it was probably some stunt to do with the shin-dig that he and Mr. Dawes were putting on for the North Church. I figured out that it was a little publicity stunt.

Finally, just as I got into Lexington, I saw my man getting off his horse at a house right alongside the Green. I rushed up and caught him just as he was going in. I introduced myself and told him that I represented the Juno Acid Bath Corporation of New York and asked him if he could give me a few minutes, as I had been following him all the way from Charlestown and had been to his office three days in succession. He said that he was busy right at that minute, but that if I wanted to come along with him upstairs he would talk business on the way. He asked me if I wasn't the man he had been talking to at "The Bell in Hand" and I said yes, and asked him how Podunk was. This got him in good humour and he said that we might as well sit right down then and that he would get someone else to do what he had to do. So he called a man-servant and told him to go right upstairs, wake up Mr. Hancock and Mr. Adams and tell them to get up, and no fooling. "Keep after them, Sambo," he said, "and don't let them roll over and go to sleep again. It's very important."

So we sat down in the living room and I got out our statement of sales for 1774 and showed him that, in face of increased competition, Juno had practically doubled its output. "There must be some reason for an acid outselling its competitors three to one," I said, "and that reason, Mr. Revere, is that a Juno product is a guaranteed product." He asked me about the extra sixpence a tin and I asked him if he would rather pay a sixpence less and get an inferior grade of acid and he said, "No." So I finally landed an order of three dozen tins of Vulcan No. 2 and a dozen jars of

Acme Silver Polish, as Mr. Revere is a silversmith, also, on the side.

Took a look around Lexington before I went back to Boston, but didn't see any engraving plants. Lexington is pretty quiet right now.

Respectfully submitted,

THADDEUS OLIN.

Attached.

Expense Voucher

Juno Acid Bath Corp., New York

Thaddeus Olin, Agent.

Hotel in Boston		15s.
Stage fare		30s.
Meals (4 days)		28s.
Entertaining prospects	£3	4s.
Horse rent. Charlestown to Lexington and return	£2	6s.
Total Expense	£9	3s.
To Profit on three dozen tins of Vulcan No. 2		18s
and One dozen jars Acme Silver Polish		4s.
	£1	2s.
Net Loss	£8	1s.

Shakespeare
Explained

Carrying on the System of Footnotes to a Silly Extreme

PERICLES

ACT II.   SCENE 3

Enter first Lady-in-Waiting (Flourish,[1] Haut-boys[2] and[3] torches[4]).

First Lady-in-Waiting—What[5] ho![6] Where[7] is[8] the[9] music?[10]

NOTES

1. *Flourish:* The stage direction here is obscure. Clarke claims it should read "flarish," thus changing the meaning of the passage to "flarish" (that is, the King's), but most authorities have agreed that it should remain "flourish," supplying the predicate which is to be flourished. There was at this time a custom in the countryside of England to flourish a mop as a signal to the passing vender of berries, signifying that in that particular household there was a consumer-demand for berries, and this may have been meant in this instance. That Shakespeare was cognizant of this custom of flourishing the mop for berries is shown in a similar passage in the second part of King Henry IV, where

202

he has the Third Page enter and say, "Flourish."
Cf. also Hamlet, IV, 7:4.

2. *Hautboys,* from the French *haut,* meaning
"high" and the Eng. *boys,* meaning "boys." The
word here is doubtless used in the sense of "high

*Might be one of the hautboys bearing a box of
"trognies" for the actors to suck*

boys," indicating either that Shakespeare intended
to convey the idea of spiritual distress on the part
of the First Lady-in-Waiting or that he did not. Of
this Rolfe says: "Here we have one of the chief in-
dications of Shakespeare's knowledge of human nature, his remarkable insight into the petty foibles

203

of this work-a-day world." Cf. T. N. 4:6, "Mine eye hath play'd the painter, and hath stell'd thy beauty's form in table of my heart."

3. *and.* A favorite conjunctive of Shakespeare's in referring to the need for a more adequate navy for England. Tauchnitz claims that it should be pronounced "und," stressing the anti-penult. This interpretation, however, has found disfavor among most commentators because of its limited significance. We find the same conjunctive in A. W. T. E. W. 6:7, "Steel-boned, unyielding *and* uncomplying virtue," and here there can be no doubt that Shakespeare meant that if the King should consent to the marriage of his daughter the excuse of Stephano, offered in Act 2, would carry no weight.

4. *Torches.* The interpolation of some foolish player and never the work of Shakespeare (Warb.). The critics of the last century have disputed whether or not this has been misspelled in the original, and should read "trochies" or "troches." This might well be since the introduction of tobacco into England at this time had wrought havoc with the speaking voices of the players, and we might well imagine that at the entrance of the First Lady-in-Waiting there might be perhaps one of the hautboys mentioned in the preceding passage bearing a box of "troches" or "trognies" for the actors to suck. Of this entrance Clarke remarks: "The noble mixture of spirited firmness and womanly modesty, fine sense and true humility, clear sagacity and absence of conceit, passionate warmth and sensi-

tive delicacy, generous love and self-diffidence with
which Shakespeare has endowed this First Lady-
in-Waiting renders her in our eyes one of the most
admirable of his female characters." Cf. M. S.
N. D. 8:9, "That solder'st close impossibilities
and mak'st them kiss."

5. *What*—What.

6. *Ho!* In conjunction with the preceding word
doubtless means "What ho!" changed by Clarke to
"what hoo!" In the original MS. it reads "What
hi!" but this has been accredited to the tendency
of the time to write "What hi" when "what ho"
was meant. Techner alone maintains that it should
read "What humpf!" Cf. Ham. 5:0, "High-ho!"

7. *Where.* The reading of the folio, retained by
Johnson, the Cambridge editors and others, but it
is not impossible that Shakespeare wrote "why,"
as Pope and others give it. This would make the
passage read "Why the music?" instead of "Where
is the music?" and would be a much more probable
interpretation in view of the music of that time. Cf.
George Ade. Fable No. 15, "Why the gunny-
sack?"

8. *is*—is not. That is, would not be.

9. *the.* Cf. Ham. 4:6. M. S. N. D. 3:5. A. W.
T. E. W. 2:6. T. N. 1:3 and Macbeth 3:1, "that
knits up *the* raveled sleeves of care."

10. *music.* Explained by Malone as "the art of
making music" or "music that is made." If it has
but one of these meanings we are inclined to think
it is the first; and this seems to be favored by what

precedes, "*the* music!" Cf. M. of V. 4:2, "The man that hath no music in himself."

The meaning of the whole passage seems to be that the First Lady-in-Waiting has entered, concomitant with a flourish, hautboys and torches and says, "What ho! Where is the music?"

Fascinating Crimes

4. The Lynn Horse-Car Murders

EARLY in the morning of August 7th, 1896, a laborer named George Raccid, while passing the old street-car barns at Fleeming and Main Streets, Lynn, Massachusetts, noticed a crowd of conductors and drivers (horse-cars were all the rage in 1896) standing about a car in the doorway to the barn. Mr. Raccid was too hurried to stop and see what the excitement was, and so it was not until the following Wednesday, when the bi-weekly paper came out, that he learned that a murder had been committed in the car-barn. And at this point, Mr. Raccid drops out of our story.

The murder in question was a particularly odd one. In the first place, it was the victim who did the killing. And in the second, the killing occurred in a horse-car, an odd conveyance at best. And finally, the murderer had sought to conceal his handiwork by cramming his victim into the little stove in the middle of the car, a feat practically impossible without the aid of scissors and a good eye for snipping.

The horse-car in which the murder occurred was one of the older types, even for a horse-car. It was known in the trade as one of the "chummy roadster" models and was operated by one man only.

This man drove the horses, stoked the fire, and collected the fares. He also held the flooring of the car together with one foot braced against a "master" plank. On his day off he read quite a lot.

The murder-car and its driver, Swelf Yoffsen
—Courtesy of John Held, Jr., and Life.

The driver of the murder-car was named Swelf Yoffsen, a Swedish murder-car driver. He had come to this country four years before, but, not liking it here, had returned to Sweden. It is not known how he happened to be back in Lynn at this late date.

If we have neglected to state the name of the victim thus far, it is because nobody seemed able to identify him. Some said that he was Charlie Ross, who had disappeared shortly before. Others (the witty ones) said it was Lon Chaney. A vote taken among all those present designated him as the one least likely to succeed.

An interesting feature of this crime was that it

was the sixth of a series of similar crimes, all of which had occurred in Swelf Yoffsen's horse-car. In the other five cases, the victims had been found inadequately packed in the stove at the end of the run, but as Yoffsen, on being questioned, had denied all knowledge of how they got there, the matter had been dropped. After the discovery of the sixth murder, however, Yoffsen was held on a technical charge of homicide.

The trial was one of the social events of the Lynn Mi-Careme season. Yoffsen, on the stand, admitted that the victim was a passenger in his car; in fact, that he was the only passenger. He had got on at the end of the line and had tried to induce Yoffsen to keep on going in the same direction, even though the tracks stopped there. He wanted to see a man in Maine, he had said. But Yoffsen, according to his own story, had refused and had turned his horses around and started for Lynn again. The next he saw of him, people were trying to get him out of the stove. It was Yoffsen's theory that the man, in an attempt to get warm, had tried to crowd his way into the stove and had smothered. On being reminded that the affair took place during a very hot week in August, Yoffsen said that no matter how hot it got during the day in Lynn, the nights were always cool.

Attorney Hammis, for the State, traced the movements of Yoffsen on the morning of the murder and said that they checked up with his movements on the occasions of the five other murders.

He showed that Yoffsen, on each occasion, had stopped the horse-car at a particularly lonely spot and asked the occupants if they minded making a little detour, as there was a bad stretch of track ahead. He had then driven his horses across a cornfield and up a nearby hill on the top of which, in the midst of a clump of bayberry bushes, stood a deserted house. He pointed out that on four out of the six occasions Yoffsen had driven his horses right into the house and asked the passengers (when there were any, other than his victim) if they would step into the front room for a few minutes, giving them some magazines to read while they waited. According to the testimony of seven of these passengers, after about fifteen minutes Yoffsen had appeared and yelled "All aboard!" in a cheery voice and everyone had piled back into the horse-car and away they had gone, over the cornfield and down the hill to Lynn. It was noted that on each occasion, one of the passengers was missing, and that, oddly enough, this very passenger was always the one to be found in the stove on the way back.

It was the State's contention that Yoffsen killed his victims for their insurance, *which is double when the deceased has met his death in a common carrier.*

On April 14th, the ninth day of the trial, the jury went out and shortly after asked for a drink of water. After eighteen hours of deliberation they returned with a verdict of guilty, but added that, as it was not sure whether Yoffsen had actually killed his victims *in* the car or had killed them outside and *then* stuffed them in the stove, he was not entitled to the double insurance.

When they went to inform Yoffsen of the verdict, he was nowhere to be found.

What College
Did to Me

An Outline of Education

MY COLLEGE education was no haphazard affair. My courses were all selected with a very definite aim in view, with a serious purpose in mind—no classes before eleven in the morning or after two-thirty in the afternoon, and nothing on Saturday at all. That was my slogan. On that rock was my education built.

As what is known as the Classical Course involved practically no afternoon laboratory work, whereas in the Scientific Course a man's time was never his own until four p. m. anyway, I went in for the classic. But only such classics as allowed for a good sleep in the morning. A man has his health to think of. There is such a thing as being a studying fool.

In my days (I was a classmate of the founder of the college) a student could elect to take any courses in the catalogue, provided no two of his choices came at the same hour. The only things he was not supposed to mix were Scotch and gin. This was known as the Elective System. Now I understand that the boys have to have, during the four years, at least three courses beginning with the same letter. This probably makes it very awkward for those who like to get away of a Friday afternoon for the week-end.

Under the Elective System my schedule was somewhat as follows:

Mondays, Wednesdays and Fridays at 11:00:
    Botany 2a (The History of Flowers and Their Meaning)
Tuesdays and Thursdays at 11:00:
    English 26 (The Social Life of the Minor Sixteenth Century Poets)
Mondays, Wednesdays and Fridays at 12:00:
    Music 9 (History and Appreciation of the Clavichord)
Tuesdays and Thursdays at 12:00:
    German 12b (Early Minnesingers—Walter von Vogelweider, Ulric Glannsdorf and Freimann von Stremhofen. Their Songs and Times)
Mondays, Wednesdays and Fridays at 1:30:
    Fine Arts 6 (Doric Columns: Their Uses, History and Various Heights)
Tuesdays and Thursdays at 1:30:
    French 1c (Exceptions to the verb *être*)

This was, of course, just one year's work. The next year I followed these courses up with supplementary courses in the history of lace-making, Russian taxation systems before Catharine the Great, North American glacial deposits and Early Renaissance etchers.

This gave me a general idea of the progress of civilization and a certain practical knowledge

213

which has stood me in good stead in thousands of ways since my graduation.

My system of studying was no less strict. In lecture courses I had my notebooks so arranged that one-half of the page could be devoted to drawings of five-pointed stars (exquisitely shaded), girls' heads, and tick-tack-toe. Some of the drawings in

Some of the drawings in my economics notebook were
the finest things I have ever done

my economics notebook in the course on Early English Trade Winds were the finest things I have ever done. One of them was a whole tree (an oak) with every leaf in perfect detail. Several instructors commented on my work in this field.

These notes I would take home after the lecture, together with whatever supplementary reading the course called for. Notes and textbooks would then be placed on a table under a strong lamplight. Next came the sharpening of pencils, which would take perhaps fifteen minutes. I had some of the best sharpened pencils in college. These I placed on the table beside the notes and books.

At this point it was necessary to light a pipe, which involved going to the table where the tobacco was. As it so happened, on the same table was a poker hand, all dealt, lying in front of a vacant chair. Four other chairs were oddly enough occupied by students, also preparing to study. It therefore resolved itself into something of a seminar, or group conference, on the courses under discussion. For example, the first student would say:

"I can't open."

The second student would perhaps say the same thing.

The third student would say: "I'll open for fifty cents."

And the seminar would be on.

At the end of the seminar, I would go back to my desk, pile the notes and books on top of each other, put the light out, and go to bed, tired but happy in the realization that I had not only spent the evening busily but had helped put four of my friends through college.

An inventory of stock acquired at college discloses the following bits of culture and erudition which have nestled in my mind after all these years.

THINGS I LEARNED FRESHMAN YEAR

1. Charlemagne either died or was born or did something with the Holy Roman Empire in 800.

2. By placing one paper bag inside another paper bag you can carry home a milk shake in it.

3. There is a double l in the middle of "parallel."

4. Powder rubbed on the chin will take the place of a shave if the room isn't very light.

5. French nouns ending in "aison" are feminine.

6. Almost everything you need to know about a subject is in the encyclopedia.

7. A tasty sandwich can be made by spreading peanut butter on raisin bread.

8. A floating body displaces its own weight in the liquid in which it floats.

9. A sock with a hole in the toe can be worn inside out with comparative comfort.

10. The chances are against filling an inside straight.

11. There is a law in economics called *The Law of Diminishing Returns,* which means that after a

certain margin is reached returns begin to diminish. This may not be correctly stated, but there *is* a law by that name.

12. You begin tuning a mandolin with A and tune the other strings from that.

1. A good imitation of measles rash can be effected by stabbing the forearm with a stiff whiskbroom.

2. Queen Elizabeth was not above suspicion.

3. In Spanish you pronounce z like th.

4. Nine-tenths of the girls in a girls' college are not pretty.

5. You can sleep undetected in a lecture course by resting the head on the hand as if shading the eyes.

6. Weakness in drawing technique can be hidden by using a wash instead of black and white line.

7. Quite a respectable bun can be acquired by smoking three or four pipefuls of strong tobacco when you have no food in your stomach.

8. The ancient Phœnicians were really Jews, and got as far north as England where they operated tin mines.

9. You can get dressed much quicker in the morning if the night before when you are going to bed you take off your trousers and underdrawers at once, leaving the latter inside the former.

1. Emerson left his pastorate because he had some argument about communion.

2. All women are untrustworthy.

3. Pushing your arms back as far as they will go fifty times each day increases your chest measurement.

4. Marcus Aurelius had a son who turned out to be a bad boy.

5. Eight hours of sleep are not necessary.

6. Heraclitus believed that fire was the basis of all life.

7. A good way to keep your trousers pressed is to hang them from the bureau drawer.

8. The chances are that you will never fill an inside straight.

9. The Republicans believe in a centralized government, the Democrats in a de-centralized one.

10. It is not necessarily effeminate to drink tea.

SENIOR YEAR

1. A dinner coat looks better than full dress.

2. There is as yet no law determining what constitutes trespass in an airplane.

3. Six hours of sleep are not necessary.

4. Bicarbonate of soda taken before retiring makes you feel better the next day.

5. You needn't be fully dressed if you wear a cap and gown to a nine-o'clock recitation.

6. Theater tickets may be charged.

7. Flowers may be charged.
8. May is the shortest month in the year.

The foregoing outline of my education is true enough in its way, and is what people like to think about a college course. It has become quite the cynical thing to admit laughingly that college did one no good. It is part of the American Credo that all that the college student learns is to catch punts and dance. I had to write something like that to satisfy the editors. As a matter of fact, I learned a great deal in college and have those four years to thank for whatever I know today.

(The above note was written to satisfy those of my instructors and financial backers who may read this. As a matter of fact, the original outline is true, and I had to look up the date about Charlemagne at that.)

Uncle Edith's
Ghost Story

"TELL us a ghost story, Uncle Edith," cried all the children late Christmas afternoon when everyone was cross and sweaty.

"Very well, then," said Uncle Edith, "it isn't much of a ghost story, but you will take it—and like it," he added, cheerfully. "And if I hear any whispering while it is going on, I will seize the luckless offender and baste him one.

"Well, to begin, my father was a poor wood-chopper, and we lived in a charcoal-burner's hut in the middle of a large, dark forest."

"That is the beginning of a fairy story, you big sap," cried little Dolly, a fat, disagreeable child who never should have been born, "and what we wanted was a *ghost* story."

"To be sure," cried Uncle Edith, "what a stupid old woopid I was. The ghost story begins as follows:

"It was late in November when my friend Warrington came up to me in the club one night and said: 'Craige, old man, I want you to come down to my place in Whoopshire for the week-end. There is greffle shooting to be done and grouse no end. What do you say?'

"I had been working hard that week, and the

prospect pleased. And so it was that the 3:40 out of Charing Cross found Warrington and me on our way into Whoopshire, loaded down with guns, plenty of flints, and two of the most beautiful snootfuls ever accumulated in Merrie England.

"It was getting dark when we reached Breeming Downs, where Warrington's place was, and as we drove up the shadowy path to the door, I felt Warrington's hand on my arm.

" 'Cut that out!' I ordered, peremptorily. 'What is this I'm getting into?'

" 'Sh-h-h!' he replied, and his grip tightened. With one sock I knocked him clean across the seat. There are some things which I simply will not stand for.

"He gathered himself together and spoke. 'I'm sorry,' he said. 'I was a bit unnerved. You see, there is a shadow against the pane in the guest room window.'

" 'Well, what of it?' I asked. It was my turn to look astonished.

"Warrington lowered his voice. 'Whenever there is a shadow against the windowpane as I drive up with a guest, that guest is found dead in bed the next morning—dead from fright,' he added, significantly.

"I looked up at the window toward which he was pointing. There, silhouetted against the glass, was the shadow of a gigantic man. I say, 'a man,' but it was more the figure of a large weasel except for

221

a fringe of dark-red clappers that it wore suspended from its beak."

"How do you know they were dark red," asked little Tom-Tit, "if it was the shadow you saw?"

"You shut your face," replied Uncle Edith. "I could hardly control my astonishment at the sight of this thing, it was so astonishing. 'That is in my room?' I asked Warrington.

" 'Yes,' he replied, 'I am afraid that it is.'

"I said nothing, but got out of the automobile and collected my bags. 'Come on,' I announced cheerfully, 'I'm going up and beard Mr. Ghost in his den.'

"So up the dark, winding stairway we went into the resounding corridors of the old seventeenth-century house, pausing only when we came to the door which Warrington indicated as being the door to my room. I knocked.

"There was a piercing scream from within as we pushed the door open. But when we entered, we found the room empty. We searched high and low, but could find no sign of the man with the shadow. Neither could we discover the source of the terrible scream, although the echo of it was still ringing in our ears.

" 'I guess it was nothing,' said Warrington, cheerfully. 'Perhaps the wind in the trees,' he added.

" 'But the shadow on the pane?' I asked.

"He pointed to a fancily carved piece of guest soap on the washstand. 'The light was behind that,' he said, 'and from outside it looked like a man.'

222

" 'To be sure,' I said, but I could see that Warrington was as white as a sheet.

" 'Is there anything that you need?' he asked. 'Breakfast is at nine—if you're lucky,' he added, jokingly.

" 'I think that I have everything,' I said. 'I will do a little reading before going to sleep, and perhaps count my laundry. . . . But stay,' I called him back, 'you might leave that revolver which I see sticking out of your hip pocket. I may need it more than you will.'

"He slapped me on the back and handed me the revolver as I had asked. 'Don't blow into the barrel,' he giggled, nervously.

" 'How many people have died of fright in this room?' I asked, turning over the leaves of a copy of *Town and Country*.

" 'Seven,' he replied. 'Four men and three women.'

" 'When was the last one here?'

" 'Last night,' he said.

" 'I wonder if I might have a glass of hot water with my breakfast,' I said. 'It warms your stomach.'

" 'Doesn't it though?' he agreed, and was gone.

"Very carefully I unpacked my bag and got into bed. I placed the revolver on the table by my pillow. Then I began reading.

"Suddenly the door to the closet at the farther end of the room opened slowly. It was in the shadows and so I could not make out whether there was a figure or not. But nothing appeared. The door shut again, however, and I could hear footfalls coming across the soft carpet toward my bed. A chair which lay between me and the closet was upset as if by an unseen hand, and, simultaneously, the window was slammed shut and the shade pulled down. I looked, and there, against the shade, as if thrown from the *outside*, was the same shadow that we had seen as we came up the drive that afternoon."

"I have to go to the bathroom," said little Roger, aged six, at this point.

"Well, go ahead," said Uncle Edith. "You know where it is."

"I don't want to go alone," whined Roger.

"Go with Roger, Arthur," commanded Uncle Edith, "and bring me a glass of water when you come back."

"And whatever was this horrible thing that was in your room, Uncle Edith?" asked the rest of the children in unison when Roger and Arthur had left the room.

"I can't tell you that," replied Uncle Edith, "for I packed my bag and got the 9:40 back town."

"That is the lousiest ghost story I have ever heard," said Peterkin.

And they all agreed with him.

More Songs for Meller

AS SENORITA RAQUEL MELLER sings entirely in Spanish, it is again explained, the management prints little synopses of the songs on the program, telling what each is all about and why she is behaving the way she is. They make delightful reading during those periods when Señorita Meller is changing mantillas, and, in case she should run out of songs before she runs out of mantillas, we offer a few new synopses for her repertoire.

(1) ¿ Voy Bien?
(AM I GOING IN THE RIGHT DIRECTION?)

When the acorns begin dropping in Spain there is an old legend that for every acorn which drops there is a baby born in Valencia. This is so silly that no one pays any attention to it now, not even the gamekeeper's daughter, who would pay attention to anything. She goes from house to house, ringing doorbells and then running away. She hopes that some day she will ring the right doorbell and will trip and fall, so that Prince Charming will catch her. So far, no one has even come to the door. Poor Pepita! if that is her name.

(2) Camisetas de Flanela
(flannel vests)

Princess Rosamonda goes nightly to the Puerta del Sol to see if the early morning edition of the papers is out yet. If it isn't she hangs around humming to herself. If it is, she hangs around humming just the same. One night she encounters a young matador who is returning from dancing school. The finches are singing and there is Love in the air. Princess Rosamonda ends up in the Police Station.

(3) La Guia
(the time-table)

It is the day of the bull fight in Madrid. Everyone is cock-eyed. The bull has slipped out by the back entrance to the arena and has gone home, disgusted. Nobody notices that the bull has gone except Nina, a peasant girl who has come to town that day to sell her father. She looks with horror at the place in the Royal Box where the bull ought to be sitting and sees there instead her algebra teacher whom she had told that she was staying at home on account of a sick headache. You can imagine her feelings!

(4) No Puedo Comer Eso
(I CAN NOT EAT THAT!)

A merry song of the Alhambra—of the Alhambra in the moonlight—of a girl who danced over the wall and sprained her ankle. Lititia is the ward of grouchy old Pampino, President of the First National Banco. She has never been allowed further away than the edge of the piazza because she teases people so. Her lover has come to see her and finds that she is fast asleep. He considers that for once he has the breaks, and tiptoes away without waking her up. Along about eleven o'clock she awakes, and is sore as all get-out.

(5) La Lavandera
(THE LAUNDRYMAN)

A coquette, pretending to be very angry, bites off the hand of her lover up to the wrist. Ah, naughty Cirinda! Such antics! However does she think she can do her lessons if she gives up all her time to love-making? But Cirinda does not care. Heedless, heedless Cirinda!

(6) Abra Vd. Esa Ventana
(OPEN THAT WINDOW)

The lament of a mother whose oldest son is too young to vote. She walks the streets singing: "My son can not vote! My son is not old enough!" There seems to be nothing that can be done about it.

The Boys' Camp
Business

THERE seems to be an idea prevalent among parents that a good way to solve the summer problem for the boy is to send him to a boys' camp. At any rate, the idea seems to be prevalent in the advertising pages of the magazines.

If all the summer camps for boys and girls turn out the sterling citizens-in-embryo that they claim to do, the future of this country is as safe as if it were in the hands of a governing board consisting of the Twelve Apostles. From the folders and advertisements, we learn that "Camp Womagansett —in the foothills of the White Mountains" sends yearly into the world a bevy of "strong, manly boys, ready for the duties of citizenship and equipped to face life with a clear eye and a keen mind." It doesn't say anything about their digestions, but I suppose they are in tiptop shape, too.

The outlook for the next generation of mothers is no less dazzling. "Camp Wawilla for Girls," we learn, pays particular attention to the spiritual development of Tomorrow's Women and compared to the civic activities of the majority of alumnæ of Wawilla, those of Florence Nightingale or Frances Willard would have to be listed under the head of "Junior Girls' Work."

*Holding you under water until you are as good as
drowned*

Now this is all very splendid, and it is comforting to think that when every boy and girl goes to Womagansett or Wawilla there will be no more Younger Generation problem and probably no crime waves worth mentioning. But there are several other features that go hand in hand with sending the boy to camp which I would like to take up from the parents' point of view, if I may. I will limit myself to twenty minutes.

In the first place, when your boy comes home from camp he is what is known in the circular as "manly and independent." This means that when you go swimming with him he pushes you off the raft and jumps on your shoulders, holding you under water until you are as good as drowned— better, in fact. Before he went to camp, you used to take a kindly interest in his swimming and tell him to "take your time, take it easy," with a feeling of superiority which, while it may have had no foundation in your own natatorial prowess, nevertheless was one of the few points of pride left to you in your obese middle-age. After watching one of those brown heroes in one-piece suits and rubber helmets dive off a tower and swim under water to the raft and back, there was a sort of balm in being able to turn to your son and show him how to do the crawl stroke, even though you yourself weren't one of the seven foremost crawl experts in the country. You could do it better than your son could, and that was something.

It was also very comforting to be able to stand

on the springboard and say: "Now watch Daddy. See? Hands like this, bend your knees. See?" The fact that such exhibitions usually culminated in your landing heavily on the area bounded by the knees and the chest was embarrassing, perhaps, but at that you weren't quite so bad as the boy when he tried the same thing.

But after a summer at camp, the "manly, independent" boy comes back and makes you look like Horace Greeley in his later years. "Do this one, Dad!" he says, turning a double flip off the springboard and cutting into the water like a knife blade. If you try it, you sprain your back. If you don't try it, your self-respect and prestige are shattered. The best thing to do is not to hear him. You can do this by disappearing under the surface every time it looks as if he were going to pull a new one. After a while, however, this ruse gets you pretty soggy and waterlogged and you might better just go in and get dressed as rapidly as possible.

The worst phase of this new-found "independence" is the romping instinct that seems to be developed to a high state of obnoxiousness at all boys' camps. I went to camp when I was a boy, but I don't remember being as unpleasant about my fun as boys today seem to be. I have done many mean things in my time. I have tortured flies and kicked crutches out from under cripples' arms. But I have never, so help me, Confucius, pushed anybody off a raft or come up behind anyone in the water and

"Now watch Daddy. See? Hands like this, bend your knees. See?"

jumped up on his shoulders. And I don't think that Lincoln ever did, either.

There is evidently a course in raft pushing and back jumping in boys' camps today. Those photographs that you see in the camp advertisements, if you examine them closely, will disclose, in nine cases out of ten, a lot of boys pushing each other off rafts. You can't see the ones who are jumping on others' shoulders, as they are under water. But I want to serve notice right now that the next boy who pushes me off a raft when I am not looking, or tries to play leapfrog over me in ten feet of water, is going to be made practically useless as Tomorrow's Citizen, and I am going to do it myself, too. If it happens to be my own son, it will just make the affair the sadder.

Another thing that these manly boys learn at camp is a savage habit of getting up at sunrise. The normal, healthy boy should be a very late sleeper. Who does not remember in his own normal, healthy boyhood having to be called three, four, or even five times in the morning before it seemed sensible to get up? One of the happiest memories of childhood is that of the maternal voice calling up from downstairs, fading away into silence, and the realization that it would be possibly fifteen minutes before it called again.

All this is denied to the boy who goes to a summer camp. When he comes home, he is so steeped in the pernicious practice of early rising that he can't shake it off. Along about six o'clock in the

morning he begins dropping shoes and fixing up
a new stand for the radio in his room. Then he
goes out into the back yard and practices tennis
shots up against the house. Then he runs over a
few whistling arrangements of popular songs and

*You'd be surprised at the sound two bicycle wheels can
make on a gravel path*

rides his bicycle up and down the gravel path.
You would be surprised at the sound two bicycle
wheels can make on a gravel path at six-thirty in
the morning. A forest fire might make the same
crackling sound, but you probably wouldn't be
having a forest fire out in your yard at six-thirty
in the morning. Not if you had any sense, you
wouldn't.

Just what the boys do at camp when they get up

at six is a mystery. They seem to have some sort of setting-up exercises and a swim—more pushing each other off the raft—but they could do that by getting up at eight and still have a good long day ahead of them. I never knew anyone yet who got up at six who did anything more useful between that time and breakfast than banging a tennis ball up against the side of the house, waiting for the civilized members of the party to get up. We have to do enough waiting in this life without getting up early to wait for breakfast.

Next summer I have a good mind to run a boys' camp of my own. It will be on Lake Chabonagog-chabonagogchabonagungamog—yes, there is, too, in Webster, Massachusetts—and I will call it Camp Chabonagogchabonagogchabonagungamog f o r Manly Boys. And by the word "manly," I will mean "like men." In other words, everyone shall sleep just as long as he wants, and when he does get up there will be no depleting "setting-up" exercises. The day will be spent just as the individual camper gosh-darned pleases. No organized "hikes" —I'd like a word on the "hike" problem some day, too—no camp spirit, no talk about Tomorrow's Manhood, and *no pushing people off rafts.*

Goethe's Love Life

LOVERS of Goethe will rejoice in the recently discovered series of letters which have been added to the world's collection of Goethiana by Dr. Heimsatz Au of Leipzig.

Dr. Au had spent fifteen years searching through bureau-drawers and things for these missing links in the chain of the poet's love-life, and was at last rewarded by finding them in the pocket of an old raincoat belonging to Hugo Kranz. Goethe had evidently given them to Kranz to mail, and the lovable old fellow had completely forgotten them. So the letters were never received by the people to whom they were addressed, which accounts for several queer things that happened subsequently, among them the sudden birth of a daughter in the family of Walter Tierney.

We must remember that at the time these letters were written, Goethe was in delicate health and had seriously contemplated suicide. At least, that was what he said. More likely he was just fooling, as there is no record that he ever succeeded. At any rate, not the Goethe of whom we are speaking. There was a George Goethe who committed suicide in Paris in 1886, but it is doubtful if he was the poet. The first of the Au collection of letters was

238

written on August 11, 1760, four days after Goethe had returned from his operation. It was addressed to Leopold Katz, his old room-mate in the Kindergarten. ". . . I have never been so sore at anyone in my life," writes Goethe, "as I was at Martha last Friday."

In closing Goethe promised to send Katz the flowered slippers he had promised him and bade him be "a good boys (*ein gutes Kind*)."

On November 26 he wrote to the Gebrüder Feigenspan, Importers of Fine Mechanical Toys, 1364 Ludwigstrasse, München:

"Gentlemen. . . . On September 12, I sent you a letter, together with fifteen cents in stamps, requesting that you send me for inspection one of your wheeled ducks as per your advertisement. Our Herr Rothapfel informs me that the shipment has never reached us. It is not the money that I object to, as fifteen cents in stamps is only fifteen cents in stamps, no matter how you should look at it, but it strikes me as very funny that a firm of your standing should be so sloppy in its business transactions. Please oblige."

That is all. Not a word of his heart-aches. Not a word of his emotional crises. Not a word of Elsa von Bahnhoff. In fact, not a word about anything but the wheeled duck. No wonder that, in January, we find him writing piteously to Lena Lewis, his teacher:

". . . Well, Lena, this is a fine sort of a day I must say. Rain, rain, rain, is about all it seems to

239

know how to do in this dump. And the food. Say! The worst you ever see (*sehen*)."

Thus we are able to piece together those years of Goethe's life when he was in a formative frame of mind and facing his first big problems. In the light of these letters several of the passages in *"Dichtung und Wahrheit"* which have hitherto been clouded in mystery may now be read with a clearer understanding. We cannot thank Dr. Au too much—if at all.

Old Program
from the Benchley Collection

*A Glance Backward in the Manner of the Authors of
Theatrical Reminiscences*

FEW, probably, of my readers, will remember
the time when the old Forrest Theater stood
where the Central Park Reservoir now is. In those
days, Central Park was considered 'way downtown,
or "crosstown," as they called it then, and one of
the larks of the period was going "down to Central
Park to see the turtles." There was a large turtle
farm in the Park at that time, run by Anderson M.
Ferderber, and it was this turtle farm, expanding
and growing as the turtles became more venture-
some, which later became the Zoological Exhibit.

I remember very well the night when it was
announced at the Forrest Theater that the building was to be torn down to make way for the new
Reservoir. It was, as I recall, H. M. Ramus
("Henry" Ramus) who made the announcement.
He was playing *Laertes* at the time (*Laertes* was
played with the deuces wild and a ten-cent limit)
when the manager of the theater (Arthur Semden,
who later became Harrison Blashforth) came into
the dressing-room and said: "Well, boys, it's all
over. They're going to build the Reservoir here!"

There was a silence for a full minute—probably more, for the manager had come into the wrong dressing-room and there was nobody there.

At any rate, "Henry" Ramus was selected to go out and tell the audience. He did it with infinite tact, explaining that there was no need for alarm or panic, as the water could not possibly be let in until the theater was down and the Reservoir constructed, but the audience was evidently taking no chances on being drowned, for within three minutes from the time Ramus began speaking everyone in the theater was outdoors and in a hansom cab. Audience psychology is a queer thing, and possibly this audience knew best. At any rate, the old Forrest Theater is no more.

Speaking of "Henry" Ramus, an amusing anecdote is told of Whitney Hersh. Hersh was playing with Booth in Philadelphia at the time, and was well known for his ability to catch cold, a characteristic which won him many new friends but lost him several old ones. The theater where Booth was playing in *The Queen's Quandary, or What's Open Can't Be Shut,* was the old Chestnut Street Opera House which stood at the corner of what was then Arch, Chestnut, Spruce, Pine and Curly Maple Streets. This theater was noted in the profession for its slanting stage, so much so, in fact, that Booth, on hearing that they were to play there, is said to have remarked: "The Chestnut Street, eh?" On being assured that he had heard correctly, Booth simply smiled. He later founded the Player's Club.

In *The Queen's Quandary, or What's Open Can't Be Shut,* Hersh had to play the part of *Rod-*

ney Ransome, the father of several people. In the second act there was a scene in which *Rodney* had to say to *Marian:*

"But I thought you said the Duke *had* no moustache!"

To which *Marian* was supposed to reply: "I never was more serious in all my life."

On the night of the opening performance Hersh was, as usual, very nervous. He got through the first act all right, with the aid of several promptings from his mother who was sitting in the balcony. But when the second act came along, it was evident to the other members of the company that Hersh could not be relied upon. This feeling was strengthened by the fact that he was nowhere to be found. They searched high and low for him but, like the sword of Damocles, he had disappeared. At the curtain to the second act, however, he was discovered sitting out front in D-113 applauding loudly and calling out: "Hersh! We-want-Hersh!" The only way they could get him back on the stage was a ruse which was not without its pathetic side. The manager of the house stepped out in front of the curtain and asked if any member of the audience would volunteer to come upon the stage and be hypnotized. Hersh, who had always wanted to go on the stage, was one of the first to push his way up. Once behind the footlights again his nervousness left him and he went on with his part where he had left off. It did not fit in with the rest of the play, but they were all so glad to have him back in the cast again that they said nothing about it to him, and whenever, in later years, he himself mentioned the affair, it was always as "that time in Philadelphia when I was so nervous." . . . And that little girl was Charlotte Cushman.

It was at this time that Stopford's *A New Way With Old Husbands, or The Mysterious Drummer-Boy,* was given its first performance at the old Garrick Theater in New York. The old Garrick Theater was torn down in 1878 to make way for the new Garrick Theater, which, in its turn, was torn down in 1880 to make way for the old Garrick again. It is the old, or new, Garrick which now stands at Broadway and Tenth Street on the spot known to passers-by as "Wanamaker's." Thus is the silver cord loosed and the pitcher broken at the well.

A New Way With Old Husbands, or The Mysterious Drummer-Boy was written for Ada Rehan, but she was in Fall River at the time; so the part was given to a young woman who had come to the theater that morning asking if a Mr. Wasserman lived there. On being told that it was not a private dwelling and that there was no one there named Wasserman, she had said.

"Well, then, does anyone here want to subscribe to the *Saturday Evening Post*?"

Those members of the cast who had gathered on the bare stage for rehearsal were so impressed by the young woman's courage that a purse was taken up for her children in case she had any and, in case she had no children, for her next of kin.

"I do not want money," she said, taking it. "All I want is a chance to prove my ability on the stage."

"Can you make the sound of crashing glass?" asked Arthur Reese, the stage manager.

"I think so," replied the young woman without looking up.

Reese looked at Meany, the assistant stage manager. "She is the one we want," he said quietly.

So the young woman was engaged. . . . Some thirty years later the Empire Theater in New York was aglow with lights on the occasion of the opening of *Call the Doctor*. Gay ladies, bejeweled and bejabbered, were running back and forth in the lobby, holding court, while tall, dark gentlemen in evening dress danced attendance. Those who couldn't dance sat it out. It was the metropolitan season at its height.

Suddenly a man burst excitedly through the crowd and made his way to the box-office.

"This seat is ridiculous," he exclaimed to the Treasurer of the theater (Roger M. Wakle, at the time). "I can't even see the stage from it."

"That is not so strange as it may seem to you at first," replied Wakle, "for the curtain is not up yet."

A hush fell over the crowded lobby. This was followed somewhat later by a buzz of excitement. This, in turn, was followed by a detail of mounted police. Men looked at women and at each other.

. . . For that young man was Charlotte Cushman.

It was about this time, as I remember it (or maybe later) that the old Augustin Daly Stock Company was at the top of its popularity and everyone was excited over the forthcoming production of *Up and Away*. It had been in rehearsal for several weeks when Tom Nevers asked Daly how much longer they were going to rehearse.

"Oh, about another week," replied Daly, with that old hat which later made him famous.

You can imagine Nevers' feelings!

A glance at the cast assembled for this production might be of interest in the light of subsequent events (the completion of the vehicular tunnel and the Centennial Exposition). So anyway it is in the middle of page 57 to look at if you want to.

As it turned out, *Up and Away* was never produced, as it was found to be too much trouble. But the old Augustin Daly Stock Company will not soon be forgotten.

My memories of St. Louis are of the pleasantest. We played there in Dante's *Really Mrs. Warrington*—and *Twelfth Night*. The *St. Louis Post-Dispatch*, on the morning following our opening, said:

"It is quite probable that before the end of the year we shall see the beginning of the end of the work on the McNaffen Dam. The project has been under construction now for three years and while there can be no suspicion thrown on the awarding of the contracts, nevertheless we must say that the work has progressed but slowly."

It was while we were playing in St. Louis that the news came of the capture of J. Wilkes Booth. A performance of *Richelieu* was in progress, in which I was playing *Rafferty*, and Fanny Davenport the *Queen*. In the second act there is a scene in which *Rafferty* says to *La Pouce*:

> *"I can not, tho' my tongue were free,*
> *Repeat the message that my liege inspires,*
> *And tho' you ask it, were it mine,*
> *And hope you'll be my Valentine."*

Following this speech, *Rafferty* falls down and opens up a bad gash in his forehead.

We had come to this scene on the night I mention, when I noticed that the audience was tittering. I could not imagine what the matter was, and naturally thought of all kinds of things—sheep jumping over a fence—anything. But strange as it may seem, the tittering continued, and I have never found out, from that day to this what amused them so. . . . This was in 1878.

And now we come to the final curtain. For, after all, I sometimes think that Life is like a stage itself. The curtain rises on our little scene; we have our exits and our entrances, and each man in his time plays many parts. I must work this simile up sometime.

Life and the Theater. Who knows? *Selah.*

The Low State
of Whippet Racing

I T DOES not seem too soon now to begin for-
mulating plans for next year's whippet racing.
While there are still a few more races on the 1928
schedule, most of the important ones have been run
off and the leading whippets have practically all
broken training.

Whippet racing in recent years has deteriorated
into a sordid spectacle, productive only of gigantic
gate receipts for the promoters. At one whippet
race on Long Island last summer, it is estimated
that forty people lined the course, and, as each of
these forty paid something in the neighborhood of
a quarter for parking their cars in a nearby field,
it will be seen that the thing has already got out of
hand and is now in the class of mad sport carnivals.

This has naturally had its reaction on the whippets themselves. They have become mercenary and
callous. All they think of is money, money, money.
The idea of sport for sport's sake is a dream of the
past as far as whippets are concerned. In order to
make the game what it used to be, we shall have to
bring up a whole new breed of whippets and send
the present success-crazed organization out on the
road in circuses where they may indulge their lust
for gain without hindrance of any considerations of
sportsmanship.

Perhaps a few examples may serve to illustrate my point. I witnessed a whippet race in California recently at which the gate happened to be very small. There had been no publicity worthy of the name and the word had simply got around among the racetrack gang that some whippets were going to race at three o'clock. This brought out a crowd of perhaps six people, exclusive of the owners and trainers. Four of the six were chance passers-by and the other two were state policemen.

Now evidently the small size of the crowd enraged the whippets or, at any rate, threw them into such a state of mind that they gave up all idea of racing and took to kidding. In the first race they were not halfway down the lanes when two of them stopped and walked back, while the other two began wrestling good-naturedly. The owners at the finish line called frantically, but to no avail, and the race had to be called off.

In the second race they would not even start. When the gun was fired, they turned as if by pre-arranged mutiny and began jumping up and kissing their trainers. This race also had to be called off.

By this time the crowd was in an ugly humor and one or two started to boo. The state police, scenting trouble, went home. This left four spectators and further upset the whippets. A conference of the owners and trainers resulted in what you might call practically nothing. It got along toward supper time and even I went home. I looked in the papers

By this time the crowd was in an ugly humor

the next morning but could find no news of the races, so I gathered that the rest of the heats had been called off too.

This pretty well indicates the state in which whippet racing now finds itself in this country. The remedy is up to those of us old whippet fanciers who have the time and the means to reform the thing from the ground up.

First, I would recommend a revision of the system of whippet-calling. As you no doubt know, a whippet race is at least one-third dependent on calling. The trainer leads the whippet from the finish line up the lane to the starting point (a silly procedure to begin with) and then holds him in leash until the gun. The owner, or some close personal friend, stands at the finish line and calls to the whippet, which is supposed to drive him crazy and make him run like mad back down the lane again in a desire to reach his owner. As we have seen, the whippet can take it or leave it and is by no means certain to show any desire at all to get back to the caller. Now this must be due to the calling. If the thing were made attractive at all for the whippet to reach the finish line, we would see no more of this hopping up and kissing trainers at the start.

As near as I could distinguish, most of the owners called out, "Come on, Luke!" or "Here, Bennie, here!" Now obviously there was nothing very exciting about these calls. You or I wouldn't run like mad down a lane to get to someone who was calling, "Come on, Charlie!" or "Here, Bob, here!" (unless, of course, it was Greta Garbo who was doing the calling. In that case, a short, sharp whistle would be O.K.).

There must be some more attractive sounds made to entice the whippets down the lanes. Not knowing exactly what it is that whippets like best, it is a little difficult for me to make suggestions. I don't know and I don't pretend to know. All I am sure of is that the whippets aren't particularly attracted by what is being held out to them now.

Now in the matter of blankets. On the way up the lanes to the starting point, the whippets are forced to wear blankets like race horses. This saps not only their vitality but their self-respect. It is all right for a race horse to wear a blanket if he wants to, because he is big and can carry it off well. But when you get a whippet who, even with everything showing, can hardly be seen unless you have him in your lap, and then cover him up in a blanket, it just makes a nance out of him, that's all. They look like so many trotting blankets, and they must know it. A whippet has feelings as well as the rest of us. You can't make a dog ashamed to appear in public and then expect him to run a race. If they have to be kept warm, give each one a man's-size shot of rye before he starts up the course. You'd get better racing that way, too. With a good hooker of rye inside him, a whippet might not really be running fast but he would think that he was, and that's something. As it stands, they are so ashamed

It just makes a nance out of him

of their blankets that they have to do something on
the way down the lanes to appear virile. So they
stop right in the middle of the race and wrestle.

This wrestling business calls for attention, too.
It is all right for dogs to kid, but they don't have
to do it in the middle of a race. It is as if Charlie
Paddock, while running the hundred, should stop
after about fifty yards and push one of his oppo-
nents playfully on the shoulder and say, "Last tag!"
and then as if his opponent should stop and chase
Charlie around in the track trying to tag him back.
What kind of time would they make in a race like
that?

I don't think that the thing has ever been put
up to the whippets quite frankly in this manner.

255

*The owner or some close personal friend stands at the
finish line and calls to the whippet*

If someone could take a few whippets to a track
meet and (the whole gag having been worked up
before, of course, among the runners) the thing
should deteriorate into a rough-and-tumble clown-
ing match of pushing and hauling one another, the
whippets might see what it looks like. You could
say to them: "Now you see, that's how *you* look
when you stop in the middle of a race and wrestle
all over the track." They would be pretty ashamed,
I should think.

The less said about their jumping up and kissing their trainers at the start, the better. This
is something that a good psychoanalyst ought to

handle. But so long as it is allowed to go on, whippet racing will be in the doldrums. And so long as whippet racing is in the doldrums—well, it is in the doldrums, that's all.

Better in the doldrums, say I, than for the whippets to so far forget the principles of good, clean amateur sport as to pursue a mechanical rabbit.

The Cooper Cycle
in American Folk Songs

A STUDY of the folk-songs of—and indigenous to—the Ohio River Valley (and just a teeny-weeny section of Illinois) discloses the fact that, between 1840 and half-past nine, coopering was the heroic occupation and coopers the legendary heroes of local song and story.

On all sides we come across fragments of ballads, or even the ballads themselves, dealing with the romantic deeds of such characters as *Cris the Cooper*, or *Warburton the Barrel-Maker*, with an occasional reference to *William W. Ransome*, although there is no record of *Ransome's* having been a cooper.

The style in which these cooper-ballads were written would indicate that they were all written by members of the same family, possibly the Jukes. There is the same curious, stilted rhyme-scheme, more like a random idea than a scheme, and a mannerism of harmony which indicates clearly that they were composed on a comb.

Probably the most famous of all these ballads in praise of coopering is the one called "Ernie Henkle," which begins as follows:

"Oh, my name is Ernie Henkle,
    Oh, in Rister I was born,
  Oh, I never let up with my coopering
    Oh, till I get my rintle on."

(A rintle was the special kind of thumb-piece that coopers used to thumb down the hoops, before the invention of the automatic hooper.)

"Oh, one day 'twas down in Georgia,
    And that I won't deny,
  That I met a gal named Sadie Fried,
    And—*(line lost)*

"Oh, she stole my heart completely,
    And that I can't deny,
  And it wasn't the tenth of August
    Or the eighteenth of July."

(Here the singer interjects a whistling solo.)

"When up stepped Theodore Munson,
    And unto me did say,
  'Oh, you can't go back on your promised word,'
    And unto me did say.

"Oh, I killed that Theodore Munson,
    And unto him did say,
  'Oh, the only gal is Henrietta Bascome,
    And that you can't deny.'"

This goes on for thirty-seven verses and then begins over again and goes over the entire thirty-seven for the second time. By this time every one is pretty sick of it.

But there we see the cooper-ballad at its best. (If you don't believe it, you ought to hear some of the others.) *Ernie Henkle* came to stand for the heroic cooper and, even in later songs about baggage-men, we find the *Henkle* motif creeping in—and out again.

For example, in the famous song about "Joe McGee, the Baggage-Man":

> " 'Twas in the gay December,
>   And the snow was up to your knees,
> When Number 34 pulled 'round the bend
>   As pretty as you please.
> Lord, Lord. As pretty as you please.

> "Now Joe McGee was the baggage-man,
>   On Number 34,
> And he sat right down on the engine step
>   And killed that Sam Basinette."

(There seems to be some confusion here as to just *what* Sam Basinette is meant. He must have been referred to in an earlier verse which has been lost.)

> "Now Sam Basinette said before he died,
>   'This ain't no treat to me,
> For the only gal is Henrietta Bascome,
>   And that you will agree.' "

It seems that *Henrietta Bascome* was more or less

of a prom-girl who rotated between the coopers and the baggage-men in their social affairs, and even got as far north as Minnesota when the roads were clear.

It will be seen that in all these folk-songs the picaresque element is almost entirely lacking: that is, there is very little—perhaps I mean "picturesque" instead of "picaresque." In all these songs the *picturesque* element is lacking; that is, there is very little color, very little movement, very little gin, please. The natives of this district were mostly rude people—constantly bumping into each other and never apologizing—and it is quite likely that they thought these to be pretty good songs, as songs go. That they aren't, is no fault of mine. You ought to know better than to read an article on American folk-songs.

Fascinating Crimes

5. The Strange Case of the Vermont Judiciary

RESIDENTS of Water Street, Bellows Falls (Vt.), are not naturally sound sleepers, owing to the proximity of the Bellows Falls Light and Power Co. and its attendant thumpings, but fifteen years before the erection of the light-and-power plant there was nothing to disturb the slumbers of Water Streetites, with the possible exception of the bestial activities of Roscoe Erkle. For it was Mr. Erkle's whim to creep up upon people as they slept and, leaping on their chests, to cram poisoned biscuits into their mouths until they died, either from the poison or from choking on the crumbs.

A tolerant citizenry stood this as long as it could decently be expected to, and then had Roscoe Erkle arrested. It is not this phase of his career in which we are interested, however, so much as the remarkable series of events which followed.

His trial began at St. Albans, Franklin County, on Wednesday morning, May 7, 1881. Defending Erkle was an attorney appointed by the Court, Enos J. Wheefer. Mr. Wheefer, being deaf, had not heard the name of his client or he would never have taken the case. He thought for several days that he was defending Roscoe Conkling and had drawn up his case with Conkling in mind.

Atty. Herbert J. McNell represented the State

and, as it later turned out, a tragic fate gave the case into the hands of Judge Alonso Presty for hearing.

Judge Presty was one of the leaders of the Vermont bar at the time and a man of impeccable habits. It was recalled after his untimely death that he had been something of a rounder in his day, having been a leader in barn-dancing circles while in law school, but since donning the sock and buskin his conduct had been propriety itself. Which make the events that we are about to relate all the more puzzling.

On the opening day of the trial, Atty. McNell was submitting as evidence passages from the prisoner's diary which indicated that the murders were not only premeditated but a source of considerable delight to Mr. Erkle. It might perhaps be interesting to give a sample page from the diary:

"*Oct.* 7—Cool and fair. Sharp tinge of Fall in the air. New shipment of arsenic arrived from W. Spent all day powdering biscuits and then toasting them. Look good enough to eat.

"*Oct.* 8—Raw, with N. E. wind. Betsy came in for a minute and we did anagrams. (EDITOR'S NOTE: *Betsy was Erkle's cow.*)

"*Oct.* 9—Still raw. Cleaned up Water Street on the left-hand side, with the exception of old Wassner who just wouldn't open his mouth. Home and read till after midnight. That man Carlyle certainly had the dope on the French Revolution, all right, all right."

As Atty. McNell read these excerpts from the diary in a droning voice, the breath of Vermont May-time wafted in at the open windows of the courtroom. Now and then a bee hummed in and out, as if to say: "Buz-z-z-z-z-z!" Judge Presty sat high above the throng, head resting on his hand, to all intents and purposes asleep.

Suddenly the attorney for the defendant arose and said: "I protest, Your Honor. I cannot hear what my learned colleague is saying, but I don't like his expression!"

There was silence while all eyes turned on the Judge. But the Judge did not move. Thinking that he had fallen asleep, as was his custom during the May term, the attorneys went on. It was not until he had gradually slipped forward into the glass of water which stood before him on his desk that it was discovered that he was dead!

The trial was immediately halted and an investigation begun. Nothing could be discovered about the Judge's person which would give a clue to his mysterious lapse except a tiny red spot just behind his right ear. This, however, was laid to indigestion and the Judge was buried.

Another trial was called for October 10, again in St. Albans. This time Judge Walter M. Bondy was presiding, and the same two attorneys opposed each other. Roscoe Erkle had, during the summer, raised a red beard and looked charming.

On the second day of the trial, while Atty. McNell was reading the prisoner's diary, Judge Bondy passed away quietly at his bench, with the same little red spot behind his right ear that had characterized the cadaver of his predecessor. The trial was again halted, and a new one set for the following May.

By this time, the matter had become one for serious concern. Erkle was questioned, but his only reply was: "Let them mind their own business, then." He had now begun to put pomade on his beard and had it parted in the middle, and, as a result, had married one of the richest spinsters in that section of Vermont.

We need not go into the repetitious account of the succeeding trials. Suffice it to say that the following May Judge Rapf died at his post, the following October Judge Orsenigal, the May following that a Judge O'Heel, who had been imported from New Hampshire without being told the history of the case, and the succeeding solstices saw the mysterious deaths of Judges Wheefer (the counsel for the defense in the first trial, who had, in the meantime, been appointed Judge because of his deafness), Rossberg, Whelan, Rock, and Brady. And, in each case, the little telltale mark behind the ear.

The State then decided to rest its case and declare it *nol-prossed*. Judges were not so plentiful in Vermont that they could afford to go on at this rate. Erkle was released on his own recognizance, took up the study of law, and is, at latest accounts,

a well-to-do patent attorney in Oldham. Every
May and every October he reports at St. Albans
to see if they want to try him again, but the Court
laughingly postpones the case until the next term,
holding its hand over its right ear the while.

The Passing of the Cow

(With Wild West Sketches from the Author's Notebook)

ONE of the signs of the gradual deterioration of the West is the even more gradual disappearance of the cow. By "cow" is meant any heavy animal that lumbers along mooing, regardless of sex. There has been too much attention paid to sex lately.

According to the startling statistics of the U. S. Cow-Counting Bureau issued on Monday (for release Wednesday), there are not more than six or seven real cows left in the West. This, at first blush, would seem to be an understatement when one thinks of the number of animals that *look* like cows that one sees from the back of the prairie-schooner as one drives across the plains. But certainly the U. S. Cow-Counting Bureau ought to know a cow when it sees one. These other animals must be impostors.

Accepting these statistics—or this statistic—as genuine, we find ourselves confronted by a pretty serious situation. The cow has been called "Man's best friend." No, that is the dog. . . . Sorry.

The situation is serious, regardless of who Man's

best friend is. Without cows (and if, when these figures were compiled, there were only six or seven

Horse and rider

(*If I were doing this over again, I would put a large cactus in to hide the horse's front legs. And maybe his hind ones, too. Perhaps I would just have the cowboy standing there.*)

left in the West, it is safe to assume that even these are gone by now) things look pretty black. It sometimes seems as if it were hardly worth while going on.

Ever since 1847 the cow has been the feature of the West that most appealed to the imagination. Prior to 1847 it was thought that all these animals were horses. You can imagine the surprise of the man who first discovered otherwise.

With the discovery of cows came the cowboy.

268

One of the steers that has disappeared
(*This is easily the worst drawing of the lot. It has, however,
caught something of the spirit of the old West.*)

And with the cowboy came the moving picture.
So you see!

It is related, in an old cowboy ballad, how the
first cow was lassoed. It seems that Ernest Guilfoil, known as "Mr. Ernest Guilfoil," was practicing
swinging his rope one day, trying to synchronize
gum-chewing with rope-twirling so that he could
work in a monologue between the two and go on
the stage. He had the gum-chewing and monologue
all synchronized, but was having trouble with the
rope. Suddenly, after a particularly complicated
session with the "pesky" thing, he felt a tug on the
other end and, on reeling it in, discovered that he
had entangled a cow in the noose. Terrified, he
jumped on his pony and rode to the nearest corral,
dragging the luckless cow behind him. Thus "Mr.
Ernest Guilfoil" became the first cowboy.

The first inkling that the world at large had of

269

Cowboy chasing cow

(It has never been very easy for me to draw animals, and it seems to be getting harder and harder as I grow older. For instance, that cow is not right and I know it. The horse is a little better, but seems to have too much personality. At any rate, the etching has action. Perhaps it would have been better to write an article just about cowboys themselves.)

the lack of cows was the concentration of cowboys in rodeos and Wild West shows. Here it was possible for a dozen or so cowboys to work on one cow, using the same one over and over at each performance. But it was not until the Bureau of Cow-Counting made its staggering analysis that the public finally realized what had happened. And now it is too late. Just what is to be done about it is a problem. Some suggest moving a lot of cows on from the East, but old-time Westerners feel that this would be adding insult to injury. The alternative seems to be to bring the cowboys on to where the cows are, but that wouldn't work out either, because—oh, because it *wouldn't*, that's all.

And so it comes about that romance dies and Civilization charges ahead. But some of us are wondering, "Is it all worth it?"

A Short (What There Is of It) History of American Political Problems

IN OUR two introductions to this history (one of which was lost) we made a general survey of the development of political theory and practice from Plato down to Old Man ("He Must Know Nothin' ") River. In beginning our history proper, it might perhaps be wise to forget all that we have said before and start fresh, as a lot of new things have come up since the last introduction was written (such as the Abolition of Slavery and the entire Reconstruction Period) which have changed the political aspect considerably.

We will begin our history, therefore, with the year 1800; in the first place, because 1800 is a good round number and easily remembered (Vanderbilt 1800, for instance), and in the second place, because it marked the defeat of the Federalist Party under Hamilton by the Republicans under Jefferson.

Now you are going to start back in astonishment when I say "Republicans under Jefferson" and most likely will write in and say, "What do you mean, *Republicans* under Jefferson, you big old gump you! Everybody knows that it was Jefferson who founded the *Democratic* Party. . . . Yours truly (whatever your name happens to be). . . ."

And here is where I will have the laugh on you, because you will have forgotten what I told you in one of our introductions to this history about the present Democratic Party having once been called the Republican Party. So when I say "Republicans under Jefferson" I *mean* "Republicans under Jefferson" and no more back talk out of you, either. If you had devoted half the time to reading one, or both, of the introductions to this history that you devote to jazz and petting-parties you would know something about the political history of your country instead of being such a nimcompoop. (There was a political party named the "Nimcompoops" a little later on, and I can hardly wait to tell you about it. . . . Perhaps I won't wait. I may tell about it any minute now. [ADV.])

Now the reason for the defeat of the Federalists in 1800 was based on several influences which have a rather important bearing on our story. They were:

1. The Federalists (as I have told you again and again until I am sick of it) thought that the Federal Government ought to have the power to rule the various states with a rod of iron. A good way to remember this by means of an old rhyme: "The Federalists thought that the Federal Government ought to have the power to rule the various states with a rod of iron. Rum-tiddy-um-tum-tum-tiron!"

2. Hamilton himself was very snooty.

3. Adams (John), the Federalist President, was very snooty and a Harvard man into the bargain.

4. No one ever had any fun.

Jefferson, on the other hand, believed that the various states ought to be allowed to govern themselves, using the Federal Government only when company came or when there was a big reception or something. This appealed to the various states, and as, after all, the various states were made up of the voters themselves and the Federal Government consisted chiefly of Hamilton and Adams and their families, it is little wonder that, on a majority vote, the various states won.

So, in 1801, Thomas Jefferson took over the reins of the government and the Republican Party had its first opportunity to show the strength of its principles.

But we are getting ahead of our story.

In our next chapter we will take up the final collapse of the Federalists and the appearance of the Whigs.

Back
to the Game

THIS is about the time of year (it would be a good joke on me if this chapter were held over until Spring) when the old boys begin thinking of going back to college to the Big Game. All during the year they have never given a thought to whether they were alumni of Yale or the New York Pharmaceutical College, but as soon as the sporting pages begin telling about O'Brienstein of Harvard and what a wonderful back he is, all Harvard men with cigar-ashes on their waistcoats suddenly remember that they went to Harvard and send in their applications for the Yale Game. There is nothing like a college education to broaden a man.

Going back to the old college town is something of an ordeal, in case you want to know. You think it's going to be all right and you have a little dream-picture of how glad the boys will be to see you. "Weekins, 1914" you will say, and there will be a big demonstration, with fire-works and retchings. The word will go round that Weekins, 1914, is back and professors in everything but Greek will say to their classes: "Dismissed for the day, gentlemen. Weekins, 1914, is back!" And a happy crowd of boys will rush pell-mell out of the recitation-hall and down to the Inn to take the horses from your carriage (or put horses into it) and drag you all around the Campus. (My using the word "Campus" is just a concession to the rabble. Where I come from "Campus" is a place where stage-collegians in skull-caps romp around and sing "When Love Is Young in Springtime" in four-part harmony. The reservation in question is known as "the Yard," and I will thank you to call it that in future.)

Anyone who has ever gone back to the old college town after, let us say, ten years, will realize that this country is going to the dogs, especially as regards its youth in the colleges. You get your tickets for the Big Game and you spend a lot of money on railroad fare. (That's all right; you have made a lot of money since getting out. You can afford it.) When you get to the old railroad station you can at least expect that Eddie, the hack-driver, will remember you. Eddie, however, is now pretty fat and has five men working for him. You can't even get one of his cabs, much less a nod out of him. "O. K. Eddie! The hell with you!"

You go to the fraternity house (another concession on my part to my Middle West readers) and announce yourself as "Weekins, 1914." (My class was 1912, as a matter of fact. I am giving myself a slight break and trying to be mysterious about this whole thing.) A lone Junior who is hanging around in the front room says "How do you do? Come on in," and excuses himself immediately.

The old place looks about the same, except that an odd-looking banner on the wall says "1930," there being no such year. A couple of young men come in and, seeing you, go right out again. Welcome back to the old House, Weekins!

A couple of young men come in and, seeing you, go right out again

A steward of some sort enters the room and arranges the magazines on the table.

"Rather quiet for the day of the Big Game," you say to him. "Where is everybody?"

This frightens him and he says: "Thank you, sir!" and also disappears.

Well, after all, you *do* have a certain claim on this place. You helped raise the money for the mission furniture and somewhere up on the wall is a stein with your name on it. There is no reason why you should feel like an intruder. This gives you courage to meet the three young men who enter with books under their arms and pass right by into the hall.

"My name is Weekins, 1914," you say. "Where is everybody?"

"Classes are just over," one of them explains. "Make yourself at home. My name is Hammer-biddle, 1931."

Somehow the mention of such a year as "1931" enrages you. "1931 what? Electrons?" But the three young men have gone down the hall; so you will never know.

A familiar face! In between the bead portières comes a man, bald and fat, yet with something about him that strikes an old G chord.

"Billigs!" you cry.

"Stanpfer is the name," he says. "Think of seeing you here!"

You try to make believe that you knew that it was Stanpfer all the time and were just saying Billigs to be funny.

"It must be fifteen years," you say.

"Well, not quite," says Stanpfer, "I saw you two years ago in New York."

"Oh, yes, I know, *that!*" (Where the hell did you see him two years ago? The man is crazy.) "But I mean it must be fifteen years since we were here together."

"Fourteen," he corrects.

"I guess you're right. Fourteen. Well, how the hell are you?"

"Great! How are you?"

"Great! How are you?"

"Great! Couldn't be better. Everything going all right?"

"Great! All right with you?"

"Great! All right with you?"

"You bet."

"That's fine! Kind of quiet around here."

"That's right! Not much like the old days."

"That's right."

"Yes, sir! That's right!"

Perhaps it would be better if the 1931 boys came back. At least, you wouldn't have to recall old days with them. You could start at scratch. Here comes somebody! Somebody older than you, if such a thing is possible.

"Hello," he says, and falls on his face against the edge of the table, cutting his forehead rather badly.

"Up you get!" you say, suiting the action to the word.

"A very nasty turn there," he says, crossly. "They should have that banked."

"That's right," you agree. You remember him as

278

a Senior who was particularly snooty to you when you were a sophomore.

"My name is Feemer, 1911," he says, dabbing his forehead with his handkerchief.

"Weekins, 1914," you say.

"Stanpfer, 1914," says Billigs.

"I remember you," says Feemer, "you were an awful pratt."

You give a short laugh.

Feemer begins to sing loudly and hits his head again against the table, this time on purpose. Several of the undergraduates enter and look disapprovingly at all three of you.

By this time Feemer, through constant hitting of his head and lurching about, is slightly ill. The general impression is that you and Stanpfer (or Billigs) are drunk too. These old grads!

The undergraduates (of whom there are now eight or ten) move unpleasantly about the room, rearranging furniture that Feemer has upset and showing in every way at their disposal that they wish you had never come.

"What time is the game?" you ask. You know very well what time the game is.

Nobody answers.

"How are the chances?" Just why you should be making *all* the advances you don't know. After all, you are fourteen years out and these boys could almost be your sons.

"I want everybody here to come to Chicago with me after the game," says Feemer, tying his tie. "I

279

live in Chicago and I want everybody here to come to Chicago with me after the game. I live in Chicago and I want everybody here to come to Chicago with me after the game."

Having made this blanket invitation, Feemer goes to sleep standing up.

The undergraduate disapproval is manifest and includes you and Billigs (or Stanpfer) to such an extent that you might better be at the bottom of the lake.

"How are the chances?" you ask again. "Is Derkwillig going to play?"

"Derkwillig has left college," says one of the undergraduates, scornfully. "He hasn't played since the Penn State game."

"Too bad," you say. "He was good, wasn't he?"

"Not so good."

"I'm sorry. I thought he was, from what I read in the papers."

"The papers are crazy," says a very young man, and immediately leaves the room.

There is a long silence, during which Feemer comes to and looks anxiously into each face as if trying to get his bearings, which is exactly what he is trying to do.

"We might as well clear the room out," says one of the undergraduates. "The girls will be coming pretty soon and we don't want to have it looking messy."

Evidently "looking messy" means the presence of you, Feemer and Stanpfer. This is plain to be

There is no sign of recognition on either side

seen. So you and Stanpfer each take an arm of Feemer and leave the house. Just as you are going down the steps (a process which includes lurching with Feemer from side to side) you meet Dr. Raddiwell and his wife. There is no sign of recognition on either side.

There is a train leaving town at 1:55. You get it and read about the game in the evening papers.

The Four-in-Hand
Outrage

WHAT has happened to four-in-hand ties that they refuse to slide around under the collar any more? Or am I just suffering from a persecution complex?

For maybe ten years I have been devoted to the soft collar or sport model, the polo shirt, and other informal modes in collarings affected by the *jeunesse dorée*. They have not been particularly adapted to playing up my good points in personal appearance, but they are easy to slip into in the morning.

With the approach of portly middle-age, however, and the gradual but relentless assumption of power in the financial world, it seemed to me that I ought to dress the part. When a man goes into a bank to ask to have his note extended he should at least wear a stiff collar and a four-in-hand of some rich, dark material, preferably a foulard. He owes it to himself.

So I laid in a stock of shirts (two) which called for either stiff collars or a knotted bandana, and then set about digging up some collars to go with them. My old stock of "Graywoods 14½" which I used to wear in high-school proved useless. They were of the mode, so flashy in those days, which

I have been devoted to informal modes of Collarings affected by the jeunesse dorée

came close together in front, allowing just a tip of the knitted club-tie to peek out from under the corners. And, owing to a temporary increase in neck-size (I can reduce it at any time by dieting for two or three days), 14½ is no longer my number. So I bought several styles of a more modern collar and prepared to throw the world of fashion into a tumult by appearing in formal neckwear on, let us say, the following Wednesday at high noon.

But in the ten years which have elapsed since I last tied a four-in-hand under a stiff collar something perverse has been injected into the manufacture of either the ties or the collars. My male readers will recognize a manœuvre which I can best designate as the Final Tug, the last short pull-around of the tie under the collar before tightening the knot. This, under the present system, has become practically impossible. The tie refuses to budge; I pull and yank, take the collar off and re-arrange the tie, try gentle tactics, followed suddenly by a deceptive upward jerk, but this gets me nothing. The knot stays loosely off-center and the tie appears to be stuck somewhere underneath the collar at a point perhaps three inches to the right. After two minutes of this mad wrenching one of three things happens—the tie rips, the collars tears, or I strangle to death in a horrid manner with eyes bulging and temples distended, a ghastly caricature of my real self.

Now this is a very strange thing to have happened in ten years. It can't be that I have forgotten how.

The tie refuses to budge

It can't be that I have lost that amount of strength through loose living. It must be that some deliberate process has been adopted by the manufacturers to prevent four-in-hands from slipping under collars. What their idea can be is a mystery. You'd think they would *want* to make things as easy for their patrons as possible. But no! Modern business *efficiency*, I suppose! The manufacturers were

288

in conference, I suppose! Rest-rooms for their women employees . . . oh, yes! Time clocks, charts, paper drinking-cups . . . oh, yes! But collars that hold ties immovable, and ties that stick in collars. That's what *we* get. That's what the Public gets. Prohibition was foisted on our boys while they were overseas, and while I was wearing soft collars the Powers-That-Be were putting the devil into stiff ones, so that when I come back to wearing them again I strangle myself to death. A fine civilization, I must say!

A Christmas Garland
of Books

AMONG the little bundle of books especially selected for Christmas-Wistmas, perhaps the most pat is "Rubber Hand Stamps and the Manipulation of India Rubber" by T. O'Conor Sloane. Into it Mr. Sloane has put the spirit of Yuletide which all of us must feel, whether we are cynical enough to deny it or not.

Beginning with a short, and very dirty, history of the sources of India Rubber, the author takes us by the hand and leads us into the fairy-land of rubber manipulation. And it is well that he does, for without his guidance we should have made an awful mess of the next rubber-stamp we tried to make. As he says on page 35: "It will be evident from the description to come that it is not advisable for anyone without considerable apparatus to attempt to clean and wash ("to sheet"), to masticate, or to mix india rubber." Even if we had the apparatus, we would probably be content with simply "sheeting" and mixing the india rubber and leave the masticating for other less pernickety people to go through with. We may be an old maid about such things, but it is too late now for us to learn to like new things.

It seems that in the making of rubber stamps a

preparation known as "flong" is necessary. Mr. Sloane assures us that anyone who has watched the stereotyping of a large daily newspaper knows what "flong" is. Perhaps our ignorance is due to the fact that we were on the editorial end of a daily newspaper and went down into the composing-room only when it was necessary to rescue some mistake we had made from the forms. At any rate, we didn't know what "flong" was and we don't want to know. A man must keep certain reticences these days or he will just have no standards left at all.

It is not generally known how simple it is to make things out of rubber. "The writer has obtained excellent results from pieces of an old discarded bicycle tire. The great point is to apply a heavy pressure to the hot material. Many other articles can be thus produced extemporaneously." (Page 78.) This should lend quite a bit of excitement to the manipulation of india rubber. Imagine working along quietly making, let us say, rubber type and then finding that, extemporaneously, you had a rubber Negro doll or balloon on your hands! A man's whole life could be changed by such a fortuitous slip of the rubber.

Not the least of Mr. Sloane's contributions to popular knowledge is his sly insertion, under the very noses of the authorities, of what he calls the "Old Home Receipt" (ostensibly for "roller-composition," but we know better, eh, Mr. Sloane?). The "Old Home Receipt" specifies "Glue 2 lbs. soaked over night, to New Orleans molasses 1

gallon. Not durable, but excellent while it lasts."
We feel sure that we have been served something
made from this "Old Home Receipt," but would
suggest to Mr. Sloane that he try putting in just a
dash of absinthe. It makes it more durable.

We can recommend Laurence Vail Coleman's
"Manual for Small Museums" to all those who have
received or are about to give small museums for
Christmas. Having a small museum on your hands
with no manual for it is no joke. It sometimes seems
as if a small museum were more bother than a large
one, but that is only when one is tired and cross.

From Mr. Coleman's remarkably comprehensive
study of small museums, we find that, as is so often
the case, income is a very serious problem. In
financing special projects for the museum, such as
the purchase of bird groups (if it is a museum that
wants bird groups), there is a great play for in-
genuity, and Dr. Abbott of the San Diego Museum
of Natural History, tells of how they, in San Diego,
met the problem:

The little cases containing bird-groups were
offered to tradespeople in the city for display in
their windows, the understanding being that the
store should pay $50 for the advertising value.
Thus, a meadowlark group, representing the male
in very bright dress, the female, the nest and eggs,
was paid for by a men's and women's clothing store
and displayed in its window in the early spring with
the slogan: "Take a pointer from the birds. Now
is the time for your new spring clothes." A savings-

bank took a woodpecker group, showing the storing away of acorns, and a California shrike group (Dr. Abbott ought to know) showing a rather sanguinary example of impaling surplus prey on the spines of a cactus, both displayed under the euphemistic caption "The Saving Instinct" and "Are You Providing for the Future by storing up your dollars [or cadavers] now?" A bush-tit's nest was taken by a real-estate firm and a mockingbird group by a music house. The local lodge of Elks gave $1200 for a case holding four elks (not members) and so, in time, the entire housing of the groups was accomplished and paid for. We are crazy to know what business houses paid for the rabbit and owl exhibits.

In the chapter on "Protection from Pests" we looked for a way of dealing with the man in an alpaca coat who grabs your stick away from you as you enter the museum and the young people who use museums for necking assignations, but they were not specified. A blanket formula is given, however, which ought to cover their cases. "The surest way to get rid of pests is to fumigate with hydrocyanic acid in an airtight compartment, but this is a dangerous procedure which has resulted in a loss of human life. [Why "but"?] Another fumigant that is widely used is carbon bisulphide, but this is highly explosive and has caused serious accidents." This presents a new problem to museum-visitors and would seem to make the thing one of the major risks of modern civilization. If a person can't be safe from asphyxiation and mutilation while looking at bird-groups, where *is* one to be safe? It would almost be better to let the pests go for a while, at least until the museum gets started.

A collection of verse entitled "Through the Years with Mother," compiled by Eva M. Young, makes a nice gift which might perhaps be given to Father. It contains most of the little poems which have been written about mothers and the general tone of the thing is favorable to motherhood. One, entitled "A Bit O' Joy," wears off a little into child-propaganda, but probably would rank as a mother-poem too, for it is presumably the mother who speaks:

> Just a Bit-a-Feller,
>   Lips a bit o' rose,
> Puckered sort o' puzzled like,
>   Wonder if he knows—

There is one more verse explaining what the Bit-a-Feller might possibly know, but we didn't go into that. Another one which we left for reading on the train was entitled: "Muvvers" and begins:

> One time, I wuz so very small,
>   I prit' near wuzn't there at all—

We can not even tell you what the first two lines are of "Mama's Dirl."

The introduction to "Are Mediums Really Witches?" by John P. Touey begins by saying: "The sole purpose of this book, as its title suggests, is to prove the existence of a personal evil force and

294

demon intervention in human affairs." This frightened us right at the start, for we are very susceptible to any argument which presupposes a tough break for ourself. There must be *some* explanation for what happens to us every time we stick our head out doors—or in doors, for that matter.

Mr. Touey begins with witchcraft in ancient times and comes right straight down to the present day. Even though he quoted "no less an authority than Porphyrius" in his earlier chapter, it was not until we got into the examples of modern people having their bed-clothes pulled off and their hats thrown at them that we began to feel uneasy. The story of the terrible time had by the Fox Sisters in Hydesville, N. Y., seemed pretty conclusive to us at the time of reading (2:15 A.M. this morning) and, frankly, we stopped there. And, believe it or not, a couple of hours later, during our troubled sleep, *some*thing pulled the bed-clothes out from the foot of *our* bed, and we awoke with a nasty head-cold.

We will pay $100 to Mr. Touey or Sir Oliver Lodge or anyone else who can help us locate the personal demon who has been assigned to us. We would just like to talk to him for five minutes, the big bully!

We can quote but one example of the fascinating problems presented in John A. Zangerle's "Principles of Real Estate Appraising" as we are limited in our space assignment, but perhaps from it the reader may get some idea of the charm of the book:

"Mr. Flanagan of New Zealand values this interest on the basis of an annuity using the 5% interest tables. Calculating the value on a 6% basis he would proceed as follows: Lessor receives $6,000 per annum for ten years, the present value of which is 6,000 x 7.36 equals $44,160; plus the present value of $12,000 per annum for 89 years commencing ten years hence which is 12,000 x 9.254 (16.614—7.36) equals $111,048. Lessor is also entitled to receive either possession or rent after 99 years have expired, the reversionary value of which can be taken at $12,000 x 16.667 less 16.614 or .053 equals $636. Thus $11,048 plus $44,160 equals $155,844, the value of the lessor's interest."

How do you mean 16.614, Mr. Flanagan? Aren't you forgetting depreciation?

For those who like to browse along lazily with British royalty, we can think of no less charming way than to accompany Helen, Countess-Dowager of Radnor through her 361-page book: "From a Great-Grandmother's Armchair." We had almost decided not to begin it at all, until we read in the Countess-Dowager's preface: "At the present time I am resting 'on my oars' (or rather, in my Armchair) at my quiet country home, which, amongst those of the third generation, goes by the name of 'Grannie's Peace-pool.' " This gave us incentive to read further.

And what a treat! "Grannie" certainly has earned her "peace-pool" after the exciting life she has led. Every year of her long career is given here in detail and it must make fascinating reading for the Radnors if only as a record of where the Countess left her umbrella that time in Godalming and who played zither in her "Ladies' String Band and Chorus" in 1879.

Among other things that are cleared up in this volume is the question of what the Countess did during those first hectic weeks of July, 1901.

"A good many engagements were crowded into the first fortnight of July," she writes modestly, "before going back to Venice. Among other things I passed a very pleasant week-end at Wendover Lodge with Alfred and Lizzie Gatty."

But the book does not dwell entirely in the past. Right up to the present day we have disclosures of equal importance. In September, 1920, while visiting in Bath, the following incident occurred:

"One Sunday I started off in the car to go and lunch with Mrs. Knatchbull. When we had gone a few miles, however, the car broke down, a 'rubber-washer' having perished and let the water through! We telephoned for a 'Taxi' which took me back to Bath, and the car was towed back. Later in the afternoon Mrs. Knatchbull sent a car for me to go over to tea, and I flew over hill and dale and reached her place in Babington in half an hour."

So you see, the Countess really *had* intended to lunch with Mrs. Knatchbull!

We neglected to mention that the authoress is by birth a Chaplin; so she probably can get free seats whenever Mary's boy Charlie comes to town in a picture.

The Woolen Mitten Situation

BEING A CONFIDENTIAL REPORT

This great historical document, sometimes referred to as the Epic of Advertising, is here presented, complete and unexpurgated, as delivered to the A. N. A. in Atlantic City.

I HAVE some very important data for all advertising men. I might as well admit right at the start that my first job on leaving college was with the advertising department of the Curtis Publishing Co. I am probably the only ex-Curtis advertising man who has not gone into the agency business for himself. As a matter of fact, when I left Curtis (I was given plenty of time to get my hat and coat) I was advised not to stick to advertising. They said that I was too tall, or something. I forget just what the reason was they gave.

But one of my last jobs before leaving Curtis was to go out on a commercial research trip for Mr. Charles Coolidge Parlin, the well-known Curtis commercial research sharp. Most of you have been shown some of Mr. Parlin's reports—in strict confidence—giving you the inside dope on the distribution of your own product and proving that, by using exclusively the Curtis publications—their names

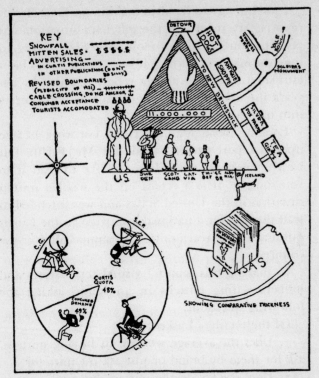

This chart shows something or other pretty graphically—we don't know just what except that Curtis is right, as usual. If the chart is correct there is certainly nothing like the Curtis Publications. At that you ought to have seen some of the dandy charts in Mr. Benchley's gingham report.

escape me at the moment—you will not only reach all the public that you want to reach but will have enough people left over to give an amateur performance of "Pinafore."

I used to have a hand in making up these Parlin reports. My report on the gingham situation was perhaps considered my most successful, owing to the neat manner in which it was bound. It has been estimated that my gingham report retarded by ten years the entrance of the gingham manufacturers into national advertising.

Looking through an old trunk last week I came upon a report which I made for Mr. Parlin, but which was never used. I would like to read it to you tonight. It is a report on the woolen mitten situation in the United States and was intended to lead the way for a national campaign in the Curtis publications to reach mitten consumers all over the country.

In making this report I visited retail stores and jobbers selling mittens in 49 states, asking the following questions:

Of the retailers I asked:

1. Does the average woman, in buying mittens, ask for them by brand or just ask for mittens?

2. Does she try on the mittens for size?

3. Is there any appreciable consumer demand for mittens during the summer? If so what the hell for?

4. Is there any appreciable consumer demand for mittens during the winter?

5. Isn't it true that a mitten with a nationally advertised trade-name—like "Mitto" or "Paddies" —provided the Curtis publications were used exclusively—would sweep the field?

6. How many mitten buyers demand that the mittens be attached together with a string?

Of the jobbers we asked the following questions:

1. How do you like jobbing?

2. Are you a college man?

3. Wouldn't you be happier doing something else?

4. Do you ever, by any chance, sell any mittens?

Out of 4,846 jobbing establishments visited, only eight jobbers were found in. Jobbing establishments are always on such dark streets and there never seems to be anybody in the store. I finally got so that I would sit in my hotel and make up the jobbers' answers myself.

Now, as a result of this investigation, the Curtis Company was able to place the following facts at the disposal of the various mitten manufacturers. Each mitten manufacturer was blindfolded and taken into a darkened room where he was made to promise that he would never tell any one the facts about his own business that he was about to be told. Then he was turned around and around until he was dizzy, and then hit over the head by the Curtis Advertising Director.

Following is the result of the mitten investigation:

1. In 49 states it was found that 615,000 women do not buy mittens at all. At first, these statistics would seem to be confusing. But, on being analyzed, it is found that 82 per cent. of these 615,000 women live in towns of a population of

50,000 or over, which means that they can keep their hands in their pockets and do not need mittens. Here, then, a consumer demand must be created.

2. From 5.6 per cent. to 95 per cent. of the department store sales of men's mittens are made to women. This just shows what we are coming to.

3. In the New England states one woman in ten buys ready-to-wear mittens instead of piece-goods from which to make her own mittens.

4. In the Middle West, one woman in eleven buys mitten piece-goods. This extra woman is accounted for by the fact that an aunt of mine went to live in Wisconsin last year.

In the South, they had never heard of mittens. At one place in Alabama we were told that they had drowned the last batch they had, thinking the inquiry had been for "kittens." This gave us an idea, and we made a supplementary report on kitten distribution. In this investigation it was found:

A. That there is no general consumer knowledge of breeds of kittens. In other words, a kitten is a kitten and that's all.

B. Four out of five kittens never do anything worthwhile in the world.

C. The market for kittens is practically negligible. In some states there are no dealers at all, and hardly any jobbers.

D. A solution of the kitten dealer-problem might lie in the introduction of dealer helps. In other words, improve the package so that the dealer can play it up. Give him a kitten he will be proud to display.

But to return to our mittens:

We have shown that a nationally advertised brand of mittens, *if* given the proper distribution and *if* adapted to the particular consumer demand in the different mitten localities throughout the country, ought to dominate the field.

We now come to the problem of the proper medium for such a campaign.

In the chart on page 299 we have a pyramid representing the Curtis circulation. Eleven million people, of whom 25,000 are able to lift the paper high enough to read it. In this shaded section here is where the country club is going to be. This is all made land. . . . We come down here to a circle showing consumer demand, 49 per cent. . . . Curtis quota 48 per cent. and here is the State of Kansas which was admitted as a free state in 1856.

To continue: in 1902, the year of the war, there were 160,000 of these sold in Michigan alone. Bring this down to present-day values, with time and a half for overtime, and you will see what I mean. Of these, 50,000 were white, 4,600 were practically white and 4,000 were the same as those in Class A—white.

We have now pretty well lined up the channels of distribution for mittens and have seen that there is only one practical method for reaching the mitten consumer, namely, 52 pages a year in the *Post*, and 12 pages in color in the *Journal* and *Country*

Gentleman. There will be no duplication here as the readers of the *Country Gentleman* go to bed so early.

In addition to the benefit derived from all this, the mitten manufacturers will be shown all over the Curtis building in Philadelphia and allowed to peek into Mr. Lorimer's office. And, if they don't like this plan for marketing their product, they can lump it, because it's all they are going to get.

This report was the start of the big campaign which put the Frivolity Mitten Co. where it is today. And, for submitting it, I was fired.

The World
of Grandpa Benchley

Thinking Out Loud in the Manner of Mr. Wells' Hero

§1

I AM eighty-nine years old, and I think I would like to write a book. I don't know—maybe I wouldn't.

§2

Eighty-nine this year, ninety next year, eighty-eight last year. That makes three years accounted for. Three into fourteen goes four times and two to carry. The Assyrians were probably the first people to evolve mathematics. I sometimes get to thinking about mathematics.

The average Englishman at the age of eighty-nine is dead—has been dead for several years. The average depth of the Caspian Sea is 3,000 feet. The average rainfall in Canada is 1.03 inches. During the Inter-Glacial Period it was 9.01 inches. Think of that—9.01 inches!

§3

All this has made me stop and think, think about the world I live in. I sometimes wonder what it is all about—this world I mean. I am not so sure about the next world. Sometimes I think there is one and sometimes I think there isn't. I'll be darned if *I* can make it out.

Grandpa Benchley

I am not so sure about my wanting to write a book, either. But something has got to be done about this world—something explanatory, I mean. Here I am, eighty-nine years old, and I haven't explained about the world to anyone yet—that is, not to anyone in this room.

§4

It is a beautiful day outside. The sun, that luminous body 95,000,000 miles from the earth, without which we should never be able to dry hides or bake biscuits, is shining through the trees outside my window, much as it used to shine through the trees outside the cave of Neolithic Man, ten thousand years before Christ. In fact, Neolithic Man sometimes built himself houses on piles driven in the water, but this was not until almost five thousand years before Christ.

Sometimes I get to thinking about Neolithic Man. Sometimes I get to thinking about Cro-Magnon Man. Sometimes it just seems as if I should go crazy thinking about things. There are so *many* things! And I am only eighty-nine.

§5

I remember when I was a very small boy my mother used to forbid me to go out when it was raining. My mother was a very quiet woman, who never spoke unless it was to figure out how long it would take to reach the nearest star by train.

"Nipper," she would say to me on such days as the rain would prevent my going out, "Nipper, I guess you don't know that thousands of years before modern civilization there was a period known as the Pluvial or Lacustrine Age, the rain or pond period."

I remember my crying myself to sleep the first night after she told me about the Pluvial or Lacustrine Age. It seemed so long ago—and nothing to be done about it.

§6

One night my father came home with a queer light in his eyes. He said nothing during dinner, except to note, as he passed me the salt, that salt is an essential to all grain-consuming and herbivorous animals but that on a meat-diet man can do without it. "There have been bitter tribal wars," he said, "between the tribes of the Soudan for possession of the salt deposits between Fezzan and Murzuk."

"Arthur," said my mother, quietly, "remember the boys are present."

"It is time they knew," was his reply.

At last my mother, sensing that something was troubling him, said:

"Arthur, are you holding something back from me?"

He laid down his knife and fork and looked at her.

"I have just heard," he said, "that the molecule is no longer the indivisible unit that it was supposed to be."

My mother bit her lip.

"You tell me this," she said, "after all these years!"

"I have just learned it myself," replied my father. "The National Molecule Society found it out themselves only last month. The new unit is to be called the 'atom.'"

"A fine time to tell me!" said my mother, her eyes blazing. "You have known it for a month."

"I wasn't sure until just now," said my father. "I didn't want to worry you."

My mother took my brother and me by the hand. "Come, boys," she said, "we are going away."

Two days later the three of us left for the Continent. We never saw my father again.

§7

This set me to thinking about atoms. I don't think that I have it straight even now. And then, just as I was getting accustomed to the idea that molecules *could* be divided into atoms, along comes somebody a few years ago and says that you can divide atoms into electrons. And, although I was about seventy-five at the time, I went out into the park and had a good cry.

I mean, what is an old fellow going to do? No sooner does he get something all thought out than something happens to make him begin all over again. I get awfully sore sometimes.

§8

Then there is this question of putting studs in a dress-shirt. Here is the problem as I see it:

If you put the studs in *before* you put the shirt on, you muss your hair putting it on over your head. If you wait until you have the shirt on before putting in the studs, you have to put your hand up under the front of the shirt and punch them through with the other. This musses the shirt bosom nine times out of ten. Eight times out of ten, perhaps.

All right. Suppose you put the studs in first and muss your hair. Then you have to brush it again. That is not so hard to do, except that if you put tonic on your hair before you brush it, as I do, you are quite likely to spatter drops down the bosom. And there you are, with a good big blister right where it shows—and it's 8 o'clock already.

Now here *is* a problem. I have spent hours trying to figure some way to get around it and am nowhere near the solution. I think I will go to the Riviera where it is quiet and just think and think and think.

§9

I am sitting at my window in the *Villa a Vendre* at Cagnes. If it were not for the Maritime Alps I could see Constantinople. How do you suppose the Alps got there, anyway? Some giant cataclysm of Nature I suppose. I guess it is too late to do anything about it now.

Irma is down in the garden gathering snails for dinner. Irma is cross at me because this morning, when she suggested running up to Paris for the shooting, I told her that the ancient name of Paris was Lutitia.

I get to thinking about women sometimes. From eight in the evening on. They are funny. Female characteristics differ so from male characteristics. This was true even in the Pleistocene Age, so they tell me.

§10

Next Wednesday I am going back to thinking about God. I didn't anywhere near finish thinking about God the last time. The man came for the trunks and I had to go with him to the station.

It is quite a problem. I don't think there is any doubt about there being some Motive Power which governs the World. But I can't seem to get much beyond that. Maybe I'll begin again on that Monday. Monday is a good day to begin thinking. Your laundry is just back and everything is sort of pristine and new. I hope that, by beginning Monday, I can get everything cleaned up by Friday, for Friday I am going over to Monte Carlo.

§11

It is six years now since I began writing this book. I am almost ninety-seven. According to the statistics of the Royal Statistical Society I can't expect much longer in which to think things over.

The big thing that is worrying me now is about putting sugar on my oatmeal. I find that if I put the sugar on first and then the cream, the sugar all disappears, and I like to see it, nice and white, there on the cereal. But if I put the cream on first and *then* the sugar, it doesn't taste so good. I asked Irma about this the other day and she told me to shut up and go back to bed.

§12

After thinking the whole thing over, I have come to the conclusion that I don't want to write a book at all. When a man is ninety-seven it is high time he was doing something else with his time besides writing books. I guess I'll go out and roll down hill.

GLOSSARY OF KIN, NATIVE, AND TECHNICAL TERMS

Kin Terms

arndi—mother.

bapa—father.

dué—father's sister's son (husband); father's sister's daughter.

dumungur—father's sister's daughter's daughter's son; father's sister's daughter's daughter's daughter.

galle—mother's brother's son; mother's brother's daughter (wife).

gatu—son; daughter.

gawel—mother's brother.

gurrong—father's sister's daughter's son; father's sister's daughter's daughter.

kaminyer—daughter's son; daughter's daughter.

kutara—sister's daughter's son; sister's daughter's daughter.

maraitcha—son's son; son's daughter.

marelker—mother's mother's brother's son.

mari—mother's mother's brother; mother's mother.

marikmo—father's father; father's father's sister.

mokul bapa—father's sister.

mokul rumeru—mother's mother's brother's daughter (mother-in-law).

momelker—mother's mother's mother's brother's daughter.

momo—father's mother.

nati—mother's father.

natjiwalker—mother's mother's mother's brother's son.

waku—sister's son; sister's daughter; father's father's sister's son; father's father's sister's daughter.

wawa—older brother.

yeppa—sister.

yukiyuko—younger brother.

Native Terms

Bamun—the mythological period when "things were different" and the totemic spirits and the ancestors of man inhabited the land.

Bapa Indi—*see* Muit.

baperu—native name for moiety, meaning four subsections that belong to each moiety.

billibong—a general term used by the Australian whites for a small lake or pool.

bilmel, bilmal—singing sticks.

birimbir—the totemic soul of man (*see* mokoi).

corroboree—a general term used by the Australian whites for native ceremonies.

313

ABBREVIATIONS

A. OLD TESTAMENT

Am.	Amos	Josh.	Joshua
Cant.	Canticles (Song of Sol.)	Judg.	Judges
Chron.	Chronicles	Kings	Kings
Dan.	Daniel	Lam.	Lamentations
Deut.	Deuteronomy	Lev.	Leviticus
Eccles.	Ecclesiastes	Mal.	Malachi
Esth.	Esther	Mic.	Micah
Ex.	Exodus	Nah.	Nahum
Ez.	Ezekiel	Neh.	Nehemiah
Ezra	Ezra	Num.	Numbers
Gen.	Genesis	Obad.	Obadiah
Hab.	Habakkuk	Pr.	Proverbs
Hag.	Haggai	Ps.	Psalms
Hos.	Hosea	Ruth	Ruth
Is.	Isaiah	Sam.	Samuel
Jer.	Jeremiah	Song	Song of Songs (Cant.)
Job	Job	Zech.	Zechariah
Joel	Joel	Zeph.	Zephaniah
Jonah	Jonah		

B. NEW TESTAMENT

Acts	Acts of the Apostles	Mark	Mark
Col.	Colossians	Matt.	Matthew
Cor.	Corinthians	Pet.	Peter
Eph.	Ephesians	Phil.	Philippians
Gal.	Galatians	Philem.	Philemon
Hebr.	Hebrews	Rev.	Revelation
Jam.	James	Rom.	Romans
John	John	Thess.	Thessalonians
Jude	Jude	Tim.	Timothy
Luke	Luke	Tit.	Titus

C. APOCRYPHA

Bar.	Baruch	Macc.	Maccabees
Bel	Bel and the Dragon	Sus.	Susanna
Ecclus.	Ecclesiasticus	Tob.	Tobit
Esd.	Esdras	Wisd. of Sol.	Wisdom of Solomon
Jth.	Judith		

314

BIBLIOGRAPHY

ABRAHAM, K. Selected Papers. London, Hogarth Press, 1927.

ADLER, A. The Practice and Theory of Individual Psychology. New York, Harcourt, Brace & Co., 1924.

ALEXANDER, F. The Psychoanalysis of the Total Personality. New York, Nervous and Mental Disease Pub. Co., 1930.

ALLPORT, G. W. Personality: A Psychological Interpretation. New York, Henry Holt & Co., 1937.

BAKER, H. J., and TRAPHAGEN, V. The Diagnosis and Treatment of Behavior Problem Children. New York, Macmillan Co., 1935.

BENDER, L., and BLAU, A. Reaction of children to sexual relations with adults. Am. J. Orthopsychiat., 7: 500-518, 1937.

BOLLES, M. M., and ZUBIN, J. A graphic method for evaluating differences between frequencies. J. Applied Psychology, 23: 440-449, 1939.

BREUER, J., and FREUD, S. Studien über Hysterie. Leipzig, F. Deuticke, 1895.

BROMLEY, D. D., and BRITTEN, F. H. Youth and Sex. New York, Harper & Brothers, 1938.

BURGESS, E. W., and COTTRELL, L. S., JR. Predicting Success or Failure in Marriage. New York, Prentice-Hall, Inc., 1939.

CALDWELL, W. E., and MOLOY, H. C. Anatomical variations in the female pelvis and their effect in labor with a suggested classification. Am. J. Obst. & Gynec., 26: 479-505, 1933.

CALDWELL, W. E., MOLOY, H. C., and D'ESOPO, D. A. Further studies on the pelvic architecture. Am. J. Obst. & Gynec., 28: 482-497, 1934.

CHENEY, C. O. Outlines for Psychiatric Examination. Utica, State Hospitals Press, 1934.

DAVIS, K. B. Factors in the Sex Life of Twenty-Two Hundred Women. New York, Harper & Brothers, 1929.

DICKINSON, R. L. Human Sex Anatomy. Baltimore, Williams and Wilkins, 1933.

DICKINSON, R. L., and BEAM, L. A Thousand Marriages. Baltimore, Williams & Wilkins Co., 1931.

DICKINSON, R. L., and BEAM, L. The Single Woman. Baltimore, Williams & Wilkins Co., 1934.

DIETHELM, O. Treatment in Psychiatry. New York, Macmillan Co., 1936.

ELLIS, H. Studies in the Psychology of Sex. Ed. 3. Philadelphia, F. A. Davis Co., 1910. Vol. 1.